VeriSM™: Unwrapped and Appli

Other publications by Van Haren Publishing

Van Haren Publishing (VHP) specializes in titles on Best Practices, methods and standards within four domains:
- IT and IT Management
- Architecture (Enterprise and IT)
- Business Management and
- Project Management

Van Haren Publishing is also publishing on behalf of leading organizations and companies: ASLBiSL Foundation, BRMI, CA, Centre Henri Tudor, Gaming Works, IACCM, IAOP, IFDC, Innovation Value Institute, IPMA-NL, ITSqc, NAF, KNVI, PMI-NL, PON, The Open Group, The SOX Institute.

Topics are (per domain):

IT and IT Management	Enterprise Architecture	Project Management
ABC of ICT	ArchiMate®	A4-Projectmanagement
ASL®	GEA®	DSDM/Atern
CATS CM®	Novius Architectuur	ICB / NCB
CMMI®	Methode	ISO 21500
COBIT®	TOGAF®	MINCE®
e-CF		M_o_R®
ISO/IEC 20000	**Business Management**	MSP®
ISO/IEC 27001/27002	BABOK® Guide	P3O®
ISPL	BiSL® and BiSL® Next	PMBOK® Guide
IT4IT®	BRMBOK™	PRINCE2®
IT-CMF™	BTF	
IT Service CMM	EFQM	
ITIL®	eSCM	
MOF	IACCM	
MSF	ISA-95	
SABSA	ISO 9000/9001	
SAF	OPBOK	
SIAM™	SixSigma	
TRIM	SOX	
VeriSM™	SqEME®	

For the latest information on VHP publications, visit our website: www.vanharen.net.

VeriSM™

Unwrapped and Applied

Claire Agutter
Suzanne Van Hove
Johann Botha

Colophon

Title:	VeriSM™: Unwrapped and applied
A publication of:	IFDC (International Foundation of Digital Competences)
Authors team:	Claire Agutter
	Suzanne Van Hove
	Johann Botha
Publisher:	Van Haren Publishing, Zaltbommel, www.vanharen.net
Design and Layout:	Coco Bookmedia, Amersfoort – NL
NUR code:	981 / 123
ISBN Hard copy:	978 94 018 0335 9
ISBN eBook (pdf):	978 94 018 0334 2
Edition:	First edition, first impression, October 2018
Copyright:	© Van Haren Publishing, 2018

Trademark notices:
Adaptive Service Model™ is a trademark of Taking Service Forward
BiSL® is a registered trademark of ASL BiSL Foundation.
COBIT® is a registered trademark of ISACA.
ISO/IEC 20000® is a registered trademark of ISO.
ITIL® is a registered trademark of AXELOS Limited.
IT4IT® is a registered trademark of The Open Group.
SIAM® is a registered trademark of EXIN.
VeriSM™ is a registered trademark of IFDC.

Preface

The world we live in today is changing more quickly than most of us still realize. New and very disruptive technologies, such as Artificial Intelligence and advanced robotics, are developing at an accelerated pace. These and other (also already existing) digital technologies have the potential to transform not only the business world and the global economy, but society as a whole and the very way in which we live our daily lives.

We know this well in Estonia, where we have been building up a digital government and society for the last 20 years. Sometimes our country is even called e-Estonia to mark the high level to which digital tech penetrates and eases the life of Estonians (and these days also our global e-Residents!).

Technology-driven solutions are already everywhere we look, right from the way our city is being redesigned and the car we drive, to the way we make individual purchases and communicate with those close to us. The best of governments are embracing technology to digitize services to citizens, companies are embracing technology to digitize services to customers. Technology is used to cut down on costs, create new value offerings, literally improve lives.

So what are the implications of this new world? Well, from a management perspective it's quite simple. The ability of both public and private sector to adapt to this new reality and embrace the possibilities of new technologies in a timely way is no longer a nice-to-have. It is essential if they are to stay relevant and so ultimately, it is a question of pure relevance or even survival.

There are enough examples around of organizations which have not adapted to the digital age and have paid the ultimate price. However, what makes this reality even more complex is that it's not just technology which is changing. The digital age has resulted in new demands on organizations and professionals which stretch much further than understanding the implications of and how to apply the new technologies. To thrive in this new world requires changed behaviors, different organization structures, new ways of collaborating, and fresh attitudes towards those we are serving: the end consumers. In short, we need to develop the right *mindset*.

This is why a new approach to service management is essential. An approach which recognizes the challenges and opportunities of the digital age we are living in; which acknowledges that the IT department can no longer operate outside of the business as a separate entity; and which focuses on the behaviors and attitudes to make a successful digital transformation.

VeriSM™ is an attempt to embrace all these elements, which is why I hope you find this practical guide a useful source of aid to start or continue your organization's digital journey – be it in government, business or beyond.

Siim Sikkut
Government CIO, Republic of Estonia

Authors' Preface

What would you do if someone told you that you could change your organization for the better by adopting just one simple new behavior? Or one amazing new technology? You'd do it, wouldn't you?

But what if that person came back the next day with another quick tip, and then another and another; and some of the tips started to contradict each other?

This is the situation for most of us in today's business environment. We are overwhelmed by new ways of working, technological changes and an onslaught of information. So how do we respond? How do we deliver value through products and services in the digital age?

Suzanne, Johann and I were all contributors to the first VeriSM publication in 2018. Sponsored by the IFDC and working in collaboration with a large global author group, we proposed a service management approach for the digital age. The feedback we received was positive, but we got one question over and over again: "how can I 'do' VeriSM in *my* organization?"

In this book, we've worked hard to bring you the equipment to answer that question. You'll find much more detail about applying the VeriSM model, inspirational case studies, stories, interviews and examples from VeriSM early adopters around the world. We know there isn't a perfect answer that will work for every organization, so what we've done here is give you the tools to help you find the answer that's right for you. The stories we share aren't meant to be copied without question or without the application of critical thinking, but we hope that they give you some examples of how you could do things differently.

Enjoy the book; we wish you success on your digital journey.

Claire Agutter
Suzanne Van Hove
Johann Botha

Contents

Table of Figures

Contributors

Name	Company
Claire Agutter	Scopism Limited
Suzanne van Hove	SED-IT
Johann Botha	getITright
Abbey Wiltse	SMV Inc & Ahead Technology Inc
Aleksandr Zhuk	Independent
Alexander Guilherme Couceiro	LOGICALIS
Alison Cartlidge	Sopra Steria UK
Alistair Doran	Architecting Solutions Ltd
Allen Dixon	Independent Consultant
Andrea Kis	Deloitte
Andrew Humphrey	Auto Trader UK
Anna Leyland	Sopra Steria
Aprill Allen	Knowledge Bird
Aureo Antunes	Citsmart Corporation
Catherine Chalmers	CTC Management Services (UK) Ltd.
Chris Pope	ServiceNow
Chris Taylor-Cutter	CTC Management Services (UK) Ltd.
Clare McAleese	VocaLink (a Mastercard Company)
Daniel Breston	Virtual Clarity
David Bentley	Cranford Group
David Johnston	Two Rivers Meet
Doug Tedder	Tedder Consulting
Dragos Malihin	CWSI
Eppo Lupes	Octopus Learning
George Nawara	Nawara & Assoc ITSM/Governance Consultancy
Gerry Sweeney	Hornbill
Helen Morris	Helix SMS
Ian Aitchison	Ivanti

Name	Company
James Gander	Gander Service Management Ltd
James Harvey	DevOpsGroup
Jan Bouman	Sogeti Netherlands
Jon Hall	BMC
Karen Ferris	Macanta Consulting
Krzysztof Politowicz	BEI Krzysztof Politowicz i Partnerzy
Kylie Fowler	ITAM Intelligence
Leo van Selm	Vaseom b.v.
Liz Gallacher	Helix SMS
Luis Anderson	Independent
Luke Koichiro Toda	Strategic Staff Services Corporation
Maarten Bordewijk	Bordewijk Training & Advies
Marcos Weiss, PhD	Independent Consultant
Mark Flynn	Felix Maldo Ltd
Mark Smalley	Smalley.IT
Marlon Molina	Computerworld
Martijn Adams	4me, Inc.
Mathias Traugott	Punctdavista AG
Michelle Major-Goldsmith	Kinetic IT
Nikola Gaydarov	NiganiConsulting
Patrick Bolger	Hornbill
Penny Emmett	Cranford Group
Peter Brooks	Independent
Randy Steinberg	Concurrency
Reni Friis	Valcon Consulting
Richard de Kock	Microsoft
Richard Sharp	NashTech Limited
Rob Akershoek	Fruition Partners, DXC technology company
Robert den Broeder	Trigono BV
Rory Canavan	SAM Charter
Sachin Bhatnagar	South32
Sandra Whittleston	University of Northampton
Satya Misra	HCL Technologies
Simon Dorst	Kinetic IT
Simon Kent	Sollertis
Simone Jo Moore	SJM
Stephen Thair	DevOpsGuys and Microsoft
Steve Matthews	DorLind Solutions
Vincent Douhairie	Amettis
Neil M Forshaw	Fujitsu

Name	Company
Rita Pilon	EXIN
Case studies/Extra bits Authors	
Liz Whitefield	Hippo Digital
Rob England	Two Hills Ltd
Jannis de Visser	QNH Consulting
Caspar Miller	Westergaard A/S
Rachel Watson	Sky Betting and Gaming
Steve Chambers	Cloudsoft Corporation
Steve Leach	6point6 Cloud Gateway
Maryvonne Hassall	Aylesbury Vale DC
Don Page	Marval
Jack D. Bischof	Technology Business Management Council
Dave Snowden	Cognitive Edge
Suzanne Galletly	IFDC
Rachel McElroy	Social Revolution Marketing
Rogier Kuijpers	ASML
David Krieg	Kinetic IT
Song Xiang	CITIC Technology Co., Ltd.
Deng Hong	Beijing Trendsetting Consulting Co., Ltd.
Xing Jie	WuXi AppTec

1 Using this Book

VeriSM™: Unwrapped and Applied develops and builds on the content in the first VeriSM book, *VeriSM™: A Service Management Approach for the Digital Age*. To use this publication effectively, concepts from the initial book should be understood. While repeating the concepts is not the intent of this volume, Section 1.1 provides a brief summary for those who are new to the approach.

■ 1.1 OVERVIEW OF THE VERISM APPROACH

VeriSM provides a value-driven, evolving, responsive and integrated approach for service management in the digital age. Key concepts for VeriSM begin with the idea that the entire organization is a service provider, not a single department such as the IT department. Expanding service management beyond one department (typically IT) to include the rest of the organization is important for the digital organization. Doing this means that all of an organization's resources and capabilities are engaged in delivering value to the consumer through products or services.

This supports the next VeriSM key concept: whatever is delivered by the service provider, products or services, does not really matter. What matters is that the needs of the consumer (a much broader and more inclusive term than customer) drive what the service provider delivers. Consumer is used as a term throughout the book, except where 'customer' is the normally accepted term (for example, when talking about customer service). VeriSM also requires products and services to be aligned with enterprise governance and supporting Service Management Principles.

VeriSM focuses on the people and culture aspects of service management including leadership and organizational culture as well as the need for continued professional development. These concepts are interwoven throughout the next chapters. An organization's leaders set the tone for success, so their role is essential and covered in detail.

The VeriSM model is a service management operating model for an organization, which includes:

- Governance;
- Service Management Principles;
- The Management Mesh, which allows for flexibility and an integrated application of multiple management practices;
- Four stages (Define, Produce, Provide, Respond) supporting the products or services delivered to the consumer;
- The consumer, who drives what the service provider does and provides feedback on what is delivered.

There is a two-way relationship between the organization's strategy and the service management operating model. In one direction, design of the operating model is derived from the strategy. In the other direction, the organization's strategy may be influenced by operating model improvements and changes, or by signals from consumer feedback that resonate with the leadership, causing changes to the overall operating model (shown in Figure 1).

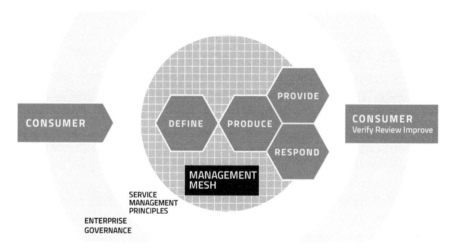

Figure 1 The VeriSM model

Full descriptions of these are found in *VeriSM™: A Service Management Approach for the Digital Age*. Briefly, each area is defined as follows:

- **Governance** – the underpinning system of directing and controlling the activities of an organization;
- **Consumer** – provides the requirements for products and services, receives products and services, gives feedback, and participates in verify/review/improve activities;
- **Service Management Principles** – based on the organizational governing principles, the 'guardrails' for the products and services delivered, addressing areas such as quality and risk;

- **Management Mesh** – how an organization combines its resources, environment and emerging technologies with different management practices to create and deliver products and services;
- **Define** – design of a solution (product or service) using agreed requirements;
- **Produce** – the creation of the solution (build, test, deploy) ensuring the outcome meets the needs of the consumer;
- **Provide** – the new/changed solution is available for use;
- **Respond** – support the consumer during performance issues, unexpected occurrences, questions or any other requests; read the consumer's signals and act accordingly.

Within the VeriSM model, governance and Service Management Principles are relatively stable elements, only changing when the organization's needs or consumer requirements change. The Management Mesh is flexible and is adjusted as required for products and services, for example to integrate a new management practice or a new technology. The four stages reflect the defined organizational management practices.

1.2   PART A: CHAPTERS 1 – 18

This book is divided into two sections. Part A discusses the impact of digital transformation on organizations and people. It provides practical guidance on how to respond, including techniques, approaches and applying the VeriSM model.

1.3   PART B: CHAPTERS 19 – 29

Part B builds on Part A with practical examples, case studies, interviews and industry perspectives. It includes a wide range of material from around the world that will be a source of inspiration and advice for your own digital journey.

1.4   THE 2018 DIGITAL TRANSFORMATION SURVEY

Whilst preparing the content in this book, IFDC conducted a survey in 2018 of more than 1,200 people to ask for their views on digital transformation and how it is affecting their workplace. Throughout the book survey extracts are used to develop concepts where they are relevant.

The 2018 Digital Transformation Survey

There were responses from many countries; the top 8 are shown in Figure 2.

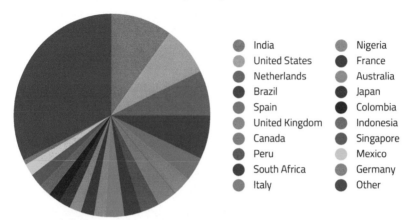

	Which country are you located in?				
1	India	10%	11	Nigeria	2%
2	United States	8%	12	France	2%
3	Netherlands	7%	13	Australia	2%
4	Brazil	7%	14	Japan	2%
5	Spain	4%	15	Colombia	2%
6	United Kingdom	3%	16	Indonesia	2%
7	Canada	3%	17	Singapore	2%
8	Peru	3%	18	Mexico	2%
9	South Africa	3%	19	Germany	1%
10	Italy	3%	20	Other	32%

Figure 2 Location of survey respondents of the 2018 Survey

Industry types and organization sizes are shown in Figures 3 and 4.

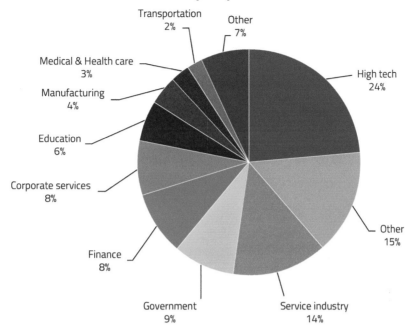

Figure 3 Respondent industries of the 2018 Survey

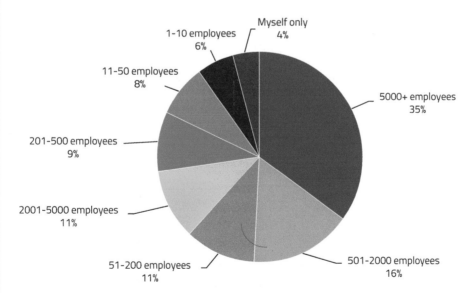

Figure 4 Respondent size of organization of the 2018 Survey

The survey shows that the trajectory of digital transformation has increased significantly over the last few years with 91% of respondents claiming they have heard the term digital transformation before; 81% of the respondents claimed their organizations have included digital transformation as part of their strategy and 61% of respondents indicated that their organizations frequently evaluate emerging technologies for their impact on products and services. It comes as no surprise that organizations are taking digital transformation more seriously when 85% of the respondents claimed that their competitors/peer organizations are embracing technology to improve their products and services. Digital transformation is no longer 'nice to have', but something organizations need to pursue to remain competitive. Further to these results, respondents claimed multiple benefits their organizations were trying to achieve through these digital transformation efforts. These are illustrated in Figure 5.

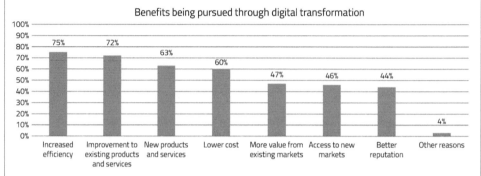

Figure 5 Benefits being pursued through digital transformation in the 2018 Survey

47% of respondents have indicated that over the last five years, the volume of the organization's products and services that depend on technology has increased significantly. Figure 6 illustrates that majority of organizations running digital initiatives fall between 10 or more initiatives or three to five initiatives:

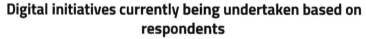

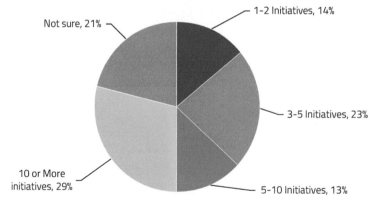

Figure 6 Number of digital initiatives in the 2018 Survey

This understandably has resulted in 73% of respondents claiming that the time spent interacting with technology within their role has increased. 90% of respondents felt that senior managers need new skills to take advantage of digital technology, with respondents indicating their organizations carry out activities relating to the emergent technologies described in Figure 7.

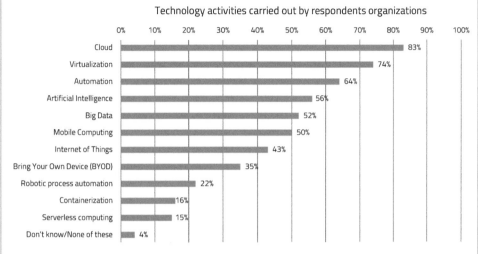

Figure 7 Technology activities carried out by respondent's organization in the 2018 Survey

Only 49% of respondents indicated that their organizations frequently evaluated new and or changed management practices, standards and frameworks amidst their digital transformation efforts. This is interesting, because emergent technologies require new management practices, standards and baselines to be effective in delivering, managing or supporting services. Organizations that are not evaluating new management practices, standards and frameworks to complement their digital transformation initiatives are likely to have difficulty in achieving the benefits they intended. These include increased efficiency, the ability to create or improve products rapidly and effectively and improving services while lowering costs.

PART A

This section of the book discusses the impact of digital transformation on organizations and people. It provides practical guidance on how to respond, including techniques, approaches and applying the VeriSM model.

2 Digital transformation in context

Introduction

Why should organizational leaders care about VeriSM? What does it mean for them, for digital transformation, and for digital optimization? This chapter assesses how VeriSM helps organizations thrive in a digital world.

Organizations, regardless of their sector and what they do or sell, can grow by embracing the digital world. Those that do not run the risk of becoming inconsequential. Household names who did not anticipate the changes that digital transformation brings or thought they would not be affected are now just distant memories in the minds of aging consumers who reminisce about the 'good old days'.

Blockbuster, Kodak, Borders Books and a long list of others are no more – they either did not see, listen or understand that the world is changing, and they paid the ultimate price. Yet there are others that were in the same – or worse – position that managed to reinvent themselves and are now shining examples of what is possible for organizations that are willing and prepared. Their journeys were not simple, easy or straightforward. These pioneers can serve as examples.

Real world examples

The Wall Street Journal was first printed on 8 July 1889. When the internet destroyed its business model, its response was typical – let's hunker down, let's consolidate. They did everything that conventional business theory said they must do and yet the bleeding continued until they truly reinvented themselves in the late 2000s. Today, it has a circulation of about 2.277 million copies, of which 1,270,000 are digital subscriptions.

Barnes and Noble started in 1873 – they had to deal with Amazon just like Borders Books. B&N is arguably one of the most successful online bookstores, Borders Books was liquidated in 2011 and 11,000 employees lost their jobs.

In 2009, Pages Jaunes, the French market leader in the Yellow Pages Industry was in trouble. The market for printed products was dying because of widespread use of the internet. The organization had to adapt to the new digital reality or, in case of failure, go out of business and cease to exist. The board developed a strategy to safeguard the organization by redefining its mission. It said that Pages Jaunes had never has been in the business of producing heavy printed books. It is (and always was) in the business of connecting small businesses to local customers. And what could do the job better that new digital technology? Within five years, more than 75% of the revenues came from digital business, thanks to a strong, simple and appealing vision and through perseverance and exemplary behavior of the leadership[1].

It is important to consider how some organizations survive, whilst others do not. More interesting is to explore how people with a good idea could not deliver that concept because the world has changed around them.

Even the most traditional 'brick and mortar' organizations can learn to outperform competitors by embracing the digital world, in a practical and pragmatic way. Some observers say that, when it comes to digital transformation, "some industries can, and others cannot", often citing examples such as government organizations. However, public sector organizations including the Estonian government administration, and the cities of Boston, New York, Chicago and Seattle have transformed. They now provide better services to citizens, engage more, and have created a sense of community by embracing the change that digital technology brings. They have indeed made their cities a better place for their citizens[2].

Case study: Aylesbury Vale District Council
For more about digital transformation in a local government organization, go to Chapter 21 to learn about Aylesbury Vale District Council and how it transformed its services in the face of severe budget cuts.

"AVDC is an ambitious council with a strong culture, based on clearly defined values and underpinned by a new commercial behavioral framework."

Andrew Grant, Chief Executive, AVDC

---

1   Bonnet, D., Westerman, G., & McAfee, A. (2014). *Leading digital: Turning technology into business transformation*. Boston: Harvard Business Review.
2   (2016, March 23). *How cities score*, (Online). https://www.economist.com/special-report/2016/03/23/how-cities-score [2018 January].

The 2018 Digital Transformation Survey

As shown in Figure 8, respondents believe that 76% to 100% of their organizations' products and services rely heavily on technology.

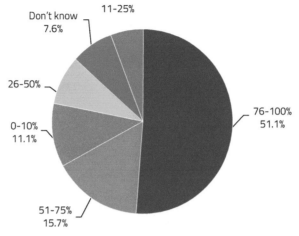

Percentage of organization's products or services supported by or couldn't operate without technology

Figure 8 Products and services supported by technology in the 2018 Survey

They also feel that the percentage of products and services that rely on technology is increasing rapidly, as shown in Figure 9.

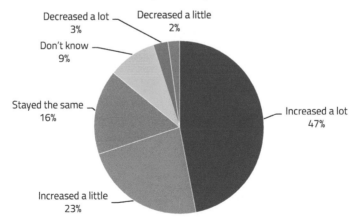

How has the percentage changed in the last 5 years?

Figure 9 Percentage change in products and services that rely on technology in the 2018 Survey

■ 2.1   VERISM AND DIGITAL TRANSFORMATION

VeriSM enables an organization to work as a single entity to provide products and services to consumers. It facilitates an organization where everybody understands their contribution to serving consumers and to achieving organizational goals and objectives. The key benefit of VeriSM for C-level executives is how the organization and its constituent parts act and think as a collective whole, ensuring that the entire organization is focused on the achievement of defined goals.

VeriSM is an evolutionary, not a revolutionary approach. An organization can start where it is and evolve into its unique digital future. It is important to remember that the role of leadership is to enable digital transformation and to ensure that managers have the resources, direction and authority to act on the direction given and make it a reality. Without support and input from the leadership level, managers' efforts will be worthless.

■ 2.2   DEFINING THE DIGITAL AGE

VeriSM does not endorse one definition of the digital age. How the digital age is defined will vary, depending on people's location, background, industry, role and age. Adding to the range of possible definitions and interpretations are phenomena and concepts such as:
- Digitization;
- Digital transformation;
- Automation;
- The Internet of Things (IoT);
- Socio-technical evolution;
- Generations;
- Big Data;
- Bring-your-own-device (BYOD);
- The proliferation of the internet;
- Knowledge management, learning and education;
- Artificial Intelligence (AI);
- The influence of social media;
- New means of communication;
- Transacting, paying and unique views on what constitutes value, especially within the context of the digital age, all of which are continually evolving.

As quickly as technologies change, so do terms. Today's definition may be described differently from tomorrow's. Ensure there is consistency in understanding in each organization – define terms and communicate the definitions. If this is not done (and there are abundant examples where actions are taken without clear understanding), stakeholder decisions and actions become unexpected and potentially contradictory. To illustrate this point, consider the fact there is no single, accepted definition of 'digital transformation'.

Any organization that is concerned with digital transformation needs to consider:
- The meaning of the 'digital age' – how it affects the organization, the context of the impact and how that effect will be embraced and managed;
- Governance and the role leaders play in helping the organization to transform, as well as how leadership can enable and facilitate organizational change;
- Ways in which the organization needs to respond to survive;
- The skills, competences and actions of leaders to be effective in a digital age;
- Knowledge and data and how organizations need to understand and utilize them in a digital age.

Each individual organization will view 'the digital age' differently. That view will have a material impact on governance, strategy, the portfolio of services and products, the way organizations manage and realize products and services and the way these translate into management activities. These management activities include creating Service Management Principles, the definition of the Management Mesh, processes, procedures, capabilities, and technologies used.

Real world perspectives

While writing this book, the author team have heard people and organizations express such divergent views as: "We have been digitally transforming since the 1950s, so what's the big deal?" to "Digital transformation is a socio-economic or/and socio-technical phenomenon that affects not only products and services but also markets and society as a whole."

How each organization views the digital age will influence how it digitally transforms or optimizes its products, services and ways of working.

The digital age, like any other preceding age, is defined as an 'age' because it represents a fundamental socio-economic and behavioral shift. The digital age is an evolution within the information age – where technology serves as the catalyst for creating a knowledge-based society surrounded by a high-tech global economy.

The digital age also means the realization of a commercialized society that allow individuals to explore their personalized needs, simplifying decision-making and transacting with counterparts on a global scale. Air travel has made the world a small place, the digital age takes this further and makes it fit on a handheld device or a desktop computer. The outcome of the digital age is an entirely new way of transacting, learning, and socializing – necessitating a fundamental rethink of how organizations operate. No business unit is immune, including any of the traditional supporting functions (e.g., HR, finance, IT, marketing, etc.) that were previously seen as non-core activities.

3 The digital age and the digital organization

Introduction

What does the digital age mean for organizations? This chapter looks at what is meant by a 'digital organization', the impact of digital transformation on systems of record and systems of engagement, people and the digital age and digital products and services.

This chapter also introduces digital transformation approaches and options.

■ 3.1 WHAT IS A DIGITAL ORGANIZATION?

A 'digital organization' is more than just the use of technology or digitizing existing ways of doing things. A digital organization enables existing business models or results in new business models and ecosystems of consumers and collaborators (and possibly competitors). A digital organization requires clearly defined and efficient processes that are data-driven. Additionally, the organization must have the ability to react quickly to changes within its ecosystem based on consumer demand and business model changes.

One significant distinction between the organizations of the past and the digital organization is a more flexible culture, involving continuous improvement, experimenting and learning new ways of working. This includes technical flexibility as well as flexibility in design. A digital organization must take steps to make progress in these areas. Not all aspects, as listed below[3], need to be fully realized in each organization. The level to which each organization aspires will depend on specific market conditions, enterprise governance and relevant products and services. For each organization, a gap analysis can be conducted, based on these aspects, to compare the desired and current situations.

---

3 Bouman, J. F., Teunissen, W., Eusterbrock, T., van Steenbergen, M., & Flikweert, J. (2017, September 30). *Imperatives of a digital enterprise*, (Online). https://bouman.home.xs4all.nl/Artikelen/20170930_Sogeti_ Imperatives_of_a_Digital_Enterprise.pdf

1. **Consumer focus:** The digital organization thoroughly knows its consumer (e.g., habits, preferences, needs, requirements...) before those needs are expressed. The organization must understand what will contribute to the achievement of the consumer's goals and then deliver that in its products and services. Creating personalized products and services while maintaining consumer privacy supports the consumer's digital 'happiness'.

2. **Everything by design:** The digital organization designs consumer value and outcomes (e.g., addressing consumer ambitions, tastes, feelings, concerns...) rather than products and services. Design experiences that are sustainable and create lasting added value.

3. **Learn by experiment:** The modern world changes faster than traditional training and ways of working can be developed and delivered. So, the digital organization must experiment, fail, succeed and most importantly, learn by doing. Learning through trial-and-error while processing feedback is key to a successful digital organization. This 'learning by experimentation' often creates the new product or service and certainly influences working practices and principles.

4. **Automation:** Consumer demands change constantly, so time-consuming design, development and production cycles may not be suitable. The digital organization automates activities from demand to delivery, reducing waiting time as well as errors. There is, however, a risk to be aware of. Radically applying automation to the delivery of products and services may create a disconnection between the service provider and the consumer as the consumer focus becomes lost.

5. **Continuous renewal:** Today's consumer will have different needs tomorrow, so developing and delivering new products and services to meet those needs is a continuous process. The digital organization will embrace continuous learning to ensure it remains relevant to its consumer base.

6. **Immediacy (Now):** The world sits in the palm of the consumer's hand. Connectivity and immediacy are expected by the consumer, who often has less time and expects instant response and satisfaction. The digital organization must be able to deliver requested products and services immediately. And, should the consumer change their mind, the digital organization will immediately adjust – all from the swipe of a finger. Consumer loyalty cannot be relied on in the digital age.

7. **Open network player:** The digital organization embraces the openness of the network. Through digitalization, distance no longer exists. Factories and offices disappear. Co-creation is the new norm, allowing organizations to create business models that are not limited by geography and can include multiple suppliers and partners.

"Technology doesn't provide value to a business. It never has (except for technology in products). Instead, technology's value comes from doing business differently because technology makes it possible."

George Westerman, Principal Research Scientist with the MIT Sloan Initiative on the Digital Economy

Embracing the concept of being a digital organization drives the 'how' of product or service delivery. Even physical products have digital aspects involved in their lifecycle. The digital organization ensures all aspects operate effectively in the creation and support of the products and services.

But the digital organization has challenges. Often, there is a remote and distributed workforce, which can make communication and process standardization difficult. There may be an ecosystem of subscription services which teams rely on, often with untapped integration opportunities and duplicated service offerings.

To transform successfully, an organization must effectively establish and embed the following digital capabilities through all of its organizational capabilities (Sales, Marketing, HR, etc.):
■ Consumer centricity and focus;
■ A focus on operational excellence;
■ An overall strategy defined in digital terms;
■ Leadership involved with and driving the organization from above;
■ Governance models and structures that support the new approach[4].

These capabilities and their associated practices will ensure an organization is nimble enough to exploit opportunities and achieve sustained competitive advantage. Disruptive technologies can be copied by competitors; digital capabilities are substantially more difficult to replicate.

Real world perspective
Steve Chambers is the Chief Operating Officer at Cloudsoft Corporation. Having worked with dozens of organizations in a career spanning more than 20 years, Steve shared some characteristics of organizations that will struggle to transform, based on his experience. These include organizations that:
• Think 'IT' is not core to their business and outsource it;
• Expect vendors to 'innovate' on their behalf;
• Fail to reward IT staff for agility, resilience and innovation and instead punish them for change, outages, and experimentation;

---

4   de Kock, R. (2017). *Digital Transformation Enablement: An assessment of IT Service Management as an enabler.* Unpublished master's thesis, University of Northampton, Northampton, United Kingdom.

- Favor status-quo over reinvention;
- Leave 'agility and innovation' to a small unsupervised 'special squad' who do not understand the big picture;
- Talk a good game about consumers but have no evidence of consumer obsession in their execution.

Real world perspective: Technology Business Management, Jack Bischof

In Chapter 23 Jack Bischof from the TBM Council shares his perspective on how the world has changed, the new skills that are needed, and how businesses need to adapt.

"Without your finger on cost, risk, value, volume, demand, and consumption of resources, services, products, and vendors, by consumer, operating or legal entity, you're not making intelligent choices."

■ 3.2   DIGITAL TRANSFORMATION AND THE DIGITAL ORGANIZATION

VeriSM defines digital transformation as "the changes associated with the application of digital technologies across all areas of an organization, from sales to marketing, products, services and new business models".

For many business people, words like 'digital' and 'systems', mean that they can 'switch off' and let the IT department solve the problem. In the digital age, nothing can be further from the truth – digital systems, products and services are just different representations of what the organization is doing. In real terms, they are the enablers of everything that happens in the business.

3.2.1   Systems and digital transformation

Digital transformation (or optimization) affects an organization's systems. To understand what this means, start with clarity about what a system is.

 System

Systems are generally described in two ways:

1. a set of things working together as parts of a mechanism or an interconnecting network; a complex whole, or, more operationally;
2. a set of principles or procedures according to which something is done; an organized scheme or method.

People often talk about the railway system or a system of government. How often has the phrase, "Don't buck the system!" come up in the workplace? These terms and phrases illustrate that a system does not solely rest in IT, an application or technology and rightly so. The word 'system' comes from the Greek *sun* (with), *histania* (set up) to form *sustema* (in Latin *systema*). A system describes how a set of 'things' are set up to make sense within a particular context.

Having an understanding and an appreciation of organizational systems is important for the leader, the executive and the manager, regardless of their area of responsibility or specialization. The organization itself is a system, truly, an ecosystem – hence the term 'organization'. To embrace the digital organization fully, understanding a system is critical in order to understand how to 'do' business.

3.2.2 Systems of record and systems of engagement

To start to understand the impact of digital transformation on an organization's 'systems', consider the definitions of systems of record (SoR) and systems of engagement (SoE)[5] drawn from Geoffrey Moore's book, *Crossing the Chasm*[6].

Systems of record

Traditional IT systems (in business terms) are systems of record. They represent how business transactions are 'done'. The business transactions are a digital representation of a business system and its processes and procedures. The main advantage of using IT systems to facilitate what happens in the business system is that it helps to manage large volumes of data and, to some extent, make better decisions by transforming the data into knowledge using analytics.

Systems of record form the main part of organizational digitization that has taken place since the advent of computing. They have grown from applications and IT infrastructure supporting a very specific business procedure or process to applications and related infrastructure that support a business ecosystem such as Material Requirements Planning (MRP) systems in manufacturing or Enterprise Resource Planning (ERP). This type of IT system can potentially digitize every process in an organization. Systems of record are very efficient but rely on pre-existing order, processes and procedures.

Systems of record are relatively easy to understand if there is clarity about the business system they represent. They bring solid gains to organizations, mostly through increased efficiencies and sometimes because they highlight systemic problems, prompting the organization to improve the way they do things (process improvement, re-engineering, etc.). Another potential gain from understanding and using systems of record is that they serve as an enabler for future automation, as new and more sophisticated technologies become available. Automation is an area where virtually all organizations can unlock gains. It enables faster and better

---

5   Moore, G. A. (2011). *Systems of engagement and the future of enterprise IT: A sea change in enterprise IT*, (Online). http://info.aiim.org/systems-of-engagement-and-the-future-of-enterprise-it. [2018 March].
6   Moore, G. A. (1991). *Crossing the chasm (3rd ed.)*. New York: HarperCollins.

(increased consistency and less variance) products and services while unlocking scalability not previously possible.

Systems of engagement

Systems of engagement (SoE) represent a new way of engaging with consumers, users, customers, or a community. This new and often unexpected engagement happens when something is used in a completely different manner from what was intended. The impact is usually completely unknown and has unforeseen consequences, even if the original system was well-planned and designed. When a new SoE is introduced, its designers will not know how it will affect the socio-economic environment – in other words, they learn its impact through consumer experimentation.

Real world example

System of engagement: email

Email was not originally designed as a business tool but as a way for scientists on different University campuses to communicate in a Defense Advanced Research Projects Agency (DARPA) sponsored project. Commercially, email was initially intended to replace letters and memos in an office environment. It later grew to include scheduling, analytical tools (surveys), a way of socializing, a means to share data beyond text, including very complex data, as a delivery mechanism for products and services, a political tool, a marketing and sales tool and many other uses and applications.

If the original designers were asked what email could – and will – do, their answer would be limited to the design specification.

With hindsight, it is easy to assume that email does all the things mentioned, as we have experienced the expanded social influence of email. It now seems only natural and logical to use email in this way.

When email is used in many different ways, organizations experience so-called 'email pollution'. Email pollutes working environments and encroaches into personal lives.

Some organizations take actions to reverse this trend and try to become email-free (see Chapter 6 – Collaboration)

As an early adopter using email on Fidonet[7] in the early 1980s, email was both innovative and utilitarian. Fidonet became the new HAM Radio network (already an unintended

---

7   FidoNet was a store-and-forward, privately funded, dial-up network operated by hobbyists across the globe. By the mid-1990s there were almost 40,000 FidoNet systems in operation, and it was possible to communicate with millions of users around the world. Only UUCPNET came close in terms of breadth or numbers; FidoNet's user base far surpassed other networks like BITNET (the precursor for the internet as we know it today).

use) for electronic hobbies and computer enthusiasts. Even in those early days, email morphed into a system of engagement.

Today, most people would probably say that email is part of the business fabric, a necessity without which organization cannot operate. Some may even say that email is a human right.

No-one has ever said the same for a financial application or ERP system. Systems of engagement become part of the fabric of society, or a community, and continuously morph into new and interesting areas of application. Consider the impact of the introduction of cell phones, the internet, email and social media platforms – there is no denying their significance.

SoE/SoR example

Consider the purchase of car insurance:
- An application used by a car insurance salesperson, where information is gathered from customers via phone calls or a face-to-face meeting would be an example of a *system of record;*
- An online portal allowing the customer to pick and choose their own policy, its features and complete the transaction, would be a *system of engagement* (particularly if it involves the user creating a user-id on the system for future relationship building or sales).

Just 10 years ago, most static consumer data was stored in SoRs (such as databases and spreadsheets). Today, the same information is stored in SoEs like collaboration systems that are used by customers, providers and other stakeholders and have direct connections to social media or other Big Data sources. These systems might use artificial intelligence and learning algorithms to optimize consumer engagement.

This does not mean, however, that systems of engagement are more important than systems of record, or that they should receive the service provider's total focus. The gains possible from digitization and automation of systems of record are similarly astounding and quite often the starting point for digital transformation initiatives. Organizations may build 'digital twins' of their current organizational capability that serve as a platform for innovation and, which in turn, identify and highlight opportunities to create systems of engagement. A digital twin is a replica of a physical object that can be manipulated to find different ways of using/ managing it.

Organizations should ideally give attention to systems of record and engagement, as both play an essential role in digital transformation. The creation of systems of engagement will almost always be an empirical process including experimentation, experience and observation. The emergent practices introduced in the first VeriSM publication may become part of an organization's Management Mesh as part of its journey in a digital age.

The Gartner view of systems

Gartner has a slightly different view that was influenced by Moore's thinking. Gartner focuses on three application categories, or 'layers'. Using this 'Pace Layered View' of systems, business applications can be categorized by the nature of the problem they address, their rate of change and the distinctiveness of the solution, helping organizations develop more appropriate strategies for each[8]:

- Systems of record: established packaged applications or legacy systems that support core transaction processing and manage the organization's critical master data;
- Systems of differentiation: applications that enable unique organizational processes or industry-specific capabilities;
- Systems of innovation: new applications that are built on an ad hoc basis to address new business requirements or opportunities.

These three layers are not fixed and will change over time. SoRs may shrink as they are transformed or modernized, becoming SoD or SoI. SoD and SoI may become SoRs as they become stable and predictable.

■ 3.3   PEOPLE AND THE DIGITAL AGE

For an organization to survive in the digital age, its leadership and management must deal with changes in technology along with changes in its consumers and staff, their attitudes and behaviors. Until very recently, the attitudes and behaviors of Generation X dominated commerce: the individual and individual advancement (to a large extent) drove attitudes in the workplace and choices made by consumers. (For more on Generations X, Y and Z – refer to *VeriSM™: A Service Management Approach for the Digital Age*.)

This Gen X focus on individual advancement is no longer as dominant. Managers from Gen X may find it difficult to deal with millennials (Generation Y) and Generation Z employees and consumers[9]. Although financial stability is still one of the main concerns of Gen Y and Gen Z, a much stronger emphasis is placed on work being meaningful and creative. Staff from these generations expect instant feedback from teachers, parents, managers and supervisors. Therefore, leaders

---

8   Gartner. (2012, February 14). *Gartner says adopting a pace-layered application strategy can accelerate innovation*, (Online). https://www.gartner.com/newsroom/id/1923014. [2018 February].
9   There are some subtle differences between the two latter generations; they however do have a lot in common

and managers need to adapt their working practices to create, facilitate and maintain the environment that will engage these characteristics.

> **Real world perspective**
> Although data changes from year to year, the generalizations stated above continue to repeat. Review the Deloitte Millennial Survey[10] on an annual basis to keep track of trends.

From a product and service perspective, these needs and ideals must be engrained within the product and service design as well as in consumer engagement. Services now need to provide virtually instantaneous results, and gratification.

> "To prosper over time, every company must not only deliver financial performance but also show how it makes a positive contribution to society."
>
> Larry Fink, CEO of BlackRock

3.3.1   Generation Y and Z as consumers

Generation Y and Z consumers display similar behavior and attitudes, making life complicated for a product or service provider. Products and services need to enable flexibility and potentially have the ability for the consumer to reconfigure the product, service or workflow in new ways they find meaningful at the time – and be able to change it again tomorrow. This makes what service providers have to offer much more dynamic, but also less predictable. Consumption of digital products or services should have a much higher social context, perhaps integrating with social platforms to provide a rich and seamless experience.

From a marketing perspective, Gen Y and Z consumers want instant service. They are less likely to spend disproportionate amounts of money on items that are perceived as non-utilitarian (traditional status symbols) and they are acutely aware of the environmental impact of their spending habits. Providers of digital products and services need to be sensitive about how these are promoted, sold and marketed. If the product or service fulfils a social or environmental need, consumers can become willing participants in the promotion and selling of the product or service. This is achieved without expecting any compensation or, perhaps, just receiving a simple form of social recognition, such as a digital badge.

---

10 Deloitte. (2018, May 15). *The Deloitte millennial survey 2018*, (Online). https://www2.deloitte.com/global/en/pages/about-deloitte/articles/millennialsurvey.html [2018 May].

> **Real world example: Tribesports**
>
> Tribesports is an example of a brand appealing to the Gen Y and Z community and using the power of digital technology.
>
> Tribesports launched its product on the Kickstarter platform in August 2013, aiming to create high quality sportswear using feedback from real consumers.
>
> Now a global brand, it maintains a strong relationship with its customer base, requesting input into products and features and feedback on its products, evolving the products continually in response.

3.3.2   Generation Y and Z as staff

To be effective when working with Gen Y and Z, managers or supervisors need to adopt a new management skillset to make the workplace function effectively. These managers and supervisors need to focus on coaching and leadership, reducing micromanagement. Additionally, organizations need to consider flatter hierarchies. The 'command and control' way of managing an organization has proven to be less effective with the Gen Y or Gen Z workers. (See Section 5.1 – Kill the hierarchy.)

The prevalence of social media use by Gen Y or Gen Z workers has augmented collaboration skills and created the need for either a team-oriented workplace or, at least, the ability to work in defined (social) groups. Another significant shift is the need for frequent feedback and, conversely, the need to be left alone to do what they need to do. These two generations are highly-educated and, consequently, they have a low tolerance for doing repetitive non-knowledge work or being micromanaged.

A major commonality of Gen Y and Z is that they are both digital natives – technology and access to technology is part of their professional and social make-up. They become extremely frustrated by education and work practices that do not reflect their perpetual interconnectedness. Further, they do not see the need for inhumane work practices (like overtime) and favor work-life balance over traditional working patterns. Conversely, they also want to be able to connect, receive service and work at times they choose.

The 2018 Digital Transformation Survey

As shown in Figure 10, the majority of survey respondents feel the amount of time they spend interacting with technology is increasing.

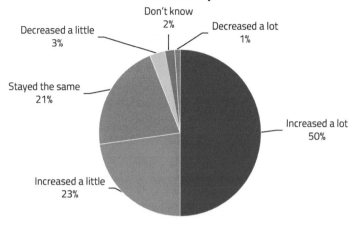

Changes in the amount of time technology is interacted with in your role?

Don't know 2%

Decreased a lot 1%

Decreased a little 3%

Stayed the same 21%

Increased a lot 50%

Increased a little 23%

Figure 10 Changing interaction with technology in the 2018 Survey

People who behave according to the stereotypes of baby-boomers and Gen X are misunderstood and seen as migrants and intruders in a digital native's world where they are, at best, tolerated. The implication is that 'traditional' methods and values are distrusted. For example, dressing up an old service with a shiny mobile interface is likely to be mistrusted and discarded. For example, after the launch of Uber, many traditional cab companies launched 'pay by mobile' apps to entice consumers. The change did not resonate with Uber's consumer base, because it only addressed the interface, not the social enterprise element underpinning the Uber service: individuals connecting with other individuals for a ride (as opposed to the traditional cab company structure).

Real world perspective

In addition to generational themes, leaders and managers always need to be aware of unique cultural and geographic differences. Cultural dynamics should not be underestimated or ignored.

A good source by which to understand cultural differences is the work of Gert Hofstede[11]. 'Cultural Dimensions Theory' is a framework for cross-cultural communication and describes the effects of a society's culture on the values of its members and how these values relate to behavior.

---

11 https://www.hofstede-insights.com/models/organisational-culture/

This is also true for those who are digital natives. In some environments socio-economic circumstances may negate generational observations. For example, it is not possible to be a digital native if you are not 'wired', so in societies with low levels of digital penetration, many of the above observations may not be consistent with reality.

Digital natives – in general – dislike control. They like to share, but also understand that some things should not be shared. They are fiercely politically correct, generally liberal in their views, more likely to work in the public sector or for organizations with charitable aims. They are prepared to work for substantially less money than peers in other roles, if they feel they make a social contribution and a difference in the world. This creates opportunities for organizations to engage workers in line with their corporate social responsibility programs.

Real world perspective: Deloitte University Press
The digital age makes new demands of organizations to keep up with the pace of change and exploit opportunities for digital innovation. It also makes new demands of the professionals working within them. The professional operating in today's digital world will still need specialist knowledge but will also need to have a much broader scope of competences than ever before. This leads to the so-called T-shaped professional. Figure 11 illustrates the skills necessary for the digital age.

Figure 11 Skills for the digital age (source: Deloitte University Press| DUPress.com)

Technical IT knowledge is more relevant than ever. This type of knowledge is crucial in ensuring that new technologies can be exploited and managed effectively. However, technological savviness is just one piece of the bigger puzzle; much more is demanded from today's professional. This includes competences related to shifts in behavior, such as the move towards more collaborative ways of working (see Chapter 6 – Collaboration), the adoption of an Agile mindset to enable increased flexibility and responsiveness and user experience (UX) design skills to assure a consumer-centric approach to product and service design. It also involves an understanding of the business and an entrepreneurial spirit, so that professionals can assess organizational risk and apply their knowledge to finding innovative solutions that add true value. Possessing such a broad skill set may seem daunting – but increasingly necessary in a world where there is now no real separation between business and IT.

The high pace of change in the digital age also means that competence requirements will continue to change and evolve. Lifelong learning has become more important than ever, as professionals need to continuously evolve their skill set to reflect new developments, in the same way that organizations need to regularly update their Management Mesh and ways of working. In the digital age, the successful professional is the one who is able to adapt to this fast-changing world and recognize that what was learnt yesterday is not necessarily still relevant for tomorrow.

■ 3.4 DIGITAL PRODUCTS AND SERVICES

Although some define a digital product or service as "one that has been entirely automated and is controlled by the interaction of the customer of the service"[12], this view may be regarded as simplistic. Excluding non- or partially-automated products when discussing digital services is a mistake. VeriSM defines a digital product or service as one that is "enabled by or only possible because of the advances made in technology" and this definition seems more inclusive and appropriate.

Digital products and services are commonly online or, at the very least, have a significant online element, for example, they are marketed, sold and/ or supported online. These systems of engagement will possibly draw information from systems of record, but this will be entirely hidden from the consumer. Online features are driven by the availability of connected client devices that are increasingly both mobile and wireless.

---

12 Otchere, E. A. (No date). *Digitize services, capture value*, (Online). http://carrier.huawei.com/en/technical-topics/service/softwareservice/Helping%20Telcos%20Digitalize%20Services%20%20Emma.

> **Real world example**
>
> Online price comparison sites such as Trivago, Booking.com and Expedia all act as systems of engagement, drawing information from multiple systems of record that are not visible or accessible to the consumer.

Digital services remove many of the barriers that exist between the service provider and the service consumer. Digital services are virtually always on, available, accessible and transactable. However, they can also create barriers by removing the direct, face-to-face relationship between service provider and consumer. See Chapter 8 – Outcomes, for more information about the challenges this can pose.

Some organizations choose to focus on the digitization of systems of record, ensuring that the interface becomes more user friendly and the product or service provides a better user experience – this is defined as digital optimization. Other organizations focus on how consumers interact with them and seek new and better ways to service, communicate, market, sell and transact with a consumer – defined as digital transformation. The optimal approach typically includes elements of both.

Focusing in digital optimization may seem 'easier'. Organizations can fall into the trap of spending far too much time and effort here, with little or no focus on active transformational projects, which may even cannibalize the profitable services that are currently offered. This is addressed in Section 3.6, looking at how innovation spaces should be separated from the organization's normal operation. It is difficult to make the case to innovate and produce something that will kill the organization's existing profitable products and services.

Most experts realize that there is a difference between 'digitally optimized' and 'digitally transformed' products or services. One uses technology better and the other actually morphs in a new product or service, with a radically altered or even totally different value proposition. This distinction is important for an organization thinking about its products or services in a digital context.

■ 3.5 DIGITAL OPTIMIZATION AND TRANSFORMATION APPROACHES

Both digital optimization and digital transformation are approaches to the digitization of the organization. There is no one standard way to achieve either. However, as more and more organizations create and share ideas, standardized approaches will emerge.

Optimization is not transformation

Digital optimization describes the situation when organizations use innovative technologies and methods to augment existing business processes, products and services. Optimization is not new, in fact, every digitization effort since the advent of commercial computing has had exactly the same aim. It stands to reason that organizations and industry have, over the years, developed effective ways of optimizing their organization with the use of technology. The only difference today is that the level of technological innovation is higher and many of the tried and tested methods are no longer fit for purpose. It is perhaps for this reason that many technology-driven organizations turn to Agile and DevOps to ensure faster and better delivery of digital capabilities.

Optimization may unlock efficiencies, but it is not a source of differentiation or long-term competitive advantage. Whether the organization's goal is optimization or transformation is an important strategic decision.

Some organizations may have projects or programs that are working on both optimization and transformation, for example a project to optimize legacy infrastructure and commodity services, and a program to transform strategic assets.

Chapter 27 provides a real-world example of how digital design techniques were used to optimize volunteer onboarding at children's charity Kidz Klub.

A number of different approaches exist to help organizations support their digital transformation. Digital transformation has its roots in established concepts such as Total Quality Management (TQM), Customer Experience Management and Strategic Planning, amongst others and, as a result, definitions related to it often mimic existing definitions that apply to other disciplines. Figure 12 shows three possible approaches for optimization or transformation. The approaches each have a different focus or perspective and are suitable for organizations with different goals and levels of maturity.

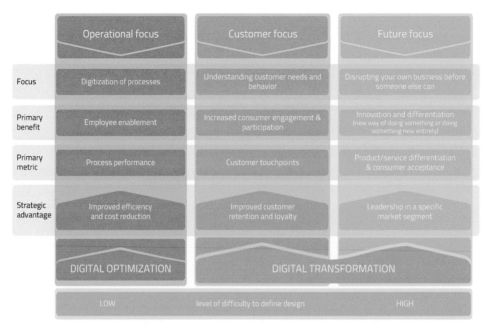

Figure 12 VeriSM Digital Optimization and Transformational approaches, their focus and benefit (source: original idea from *Digital Transformation: a Roadmap for billion dollar organizations*, 2011 MIT Centre for Digital Business and Capgemini Consulting)

The three broad approaches to digital transformation and optimization, outlined in Figure 12, are:

- An operational approach – focuses on process digitization that will facilitate process efficiency and reduce costs;
- A customer focused approach – focuses on servicing known customer needs better and emergent (observed) behaviors. The outcome is greater customer loyalty and higher levels of satisfaction;
- A future focused approach – seeks to innovate and disrupt markets to ensure long-term market segment leadership and enables the organization to survive and thrive.

Digital transformation is about much more than technology. It encompasses culture, people and behavior, organizations and markets. As such, digital transformation encompasses all areas within an organization. When defining digital transformation efforts, the organization must include the language and expectations of all organizational capabilities (e.g. HR, Finance, Sales...) to ensure each capability embraces and understands the journey. Any digital transformation effort must take into consideration the legal, regulatory and financial requirements for the organization. Products and services must operate within established legal and regulatory constraints, and not expose consumers or the organization itself to potential fines and penalties.

Some organizations may adopt a combination of approaches. Using one approach does not preclude the use of another; sometimes distinct parts of the business will use different approaches. An organization, for example, choosing the optimization approach might then use the customer and/or future focused approaches to help it solve problems.

All digital transformation efforts require dedicated leadership to ensure they are sustained, on track and achieving the agreed strategy. Direction given by senior management is key. Proper governance provides the required structure, transparency and guidelines to ensure behavior is monitored and directed effectively. This approach also allows organizations to demonstrate that the vision and industry norms are being met. (See Chapter 10 – Governance and strategy – for more detail.)

■ 3.6 FROM CONVENTIONAL TO DIGITAL SERVICES

Can a conventional (non-digital) service become a digital service? The short answer is, yes, the slightly longer answer is, yes – but projects of this nature frequently fail. The main reason for this is that most stakeholders do not realize that digitization does not guarantee success in terms of use, utility, acceptance or value. Completely different practices are required to support the consumer approach; including design and renewal of products or services and operations, automation, delivery and co-creation.

Many organizations start their digital journey with aggressive automation. This includes seeking opportunities to automate existing processes, taking systems of record online and improving the user experience (UX). Many purists will argue that this is not digital transformation, because it is not social and is only technical, economic or transactional in nature.

Some organizations build digital replicas (twins) of their physical environment to better understand how traditional services will behave in a digital context. For example, a Siemens plant in Germany uses a digital twin to test the outcome of changes to the automated manufacturing processes. Building a twin may be starting point for digitizing a service (digital optimization/operational focus – blue in Figure 13), but the real value of having a digital twin comes from the ability to use it for experimentation and learning for innovation purposes.

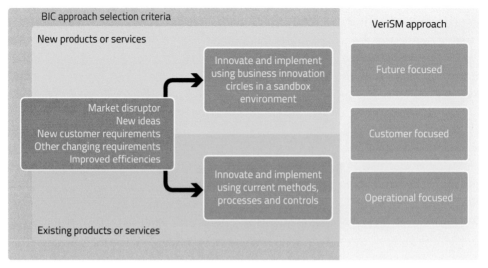

Figure 13 Mapping VeriSM approaches to Business Innovation Circles™ optimization and transformation approaches

Innovation to support a customer or future-focused transformation approach is best carried out in 'innovation spaces' (upper, light orange area to the left in Figure 13) where the replica can be exposed to rigorous experimentation and hypothesis testing. These cannot be conducted realistically in a live commercial environment. These innovation spaces should be a safe area isolated from the business environment and controls. They were originally called 'skunk-works®[13]' but now have various names and may be referred to as a 'sandbox environment'. Chapter 9 provides an example of how one innovation technique – Business Innovation Circles[14] – works.

Organizations usually find the greatest value when they design and build a digital product or service from the ground up. However, successful digital transformation still relies on existing knowledge and experience developed from the market, its consumers and within the organization.

■ 3.7 REQUIREMENTS FOR SUCCESSFUL DIGITAL PROGRAMS

What sets one digital initiative apart from the next? The following themes are commonly found in successful digital initiatives:

■ **Digital transformation is established as an organization-wide strategic program.**
Given the complex nature of transformation initiatives, they need to be managed as a program of work to ensure that all efforts are coordinated effectively. It

13 ® Skunk-Works is a registered trademark of Lockheed Martin Corporation.
14 © 2016, BIC and BUSINESS INNOVATION CIRCLES™ is a trademark and copyright of getITright® Skills Development www.get-it-right.com and the content made available in documents is subject to this notice being included in the text.

is essential that digital transformation is not run as a single initiative or project. Transformation should be expected to take several years, carried out as a series of small incremental projects, leading to a permanent culture change.

■ **The role of IT (technology) as part of the business is pivotal.** Attempting digital transformation as an IT project alone will not be successful. There needs to be a robust and integrated bond to build trust and continuous collaboration between technical and business knowledge, across the organization. Without collaboration, technology will not be used effectively to enhance business capabilities and the consumer experience. It is important to realize that digital transformation is a business initiative supported by technology – it is not 'an IT project'. The definition of 'IT' needs to be clear; this is about the technology that enables the organization, not just the department.

■ **Personalized real-time feedback is essential.** To keep motivation high and maintain momentum, it is vital that personalized real-time feedback is provided to all the connected stakeholders during the entire transformational program. This can be a single page dashboard on progress or the sharing of success stories. It is essential to keep all stakeholders involved to give them a sense of ownership and connection.

■ **Providing governance for digital transformation.** The use of centers of excellence or steering committees facilitates communication, participation and success. The focus of these structures should be to identify and highlight business opportunities for transformation and candidate technologies to be used for innovation. Governing guidelines and Service Management Principles for piloting new technology in a controlled, yet unrestrictive manner also need to be established to enable innovation. Principles foster a culture of security, privacy, sharing and ownership to enable responsible management of consumer data.

■ **Focus on market leadership and building competitive capabilities through the use of emergent technologies.** Successful organizations need to be able to do this continually and rapidly. Any organization can use emergent technology, but it is the marriage of technology and digital capabilities that unlocks mastery of a market or sector.

■ **Establishing and maturing digital capabilities**. True digital transformation involves the establishment and maturity of key capabilities such as consumer centricity, operational excellence and strategic innovation as well as leadership and governance. As illustrated in Figure 14, without all the capabilities in place, sustained competitive advantage through continual transformation would not be possible.

As part of digital transformation, organizational resources should be exploited, but not necessarily the existing organizational processes. Using organizational processes may stifle innovation. It is better to create a safe place in which to experiment without the restrictions of existing controls. See Chapter 9, Business Innovation Circles, for more detail.

Figure 14 Consequences of missing capabilities

■ 3.8   DIGITAL TRANSFORMATION OPTIONS

Organizations need to experiment and identify which digital transformation approach best suits their needs. Organizations also need to consider how their chosen approach will be implemented. In Section 3.5, three approaches were described. These can be implemented by using one of these options:

■ Organization-led implementation option;
■ Consultant or vendor-led implementation option;
■ Mixed implementation option.

Most digital transformation initiatives are multi-year initiatives. It is imperative that suitable implementation methods are used to enable frequent review, learning and updates to take place. Where necessary, actions can be taken to realign initiatives that are off course.

> "Seventy percent of strategic failures are due to poor execution…it's rarely for the lack of smarts or vision."
>
> Ram Charan, *Execution: The Discipline of Getting Things Done*

3.8.1   An organization-led implementation option

If an organization wants to embed digital capabilities and transform its products and services in innovative ways and it has the essential knowledge, skills and resources and appetite to perform the transformation itself, then the organization-led option is suitable.

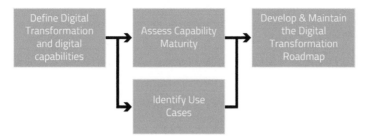

Figure 15 Organization-led implementation

> **Real world example: WuXi AppTec and ANONCORP**
>
> Chapter 20 looks at the digital transformation of WuXi AppTec, a Chinese organization in the drug and medical industry.
>
> "The whole procurement team was struggling with the manual maintenance of suppliers, quotation, and order follow-up. Simply adding more employees is becoming more difficult due to the cost pressure and low efficiency in cross collaboration."
>
> It also includes a profile of ANONCORP, an organization that provides digital services to its external customers and suppliers.
>
> "Based on the Business Information Plan priorities are set, and resources are arranged via the portfolio governance boards where both business and IT are involved to realize the required competences within the timing and resource constraints provided."

Define digital transformation and digital capabilities

Clear communication and understanding are key elements to succeeding with any large initiative. Communication starts with a definition of what digital transformation means for the organization and how it relates to the organization's strategic objectives. It is essential that digital transformation is defined in a way that resonates with the people involved. Further to this, aligning the digital transformation program to the organizational vision and mission statement will provide a clear message to the organization on its digital journey. Governance and Service Management Principles must be in place to act as guardrails and provide direction.

The organization needs to define the digital capabilities that are needed, along with a definition of what each capability means. Digital capabilities need resourcing, development and maturing across all organizational capabilities, covering:

- Consumer centricity and focus;
- A focus on operational excellence;
- An overall strategy defined in digital terms;
- Leadership involved with and driving the organization from above;
- Governance models and structures that support the new approach.

Assess digital capability maturity

If an organization wants to fully embrace holistic digital transformation, a digital maturity model can be used to benchmark its progress in building capabilities. There are many digital capability assessment models available that can be used to assess skills, processes and tools. The results would be used to define a prioritized roadmap of initiatives the organization would need to follow in order to improve digital maturity and capability.

Digital capability assessment

A gap analysis based on digital capabilities (see Section 3.1. What is a Digital Organization?) has proven to be a very useful assessment practice. For each aspect the desired and current situations can be determined, and the gaps can be 'filled' with skills, processes and tools to bridge the gaps.

Digital transformation is a strategic decision for the organization and should never be limited to a single project or initiative. Capabilities also need to be focused on the enablement of the entire enterprise and not on a single product or service. The level of maturity required for each capability will be defined by the organization's objectives. Although many organizations treat digital transformation as a project or program, organizations that embrace digital transformation at the strategic level consistently outperform organization that do not[15].

Identify digital use cases

A use case is a modelling technique that describes, either visually or through a narration, a user's perspective of how they would interact with various systems in order to achieve a specific goal. Within the context of digital transformation, use cases provide scenarios which show how technologies and digital capabilities can provide competitive advantage. They are applied to define, design, test or validate transformation initiatives.

Digital use cases can be identified and built at the same time as capabilities are built and matured. However, they cannot be used before an organization's digital capabilities are clearly defined, agreed and communicated. The organization should look for digital use cases across all products and services to identify enhancement opportunities. Use cases should be continually re-evaluated. They should be updated, or additional use cases defined, as new information becomes available and new transformational initiatives are identified. Examples could include the introduction of new digital channels for consumer communication, introducing machine learning for identifying new consumer insights, automating end-to-end processes or using orchestration for operational excellence.

---

15 Bonnet, D., Mcafee, A., Westerman, G. (2014) The Nine Elements of Digital Transformation. *MIT Sloan Management Review*. January, 1–6. [online]. Available from: http://sloanreview.mit.edu/article/the-nine-elements-of-digital-transformation/.

Digital channel

A digital channel is any means an organization can use to interact with its consumers around its products and services. Digital channels include the internet, mobile network, mail etc., but channels can also be more granular and include platforms such as Twitter, Facebook, Google ads, email, SMS, etc.

The following techniques can be used to identify possible use cases:

Table 1 Techniques to discover use cases

Techniques	Description
Engage with vendors / partners	Technology vendors or partners are a great resource to use to come up with new innovative ideas and case studies for digital capabilities. They can review your business and provide proposals for latest technology innovations etc.
Hackathons	Many organizations make use of hackathons – organization-wide competitions that encourage staff to think of innovative ways of doing things. A few criteria may be laid out to ensure ideas address innovation needs, such as being focused on consumer centricity or fitting within a certain budget. The employees would design use cases, prototypes and associated business cases to support the ideas. These are reviewed to identify the strongest candidate, with prizes awarded at events to promote excitement. Typically, these events are regular – often held every six months to a year. If repeated, they will slowly foster a culture of innovation as staff will be more likely to continually seek and present new ideas.
Innovation hubs	Another approach is to create innovation hubs: dedicated teams that focus on reviewing the organization and identifying use cases for digital transformation. Innovation hubs can be useful for coordinating digital transformation efforts. They can make use of vendor engagements, hackathons and other approaches to generate further innovative ideas and concepts.
Innovation and ideas management tools	Other techniques may include the use of innovation and ideas management tools. These tools can enable collaboration and/or wider support for innovation ideas to develop them further, across the organization or across departmental boundaries.
Digital center of excellence	An organization could establish a digital center of excellence where some of its most innovative people get together to review business opportunities and establish use cases incorporating emerging technologies and digital capabilities. These digital centers of excellence could be set up in a room or a cordoned-off space. Business people can be invited to 'ideation' sessions where innovative ideas can be generated. The digital center of excellence would need to see the ideas and resulting use cases established as projects or programs of work and run to completion.
Solution labs	Solution labs showcase the latest in services and products the organization is offering. This demonstrates a consistent and ongoing approach for business innovation and can lead to input for strategic ideas.

The techniques in Table 1 should not be seen as a definitive list. As part of building the Management Mesh, organizations need to continually assess new management practices to identify techniques that might add value.

Develop and maintain the roadmap

Assessing digital capability maturity and creating digital use cases will result in a set of initiatives that need to be prioritized and sequenced into a roadmap to form the foundation of the digital transformation program. Assessing digital capability identifies existing gaps and the work that is required to establish the skills, knowledge, processes and competences to transform effectively. The digital transformation definition should be established first, so that there is intent behind the organization's digital transformation journey. The vision drives both the setting and the measurement of capability and maturity targets. A roadmap for the sake of a roadmap will not return the desired results.

> The development of digital capabilities is the foundation upon which all digital initiatives are built. For example, there is little value in an organization implementing a new customer management solution (CMS) with multiple touch points for customers as an innovative digital solution if it has not established the skills, understanding and experience around customer journey mapping and experience management. Digital initiatives are important, but their value cannot be realized without the necessary digital capabilities in place.

The organization's transformational roadmap needs to include a plan for innovation in products and services and development of new capabilities to support innovative digital initiatives. When developing the overall roadmap, the organization needs to review all digital innovation and capability building initiatives, prioritize them and ensure alignment to the plan. Sequencing must be optimal – ensuring that the activities support each other. Prioritization criteria need to consider:

- Budget;
- Resource availability;
- Dependencies (such as skill establishment/organizational readiness before technology initiatives);
- Important competitor product or service launch dates, where relevant.

If these criteria are not carefully weighed and considered at a practical level, there is a risk the overall transformation can be severely affected by budget or resource constraints. There is also a risk that technology is deployed before the prerequisite capabilities are developed or at the right maturity level in the organization, making the initiative worthless.

3.8.2   Consultant/vendor-led implementation option

The consultant/vendor-led option is suitable for an organization that wants to start digital transformation but has limited skills, knowledge or resources or is not effective at running programs (based on the success rate of all of its previous large programs).

This option has some advantages and disadvantages that the commissioning organization needs to consider carefully.

Table 2 Advantages and disadvantages of consultant/vendor-led implementation

Advantages	The consultancy / vendor firm can share the expertise and skills that have been exposed to and matured with many other organizations and could also provide resources for many of the initiatives.
	The consultancy / vendor firm is also likely to have a higher success rate due to the accountability that comes with a signed contract with specific deliverables.
Disadvantages	Consultancy/vendors do not have deep knowledge of the organization. The digital transformation could have a negative impact if the changes are not based on accurate insights and facts.
	Vendors frequently use proprietary products or frameworks, which may not be suited to the organization.
	Using only one consultancy or vendor firm may expose the organization to dependencies that lock it in and keep the vendor involved in perpetuity.
	The easy availability of vendor expertise can lead to organizational complacency in developing in-house digital expertise, which can hold back future innovation.

If an organization chooses to use a consultant or vendor, it is important that it clearly understands where and how it wants the vendor involved in and supporting the digital transformation. At the very least, a clear engagement model, roles and responsibilities, skills transfer, capacity and capability building and exit criteria need to be defined and managed rigorously. See Chapter 16 on Sourcing for more detail.

3.8.3   Mixed implementation option

Many organizations select a mixed option for digital transformation. They may use a consulting firm to help them get started on their journey, to speed up their progress or to gain leading insight and advantage over their competition. Organizations are likely to use consulting firms and vendors throughout their innovation cycle as they create a new product or service. During digital transformation consultants are used to help define and embed new ways of working, acting as experts with a track record of success and previous experience. If an organization selects the 'mixed implementation' option, it will need to have a plan to prevent dependency on external resources, building internal skills to avoid 'vendor lock-in'. The Management Mesh can be used to identify which management practices are being carried out by external resources and identify where the organization might need to build skills internally.

■ 3.9   THE IMPACT OF DIGITAL TRANSFORMATION ON WAYS OF WORKING

Digital transformation is organization-wide (not just a technology project) and therefore has an impact on ways of working across the whole organization. The introduction of digital products and services brings unavoidable changes to the way things are done. Most transformation projects do not fail for technical reasons; they fail culturally and behaviorally. Later chapters discuss operational changes in detail, including:

■ Knowledge management (Chapter 7);
■ Collaboration (Chapter 6);
■ Organizational change management/constant change (Chapters 5 and 24).

Many organizations find that innovation or improvement in one area delivers limited value because it creates conflict with ways of working in other areas. For example, many organizations that adopt Agile software development methods find that their budgeting, business case or procurement processes do not align with Agile. The Management Mesh is a useful tool to integrate and manage new ways of working and new technologies, assessing how to incorporate them and identifying their impact on the organization as a whole. This integrated approach makes sure anything new delivers maximum value, instead of organizations chasing the latest new and 'shiny' thing.

3.9.1   Consumer centricity

Consumer centricity is an important digital capability and is at heart of digital transformation. This capability draws its roots from customer experience and marketing management and is also the main principle defined in Lean.

Consumer centricity drives new ways of working by putting the consumer at the heart of every decision, including:

■ Orienting the organization to the needs and behaviors of its consumers rather than internal drivers, such as short-term profits or cost cutting;
■ Alignment between organizational metrics (such as people reward and recognition), processes and consumer focus;
■ Creating new value for consumers in a way that also creates value for the service provider organization, such as product and service development that creates demand.

Real world perspective

Ways of working – project management

VeriSM proposes an organization-wide approach for service management. To operate effectively in the digital world, organizations need to review their business processes (not just IT or technical processes) and assess if they are fit for purpose. Funding models, budget cycles, approval processes, portfolio management, product management, and project management are all areas that may need to evolve or adapt to support better organizational outcomes and more agile, iterative ways of working.

This segment contributed by Rob England (better known as the IT Skeptic), looks at an example of this: how conventional project management thinking is no longer fit for purpose to manage software development.

What's the problem with projects?[16]
Conventional project management approaches create several challenges in a digital product or service environment:

- When funds are constrained (i.e. usually) projects call on business-as-usual staff, who do not have the time to work on project tasks;
- Digital products and services evolve continuously – there is no 'done' moment that marks the end of a project until the product or service is retired;
- When time, money and deliverables are agreed and set, only one area can vary: the quality of the outputs;
- Project teams are often disbanded at the end of the project. This prevents teams from ever getting beyond 'forming, storming and norming', and key knowledge is lost or dispersed.

Agile ways of working disrupt traditional project management
There are ten Agile principles that sit badly with conventional project management methodology:

1. 'No known defects', which means prioritizing resolving defects over new functionality;
2. Think about 'product' not 'project';
3. Bring the work to the teams, stop disbanding and reforming teams;
4. Create a single stream of work; stop making people prioritize across multiple owners;
5. Teams work to velocity, do not overburden the system, limit work in progress, never run people at 100% utilization;
6. Do the work as late as possible;
7. Maximize the work not done;
8. Deliver in as small increments as possible;
9. Experiment and failure are normal; we do not know the end state;
10. You will never get real quality until those accountable for running it are those who build it.

---

16 England, R. (2017, December 5). *Project management was the worst thing to ever happen to IT*, (Online). http://www.itskeptic.org/content/project-management-was-worst-thing-ever-happened-it. [2018 February].

What needs to change?

The emerging trend is for the organization to change its focus from projects to products and services. Staff are dedicated to the products and services they work on, allowing teams to bond and improve and to gain knowledge and experience over time. This replaces the project structure where teams are broken up as soon as the project is declared as finished.

Organizations can focus on quality, not time. Agile introduces the concept of zero known defects. The way that Agile increases velocity is through increasing quality, not through compromising quality. If new or updated products and services are of high quality, this reduces the impact on the business-as-usual staff who work with and support them and the build staff who fix and improve them. As the amount of time spent on unplanned work reduces (because quality has increased), staff have more time to spend on value adding activities, including further improving quality.

Where project management is used within an organization, focus on 'minimum viable' approaches. Challenge the excessive levels of ceremony of project management, which include:

• Hundreds of pages of requirements which everybody knew would not or could not be delivered;
• Phased approaches;
• Complex stage gates;
• Specialization of function;
• External organizations assuring risk, compliance and quality.

Many organizations will admit they do not measure anticipated outcomes or track project results. By focusing on 'just enough' project management, organizations can get the results they need while minimizing waste.

Projects are Waves[17]

Projects are transitory waves that pass through the product structure. A project is a surge in work, to deliver a defined outcome or a step-change in a product or products. Therefore, it is a surge in the number of people in the team(s) and in the velocity of the team(s) required by the organization to deliver the wave of change by the project.

---

17 England, R. (2017, September 18). *A project is a wave in a product structure*, (Online). http://www. itskeptic.org/content/project-wave-product-structure [2018 March].

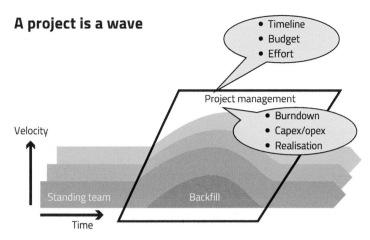

Figure 16 Projects are waves

In this way of working, the project manager role acts as a support function, helping the product teams to deliver an organizational outcome (the organization's project). The project manager will still coordinate, track, and account:
• Effort, money, timeline, milestones;
• Project burn down;
• CAPEX/OPEX.

What they do not do is:
• Hire and fire;
• Own or manage (most of the) people;
• Own the customer or owner relationship;
• Make design or quality decisions;
• Make time decisions.

Equally, they are not accountable for these things.

3.10 THE IMPACT OF DIGITAL TRANSFORMATION ON STRUCTURE

Digital transformation can also have an impact on an organization's structure. The cultural and behavior changes necessary for digital transformation may trigger structural changes. This includes assessing whether some activities would be more effectively carried out by external suppliers. For a real world example, Martijn Adams from 4me shares his experience of the organization with no IT department.

Real world perspective
Does every organization need an IT department?
Martijn Adams — General Manager, EMEA at 4me talks about how digital transformation is affecting the structure of organizations and challenging the way things are done.

Every organization has an IT department, or does it...?

Smaller organizations and start-ups often do not have an IT department. This could be because they are too small and cannot afford dedicated IT staff or they are just not organized enough yet, like start-ups who are laser focused on their 'greatest idea ever'.

In the past years I have seen these organizations grow, move from start-up to scale up and beyond and many still do not have an IT department... So, what has changed in the past years?

Today's users are more tech-savvy and have grown up in a digital world where everything is available in a heartbeat and is very customer centric. These users are in general more capable of organizing their own IT workplace. But even more important is the IT – business alignment that we have talked about for so many years is finally happening. Actually, it is not alignment, it is convergence. IT (technology) today is such an important and indispensable part of any business function and service, that it has changed the traditional approach to IT and the IT strategy.

Organizations used to define their business strategy and afterwards create the IT strategy to support it. Today IT (technology) is part of the business strategy design and is often handled by staff from the specific business function, rather than a member of the IT department. This has become possible because of the tech-savvy staff who can now be found in all departments of an organization, not just the IT department.

This does not mean these people will actually execute IT work. It often means they know where to go, on the internet or the market, to order or sign up for a certain service. The IT department has a name for this: 'Shadow IT' that often has a negative connotation. But perhaps it is a sign of the future, where IT is embedded in every business function and no longer a separate department or perhaps a hybrid model where IT takes care of infrastructure and global services, but all business-specific IT services are handled by the business functions themselves and vendor management sits with the finance department.

I am currently working for a software organization in the scale up phase. We have approximately 30 people working for us and an active partner channel of another 60 to 70 people. We have product management, development and operations, sales, marketing, HR, finance, etc. Every staff member receives a salary that allows them to arrange their own laptop, including productivity software, phone and anything else they need to do their job.

All IT business applications are cloud based and delivered to us as a service. The departments themselves have selected the services they would like to work with. These are things like email, storage, CRM, web conference, DevOps tools, service management (our own of course), bookkeeping, invoicing, etc.

The vendor management of all these applications is with the finance department but it is, in general, nothing more than paying the bills. The operational management, for example "is the service delivered as agreed?" is with the department that consumes the service. Marketing deals with CRM and the webinar tool, Development with the DevOps tools and with the data center, Finance with the invoicing tool supplier, etc.

We do have a (part time) CTO who is responsible for security and for the integration of the different services to automate as many of our processes as possible. When it comes to security, the CTO has an absolute veto. When it comes to integration, he can start discussions with the department that wants to order a service that would cause integration issues with other existing services to see if other options are available.

As we continue to grow, we expect the CTO to have a small team looking after security and Service Integration and Management (SIAM) but we have no plans for our own IT department as the current organization structure works very well and is still very scalable. The IT department may eventually disappear or get a very different role but that is only because IT has become such an indispensable part of every business function. Welcome to the world of digital transformation!

Digital transformation and its impact on organizational structure is discussed in more detail in other areas of this publication. Chapter 5 discusses moving to a flatter structure, and Chapter 21 Aylesbury Vale District Council case study includes the creation of a 'digital' team.

4 The digital leader

Introduction

What are the essential skills and competences for the digital age? In this section, we look at who the leaders are in a digital organization, the digital mindset and how the required skills change as transformation proceeds.

"Empowerment can't mean letting everyone loose to do whatever they like." Hiroshi Mikitani, Rakuten founder.

Different skills may be required to lead the program during the initial stages and the later stages. Understanding this is a key to preventing unnecessary issues as the program matures[18].

■ 4.1 WHO ARE THE LEADERS IN THE DIGITAL ORGANIZATION?

"Everything we do must represent our best understanding, but our best understanding is imperfect, and we must expose it to criticism and ridicule quickly and often to figure out where we are wrong so that we can correct that. Toyota has a community of scientists continually experimenting. Often, we think about science and knowledge work as the domain of the elites (educated in US) but if you manage properly you can harness the experimental and exploratory instincts of everybody, regardless of their pedigree. When you do that with all your people, and competitors are only doing it with 5% of their people, you're bringing a much bigger team and a much better team, so you are going to win consistently!"

Dr. Steven Spear[19]

---

18 Sieff, G., & Carstens, L. (2006). The relationship between personality type and leadership focus. *SA Journal of Human Resource Management*, **4**(1), 52-62.
19 Dekker, S., Spear, S., Cook, R., & Kim, G. (2017, November 15). *DevOps Enterprise Symposium: Lean, Safety and DevOps* (online). https://www.youtube.com/watch?v=gtxtb9z_4FY.

Ultimately, leadership is provided by the organization's governing body. A visible senior manager, probably at the C-level, must be appointed as the leader of the transformation program. This leader must have both a business and technical understanding of the program so that services can be created that are feasible, scalable and supportable. The 'technology' might change quickly, but 'technical practices' change less frequently and 'good principles' evolve much more slowly. VeriSM aims to equip leaders and professionals with a new way of thinking about organizations, services and products, the changing demographics, behavioral shifts in markets and the uncertainty new technology brings.

> VeriSM is not prescriptive – our intent is to provide readers with a highly flexible transformational model, some great ideas, some tools and techniques to see how you can adapt the good in current thinking, adopt new thinking fast and be part of evolving ideas, and yes, sometimes to be the originator of revolutionary ideas.

■ 4.2   THE DIGITAL MINDSET

A 'digital mindset' is one that leads to increased value for stakeholders across all services. How that relates to corporate culture and technology is the question. A digital mindset includes the leader having an exploratory mind and a collaborative approach that embraces diversity. The leader must be comfortable with ambiguity to bring a wider perspective. This enables a focus on abundance, growth and agility. Digital leadership has the following characteristics:

- A collaborative style that appreciates that leadership is not just about having the title or authority;
- An understanding of effective delegation that gives staff autonomy by developing the ability to take accountability;
- An openness to experimentation;
- An appropriate attitude to risk, enabling the 'fail fast' approach.

Digital leaders need to have digital awareness.

> **Digital awareness**
> 'Digital awareness' describes a curiosity and openness of mind to technological innovation. Being 'digitally aware' does not mean having the technical knowledge to build a new service using an innovative method or technology, but instead means that one can describe how the innovation could be applied to increase the value of a service.

A 'digitally aware' individual would be able to contribute to the writing of the management summary section of a business case, but not necessarily to the detailed description of the implementation in the later sections. Digital awareness is not the same as an ability to deploy the latest buzzwords, but rather an ability to explain what the latest buzzwords actually mean in the context of the organization, its services, and its stakeholders. This is an essential skill for a digital leader when mapping the organization's current Management Mesh and in knowing when and how the mesh needs to evolve.

Chapter 25 includes the real world perspective of Cranford Group, an executive sourcing organization. It shows how they are seeing digital transformation affect the types of role available at the C-level.

■ 4.3   WHAT SKILLS DO DIGITAL LEADERS NEED?

Know the possibilities! Everything is possible, but what are the parameters? A digital leader has the core skills you would expect of any leader; however, you will find digital leaders are able to extend these into the digital environment. They are imbued with a different mindset and thought pattern that goes beyond the standard practices that currently exist. They are clear on the organization's 'arc of possibility' and take them into the 'art of the possible'.

The skillset is not just a list to check-off during an interview or performance review meeting. They are actionable characteristics that work together. One always pushes or pulls on another, so it is the balance between them when applied to a particular situation and environment, which makes a difference to their negative or positive impact on outcomes and performance.

Skills for a digital leader include:
- An adaptive and responsive approach to challenges;
- An ability to delegate effectively, avoiding micromanagement;
- An ability to deal with complexity. The Cynefin framework (see Section 9.1.1) can assist with this;
- An ability to provide autonomy, space for self-management to staff at all levels;
- The ability to communicate values and deal with conflict;
- Digital awareness. This involves understanding the benefits and attributes of the technology involved, if not, necessarily, the detail of the technological 'how?';
- A shared vision of the transformation;
- Sound communication skills, across multiple channels, that are adaptable to distributed teams;
- An ability to build the right culture and other conditions, for change, along with the ability to motivate staff through the difficulties of cultural change;
- An ability to know 'when' to adopt new things, avoiding both the danger of being too early and too cautious an adopter;
- An ability to manage budgets through rapidly changing circumstances, adapting resources to immediate requirements, whilst planning to ensure that bottlenecks and other delays do not provide unacceptable constraints;

■ An understanding of when standard processes and procedures are appropriate and when a situation must, instead, be treated as a specific case;
■ An ability to recognize patterns in organizational behavior and events – possible techniques to use to understand how to recognize patterns – Value Stream Mapping and other Lean techniques such as Gemba and Catch-ball.

All require effective emotional intelligence. Measuring not only personal awareness but also social awareness, emotional intelligence is increasingly in demand in leadership roles (as well as throughout the entire organization). Bradberry and Greaves (2009) report that emotional intelligence is twice as important as IQ when achieving life goals.[20]

4.3.1   Leadership competences
Transforming and maintaining value streams successfully in the digital age requires several leadership competences to be practiced simultaneously. This section can be used as a practical guide to help define leadership competences for the digital age. These include:

Vision:
■ Leadership has a compelling and transformative digital vision that is clear to everyone and provides direction;
■ Leadership has a clear ambition for digital transformation, concerning:
  • Substitution: providing business as usual services digitally;
  • Optimization: providing better or more services based on existing value streams and;
  • Transformation: providing other and new services enabled by digital technologies;
■ Leadership vision is continuously evolving during the transformation process.

Governance:
■ The organization has 'digital' role model(s) at the C-level;
■ Leadership has defined clear goals and results for the digital transformation process;
■ Leadership organizes committees to direct and coordinate all digitalization and innovation initiatives and distributed leadership roles to drive change and assist coordination;
■ Leadership assigns value stream ownership; leadership prioritizes digitalization and innovation initiatives to give direction;
■ Leadership synchronizes digitalization and innovation initiatives to make them coherent.

---

20 Bradberry, T. & Greaves, J. (2009). *Emotional intelligence 2.0.* San Diego, CA: TalentSmart.

Culture:
- Leadership creates a 'consumer first' culture;
- Leadership creates a collaborative culture;
- Leadership allows staff to embrace risk with a culture of experimentation where failure is not punished;
- Leadership supports distributed authority and decision making.

Engagement:
- All leading staff members of the organization show positive behavior;
- Leadership collaborates with staff through open and well-organized participation (e.g. internal crowdsourcing);
- Leadership provides a platform that makes knowledge, skills, resources and results available to each staff member;
- Leadership assigns roles to each staff member related to digital transformation or digital value streams.

Knowledge and skills:
- Leadership is digitally and technologically aware;
- Leadership ensures that the organization's staff have first class digital skills;
- Leadership recognizes the bottlenecks and constraints that exist owing to old technologies in the consumers' organization;
- Leadership organizes and enables effective sharing of knowledge, skills, resources and results.

The 2018 Digital Transformation Survey

As shown in Figure 17, the majority of respondents believe some or all senior managers need new skills to be able to take advantage of digital technology.

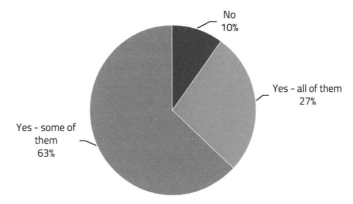

Figure 17 Do senior managers need new skills? (Source: 2018 Survey)

■ 4.4   LEADING CULTURAL TRANSFORMATION

Leading large-scale cultural transformation can benefit from a 'servant leadership' approach. Servant Leadership is a term coined by Robert K. Greenleaf in The Servant as Leader[21], an essay.

Servant leader

"The servant leader is servant first... It begins with the natural feeling that one wants to serve, to serve first. Then conscious choice brings one to aspire to lead. That person is sharply different from one who is leader first, perhaps because of the need to assuage an unusual power drive or to acquire material possessions...The leader-first and the servant-first are two extreme types. Between them there are shadings and blends that are part of the infinite variety of human nature....

...The difference manifests itself in the care taken by the servant-first to make sure that other people's highest priority needs are being served. The best test, and difficult to administer, is: Do those served grow as persons? Do they, while being served, become healthier, wiser, freer, more autonomous, more likely themselves to become servants? And, what is the effect on the least privileged in society? Will they benefit or at least not be further deprived?"

Robert K. Greenleaf

A servant leader will need to understand the vision, goals and scope of the organization or project/program and ensure that they are understood by all staff. They will need to facilitate decision-making, rather than make decisions themselves, enabling staff to be self-organizing and to find their own way to fulfil the deliverables within the guidelines set in the goals and scope. The servant leader will ensure that if the team comes across obstacles that will affect their ability to deliver the expected value, these obstacles are removed.

To foster good leadership and management in an organization there should be an active program to identify cultural differences. This includes how they relate to corporate culture and communication, how to use knowledge management to encapsulate them, and an ongoing training and awareness program to ensure that knowledge is part of the organization's ways of working.

---

21 Greenleaf, R. K. (1970). *The servant as leader*. Atlanta: Robert K. Greenleaf.

■ 4.5 LEADERSHIP IN THE INITIATION PHASE

When initiating digital transformation, a charismatic enthusiast who is taken seriously by senior people is required. The most essential skill is the ability to convince the board to embrace, support and fund the transformation program. This requires:

- A clear idea of exactly what 'digital transformation' is, and how it differs from the 'cargo cult' – that is, enabling the actual change, rather than simply the outward appearance of the change. This requires a practical understanding of what will be required to accomplish the transformation;
- A clear picture of what transformation will require from all stakeholders, and an ability to motivate those stakeholders to accept and embrace that change;
- The ability to get the ear of senior management and the board or governing body;
- Good communication skills to convey the message to the board, and convince it that the investment is worthwhile;
- The ability to follow through from convincing sufficient people to gaining support for the business case, and implementation plan;
- The ability to identify outcomes, and then communicate to all stakeholders, including across supply chains and those external to the organization.

It is recommended that one of the top leadership roles in the organization takes charge of transformational initiatives. They will act as the sponsor and be actively involved (and seen to be involved) in the initiative. Many organizations create new roles like Chief Digital Officer (CDO) or assign the role to the Chief Information Officer (CIO) (see Chapter 18), but these are not the only candidates. It really depends on the people available in an organization; their ability to get things done and to influence decisions.

■ 4.6 ONGOING LEADERSHIP

Once the program is in place, the leader has to pay close attention to detail and work through difficulties to find solutions. They must ensure that they become an enabler or facilitator for the rest of the transformational team. They also need to put their communication skills and ability to influence others to good use. Good communicators drive the culture and mentality for improving and that includes business awareness at all layers (strategic, tactical or operations). Success is more likely when supported by the consistent sharing of knowledge and information and adapted feedback loops.

Real world perspective: No more heroes

What does a leader look like in the digital age? Who do you think of? Steve Jobs? Travis Kalanick? There are many articles out there praising charismatic entrepreneurs and suggesting ways to emulate their behavior.

This is the 'founder myth' – the suggestion that great organizations exist because of one person. In reality, these 'heroes' don't do everything by themselves. They can in fact be single points of failure, and their unique approaches do not always lead to success.

Organizational leaders need to surround themselves with great people and give them autonomy. An organization should not revolve around one person.

■ 4.7 COMMUNICATE THE 'WHY'

It is essential to communicate the vision throughout the organization. A digital leader understands that this requires communicating the 'why?' of the vision, as well as the vision itself. Sometimes, however, a vision does start with the 'why?' perhaps because:

- ■ It is not necessary – the staff just need to do it and there is no need for them to worry about 'why?';
- ■ Management does not know why either – the edict has been issued from above, and they are as confused as anybody else, but do not like to admit it;
- ■ It is 'obvious'. After discussing and learning about the new idea, it is easy to forget that it was not obvious why it was a good idea to start with. A leader with a teaching mindset will understand that because something seems obvious to them, it is not necessarily clear to other people who have just heard about it for the first time;
- ■ Explaining 'why?' opens the discussion to objections. If the desire is not to communicate, but simply to order, the discussion is seen as negative and objections are simply things to be 'dealt with'. Actually, objections are valuable. They may point out flaws that were not apparent before and enable fixes to be applied before they cause a serious loss of value;
- ■ It takes too much time to explain or explaining would reveal confidential information to staff. These are usually just excuses for one of the reasons stated above. Typically, restricting information because of confidentiality provokes people into working out the impact themselves. To avoid falling into these traps, ensure that the 'why?' of the vision is well understood before communicating it.

To avoid falling into these traps, the digital leader must ensure that the 'why' of the vision is well understood before taking action or communicating plans.

■ 4.8   DIGITAL SUSTAINABILITY: GUIDANCE FOR DIGITAL LEADERS

Sustainability is the ability to do something in a way that is maintainable at a certain rate or level, avoiding the depletion of resources and maintaining a level of balance. This is an important area for digital leaders because digital transformation can be seen as a journey of learning, growing and improving that never really ends.

To plan and measure sustainability, plan for the short, medium, and long-term. That way, sustainability plans can be incorporated into continuous improvement plans. The word 'environment', as used here, includes the economic and human context within which an organization operates, including any possible positive or negative impact on any stakeholder, as well as the purely physical environment.

Technologies change, but the technologies that should be part of planning at the time of writing, include but are not limited to sustainable energy, 3D printing, drones and blockchain applications. The digital mindset considers the possible applicability of new technologies before they become commonly applied, so that existing plans include measures to move to appropriate technology when it becomes mature enough. These become part of the organization's Management Mesh.

 Sustainable development
Economic development which can be sustained in the long term; ecological use and development of natural resources in ways which are compatible with the maintenance of these resources, and with the conservation of the environment, for future generations[22].

Organizations and their leaders need to plan for digital sustainability. This includes:
■ Using appropriate technology to reduce the organization's long-term footprint;
■ Ensuring that, when a service is designed or updated, it is analyzed to establish where any negative impact on people, the economy, or the environment can be minimized;
■ Projecting the consumption of all resources; economic, environmental, and human, to ensure that current practices can continue in the long-term without depleting or negatively affecting the resources themselves;
■ Including a section on sustainability in all business cases or approvals in which innovative use of technology can reduce the impact of the organization to long-term sustainable levels;
■ Including sustainability plans, practices, innovations, successes and gaps in the organization's annual integrated governance report.

—
22 (2009). *Oxford English dictionary* (2nd ed.) [CD-ROM v4.0]. Cary, NC: Oxford University.

4.8.1   Planning and measurement: short term

In the short term, the organization should concentrate on moving away from unsustainable practices, particularly environmental ones. This includes:

- Choosing suppliers and materials that are sustainable;
- Working with purchasing and contracts to be sure that tenders and other purchasing decisions include standards for sustainability;
- Sustainable automation:
  - Planning for retraining and redeployment of staff
  - Ensuring that the costs of early retirement or redundancy are built into the business plans for automation, and new services that will potentially reduce headcount;
  - Plan to phase out old, outdated, dangerous, or unsustainable technology;
  - Plans must include security. Anything vulnerable to ransomware, spyware, viruses is not sustainable;
  - Plan to remove programmed redundancy ("planned obsolescence"), as this is not sustainable, and, in some places (for example France) is illegal.

4.8.2   Planning and measurement: medium term

The medium term involves working on efficiencies and continual improvement to reduce consumption of materials, energy, waste and goodwill. This could include:

- Move to sustainable energy sources and environmentally friendly materials (bamboo cups for staff coffee for example);
- Reducing shipping distances for raw materials, finished goods, and other shipping (shipping is a major consumer of non-renewable energy);
- Where possible, use shipping methods that use renewable energy;
- Locate facilities near consumers and near raw materials, with intelligent logistics between them:
  - Very large organizations might look at investing in sustainable digital technology, such as drones for delivery, and sailing ships for bulk goods;
  - Smaller organizations can plan to use sustainable shipping organizations, by making it a selection criterion between competing shippers;
- Technologies such as 3D printing, and blockchain, offer increased flexibility, reduced cost, and increased integrity of services.

Medium term questions to be asked include:

- Must current technology and shipping be used for any product or service?
- Can a digital, less resource-intensive method be found?
- Is all software and are all communications sustainable?
- Is it appropriately secure?
- Can data integrity be guaranteed?
- Have new security technologies, such as blockchain, been considered to improve current systems? This can be done via the organization's Management Mesh;

- As a responsible digital organization, is there sufficient investment in future technology research & development?

4.8.3   Planning and measurement – long term

This includes investment in education and training for both current and future staff, the replacement of current services with services that satisfy anticipated future needs more sustainably and plans for the graceful exit from sunset technology. Radical Design Thinking in the long term can include:

- Developing a long-term replacement / enhancement roadmap to drive short and medium-term decisions;
- Digital organizations should be investing in their future by paying for the development of open source technologies that will be needed in the future. Investing in open source development is a direct support for a sustainable and secure future. Relying on the random goodwill of developers is not sustainable;
- Open source development should include the open source development of hardware, as well as software;
- Innovative organizations may produce plans to employ retired or redundant staff in their open source development programs;
- Sustainability plans must include:
  - Retention of corporate knowledge;
  - Building a digital future;
  - Responsibility to all stakeholders;
  - Responsibility for the environment.

5 Adapting to constant change

> **Introduction**
>
> This chapter continues to consider the impact of digital transformation on the organization by looking at the world of constant change. This chapter includes practical strategies that organizations can adopt to become change-resilient and will be of particular relevance to the digital leaders discussed in Chapter 4.

Digital transformation is nothing new. The first computers were introduced in the 1930s, but humanity has been finding faster, more automated ways of doing things long before that. The dishwasher was invented in 1886 and the first electric vacuum cleaner introduced in 1901. The impact comes not so much from digital transformation, but from the disruption organizations are feeling today, as the speed of change increases and becomes less predictable and manageable. Organizations that will survive and thrive amidst the disruption are the ones that truly accept that change is now constant. These organizations embrace a world in which the volatility, uncertainly, complexity and ambiguity (VUCA) of change is ever increasing. These organizations do not view change as a 'program' in which change is dictated from the top and cascaded through the hierarchy. In these organizations, change is a platform on which everyone can initiate and execute change.

> "Producing major change in an organization is not just about signing up one charismatic leader. You need a group – a team – to be able to drive the change. One person, even a terrific charismatic leader, is never strong enough to make all this happen."
>
> John Kotter, *Leading Change*

So how can organizations get to a place where change is truly everyone's business? Organizations and their leaders need to make a fundamental shift. Organizations need to build a platform for change where everyone can initiate and drive change, and everyone can make rapid decisions based. Staff must have ownership of outcomes for themselves, their colleagues and the organization.

The 2018 Digital Transformation Survey

As shown in Figure 18, many respondents feel their organization does not respond well to major changes.

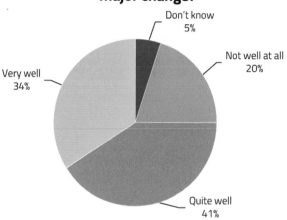

Figure 18 How well does your organization adapt to major changes? (source: 2018 Survey)

■ 5.1   KILL THE HIERARCHY

For an organization to survive and thrive in a world of constant and uncertain change, leadership is important, but more important is a collaborative workplace in which transparency and creative freedom reign over hierarchical boundaries. (See also Chapter 6 on Collaboration.) This type of organization enables innovation, creativity, experimentation, rapid decision-making, agility and employee ownership, engagement and influence. There is widespread autonomy, and everyone leads.

5.1.1   Moving to a flatter structure

The only way to enable a 'faster' organization that can respond to constant change is to flatten the structure. The organization needs to move away from a model of hierarchical control to a flatter structure, removing the bureaucracy that slows organizations down. It is not about having no structure at all and having no hierarchy – it is most likely that there will always be an element of hierarchy.

There are organizations such as Valve Corporation – a leading video game developer and digital distribution system and Morning Star – a leading food processor, that have decided to move to a completely flat structure. There are others that have moved to a 'flatter' structure such as W.L. Gore – an international industrial products organization, which has a structure that has three levels in the organizational hierarchy – the CEO (elected democratically), a handful of functional heads and everyone else. Facebook, Pixar, and Toyota are other examples of organizations with a flatter structure.

Whether organizations move to a completely flat structure or a flatter structure, informal hierarchies will emerge just as they do in nature. However, this type of hierarchy is very different from social constructs that are imposed with the sole intention of 'keeping control'. Flat organizations do not have to be truly 'flat'. They are just flatter than 'tall' organizations. Tall organizations shift the responsibility up the management ladder, whereas flatter structures allow employees to make decisions and feel responsible for the organization's success.

Characteristics of flatter structure organizations include:
- An increased level of communication between employees and management;
- Greater democracy;
- A greater level of innovation.

Communication is usually faster, more reliable and more effective than in tall structures. Direct employee input leads to more support for decisions and fewer behind-the-scenes power struggles and disagreements.

Real world examples
Flatter structures
W. L. Gore, an innovative and successful organization, has more than 10,000 employees. All decision-making is done through self-managing teams of 8-12 people. The Gore website states:

> "There are no traditional hierarchies at Gore, but we're not a completely flat organization. Our lattice structure guides how we operate and communicate; through this structure, Associates engage with whomever is needed to get our work done.
>
> We also have a leadership structure. Leaders most often emerge based on skill, capability and followership — or their potential to build followership over time. The leadership structure helps us understand expectations and scope and helps each of us stay accountable to our commitments."[23]

At Morning Star, rather than pushing decisions up, expertise is pushed down. In many organizations, senior executives trained in the science of business analytics make the key decisions. They have a wealth of data at their disposal and analytical prowess, but what they lack is context – an understanding of the reality and facts at the coalface. This is why

---

23 Gore. (No date). *Working at Gore*, (Online). https://www.gore.com/about/working-at-gore. [2018 February].

decisions that appear absolutely brilliant by the top-level executives, are seen as idiotic by those on the front line. Roughly half of the employees at Morning Star have completed courses on financial analysis and how to negotiate with suppliers. This makes the doers and the thinkers the same so that decisions are faster and wiser.

Valve, considered one of the most successful organizations within its industry, has approximately 250 employees and an estimated worth of USD $3 – $4 billion. Rather than assigning permanent managerial staff, Valve rotates its leaders on a per-team, per-project basis. Rather than creating permanent departments, Valve allows employees to choose the type of work that they want to do.

5.1.2   Why embrace a flatter structure?

According to researcher Tim Kastelle, Associate Professor at University of Queensland-Australia, the flatter approach is great for organizations that are looking to innovate, need to respond to a rapidly changing environment and have a shared purpose. In what is now termed a volatile, uncertain, complex and ambiguous (VUCA) world, organizations will have no choice but to respond to constant and unpredictable change. When employees have influence and can actively participate in decision-making, they have a sense of ownership.

The flatter structure provides employees with autonomy. As they take on a bigger role within the organization they become increasingly motivated to be successful. Reducing middle management means there are fewer layers between the most senior level and the front-line employees – making it easier to communicate and drive change.

As stated in the Morning Star article "What Is Self-Management?"[24]:
- People are generally happier when they have control over their own life (and work);
- It does not make a lot of sense to give the decision-making authority to the person that is furthest away (literally) from the actual work being done;
- When you give good people more responsibility, they tend to flourish;
- The traditional hierarchical model of organizations is not scalable—in fact, it is a recipe for a slow painful death;
- There's an undeniable link between freedom and economic prosperity in nations around the world – and, further, an undeniable link between lack of freedom and corruption at the national level. The same is true of human organizations in general.

5.1.3   Getting started

To manage the successful transition of people and the organization through constant change: remove the bureaucracy, flatten the hierarchy, speed up decision making,

---

24 (No Date). *What is self-management?* (Online). http://www.self-managementinstitute.org/about/what-is-self-management. [2018 April].

empower and involve and employees and give control to those who are actually doing the work.

■ 5.2 DECENTRALIZE DECISION MAKING

An organization that is going to be able to respond to rapid change, has to be one in which decision-making is located at the place in the organization where it is best suited. This relates to a flatter hierarchy in that the model promotes employee involvement through a decentralized decision-making process. When the levels of responsibility of employees are elevated, and unnecessary layers of middle management are eliminated, decision-making happens faster.

5.2.1 Best placed
As Peter F. Drucker wrote: "Knowledge workers themselves are best placed to make decisions about how to perform their work."[25]

Gene Kim added, "The greater the distance between the decision and the work done – the worse the outcome."[26]

Increased competitiveness means organizations have to deliver value in the shortest possible time. This requires decentralized decision-making. Decisions that have to go up the chain-of-command introduce a delay and can decrease in quality as they lack local context. Add to this the fact that change can happen during the delay, which may render the decision superfluous.

Not all decision-making is decentralized. Decisions of a strategic nature that could have a far-reaching impact must be considered the remit of (centralized) leadership who have the market, financial and business knowledge to lead the organization in the right direction. Everything else can be decentralized. When staff participate in decisions that matter to them, employee engagement and productivity increases, as does ability of the organization to respond to change.

Real world example
Go with your gut!
Ricardo Semler, CEO of Semco, a Brazilian conglomerate, urges employees to "go with your gut" with regard to their decision-making.

---

25 Drucker, P. (1996). *Landmarks of tomorrow: A report on the new*. Piscataway, NJ: Transaction.
26 Kim, G. (2015, February 25). *Mastering performance and collaboration through DevOps*, (Online). https://www.youtube.com/watch?v=cWpPmO6I064. [2018 March].

Semco does not have a mission statement, written policies, job titles or an organizational chart. Decision-making is in the hands of the employees. Semler summarized his position when he said:

"We'll send our sons anywhere in the world to die for democracy, but do not seem to apply the concept to the workplace."[27]

When Semler became the CEO of Semco in 1982 at the age of 24, he started to slowly change the organization from an autocracy to a corporate democracy.

He cut the bureaucracy from 12 layers of management to four and devised a new structure based on concentric circles to replace the traditional, and confining, corporate pyramid. The center circle comprises the top five managers called Counsellors. The second circle consists of Partners, who are in charge of the small business units. Coordinators, whose job is to supervise, represent the third circle. The rest are called Associates.

Semler devolved and distributed power. Company revenue, profit margins and salaries are totally transparent with all employees having access. Employees set their own salaries. It is all about accountability and performance over hours worked. Employees set their own working hours. Employees choose their managers and evaluate them twice a year. There are no receptionists, secretaries or personal assistants – what they would do is 'your' job.

Semco's core values are:
• Democracy – gives employees control of their work;
• Profit sharing – gives employees a reason to do work better;
• Information – tells employees what is working and what is not.

Semler talks about managing without managers.

"Managers and the status and money they enjoy—in a word, hierarchy—are the single biggest obstacle to participatory management. We had to get the managers out of the way of democratic decision-making, and our circular system does that pretty well. We insist on making important decisions collegially, and certain decisions are made by a company-wide vote."[28]

Under Semler's leadership, Semco grew from $4 million in revenue to over $160 million in about 20 years.

27 Semler, R. (1989). *Managing without managers*, (Online). https://hbr.org/1989/09/managing-without-managers. [2018 February].
28 Semler, R. (1989). *Managing without managers*, (Online). https://hbr.org/1989/09/managing-without-managers. [2018 February].

5.2.2 Getting started

Decentralized decision-making encourages motivation and creativity; it allows many minds to work simultaneously on the same problem; and it accommodates flexibility and individualization. Allowing more people to be involved in the decision-making process, increases input for solutions and innovative ideas. Decision-making is accelerated as it is handled where it needs to be. Power is placed directly into lower areas of the organization, who are best suited to make a decision. Upper management does not get involved and a response can be reached much faster. Unnecessary escalation to management is just a needless delay. Quality of decisions also diminishes if the decision does not have local context.

■ 5.3 PROVIDE AUTONOMY

There are sound business reasons for treating people with dignity, for providing autonomy and for organizing with small teams rather than large hierarchies. When as many people in the organization have as much autonomy and authority as they are capable of delivering well and consistently, the organization becomes nimbler, better able to respond to change and employees become more productive and content.

> Tracy Maylett's description of an organization without employee autonomy really sums it up. Writing for Entrepreneur, he says:
>
> "Without it, your workforce may become the "land of the working dead," roaming endlessly in zombie-like fashion, waiting to be told what to do next. Not an enjoyable workplace for employees or managers, by any stretch".[29]

5.3.1 What is autonomy?

Autonomy is about giving employees the right to do the work they want, how they want and when they want. It is about management getting out of the way and letting employees get on with their job. Autonomy could be choosing which projects to work on, who to work with, when to work and how to get the job done. In an organization with employee autonomy, the focus is on what gets done (outcomes) as opposed to how it gets done (see Chapter 8 – Outcomes for more information). Autonomy is linked directly to employee engagement and motivation. It increases feelings of ownership and loyalty. This means that talent is both retained and attracted. Increased employee engagement leads to increased productivity and profitability.

---

29 Maylett, T. (2016, March 4). *6 ways to encourage autonomy with your employees*, (Online). https://www. entrepreneur.com/article/254030 [2018 April].

Autonomy can also be applied to teams. An autonomous team is one that is self-managing with little or no direction from a manager. When team members work well together, they can build on each other's strengths, and can compensate for other's weaknesses. This sort of environment has a direct impact on increasing job satisfaction.

5.3.2 Guardrails

Autonomy does not mean that there is outright anarchy. Organizations have principles or guardrails (defined in the VeriSM model via governance and the Service Management Principles). The guardrails are comparable to lines on the road that help keep drivers safe. Guardrails keep everyone aligned to the organization's goals and objectives. They are the parameters within which employees can operate without unnecessary interference. The US military call this 'doctrine' – the mechanism for managing the fog of war, pushing decision-making closer to the ground, while providing the lines to guide decision-making and action.

Real world example

Gumroad

At Gumroad, the successful platform that enables creators to sell products directly to consumers, a focus on a bias towards action, ownership and a flat organization is baked into each of its core values (principles).

First Round Review[30] listed these values:

> **Move fast**
> Move quickly. Do not lag. Once a decision is made, execute on it as fast as possible. Ship quickly. Save words. Instead, implement and measure. Perfect is the enemy of good.

> **Change**
> Get comfortable with being uncomfortable. Nothing is sacred, everything is in a state of change. As individuals, we should look to place ourselves in a position where we are learning and getting better every day.

> **Align yourself**
> Constantly put yourself in a place where the best thing for you is the best thing for everyone else that you work with and for.

> **Be open and transparent**
> Simplify your relationships. Lose the filter. Talk openly about what you care about and the problems you are dealing with. Get feedback to get better.

---

30 (No date). *An inside look at a flat organization that serves millions*, (Online). http://firstround.com/review/An-Inside-Look-at-a-Flat-Organization-That-Serves-Millions/ [2018 April].

Stay focused

Is the thing you are working on right now the most valuable thing you could be doing? A corollary to this: trust others to execute on their objectives so that you can stay focused on your own.

Smile!

Have fun. Don't regret. Don't think too hard. Be optimistic. Assume the best. Things will work out — how could they not?

If all Gumroad employees follow these principles, the organization is in good hands!

Real world examples

About 20% of the world's websites are now on the WordPress platform – making it one of the most important internet companies. **Automatic**, the firm behind WordPress, employs a few hundred people, who all work remotely, with a highly autonomous flat management structure.

Prior to being purchased by Microsoft, another successful development platform, **GitHub**, is another highly successful firm with a similar structure. It has no middle managers, employees are beholden to no one, and are encouraged to define their roles in ways that make sense to them. They have autonomy. Shortly before publication of this book, GitHub was acquired by Microsoft. It will be interesting to see how the two organizations work together and what level of integration takes place.

At **W.L. Gore,** the American multinational manufacturing organization, all decision-making is achieved through self-managing teams of 8-12 people: hiring, pay, which projects to work on, everything. Gore has more than 10,000 employees with basically three levels in their organizational hierarchy.

At **Morning Star**, the world's leading tomato ingredient processor, the notion of empowerment assumes that authority trickles down -that power is bestowed from above, as and when the powerful see fit. In an organization built on the principles of self-management and autonomy, employees are not given power by the higher-ups -they simply have it.

The **Ritz-Carlton** is famous for its high levels of customer satisfaction achieved through its excellent customer service, which is underpinned by employee autonomy.

The Ritz-Carlton has for many years given staff $2,000 of discretion per employee per guest that can be used to solve any customer complaint in the manner the employee feels is appropriate. There is no recourse to a higher authority for approval.

The Ritz-Carlton employees are known as the Ladies and Gentlemen of the Ritz and have the autonomy to make decisions, craft special moments and resolve customer issues.

Valve Corporation, the leading video game developer and digital distribution system, is one of the best-known examples of a large organization that operates on a flat hierarchical structure. It does not assign permanent managerial staff but rather rotates leaders on a per-project, per-team basis. It does not create permanent departments but allows employees the autonomy to work where they want, on what they want and when they want. With an estimated worth of $2-4 billion, Valve is considered one of the most successful organizations within its industry. CEO Gabe Newell claims that the organization is more profitable per employee than either Google or Apple.

Google has one aspirational mission statement (we would call it a 'vision'):

> "Organize the world's information and make it universally accessible and useful."

Google has one goal:

> "Develop services that improve the lives of as many people as possible. Not just for some. For everyone."

Employees are trusted and given the autonomy to self-manage and deliver on that mission and goal. There are principles (which include guardrails):

- Innovation comes from anywhere
- Focus on the user (consumer)
- Aim to be ten times better
- Bet on technical insights
- Ship and iterate
- Give employees 20% time
- Default to open processes
- Fail well
- Have a mission that matters

Think of "Focus on the user", "Ship and iterate" and "Fail well" as guardrails. For Google, is ok to ship early rather than waiting until something is perfect. Customers will help you make if 'better' through their feedback. It is OK to do this, as long as you are focused on the user. There is no stigma attached to failure. In fact, Google treats failure like a badge of honor. If employees do not fail enough, they are not trying enough.

5.3.3 Getting started

The organizations mentioned in this section would not be the successes that they are without giving employees autonomy. Use this formula to guide efforts towards autonomy:

Autonomy = more choice, more engagement, more retention, more motivation, more innovation, more productivity, more profitability = more success.

■ 5.4 EMPLOYEE OWNERSHIP

Ownership occurs within an organization when there is enterprise-wide buy-in to a common goal. A sense of ownership holds everyone accountable for their actions and decisions.

> **Real world examples**
>
> As CEO of W.L. Gore, Terri Kelly, said: "It's far better to rely upon a broad base of individuals and leaders who share a common set of values and feel **personal ownership** for the overall success of the organization. These responsible and empowered individuals will serve as much better watchdogs than any single, dominant leader or bureaucratic structure."[31]
>
> W.L. Gore is known for its flat structure. Although there is a structure (divisions, business units, etc.), there is no organizational chart, no hierarchy and therefore no bosses.
>
> Gore's philosophy is that individuals do not need close supervision; what they need is mentoring and support.
>
> W.L. Gore is one of the most successful companies in the world and has more than 10,000 employees. Gore is most famous for its Gore-Tex fabric but actually has a large diverse product portfolio, including vacuum filters, microwave cable assemblies, guitar strings, dental floss and medical devices. Gore has earned a spot on the Fortune 100 Best Companies to Work For [32]list every year since 1998, and in 2018 was number 52.
>
> The fundamental beliefs[33] on the W.L. Gore website epitomize the principles of employee ownership.
>
> "We also believe we're all in the same boat. As Associates, we have a vested interest in the success of the company, and we share in Gore's risks and rewards while having an added incentive to stay committed to our enterprise's long-term success. As a result, we

31 Kelly, T. (2010, April 8). *No more heroes: Distributed leadership*, (Online). https://www. managementexchange.com/blog/no-more-heroes [2018 May].

32 http://fortune.com/best-companies/

33 Gore. (No date). *Our beliefs & principles*, (Online). https://www.gore.com/about/our-beliefs-and-principles. [2018 February].

feel we're all in this effort together, and believe we should always consider what's best for the enterprise as a whole when making decisions".

At Gore, 'Associates' can make decisions, choose the work they do and make commitments to their colleagues on the outcomes they will achieve. They are encouraged to experiment. As a result, they have a stake in the organization's success and a feeling of ownership.

5.4.1 Benefits
So what benefits do organizations reap when there is a sense of ownership?

When leaders entrust employees with a sense of responsibility and ownership towards their role, it fosters collaboration at work for maximized productivity. When employees have a sense of ownership of their job, they tend to become better performers. A 2014 Forbes[34] article cited a Data Freaks study that revealed how organizations can benefit from higher employee engagement, lower turnover and increased financial performance by simply increasing the feeling of ownership employees experience – regardless of whether employees have any ownership in the business itself.

Higher employee engagement not only leads to increased productivity and profitability but also increased motivation, innovation and creativity. Lower turnover reduces the cost of attrition and retains talent. Engagement and low turnover will also result in the attraction of talent as the organization is regarded as a great place to work.

High performing organizations have employees who 'own' outcomes. There is a culture of accountability, trust and mutual respect. Employees treat the business as if it were their own. They handle actions and decisions with due care and attention. Ownership is about taking initiative and doing the right thing for the business. When there is a sense of ownership, employees are aligned to the values and culture of the organization and identify with its goals and objectives. As in the Gore example, there is a sense of 'we are all in this together'.

5.4.2 Achieving a sense of ownership
The Gore example and those of other organizations in which employees have a sense of ownership have some basic things in common:
■ Actively encourage employee involvement in all aspects of the business;
■ Encourage cross-team collaboration;

---

34 Data Freaks. (2014, September 25). *Motivating employees has everything to do with giving them feelings of ownership*, (Online). https://www.forbes.com/sites/datafreaks/2014/09/25/motivating-employees-has-almost-nothing-to-do-with-their-attitude-and-almost-everything-to-do-with-feelings-of-ownership/#102957531140. [2018 May].

- Make it easy for employees to navigate the organization to support collaboration;
- Provide a supportive framework with a culture of reward and recognition;
- Encourage innovation and experimentation with a no-blame culture when things go wrong – as long as they were done with the good of the organization in mind;
- Establish common values, with which everyone can identify and live by;
- Create a common sense of purpose;
- Build trust and mutual respect;
- Hold everyone accountable;
- Allow employees to make decisions, initiate and drive changes;
- Allow everyone to challenge the status quo and enable everyone to contribute to discussions with regard to alternative approaches;
- Create continual feedback loops for all parts of the organization – up, down and across. Support this with continual learning and development;
- Give employees flexibility and choices;
- Do not tell employees they are empowered – tell them they already had the power;
- Make sure you have leaders as well as managers;
- And finally, kill the hierarchy to remove the bureaucracy – otherwise the guidance above cannot be implemented.

Most of these actions will not happen quickly, but organizations can start to move in the right direction. Take a look at some of the organizations that have challenged their status quo to obtain employee ownership. As part of a digital transformation, ensure there is a strong focus on culture and not just technology. Plan to introduce some, if not all, of the initiatives that Gore, Valve, Semco, General Electric, Caterpillar, Morning Star and Pixar have achieved to their organizations' clear benefit.

Most leaders are aware of the concept of 'virtual teams' and a geographically distributed workforce. An additional challenge that affects many digital natives and their managers is the 'loosely-coupled' workforce. Staff may not have permanent contracts, may work for more than one organization and have no expectations of a 'job for life'. Creating a sense of ownership in staff who are not permanently employed by the organization needs to be addressed directly.

> **Real world example**
> **FedEx**
> Another organization featured on the Fortune Best Companies to Work for in 2018[35] is FedEx – coming in at position 99.
>
> FedEx gives drivers ownership, which means they are in charge of figuring out the best route to serve their customers most efficiently. No one tells them how to do their job; they simply need to achieve their goal: get their deliveries to the right people quickly.

---

35 http://fortune.com/best-companies/fedex-corporation/

Tom Peters, the management guru, has made the story about a FedEx employee and a helicopter become a legend in demonstrating what can happen when employees feel 'ownership'.

The story goes that back in the 1980s, a blizzard in California took down a telephone tower located in the mountains, which served the main FedEx call center. The phone company employees were unable to get to the top of the mountain to repair it. A 'regular' FedEx employee worked out that he had the ability to fix the failure. He rented a helicopter, paid for with his own credit card, and flew to the mountaintop where he fixed the tower and in so doing, the FedEx call center came back online.

The crux of the story was that the FedEx employee felt he had 'ownership' of the problem but also of the outcome. It is also important to note that the employee was empowered and felt he could make the decision. It did not have to go up and down a hierarchy of control, which would have either led to total inertia or a considerable and unnecessary delay in restoring call center operations.

5.4.3   Getting started

Giving employees a sense of ownership will help to ensure they are motivated, innovative and creative. Employee engagement increases, which leads to increased productivity, which in turn has a positive effect on the bottom line. Profitability goes up. Use the common attributes listed above starting points for each organization.

■ 5.5   WHAT DO LEADERS NEED TO DO?

To thrive in a situation where change is constant, leaders need to make significant changes in mind-set and approach. Firstly, they need to truly accept that change is now constant and that the pace of change will not slow. They need to be able to rapidly adapt and shift direction, constantly evolving themselves and developing their teams to be adaptive. Leaders need to accept that what they know and the skills they have may not be enough to always have the right answers. In the world of constant and unpredictable change, leaders have to absorb new information and make sense of it.

"The pessimist complains about the wind. The optimist expects it to change. The leader adjusts the sails."

John Maxwell

5.5.1 Become adaptive leaders

When living in a world of volatile, uncertain, complex and ambiguous change, how do leaders chart a course when they cannot predict the outcomes of their decisions? In the digital world, every organization is an information organization. Leaders – at every level – need to be able to read the right signals and act upon them. Adaptive leaders learn through experimentation and don't blindly follow instructions. They cultivate a diversity of views to generate a multiplicity of options. They lead with empathy, reward accomplishment with autonomy and seek winning solutions for all stakeholders.

"The moment we think we have nothing to learn is the point at which failure looms large."

Sharon Whale, CEO, Oliver UK[36]

Real world example
Apollo 13
A great example of adaptive leadership and adaptation is the Apollo 13 story. What do leaders do when all their training and all their knowledge is not enough, and they have to deal with the unknown?

As described in Fire Fighter Nation:[37]

"Houston, we have a problem," is the famous line (even if it is not quite accurate) that the crew of Apollo 13 radioed back to Earth when they were halfway to the moon. That famous (and understated) line started a series of problem-solving endeavors, ones that NASA had never approached during a mission. It was quickly clear that Apollo 13 could not land on the moon, which led the ground crew to evaluate the "what-if" abort scenarios. One of those scenarios—using the Moon's gravity to return the ship to the Earth—was chosen, but even then, the crew faced enormous challenges that didn't fit any of the previous modelling—a shortage of food and water, the need to conserve all but the most essential power (which in turn limited communications with the ground crew) and insufficient resources for removing carbon dioxide.

Eventually, the Apollo 13 crew, working with engineers on the ground, was able to overcome these challenges, and they returned home safely. But their success wasn't the result of training or simulation or SOPs; it was the result of adaptation. Gene Krantz, head of mission control, recognized this: "We are throwing out the flight plan. I do not care what (space) craft was designed to do; all I care about is what it will do."

---

36 Whale, S. (2017, August 2). *Adaptive leadership lessons from Trump and advertising*, (Online). https://www.campaignlive.co.uk/article/adaptive-leadership-lessons-trump-advertising/1441056. [2108 March].
37 (2011, May 24). *Adaptive leadership: Dealing with the unknowns*, (Online). http://www.firefighternation.com/articles/2011/05/adaptive-leadership-dealing-with-the-unknowns.html [2018 January].

Adaptive leaders deal with the unknown effectively, including situations where there are no policies, processes or procedures, no known practices or solutions to fit the situation. They know what to do when they do not know what to do. See Section 9.1.1 Cynefin for more information on strategies to support this.

Qualities of an adaptive leader include:

- Self-awareness;
- Emotional intelligence;
- Ability to build relationships;
- Transparency and the ability to 'tell it how it is';
- Treat people fairly and with respect;
- Have integrity and deliver on promises; this earns them respect;
- Are open and share information;
- Not shying away from bad news or ignoring information, they make the messenger feel valued and respected;
- Know they always have something to learn;
- Know they are responsible for the development of others.

The leaders who develop these skills will be the ones that thrive in a world of constant change.

5.5.2   Adaptive leadership teams

Adaptive leaders build adaptive leadership teams. These teams need to be able to thrive despite the constant turbulence they face. Adaptive teams are ones in which everyone leads. They are cross-functional with a shared goal. They trust and have respect for each other. They are provided with the desired outcomes and have the autonomy to determine how they will achieve those outcomes. They are not just allowed, but they are encouraged to experiment, innovate and be creative.

Real world perspective

Boston Consulting Group

Boston Consulting Group (BCG) undertook research back in 2011. They reported on their findings in an article called "Five Traits of Highly Adaptive Teams".[38]

BCG studied a carefully selected sample of companies to discern what the most adaptive leadership teams do differently or better than those teams that deliver average or substandard results.

"Regardless of industry, size, location, and company life cycle, these companies with adaptive leadership teams all outperformed their peers—some just slightly and some by

---

38 Torres, R. & Rimmer, N. (2011, December 21). The five traits of highly adaptive leadership teams, (Online). https://www.bcg.com/en-au/publications/2011/people-organization-five-traits-highly-adaptive-leadership-teams.aspx. [2108 April].

a significant margin. Through their business performance in a variety of environments, all have demonstrated that agility and adaptation are, to a greater or lesser extent, part of their company DNA."

The five key traits that BCG uncovered were:
- **One voice**: the team has a shared goal that guides what they do. The goal is aligned with that of the organization as a whole.
- **Sense and respond capacity**: the team excels at being able to read the external signals, identify trends and able to respond accordingly.
- **Information processing**: they use their collective intelligence to synthesize complex insights and make high-quality decisions quickly.
- **Freedom within a framework**: They have a framework in which they can experiment. They can take risks within guardrails and failure is accepted as long as lessons are learnt.
- **Boundary fluidity**: Team members can play different roles at the drop of a hat. This build a bond and they feel that everyone has each other's back covered.

Adaptive leadership teams embrace constant change.

5.5.3   Get out of the way

Leaders have to get out of the way and let employees get on with the job in hand. Leaders have to move away from 'command and control' to a model of delegation and trust. In today's fast moving and constantly changing world, leaders have to understand that they need to relinquish control in order to gain control. The best way to lose control is, in fact, to try and control everything. 'Command and control' stifles innovation, experimentation and creativity.

Real world example
CSC
Harvard Business Review[39] talks about CSC, which went from increasing control and efficiency to relaxing control with resounding success.

"In response to poor financial performance in 2007, CSC Germany, a division of the $17 billion worldwide IT consulting and services firm, at first took the usual approach of increasing control and efficiency. The result was a further decline. When the division's leaders did the opposite—relaxed control and gave employees the freedom to do things as they saw fit—the outcome was resounding success.

Responding to an initiative by its parent company to rethink management practices, CSC Germany experimented with a no-control approach within the 60-employee Enterprise Content Management (ECM) unit. To encourage the development of a knowledge

39 Amar, A. D., Hentrich, C., & Hlupic, V. (2009). *To be a better leader, give up authority*, (Online). https://hbr. org/2009/12/to-be-a-better-leader-give-up-authority [2018 February].

culture, the division began using peer group supervision and relying on in-house coaches to do both one-on-one and team coaching at all levels. The results were so impressive that CSC Germany took the approach to its 34-employee IT Architecture Consulting unit.

In April 2009 ECM's revenue, after dipping in December 2008, rose sharply and continued upward. IT Architecture Consulting, which had been performing poorly, showed marked improvement on a productivity measure known as utilization in the months after control was relaxed."

The challenge for many leaders who have learnt to get out of the way is to remain in that place when a crisis arises. These leaders have told their employees that they can experiment, innovate, create, self-manage and that they have autonomy to do the job as they see fit. When the crisis happens, the natural tendency is to revert to the 'command and control' style of leadership. This just makes the crisis worse. Employees are confused and disengaged because leaders have set them free but are now caging them again.

When a crisis happens, employees must be able to take ownership, make decisions, innovate and experiment, take risks and be leaders themselves. Without this, the organization will not be able to respond to a crisis effectively.

5.5.4   Move away from 'empowering'
According to dictionary.com[40] empowerment means: *to give power or authority to; authorize.*

Empowerment implies that it is something given at a particular point in time based on a certain behavior. Empowerment is not something that a leader can 'give' employees – it should be something they always have. Empowerment suggests that authority trickles down through the organization, and power is bestowed from above when the powerful see fit.

Leaders need to move away from being managers and treat the workforce as adults, by trusting and respecting them to do the right thing. The empowerment conversation sounds like: "You did a good job, so I now empower you to do it next time without my help". That sounds like a conversation between an adult and a child. Leaders need to give employees true autonomy and lead from an outcome driven position. Leaders need to let those who actually know best get on with the job the way they see fit.

Clarity
One of the most important actions leaders need to take when faced with constant and complex change is to set clear objectives. 'Command and control'

—

40 http://www.dictionary.com/browse/empowerment

management makes sure orders and work requirements are carried out through plans and direction. Leadership sets clear objectives, provides autonomy, relinquishes control and gets out of the way.

Clear objectives (and shared goals) are great motivators. A good example of this is the objective set on May 25, 1961 by John F. Kennedy. He announced the objective to put a person safely on the moon by the end of the decade. Most people thought this was impossible. To everyone's amazement, the objective was achieved on July 20, 1969, when Neil Armstrong stepped onto the moon's surface. Kennedy's clear objective provided incentive and motivation for all involved to make it happen.

Research by Bersin[41] found that employees with a high level of objective clarity were four times more likely to score in the top quartile of business performance.

Clarity is provided by making the objective clear and unambiguous; continuing to provide clarity on a regular basis; and making the objective meaningful to the employee. Employees also need clarity about the fact that change is constant, volatile, uncertain, complex and ambiguous. Everyone has to be clear on the fact that the speed of change is not going to slow down and that this might have an impact on their current objectives. Objectives may have to adapt – and frequently – to respond to continual and unrelenting change.

Authority

When leaders treat people with respect and give them the autonomy and authority to get on with the job, the organization will become more nimble and better able to respond to change. Employees are more productive, innovative, creative and engaged. Leaders give employees authority and autonomy by embracing the fact that not everything will work first time and there will be failures. Celebrate failures as learning opportunities. Employees will only experiment and innovate when there is a no-blame culture. Failures should be shared as a team-failure (including the leader) and not as the failure of a single person. When recruiting, leaders should look for people who are self-starters and will demonstrate authority and autonomy. Leaders have to supply employees with guardrails, provided through direction and Service Management Principles.

Employees need to have a sense of ownership of their work, which leaders provide by letting them deliver the specified outcomes in their own way. Leaders need to ask, "what would you do if this was your business?" Thinking about the workplace as if it was theirs develops a sense of employee ownership. With this premise, employees

---

41 Garr, S. (2014, December 18). *The gift of clarity (and using goals to provide it)*, (Online). https://blog.
bersin.com/the-gift-of-clarity-and-using-goals-to-provide-it/. [2018 April].

have to be able to make decisions for themselves without recourse to unnecessary management.

A sense of ownership can also be built by allowing employees to be involved across the entire organization. If they are developing products, let them sit in the call center to find out what customers are saying. If they are sitting in the call center, let them sit with the designers to understand the design process. Assign people to different parts of the organization so that they gain an understanding of the sum of the parts. Link everything an employee does to the outcomes achieved for the business.

Real world example
Spotify
At Spotify, the belief is that alignment enables autonomy. In 2018, Spotify was a 10-year-old music, video, and podcast streaming organization with 30 million paying subscribers and about $3 billion USD in revenue.

A Harvard Business Review article[42] describes how Spotify provides employee autonomy. Spotify's 2,000 employees are organized into agile teams, called squads, which are self-organizing, cross-functional, and co-located.

"The central organizational feature that shapes Spotify's model is the concept of "loosely coupled, tightly aligned squads." The key belief here is that "alignment enables autonomy — the greater the alignment, the more autonomy you can grant." That's why the company spends so much time aligning on objectives and goals before launching into work. The leadership model at Spotify reinforces this alignment. A leader's job is to figure out the right problem and communicate it, so that squads can collaborate to find the best solution. Coordination comes through context and through a deep understanding of the company's priorities, product strategies, and overall mission. The release process decouples each element for feature squads, infrastructure squads, and client application squads. The ability to release features and then toggle them on or off enables full releases even before all features are fully operational. Here, too, the culture acts as a support. The watchword at Spotify is "be autonomous, but do not sub optimize — be a good citizen in the Spotify ecosystem." A common analogy at the company is a jazz band: Each squad plays its instrument, but each also listens to the others and focuses on the overall piece to make great music."

Another great example of employee authority and autonomy is at **The Ritz-Carlton**. It is now a widely used example when discussing employee autonomy. The Ritz-Carlton gives every employee $2000 USD per day per guest as discretionary spend to either resolve a customer issue or give the customer a 'wow' moment.

---

42 Mankins, M., & Garton, E. (2017, February 9). *How Spotify balances employee autonomy and accountability*, (Online). https://hbr.org/2018/02/how-spotify-balances-employee-autonomy-and-accountability. [2018 January].

5.5.5 Getting started

Leaders need to get out of the way and let employees get on with the job where and when they want to, and with whom. This will deliver high levels of employee engagement and low attrition and make the organization an attractive place to work.

Real world example

Valve Corporation

A shining example of this mentioned is Valve Corporation. This is an extract from the Valve Handbook for New Employees[43]. It summarizes what all leaders should aspire to if we are going to flourish in a world of constant change.

"Hierarchy is great for maintaining predictability and repeatability. It simplifies planning and makes it easier to control a large group of people from the top down, which is why military organizations rely on it so heavily.

But when you're an entertainment company that's spent the last decade going out of its way to recruit the most intelligent, innovative, talented people on Earth, telling them to sit at a desk and do what they're told obliterates 99 percent of their value. We want innovators, and that means maintaining an environment where they'll flourish.

That's where Valve is at. It's our shorthand way of saying that we do not have any management and nobody 'reports to' anybody else. We do have a founder/president, but even he isn't your manager. This company is yours to steer—toward opportunities and away from risks. You have the power to green-light projects. You have the power to ship products."

■ 5.6   ESTABLISH MUTUAL TRUST

Constant change needs a flatter organization so that things happen faster. The only way a flatter hierarchy with less managerial presence will be successful is if there is an environment of trust and mutual respect. Everyone in the organization has to trust everyone else to do the right thing for their colleagues as well as the organization as a whole.

Sahil Lavingia, co-founder and CEO at Gumroad, the successful platform that enables creators to sell products directly to consumers, was quoted in *First Round Review*:[44]

---

43 Valve Corporation. (2012). *Valve: Handbook for new employees*, (Online). https://steamcdn.a-kamaihd. net/apps/valve/Valve_NewEmployeeHandbook.pdf [2018 March].

44 (No date). *An inside look at a flat organization that serves millions*, (Online). http://firstround.com/review/ An-Inside-Look-at-a-Flat-Organization-That-Serves-Millions/ [2018 April].

> "Keeping a company flat is all about finding creative ways to achieve trust and clarity without the bureaucracy. A flat company is founded on the idea that trust shouldn't only exist between a manager and their reports. Everyone within the company should trust everyone else they work with too. That's how you end up moving really fast".

So how is trust established?

5.6.1   Sense of purpose

Organizations have to truly recognize the purpose of the organization – what is it trying to achieve and why? What are the core values that will inspire everyone in the organization so that everyone is working towards a common goal?

Real world example
Google
Google has one mission and one goal.

Mission: Organize the world's information and make it universally accessible and useful.

Goal: Develop services that improve the lives of as many people as possible. Not just for some. For everyone.

Everyone at Google has a shared purpose – to support the mission and achieve the goal. They are unified, and this unity and the sense of purpose inspires trust in everyone in the organization.

When all staff share a common goal and have a collective sense of purpose, high levels of trust are an outcome. If staff believe others have different agendas that do not support the common goal, then mistrust and suspicion permeate the organization, and everyone spends time watching their own back.

5.6.2   Walk the talk

Leaders are often expected to 'walk the talk' and lead by example, but in reality, this goes beyond just those in senior positions in the organization. Everyone should walk the talk and lead by example and when they do not, this needs to be questioned. In an organization where everyone can 'lead' then everyone is accountable to serve the purpose of the organization. Leaders trust employees and vice versa. To receive trust, it has to be given. Whilst everyone should lead by example, the charge has to be led by the CEO or the 'owner' of the organization. Everything he or she commits to doing must be done if trust is to be established. If that commitment has to be changed, then transparency and honesty are crucial if trust is to be maintained.

5.6.3 Teams

> John Mackey, co-founder and CEO of Whole Food Market Inc. writing for Management Innovation eXchange[45], said research indicates that our ability to maintain close trusting relationships with family, friends and work colleagues is constrained to probably around 150 people.
>
> "At Whole Foods we recognize the importance of smaller tribal groupings to maximize familiarity and trust. We organize our stores and company into a variety of interlocking teams. Most teams have between six and 100 team members and the larger teams are subdivided further into a variety of sub-teams".

Typically, people know more than 150 people at any one time. It is hard to develop close bonds of trust based on actual experiences with this many people. Teams need to be the right size, the right structure and have the right motivation.

> **Real world example**
> **W.L. Gore**
> W. L. Gore is a highly successful American multinational manufacturing company specializing in products derived from fluoro polymers. Gore has around 9,500 employees distributed across 30 countries.
>
> Management Innovation eXchange describes Bill Gore's vision of self-managed teams and why they are kept small.[46]
>
> "Gore's commitment to keeping its operations small and informal is one key. It generally does not allow a facility to grow to more than 200 people. That reflects another of Bill's beliefs: that once a unit reaches a certain size, "we decided" becomes "they decided".
>
> When teams become too big, "they decided" dissolves trust.

5.6.4 Enablement
Trust is demonstrated when employees are enabled to get on with their job.

As discussed in Section 5.5.4, many organizations call this empowerment, but empowerment implies that power is passed down from on high. In a flatter organizational structure, employees always have that power. Enablement,

---

45 Mackey J. (2010, March 9). Creating the high trust organization. https://www.huffingtonpost.com/john-mackey/creating-the-high-trust-o_b_497589.html?guccounter=1 [2018 February].

46 Hamel, G. (2010, September 23). Innovation democracy: W.L. Gore's original management model, (Online). https://www.managementexchange.com/story/innovation-democracy-wl-gores-original-management-model. [2018 February].

empowerment, permission – whatever you want to call it – is critical. Hierarchies with a 'command and control' managerial approach kill trust. They are driven by rules and structures to enforce those rules.

5.6.5 Transparency

If people are not transparent, there will be no trust. There may be some occasions when things cannot be shared (for example, confidential information) but this should be the exception. When people perceive that they are not being told the truth, trust will disappear rapidly. Remember that once trust is broken, it will be considerably harder to restore it than it was to establish it in the first place. Communication needs to be transparent and honest. People will see 'spin' when it happens, and, once again, trust is lost. Telling the truth, albeit sometimes through a difficult conversation, fosters trust and mutual respect.

5.6.6 Everyone is equal

Trust is soon lost when there is the perception that some people are treated more favorably than others. The perception that some are more equal than others will cause trust to quickly diminish. The good thing about transparency is that it exposes unfairness and corrective action can be taken quickly.

This equality is reflected by the removal of titles in organizations such as Morning Star where everyone is a Colleague; at W.L. Gore where everyone is an Associate and in organizations adopting Holacracy, where everyone is a Partner. All of these organizations have a flat structure.

5.6.7 Getting started

Trust is key to providing employees with autonomy, allowing them to be self-managing and distributing decision-making. Treating everyone as equal, being honest and transparent, providing a shared sense of purpose, walking the talk, and creating smaller teams to avoid *"we decided"* becoming *"they decided"*, will foster a sustainable eco-system of trust.

■ 5.7 BUILD A NETWORK OF RELIANCE ON OTHERS

Employees need to know that they can rely on each other. When teams have a shared sense of purpose and connectedness, and mutual trust and respect, they can face continual and complex change. They know that they can rely on each other. There is a feeling of resilience to constant change when someone has your back.

When we have reliance on others, there is a sense that we are all in it together with a shared sense of purpose. To foster this ability to rely on others, we need to break down silos and build cross-functional teams. Change is fluid and so are the teams addressing those changes. The composition and structure of teams can change as needed, to respond to change. Therefore, the sense of reliance on others needs to extend across teams and not just within them.

Creating a culture of trust and respect throughout the organization allows people to seek out help and advice without fear of reprimand or criticism. Employees can rely on others to solve problems, come up with innovative responses to change and work as a collective rather than as individuals.

Employees form trust networks that are adaptive and can innovate when faced with change. Support and a sense of belonging can contribute greatly to employee engagement and staff feel supported. Staff will help each other, rely on each other and build trust. When change is constant, support is crucial for the success of the organization. When employees can look to one another for guidance or support, focus can remain on the overall outcome needed. If an opportunity or problem is handled individually, there is the risk of an employee becoming overwhelmed and making irrational decisions. When employees are connected to resources across the organization, they feel supported and are therefore engaged and motivated, which leads to increased productivity.

> A Harvard Business Review[47] article stated: Some companies — among them Google, DaVita, Dropbox, and Southwest — have built reputations for fostering comradeship at work. Creating comradeship at work hinges on the leaders of organizations. That is, companies can and should create and value camaraderie as a competitive advantage for recruiting top employees, retaining employees, and improving engagement, creativity, and productivity.
>
> It is up to the leaders to foster collaboration, trust, mutual respect, and support for each other.

5.7.1 Getting started

When everyone can rely on everyone else there is increased collaboration, creativity and innovation. This is what will set the organizations that thrive through constant change apart from those that do not. When employees work together in an environment where they feel supported by each other, they have an easier time coming up with new ideas.

---

47 Riordan, C. M. (2013, July 3). *We all need friends at work*, (Online). https://hbr.org/2013/07/we-all-need-friends-at-work. [2018, March].

Creative thinking is vital to the success of the organization especially when change is constant. People can rely on each other to brainstorm new ideas. Getting different points of view allows the organization to respond to rapid change in the most effective manner as issues and challenges are seen from different angles.

Real world perspective

Chapter 24 has an interview with organizational change management expert Karen Ferris, who shares more practical insights about how organizations can thrive in a world of constant change.

"There's a famous quote "organizations do not change, people do".[48]

Organizations can only change by getting people to adopt change and drive a change forward. Many organizations have projects that fail because of lack of adoption, or not getting people ready for change.

In the past, overcoming resistance to change has been a key OCM activity, viewing resistance as a negative to be overcome. We need to see that resistance isn't necessarily a bad thing. The change itself could be wrong."

—

48 Source unknown

6   Collaboration

Introduction

Effective teams collaborate, share knowledge and communicate well. They build a body of knowledge that is invaluable to the organization, and in the same way that organizations are unique, so are these bodies of knowledge. Virtual teams, the requirement to collaborate across time zones and supply chains and the multitude of collaboration tools available all add challenges.

This chapter looks at what collaboration is, and how to improve the level of collaboration within an organization. Without collaboration, cross-functional teams will be ineffective, trust will be low, and outcomes will be poorer.

Business practices have been evolving ever since the introduction of business computers in the 1970s. The way people share information, communicate and get work done has changed beyond recognition. During this time, there has also been the rise of the knowledge worker as organizations and the services they provide are built on know-how and intellectual property.

In all this time, one thing has not changed. Something so important that nothing functions without it, so universal that it transcends best practice frameworks, technology and business changes – and that is people and their knowledge. No matter how automated, how commoditized, or how simplified systems become, people and their knowledge will always be key to an organization's success. This has been true since the first time groups of people worked together hunting mammoths. Collaborative practices can dramatically transform an organization or team's performance; driving productivity, improving staff retention, increasing general awareness and reducing the time and number of meetings required to keep staff up to speed.

The 2018 Digital Transformation Survey

As shown in Figure 19, many respondents feel that collaboration works well in their organization, although there is still space for improvement.

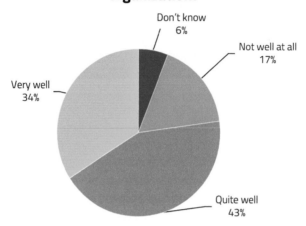

How well does collaboration work within your organization?

Don't know 6%

Not well at all 17%

Very well 34%

Quite well 43%

Figure 19 How well does collaboration work in your organization? (Source: 2018 Survey)

■ 6.1   WHAT IS COLLABORATION?

Collaboration is intangible and best described as 'a way of behaving' and 'ways of doing' important activities. These statements suggest a need to focus on intangibles and soft skills. The Oxford English Dictionary defines collaboration as "the action of working with someone to produce something". To work together and achieve common goals, people have to collaborate.

This basic definition of collaboration is so broad and open to interpretation that it is easy to appreciate why people do not always grasp the essence of what collaboration really is. The definition describes collaboration as "the action of". It is something that "occurs". It can be facilitated by leadership, direction and tools, but first and foremost it is a way of working that must be allowed, or perhaps, made to happen.

One way to understand what collaboration means is to first establish what it is not.

6.1.1   Collaboration is __not__ a tool

The most common misconception is that collaboration is (or can be achieved via) 'a tool'. Organizations assume that once a collaboration tool has been implemented, staff will start collaborating, or worse, because a tool has been implemented, they must already be collaborating. The presence, or lack, of a tool does not guarantee collaboration.

> "Technology does not automatically improve conversation, communication or behavior."
>
> Theodore Zeldin

6.1.2   Collaboration is not using social tools in the workplace

Modern social media tools may be excellent for keeping in touch with friends or digesting news, but their use in the workplace is at best distracting and, at worst, a risk to corporate confidentiality and security. While social tools have undoubtedly introduced simpler and more effective ways to communicate, using richer content and interactive real time chat and information sharing, they are not generally fit for enterprise use. Enterprise tools need security and visibility control features that are tuned to the needs of the organization rather than social sharing. Information sharing in enterprises is generally confined to employees and does not extend to friends and family in the same way that social networking tools do.

6.1.3   Collaboration is not email

Email is the primary tool for business communication. Email has many benefits; it facilitates and records conversations, but this does not mean that it is an effective tool for enterprise collaboration. The closed-loop format of information exchange means that email does a poor job of supporting and nurturing a collaborative culture.

◼ 6.2   COLLABORATION BEHAVIORS

Enterprise collaboration behavior falls into these categories:

- **Conversations** – facilitating open, transparent and inclusive one-to-one and group conversations;
- **Information sharing** – enabling and encouraging the free flow of information;
- **Tacit knowledge** – tacit knowledge is that knowledge which is known but not thought of until someone asks the question;
- **Information visualization** – providing ways of visualizing data in a way that encourages conversation, contribution and inclusion;
- **Community** – creating a culture that has a 'community' feel;
- **Governance** – systems and processes must be aligned with and support corporate security, compliance and policies.

Collaborative organizations exhibit behavioral characteristics that are tangible and measurable, which can be seen in action and act as strong indicators as to the levels of collaboration that is occurring. These include:

■ **Leadership** – a team or organization will never be truly collaborative without strong leadership. This is especially true in the early days of establishing and nurturing a collaborative culture. Once a collaborative culture takes hold, leadership focus becomes less important, as people realize the benefits and the behavior becomes self-perpetuating. It is worth noting that anyone can initiate or lead a collaboration initiative, but ultimately, they will need support and sponsorship from senior management to overcome the inevitable hurdles and objections that will be encountered.

■ **Support** – people will not collaborate in a truly open fashion unless the culture supports it. Mistakes will occur, and leadership should acknowledge and accept this. People learn from mistakes, and, typically they will own and fix any problems that arise. A supportive environment encourages people to contribute, come up with ideas and share information, without fear of retribution when things go wrong. It is worth remembering that *"If you're not making mistakes, then you're not doing anything".*

■ **Transparency** – it is almost impossible to be truly collaborative in an environment that is not transparent, open and communicative (see Section 5.6.5). Collaborative teams share what they know. They use open communication, are willing to share and will support their colleagues Transparency can be a real challenge, especially within organizations that have complex political and organizational cultures. Silos are created and ring-fenced to deal with highly specialized work and, while they serve an important purpose, the overall goals of the organization are often replaced by departmental targets, team objectives and local optimization. Although many organizations are tearing down silos, they are necessary and, where they exist, a high degree of transparency and open communication should be encouraged to ensure that collaboration between necessary silos can occur.

■ **Contribution** – if there is a good flow of information, the contribution of ideas, thoughts and comments should be encouraged. Collaborative teams solicit feedback, discuss ideas and suggestions, and will set aside a 'not invented here' mentality. If a Finance person suggests a great marketing idea, embrace it – do not discard it because it did not originate from the marketing team. Well-run organizations know instinctively that the best ideas must win every time. In a VeriSM model, this is supported by the concept of all organizational capabilities working together to support the 'organization as service provider'.

The term 'silo' typically has a negative connotation, a throwback to an era of 'command and control' hierarchies. The IT department, for example, is often perceived as a silo that operates in isolation and sees 'customers' as the people inside the organization that it serves. The corporate IT function is organized into teams (infrastructure, security, development etc.) focused on local optimization of their own processes, leading to a further siloed mentality and internal competition between teams. Collaborative organizations connect these silos, and collaborative teams see themselves as critical cogs in the organization's machine. They understand that 'customers' are external and that serving them well is paramount to an organization's success.

6.2.1   Organizational behavior characteristics

Figure 20 Organizational behavior characteristics (source: Hornbill)

Collaboration encourages a different set of behaviors. Transparency creates a flow of information that gives everyone a better insight into the organization and how it works. This, in turn, encourages the traits and behaviors of externally competitive organizations, as shown in the diagram above.

Collaboration is not just another best practice, nor is it an alternative to something else. Instead, think of collaboration as the "fitness level" of your organization, and the fitter you are, the better you can perform. In the same way as an athlete's level of fitness directly affects their level of success in a given sport, your level of collaboration has a direct impact on the level of success you are likely to achieve within your profession. However, collaboration is a team sport, not an individual sport. Knowledge hoarding and heroics have no place in a collaborative environment; it is about sharing what you know, and lifting others up, so that the entire community benefits.

■ 6.3   WHY IS COLLABORATION IMPORTANT?

Providing products or services is ultimately about people, and how well they work together, removing friction from the product or service experience and delivering value to customers. Knowledge is attained over time and through experience and learning happens as work gets done.

Service disruption or product failure is often the result of repetitive issues that could be resolved easily with good quality, easily accessible knowledge. Complex issues generally require input from several stakeholders to achieve resolution. Whether an organization has formal structures, such as first, second, and third line teams or more informal channels, such as a tech bar, or simply catching up with a subject matter expert by the coffee machine, information still needs to be shared.

A collaborative environment encourages knowledge sharing, supporting and recognizing the value of effective and free flowing communication. Unfortunately, a great deal of knowledge sharing and conversational information exchange goes unrecorded. Ideally, effective collaborative environments automatically capture and distribute knowledge for the benefit of the entire community, at zero cost, as a by-product of getting work done. This significantly enhances, optimizes and streamlines work, as knowledge accumulates during the flow of information between individuals, teams and departments.

Although every organization is different, a service management culture provides a common language and proven practices that allow organizations to learn from the experience of others. As new challenges give rise to new ideas, best practice frameworks will fall in and out of fashion, but organizations can usually adapt. Collaboration is not a replacement for any best practice, instead, it is a foundational set of cultural behaviors that enable teams to adopt, adapt and improve in a better way.

Collaborative teams are more innovative, as the free flow of information encourages contribution and generates ideas. When team members feel close to their own ideas, or contribute to the development of shared ideas, they are more inclined to create time within their schedules to implement them. By encouraging your teams to collaborate, you are creating a platform for innovation.

■ 6.4   THE DYNAMICS OF COLLABORATION IN AN ORGANIZATION

Real world perspective

Hornbill

Gerry Sweeney, Founder, Group CEO and CTO at Hornbill, shares these thoughts about the dynamics of collaboration in their organization. Hornbill are leaders in collaboration practices and contributed to this chapter extensively.

"Coming from a background where collaboration is now (almost) entirely institutionalized, it is easy for me to sing the praises of collaborative working. However, the people dynamics remain a continuous challenge, which need to be kept in check. Along the way, we have encountered unexpected behaviors and outcomes, both positive and negative. Your efforts to get collaboration established will evolve, and, just like a ship needs to adapt to the wind and changing currents, you will need to keep your hands on the wheel, continuously making minor course corrections.

It is difficult to provide generic advice on collaboration because larger organizations have a high level of diversity and scale and different teams may need a different approach. The fundamentals may be the same, but the specifics can be quite different, so it is best considered as two distinct discussions. The first, focused on collaboration within a team (team collaboration), and the second between teams (enterprise collaboration) and the behaviors, and dynamics of both are different.

Team collaboration means a single team that performs a specific function within an organization e.g. IT, Facilities, HR, Finance, Sales, Marketing etc. Team collaboration means that the people are collaborating with colleagues who work within their team, but not with other teams or departments.

Enterprise collaboration means that teams are collaborating with other teams. For enterprise collaboration, the channels of information that flow between teams require more organizations and structure, primarily to limit noise and ensure that the content remains relevant."

6.4.1   The dynamics of team collaboration

Most teams are naturally collaborative. A team is a group of people who work together to achieve a common goal. Within the team, sharing knowledge, information, and supporting each other are all part of collaboration.

However, teamwork and collaboration are not the same thing. Teamwork is usually carried out under a single authority, a team leader or manager, who organizes resources, disseminates information, prioritizes work, supports team members and resolves conflicts. In a collaborative environment, such as a large open-source project, there is no manager or single authority. Instead, seniority, experience and contribution to the project are ultimately what drives decision making. Team collaboration includes open communication, knowledge sharing and ideation and using collaboration tools as a communication platform, creating the opportunity for any individual to shine through their contribution to the work being done. Team collaboration delivers distinct advantages, which positively affect the way that the team works:

- **Conflict resolution** – this is a difficult and time-consuming job for a manager. In traditional teamwork environments, conflicts often start with an email trail, followed by a meeting, where the manager has to arbitrate to resolve the conflict. In a collaborative environment, where email is reserved for external communication, the conflict happens in an open (team) forum, where others can join the conversation, and more often than not, team consensus lead to a frictionless resolution.
- **People think twice** – when team members are encouraged to post to an open forum, instead of emailing a select audience, people think twice about what they post. This leads to better conversations, improved communication and effective knowledge capture.
- **Idea rejection** – team members are usually happy to make suggestions and propose ideas, and this should always be encouraged, but ideas might not get a fair hearing, or may be rejected unreasonably. It often falls to the manager to reject ideas tactfully, in a way that does not demotivate individuals or team morale. When team members are encouraged to submit ideas in an open forum, team consensus will separate the good from the bad quickly. An idea that initially seemed poor can plant a seed for a great idea to develop, and therefore instead of having their original idea rejected, the initiator has contributed to a better idea that can be implemented.
- **Recognition and reward** – it can be demoralizing when somebody else takes the credit for an idea that you have proposed. In an open forum, there is no question about the origin of new ideas, so people can be recognized for their contribution. An open forum creates healthy competition, providing the opportunity for anyone to shine. However, if an individual's ideas are constantly rejected, they may shy away from further participation. A supportive culture is critical to ensure that every team member has a voice and continues to contribute.
- **Team awareness** – when the entire team is collaborating in an open forum, people truly get to know each other. This is especially important for remote workers, or geographically dispersed teams, who can continue to work independently, while participating in conversations and contributing their knowledge, expertise and ideas.

Some teams are naturally collaborative and need little encouragement to participate. Software development teams are a prime example, as team members must share source code, knowledge and know-how to work effectively. The widespread adoption of open-source software is only made possible when software teams collaborate. At the other end of the spectrum, teams that carry out transactional or administrative work can often operate in isolation and have less need for collaboration.

Working in an open and collaborative environment can, initially, create perceived 'risks' for certain individuals. If a team member is failing or not contributing to objectives, the entire team will notice. To succeed within the organization, team members must contribute, as it is harder to play corporate politics in this more open context. Mistakes are highly visible, so good leadership and a solid understanding of these dynamics are essential to the creation of a supportive environment where people learn and grow.

Teams are important components of the organizational machine. Inside the machine there are many moving parts and each part has to do its job effectively for the machine to work. One malfunctioning component can break the whole machine, or at the very least, place unnecessary pressure on other moving parts, which may lead to their failure. As the machine moves, each part must perform its function and hand over to other parts to complete the process. Communication and knowledge sharing are vital lubricants that enable these parts to work together effectively. Pay close attention to how teams interact. When exceptions occur, they must be dealt with, so effective communication between teams is vital.

Finance teams, for example, must ensure that Sales teams follow a specific process, so that customers can be billed correctly and on time. In a collaborative environment, the Sales team could easily propose improvements to the Finance team's billing process – and vice-versa – and encouraging this type of interaction will deliver value across the entire organization.

6.4.2   The dynamics of enterprise collaboration

Enterprise collaboration is where different teams within the organization are collaborating with other teams or departments. Many organizations still operate a traditional 'command and control' hierarchy, with a management approach that relies on authority and instruction. Within these organizations, a significant proportion of the workforce may not need to understand the 'big picture' to carry out their work to a certain standard. A factory worker who sits on a production line may be required to assemble 2000 widgets per hour. The worker does not need to know why they are assembling them or why they need to assemble 2000 per hour. Those parameters have been defined by the management system, and workers must do their jobs and hit their targets to deliver against production plans.

> Despite having little day-to-day input into the strategy of the organization, good leaders recognize that production line workers can contribute valuable ideas to improve output and efficiency. Early initiatives, such as the 'suggestion box' were deployed to encourage workers to make suggestions for improvement, but the process was still plagued with organizational controls.

Using the hypothetical factory scenario, this section examines some of the collaboration problems that organizations may face.

A worker suggests that instead of hand assembling the widget, the organization could change the manufacturing process by introducing a magnetic binding feature, which means that two other components are no longer needed. Assembly time can be reduced, increasing production to 2700 widgets per hour. The removal of two components reduces production costs by 30 cents per widget; a remarkable win for the business and the 'suggestion box' initiative. However, the dynamics of different teams and poor collaboration come into play, leading to:

- **Not invented here** – the suggestion might be ignored by the Design team, because by acknowledging it, they must accept that their original design was not optimized. They are paid to design an efficient and cost-effective production process and it does not reflect well when someone external to the design team suggests a more efficient process. The worker is discouraged from making future suggestions because they believe that it is a waste of time.
- **A poor idea** – what seemed like a really good idea is dismissed, because while it made sense, the cost saving had a genuine knock-on effect elsewhere, which affected revenue. The idea is dismissed, and although there was a good reason for not implementing it, the worker has no idea why, and is discouraged from making further suggestions.
- **Unbalanced credit/reward/recognition** – the suggestion is adopted by someone further up the chain and the worker receives recognition from their line manager for the contribution. However, the production director is awarded a $50k bonus and gets credit for saving the organization $500k annually in production costs. The C-suite (see Chapter 18) has no knowledge that the idea actually came from a worker on the production line. The worker gets a pat on the back, while someone else gets a big bonus and a future promotion. Again, the worker is discouraged.

Although these are extreme scenarios, used to illustrate some of the problems that can be encountered with 'command and control' hierarchies, many organizations display similar behaviors. 'Command and control' hierarchical structures are not conducive to open, transparent and collaborative working.

Consider the same scenario within a collaborative organization.

In a collaborative organization, communication is open and transparent, so everyone is involved in the conversation and the flow of information. The organization has a system in place to facilitate open conversation, typically enabled by a collaboration tool where conversations are visible to anyone with permission to see the information being posted. Everyone, from the CEO down, favors open forums for conversation, instead of closed channels, such as emails or meetings. A workspace (think of this as a specific conversation topic) has been created called 'Production Improvement Ideas and Suggestions' and everyone is encouraged to submit ideas and suggestions into this workspace.

The CEO, a woman, has a keen interest in production ideas, as she built the organization upon a foundation of production innovation. Although she is no longer involved with the day-to-day production operation, she keeps her finger on the pulse, and contributes to ideas. She joins the workspace and is now part of the conversation and has visibility of the ideas being proposed. The manager, director and most of the production workers are members of the workspace.

A worker makes a suggestion, articulating their idea in the workspace, where others can comment and voice their opinions. When collaboration is adopted in the organization, the demotivating outcomes mentioned earlier are negated:

- **Not invented here** – the suggestion is liked by several employees, who also think it is a great idea. The Design team cannot simply dismiss the idea but may choose to discredit it and there may be good reasons why it should not progress any further. However, the Design team needs to explain its reasoning, because people have visibility of the conversation. In an open workspace, the ability to suppress a good idea for political reasons is eliminated. Instead, the culture requires the Design team to acknowledge and examine ideas.
- **A poor idea** – the suggestion seems like a good one, so a conversation ensues with several people commenting and expanding on the idea. They determine that, while it improves one part of the production process, there is a knock-on effect that creates a bottleneck elsewhere. Everyone involved in the conversation has been educated and, although the idea seemed good, it will not work for the organization. The worker is praised for their suggestion and understands why the idea cannot be taken further.
- **Unbalanced credit/reward/recognition** – the origin of the idea is clear from the start and nobody else can claim the credit. The worker is recognized with a 'Great Idea' comment from the CEO and is encouraged to think about how to further improve the organization's production efforts.

These simple examples show how organizational barriers can be broken down and explain how a collaborative environment can create a powerful platform for innovation and agile change, which can quickly transform an organization. Collaboration can have a profound effect on an organization's culture, opening lines of communication that are missing in non-collaborative environments.

While team collaboration is relatively easy to deploy, enterprise collaboration is more challenging to get right. Strong, top-down leadership and clear commitment is required to build a collaborative culture. Politics and team dynamics are disrupted within a collaborative environment. Some teams will resist collaboration and may find it difficult to adapt when information is flowing freely across hierarchical structures and boundaries.

■ 6.5 BENEFITS OF NURTURING A COLLABORATIVE CULTURE

There are tangible and intangible benefits to nurturing a collaborative culture within an organization. Collaboration improves overall organizational performance and creates an environment to improve products and services by enhancing organizational knowledge and workforce engagement. The benefits are:

■ **Process/ways of working improvement** – there is no better way to improve operational processes than enabling the people who run the processes to help improve, evolve and refine them. When a process can be improved, people are generally vocal, and, by embracing collaborative working, good ideas can be quickly put into practice.

■ **Intellectual capital** – although formal training is essential, most organizational learning is achieved by 'doing'. Building know-how and skills is imperative to stay ahead of the competition and the best way to build knowledge is by continuously – and automatically – keeping your people up-to-speed. It is also vital that intellectual capital and know-how does not disappear when employees leave. By encouraging the free flow of information on a suitable platform, knowledge can be retained and structured in a natural way. This makes it searchable for future use, enabling new employees to get up-to-speed quickly.

■ **Human capital** – almost without exception, a company's largest expense is its workforce. Staff who are listened to, kept well informed and who understand the purpose and challenges of the organization, are an engaged and happy workforce. A happy workforce means lower staff turnover, reduced recruitment costs and, ultimately, happy customers and consumers.

■ **Communication improvement** – staff always need to feel engaged and informed. Two remarkable dynamics occur in collaborative environments, which change the way in which an organization uses its time and resources. First, people are better informed before going to meetings, which are generally shorter and are needed less frequently. Second, the need for leadership to communicate progress, news and status information continuously is reduced substantially. People stop saying "I do not know what's going on" and management has more capacity for higher value work.

■ **Appetite for educated risk** – traditional hierarchical organizations typically discourage failure. It gives bad publicity, costs money and is inefficient. However, developments in the digital age are so fast that learning by experimenting becomes the norm. This means that risks must be taken, and failures are welcomed as lessons. The organization's culture should have an appetite for risk and it should be safe for employees to fail occasionally. In a true collaborative culture, the organization will benefit from an appetite for educated risk. Of course, there must be a balance between successes and failures. The leadership will therefore have to give the organization focus by providing direction and principles.

These benefits improve organizational efficiency, drive down costs and boost productivity, delivering measurable improvements that are visible on the bottom line.

Real world perspective
Hornbill
Pitfalls of collaboration and how to avoid them
Gerry Sweeney, Founder of Hornbill, Group CEO and CTO shares some further experiences from his organization.

"I can tell you from first-hand experience that creating a collaborative environment is transformational, in ways that almost appear magical. The benefits are immense, and amazing things happen when you get to the point where a collaborative culture has been institutionalized. However, it is not all plain sailing, and there are pitfalls to watch out for along the way. And when you have arrived, you'll need to keep some things in check to prevent your collaborative culture from failing and creating organizational problems and management overhead.

Every organization is different, so it is hard to list all the pitfalls that you may encounter. Although by no means a definitive list, here are some of the things I have seen and experienced, which should give you a starting point and some insight into the things to look out for:

- **Anti-collaborators** – not everyone likes to collaborate. Some people prefer a closed-loop, email/BCC way or working. Others feel that they have little to contribute. They simply want to keep their heads down and do their work, so choose not to collaborate. Others prefer the traditional command-and-control approach of meetings, face-to-face conversations and "taking it off-line". They believe that it is easier and faster to work this way. However, this comes at a cost, because by working this way, they are closing the door to contribution from others and failing to create reusable knowledge by refusing to use a communication platform that is designed to capture these conversations. Anti-collaborators not only avoid collaborating; they will subconsciously prevent others from doing so, by moving conversations that should be on a workspace into meetings. You will undoubtedly find anti-collaborators within your organization but be aware that too much of this behavior can undermine your collaborative culture.
- **Toxic conversations** – these will happen. Despite conversations being highly visible, people will voice their opinions, disagree and express their dissatisfaction with situations or outcomes. To some degree, you must let this happen, but be prepared to bring such conversations to an end when appropriate. Because of the open nature of conversations, this is mostly self-regulating, but heated conversations will arise from time to time. The last thing you want is a toxic conversation with no conclusion because the resolution was taken off-line, so ideally, they should always be resolved in the same open forum.

- **Non-collaborating teams** – just as you'll find individuals who are anti-collaborators, you'll find teams that are used to working in a more traditional way, through meetings and email. Often the team does not understand the importance of promoting the value they bring to a wider company audience. This behavior is common amongst teams that do not want anyone to interfere with their working practices, activities and ideas. They may perceive suggestions as criticism or think that other people have no right to tell them how to do their jobs. The good news is that in an organization where most teams are collaborating, those that are not will quickly start to feel isolated. Their lack of contribution becomes highly visible, so this situation is usually self-correcting.

- **Unwanted contributions** – this tends to be a later stage effect, which only starts to become an issue when collaborative behaviors have been institutionalized and everyone has become used to working openly and transparently. People post their ideas, invite others to comment, value their feedback and overall contribution to the outcome. However, inviting commentary and feedback too early in the conversation can be obstructive. Product development is a prime example, where ideation around new or enhanced features is likely to invite feedback, questions and suggestions. This can be time-consuming to manage, especially if people are not aware of the full picture. This is more pronounced with Enterprise collaboration and, if multiple teams are brought into the conversation too early, it can be counter-productive.

- **Distracted by 'the exciting stuff'** – alongside all the interesting work that we *want* to do, comes mundane work that we *have* to do. Although all work is important, people are generally more motivated by new and exciting things. Collaboration creates the opportunity to expose and involve more people in the new and exciting things the organization is doing. You must watch out for the tendency for people to be unproductively distracted by exciting stuff, to the point where it affects their ability to focus on the mundane, yet critical things that must be done for the organization to function. Keep this in check through clear objectives, and by recognizing and rewarding people for good efforts on business-as-usual activities.

- **Anarchy mistaken for collaborative culture** – effective collaboration needs governance and direction. In some business cultures (e.g. central Europe) peer-to-peer relationships are often considered to be more effective than hierarchal relationships. This often works very well but there is a risk that collaboration without direction degenerates into anarchy. This can be avoided by strong governance and principles that respect the local business culture."

▪ 6.6 COLLABORATING IN PRACTICE

Collaboration is a culture, a way of working, and something that organizations and teams 'do'. Tools will help, but they will not make a team, or an organization collaborate. Although collaboration will not occur because a tool has been implemented, in practice, an appropriate tool is almost mandatory. Purpose-built tools will enable your team/organization to collaborate effectively using features that are not found within email natively, chat or instant messaging applications. Any good tool should provide these basic capabilities:

- **Organized conversations** – the most fundamental capability of any collaboration tool is the ability to create 'conversation topics' that allow people to share information, ask questions, propose ideas and discuss a topic. Posts will have a title, which is the subject and comments are the thread of conversation around the subject.
- **Rich multi-media content** – people communicate well when using a combination of text, images, video, animations, so rich content is a must. The tool should make it easy to communicate and share thoughts and ideas using the media that best suit the topic.
- **Emotional communication** – people use body language and vocal expression to communicate emotional elements in face-to-face conversation. Text and images remove body language from communication, so good collaboration tools should allow you to use other media, such as emojis, animated images (Giphy), static images and other media designed to communicate emotion.
- **Membership and visibility** – organizations need the ability to control access and visibility to structured conversations, to control privacy and participation. Most collaboration tools are built with this in mind.
- **Syndication and notifications** – highly collaborative teams generate significant amounts of content, so a good tool needs to help manage this. A good tool will help users manage conversations and get visibility of what is new or relevant.
- **Chat** – a good tool will provide a chat capability, with real-time, instant messaging that facilitates one-to-one, or one-to-many 'off-topic' conversations, ideally supporting both rich text and video chat.

Collaboration tools

Although not a complete list, here are some good examples of collaboration tools:

- Atlassian Confluence;
- Google Hangouts;
- HipChat;
- Hornbill Collaboration;
- Jive[n];
- Slack;
- Skype;
- Microsoft Teams;
- Yammer (part of Office 365);
- Trello.

Collaboration solutions are a type of communication tool. Their purpose is to act as an alternative means of communicating between individuals and teams. However, many organizations that have deployed one of these tools have limited success in establishing collaborative behaviors. So why do these tools not take off in most businesses? The answer is simple – if an organization rolls out a tool and instructs people to collaborate, employees simply see this as another 'thing to do' – a change that is being forced on them.

The key adoption problem for stand-alone collaboration tools is that they are not 'destination applications' i.e. not the application that employees will open first when starting their day. For most people, their primary destination application is email. You must consider: why would your employees use email for external communication and a different tool for internal conversations? This is the primary adoption barrier for most organizations.

The need for increased collaboration is having a huge impact on supporting technologies. Many tools are now providing or working towards a convergence of document production, video, chat and conferencing. The concept of a 'file' is changing; documents might be stored in the cloud as 'pieces' to allow more than one person to work on the file at once.

The key to a successful collaboration initiative is to for your employees to collaborate while getting work done and not give them an extra thing to do, or another application to use.

Real world perspective
Hornbill
Pitfalls of collaboration and how to avoid them
Gerry Sweeney, Founder, Group CEO and CTO shares some further experiences from his organization.

"Based on my experience, here are the three key things you need to address in order to deploy effective collaboration within your organization:
1. Leadership commitment is paramount. If your leadership (at a team or organization level) is not on board, your initiative will not succeed, because people are being asked to change the way they work and communicate fundamentally.
2. You must change the culture, moving ALL and ANY internal conversations off email and onto your collaboration tool of choice. Getting your employees/teams to do this is a real challenge. Giving instruction is not enough, as people will quickly revert to old habits and use the email reply button. Each time a conversation thread appears in an email, ask the originator to 'post to the appropriate workspace' and remind everyone to use the collaboration tool to continue the discussion. Depending on the size of your team, it may take weeks or months, but persevere, and the message will eventually hit home. During this transition period you will need leadership and conviction to force behavioral change.

3. Your collaboration tool must be a destination application, the place your employees go to first, to find out what is happening, to communicate with their colleagues, and most importantly, the tool they use most to get work done.

Trying to transform the entire organization at once is a big mistake. Pick one (or more) teams and get them collaborating first. Ask them to discuss topics, share knowledge and propose ideas using the collaboration platform. People are naturally curious and will be interested in what's going on, so use this to your advantage. If people need to use email, ask them to include links to a relevant workspace/post within the email message.

The main competition to collaboration

The two main competitors to collaboration are your email system, and your employees, More specifically, your employee's reliance on email for internal communications. It's worth exploring this to understand why it is so difficult to detach people from their reliance on email. Let's break it down into simple use-case stories to illustrate the point.

- **I need to send someone a message** – this is a natural fit for email, the most obvious function and the primary thing people think of when you mention email. However, this is a limited use case, as email is used for so much more.
- **I need to send images to someone** – almost the same above, but with the addition of embedded images or attachments, and still a reasonable use of email.
- **I need to share a document with my team** – this is not sending a document via email, it is sharing a document with a number of colleagues. If it is a simple one-way exchange of a document, that is still a reasonable use of email.
- **I need to keep documents and have them to hand in case I need to share them again** – this is where things start to go wrong, when email is used as a personal document storage system. People develop their own schemes to organize their documents, from searching the Sent Items folder for the document, to remembering who they last sent the document to. Email was not designed to be an archiving system.
- **I need to have access to every message I've sent at work** – this is very common and becomes visible when quotas are placed on mailboxes. The more senior the user, the greater the objection, as everything they keep is very important. The truth is that it is just convenient for them to do it this way.
- **I need to share large files with my colleagues** – email was not designed as a document or file sharing platform, yet for the majority of the users, email is the quickest and easiest way to share files and documents with colleagues and between devices.
- **I need to retain the email addresses of every person I do business with** – arguably a function of email, but not as effective as using a CRM system to manage the data properly. With the introduction of the European General Data Protection Regulation (GDPR) and other stringent regulations around the protection of personal data, the use of email as a data store has become a real problem for organizations.
- **I need to remember how to do that thing that Dave showed me last year** – email is used to store and later retrieve knowledge, by searching for people, or keywords.

- **I need everything I have in my email on my mobile device** – when so much data is stored in a mailbox, it becomes a real challenge to the performance of the email system.

A good collaboration tool facilitates all of these requirements in a way that's simple, and more effective and efficient than email. It's important to understand these use cases, and if you choose a tool that allows you to achieve the same, you are well on your way to implementing a collaboration tool successfully.

◼ 6.7   MEASURING SUCCESS

Measuring collaboration success is easy. When staff go to the collaboration platform to get work done and almost all internal conversations are happening within the tool, it will be open at every colleague's desk, and people will not want to go back to the way things were. Other magical things start to happen once you are collaborating effectively. People, being social creatures, will simply be happier and therefore be more cooperative, motivated and creative:

- Knowledge about day-to-day operations will increase dramatically;
- People will not claim that they are 'not kept in the loop' or 'do not know what the plan is';
- Meetings will be less frequent, shorter and more productive;
- People will have a better appreciation of what the organization does, who its consumers are and what must be done to keep them happy;
- Staff will be more engaged and feel that they can contribute to the organization's success.

Case study: Sky Betting and Gaming

To get some more examples of how 'digital first' organizations are innovative in their ways of working, including collaboration, we spoke to Rachel Watson, Head of Service Operations at Sky Betting and Gaming. You can read the full interview in Chapter 22.

"Every Friday afternoon, from 1 PM, is allocated as learning and development and collaboration time; where business-as-usual work stops. This investment in the employees has led to some ideas that have been of real benefit to the organization."

---

7   Knowledge management

Introduction

Digital organizations run on knowledge. Often, a large part of the 'value' of the organization (for example, to shareholders) comes from its intellectual property and the knowledge it creates. How knowledge is shared, used and updated can be a large source of friction; or alternatively, knowledge can improve both employee and consumer experience.

This chapter explores some key concepts to give organizations a solid foundation for making better decisions in the digital age. What is provided is by no means exhaustive and it is important to note that lifelong learning is one of the most important qualities for leaders in a digital age.

Digitization in any form implies some fundamental knowledge and building blocks. This is not necessarily different from what traditionally happens – or should happen – in an organization when thinking of strategy, governance and management of its services. These elements are of even more critical importance than before.

> "The illiterate of the twenty-first century will not be those who cannot read and write, but those who cannot learn, unlearn and relearn."
>
> Alvin Toffler[49]

■ 7.1   KNOWLEDGE MANAGEMENT DEFINED

Knowledge management (KM) is the process of capturing, developing, sharing and effectively using organizational knowledge. It helps organizations make the best use

---

49 Toffler, A. (1970). *Future shock.* New York: Bantam.

of knowledge. Knowledge management is a way of working. It needs to be part of the organization's culture and how 'things are done'.

A digital mindset has been described as:

"…one that leads to an increase of value to stakeholders across all services. How that relates to corporate culture and technology is the question. A digital mindset includes the leader having an exploratory mind and a collaborative approach that embraces diversity and comfort with ambiguity to bring a wider view and value focus to abundance, growth and agility."

It is thought that this mindset comes naturally to those labeled as 'digital natives'.

"A digital native is an individual who was born after the widespread adoption of digital technology. The term digital native does not refer to a generation. Instead, it is a catch-all category for children who have grown up using technology like the Internet, computers and mobile devices."[50]

From the perspective of KM, it is the people within the organization that embrace collaboration, incorporating knowledge activities within their workflows. Search, use, and capture of knowledge is done almost subconsciously. People are tapped into the knowledge sources that are essential to their work, like a courier knowing what parcels need to be delivered each day and how that affects their route.

No matter how ingrained the knowledge activity becomes, it is necessary to elevate it into the conscious realm of the culture. The digital mindset includes awareness that each person is responsible for the knowledge with which they interact, and the value it has. Each person is responsible for correcting inaccuracies, commenting on current knowledge and, where it is missing, adding knowledge to maintain the overall health of organizational knowledge and its continued positive impact.

■ 7.2   KNOWLEDGE MANAGEMENT IN THE DIGITAL AGE

Knowledge management becomes increasingly important for organizations in the digital age. The pace of innovation and change, evolving technologies and ever-changing business requirements demand that organizations capture and share knowledge enterprise-wide and with their consumers. The digital age will put pressure on staff to perform without necessarily possessing the appropriate knowledge personally. The knowledge worker (staff member) must become adept

---

50 https://www.techopedia.com/definition/28094/digital-native

at *doing* rather than *knowing*; how to find knowledge (or the known known), how to apply that knowledge, and how to overcome the known unknowns as well as discovering the new known.

Digital transformation also presents a paradox for KM. The application of technologies (such as automation, machine learning, and natural language processing) and the emergence of collaboration platforms (e.g., Slack, Zoho Projects, LiquidPlanner, Wrike, Asana and Airtable among others) provide ways to collect and share knowledge quickly. However, the paradox is that technology will not replace human judgement. Instead, it will further unlock people's ability to apply judgement and insight into the use of knowledge; especially when faced with unknowns.

In many organizations, KM has been confined to the operational level, supporting functions like a Help Desk. In the digital era, knowledge management must happen at across the enterprise and even extend beyond the organization to consumers. Data capture can no longer follow a traditional, single-threaded approach.

Many organizations' current KM approach follows a model where data and information is captured by a Help Desk and is eventually transformed into knowledge usable by the organization. In the digital era, capturing, gathering, and disseminating knowledge must shift to the enterprise, as it is the enterprise that is the service provider and not an individual department within the organization.

Knowledge must be a core organizational capability and the foundation of effective decision-making and, therefore, necessary to all parts within the organization. In the digital workplace, activities reside in a connected, online environment, requiring integrated tools, data and information. In addition, the use of collaboration tools has expanded rapidly so that workers can easily connect, exchange ideas and get work done (see Chapter 6 – Collaboration).

Automation has had significant impact on KM. The processes for capturing and managing knowledge can be automated and the involvement of humans is changing. Other technical advances, such as intelligent information discovery enabled by content and data management tools, natural language processing and advances in search (such as natural search) also have an impact. Automation can provide the tools to find the right information easily and deliver it to those who need it.

■ 7.3 KNOWLEDGE MANAGEMENT BEHAVIORS

To support digital transformation, KM behaviors need a fundamental shift. There is no rulebook or easy answer now. Context is essential. Leaders and teams need to absorb information and ask, "Based on what I know, what do I do?" KM must enable the exposure and reuse of knowledge. To do this, it requires appropriate resources as well as leadership support.

For knowledge workers, what they know and the connections they can make are their stock in trade. Knowledge can be part of how an organization creates value for its consumers. If ideas and knowledge are raw materials, then organizations must modify systems and workflows so that they flow around the organization and out to consumers with as little friction as possible. Friction in knowledge flow is a bottleneck in a system.

Knowledge work is a human endeavor, which means knowledge flow is susceptible to all the moods and behaviors that make people human. This can make KM complex and illogical. Adding to the inherent complexity of behaviors is the changing nature of work. Contingent and distributed workforces are becoming the norm. There is a proliferation of software-as-a-service (SaaS) applications within the work ecosystem, many of which overlap in collaborative and content management functionality. Moreover, in addition to those challenges, KM can be enacted in a multitude of ways and at every level and function within the organization. How do organizations know where to focus knowledge management efforts or what skills to look for in the roles that require a focus on knowledge management capabilities?

VeriSM helps organizations define Service Management Principles related to KM and create actionable policies that connect KM efforts to strategic goals. Defining the expected outcomes and building policies to support their achievement avoids wasted effort and engages appropriate commitment to maintain the behavior change needed to assure successful and ongoing knowledge flow.

Example

KM principles and policies

Common principles and associated policies for KM include:

- Principle – Capture and Create:
  - Policy – Capture what is searched (real-time capture based on a request) – 'if the issue is worth solving, it's worth saving' and create the necessary records.
- Principle – Codify following a set structure:
  - Policy – Follow the defined template for knowledge content (typically includes: issue, environment, resolution, cause, selected metadata [date modified, key words, date created, modification history, use/reuse count).
- Principle – Share, Utilize and Re-use:
  - Policy – Search and collate – as new knowledge is created, search for similar content and link together.

- Principle – Manage and improve:
  - Policy – Review and improve – as articles are reused, improve them for clarity and accuracy.

■ 7.4 THE PURPOSE OF KNOWLEDGE MANAGEMENT IN A DIGITAL ORGANIZATION

Knowledge management has a significant role in managing internal and external knowledge to aid the organization in making better and faster decisions. It is important to recognize that KM cannot be a separate process, because knowledge activities reside at and within all organizational levels and processes that coordinate organizational activities including interaction with consumers, partners and suppliers. The intuitive and spontaneous nature of knowledge derived from these relationships provides deeper context to the knowledge captured.

Many attempts at improving knowledge management focus on technology. However, the success of such attempts has been limited as technology is only one part of the whole strategy. A core focus of KM, especially in a digital organization, must be on the value that humans attach to the knowledge. People's ability to keep pace in absorbing, analyzing and using the knowledge requires a wide collaboration. Anywhere there are relationships, KM is required. The organization must ensure KM extends across supplier networks, virtual teams, home workers, consumers and so on. To accomplish this, leaders should actively promote and encourage fundamental KM skills and attitudes for every member of staff. For specific management practices, see Appendix D2.

If an organization is truly focused on creating valuable outcomes for digital operations and transformation efforts, it must ensure ongoing knowledge management is built into its services and products. In the first instance, this involves understanding (and providing) the knowledge required by the consumer, but then expanding the view. Focus internally and externally, reviewing all interactions between the products and services, including partners and vendors, and define the necessary knowledge capture. It can be useful to visually map the knowledge relationships using specific methods such as OBASHI™.[51]

Most organizations have no clue where to start. It is big and complex, so real guidance on an approach to gather, refine, present, review, share, improve, – and dispose of – knowledge is required. Most organizations perform KM activities in an informal and almost ad hoc way, relying on good people typically working in

---

51 http://obashi.co.uk/

isolation within the organization. These organizations overlook the need for a KM strategy and a defined approach.

The 'knowledge is power' mentality is firmly embedded in most organizations – it has been the basis of reward systems within organizations for years. This mentality has created great stores of information (typically unmanaged) with varying value. Information capture and knowledge management are different, and the difference lies in its use and applicability. Change the reward system from 'what you know' (removing the emphasis on 'brain dumping') to 'what you share' and how it enhances the achievement of the organization's strategic goals and initiatives.

Ultimately, KM is about getting the right information to right person or place at the right time to enable informed decision-making.

■ 7.5 KNOWLEDGE MANAGEMENT ROLES AND COMPETENCES

There are countless ways to organize and name necessary KM roles. Remember that roles do not necessarily mean each role is an individual. One person can hold multiple roles – what is important is the activities that are fulfilled by the role. Regardless of the role name, ensure the activities that are necessary to the organization are assigned, accepted and measured. Common KM roles (see the Knowledge-Centered Service callout box for more information) to consider include:

■ Chief Knowledge Officer[52] (CKO) – responsible for ensuring the organization has a viable KM program, evangelizing the nature and value of knowledge, as well as the concept of knowledge management. The CKO is not a relabeled Chief Information Officer (CIO) as the CIO's chief responsibilities lie within Information Technology (IT), while the CKO looks across the organization.
  • Common activities include defining a formal KM program, leveraging the value of organizational knowledge in business development and operations, providing necessary knowledge to make informed decisions across all levels of the organization and exploiting knowledge as an organizational economic resource.

■ Knowledge Manager – champions KM activities and typically reports to the CKO; ensures conformity to KM policies; deploys and manages the defined KM program including structure, tools, training, measurement and reporting; consults with, and advocates collaboration within and between, organizational capabilities to promote KM.

---

52 Earl, M. J., & Scott, I. A. (1999, January 15). *What is a Chief Knowledge Officer?* Online. https://sloanreview.mit.edu/article/what-is-a-chief-knowledge-officer/. [2018 May].

■ Community Manager – supports online or virtual knowledge communities; builds and manages social networks and user groups to ensure value to the user (e.g., defines acceptable behavior, content creation and publishing, analyzes community-created information…).

Regardless of the role title, perhaps it is more important to consider the competencies required for good KM. Ghosh (2003)[53] outlines these KM competencies:
■ Establish a culture of knowledge dissemination and sharing;
■ Establish a knowledge management system;
■ Assist in codifying best practices;
■ Facilitate access to international best practices;
■ Provide support services to project managers;
■ Advance KM within the organization;
■ Assist in the development of a learning network;
■ Assist in the organization of regular program of learning and knowledge sharing.

Knowledge-Centered Service (KCS)

Knowledge-Centered Service (KCS), developed and maintained by the Consortium for Service Innovation, is an approach for knowledge management that has been developed over the past 25 years and continues to advance and improve its guidance. The Consortium describes KCS as "a set of practices for creating and maintaining knowledge in knowledge-intensive environments. Unlike the traditional add-on process of knowledge engineering, KCS is an integral part of day-to-day operation. For optimum performance, KCS practices and the tools that support them must be integrated with other support and business systems". Foundational elements for KCS include:
• Strategic framework;
• Communication plan;
• Measurement framework;
• Workflow or process definitions;
• Content standard;
• Adoption roadmap;
• Technology requirements.

These elements are typically managed by a small team dedicated to KM. The roles that will support the development and management of the above elements include:
• **Global KCS program manager** – the KCS champion or evangelist;
• **Project manager** – manages the scheduling and tracking of events that create the knowledge stores;
• **KCS trainer** – delivers training to line managers, support analysts and coaches;

---

53 Ghosh, M. (2003). *Knowledge management in the digital age: Challenges and opportunities in India*, (Online). https://www.researchgate.net/publication/264496706_Knowledge_Management_in_the_ digital_age_Challenges_and_opportunities_in_India [2018 April].

- **Lead KCS coach** – mentors and coordinates the coaches, provides training and coordinated the coaching activities;
- **KCS architect/auditor** – facilitates assessments and designs for the knowledge stores; as the organization matures, audits the system to assess compliance to the strategy and principles as well as the achieved results;
- **Business analyst** – provides data to support planning and adoption by identifying the high value/high impact areas of the organization (where will the greatest benefit occur?); defines the measurement framework and is responsible for data capture and reporting capabilities;
- **Knowledge worker** – anyone performing intellectual or cognitive work using data and information to make decisions or judgements or take action. There are two roles within the knowledge worker – the **requestor** (seeks information) and **responder** (provides information or resolution).

Additional details can be found in the *KCS v6 Adoption Guide*[54].

---

54 https://library.serviceinnovation.org/KCS/KCS_v6/KCS_v6_Adoption_Guide

8   Outcomes

Introduction

This chapter looks at the 'outcomes' of a digital product or service; how they are defined and measured and some of the specific challenges associated with them.

An outcome is the "end result of a consumer interacting with a product or service" and historically, service provider organizations have not been very good at measuring them. Outputs are often easier to measure; examples of outputs include measures such as number of widgets produced per day, response time for a website, number of calls answered on target, etc.

■ 8.1   WHAT IS AN OUTCOME?

Generic outcomes can be easy to define. An organization might say it wants:
- Happy consumers;
- Happy staff;
- Happy community.

These, however, are not particularly easy to measure. Outcomes are defined by an organization's governing body to help set strategic direction, and to ensure that progress towards that strategic direction can be measured. These then help to guide the 'monitor' activity in governance (see Section 10.5.4). Just as broad generic outcomes have limited use, so do narrow, over-defined outcomes. Organizations can become swamped in critical success factors and key performance indicators that are not helping them to achieve clarity.

The leaders of an organization are accountable for defining and communicating outcomes which teams can relate to the products and services that they are creating and delivering. Different stakeholders (suppliers, consumers, leaders etc.) will have different outcomes. Some outcomes can be negative, so organizations need to plan for their potential consequences. For example, making 'in application' purchases available on a children's game can lead to unwanted outcomes for a child's parent.

Service providers should think about the potential positive and negative outcomes of a product or service, for example:

Positive:

■ Use of the web channel by consumers results in the best customer journey experience when compared to competitors.

Negative:

■ Consumers using the web channel feel insecure as a result of using its payments process.

The positive outcome should always be described, not just potential negative outcomes. Positive descriptions can be made specific, while negative descriptions often leave a question: this is not desirable, but what is desirable? In other words, negative descriptions of outcomes will not be specific and so are not necessarily helpful.

Outcomes are often compared to outputs. Output is a term strongly associated with systems and processes and, as such, is not new. The output of any process or system is defined and measured. Output metrics are then used to check if the process or system is working as it should.

It is essential for a product or service provider to know and understand their customers' definition of outcomes. The only thing that matters is whether a product or service helped a consumer achieve their desired goals and objectives – thus whether a product or service achieved the intended outcome from a consumer's perspective. Figure 21, from the Adaptive Service Model[55], shows an example of how outcomes form part of the overall interaction between service provider and consumer.

55 Taking Service Forward. (2014). *The adaptive service model: Architectural concepts, modelling language and principles*, (Online). https://docs.google.com/document/d/1TcZqo71wDAzW2qQsAdEBE3WIFTEO34 wSOygo6zGu2xA/edit# [2018 February].

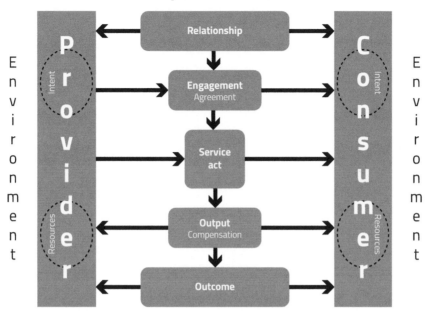

Figure 21 Outcomes form part of the interaction between service provider and consumer (source: Adaptive Service Model)

■ 8.2 WHAT IS DIFFERENT FOR PRODUCTS AND SERVICES?

Service provider organizations have been talking about outcomes for years, so what is different in the digital age? There are several factors to consider here:

- Feedback is much faster for digital products and services;
- Services can be delivered incrementally, allowing for early value and for course corrections;
- Digital products and services change more frequently;
- Digital consumers may have little/no face to face interaction with their service provider.

■ 8.3 HOW TO IDENTIFY OUTCOMES

Figure 22 shows how an organization's strategy and principles define outcomes and objectives, which lead to the creation of value through products and services.

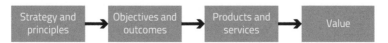

Figure 22 Strategy and principles lead to value

Outcomes can occur that are negative or risk-based. These can be measured and monitored by assessing the risk level imposed by the solution. Examples of negative outcomes might be:

- Service outages;
- Rework or waste;
- Security breaches;
- Unexpected costs.

Real world example

Outcome definition

VeriSM contributor, Peter Brooks, shares his experiences of outcome definition.

"In my experience, outcome definition starts with a workshop with the board and senior management. The aim would be to produce two lists. One list is a collection of all the possible ways that value can be delivered. The other is a prioritized list of those values that are supreme, and which have to be delivered for the organization to survive and/or thrive.

The two lists can then be refined through consultation. The first list can become the start of a service-orientated requirements register. The second, perhaps, the start of the corporate improvement register.

The way of working would be to communicate the primary list widely and help the board to own it (and changes to it) while working to make the secondary list closer to a strategy than a wish list. Moving from a wish list to a strategy would involve making business cases for items on the list, selection of items or services that address the items, then using the business cases to decide which move to the primary list, which are impractical, and which are longer-term prospects.

This will be an ongoing, iterative process, not a one-off exercise."

8.3.1   Value Stream Mapping (VSM)

Value Stream Mapping is a technique that can be used to help organizations understand outcomes. It helps organizations to understand better what they currently do, whom from across the organization is involved and how. This forces the organization to make sure what customer expectations are and, as a result of analysis, identify how things can be done better or even differently.

Value Stream Mapping (VSM) is used to improve end to end value streams that span across functions in organizations and is, therefore, an appropriate tool to use when trying to understand what an organization can do to improve its processes. The intention of VSM is operational improvement, but the tool does have strategic value. Leaders and governors can use VSM to understand services and products provided by the organization, by reviewing the processes used to produce these services or products and identifying how they can be improved.

The most significant value of this technique is that it totally disregards organizational and divisional boundaries by assessing how value is created from customer request to fulfilment. In that sense, a value stream is like a cross-functional process – the difference is that is not as focused on the activities as such, but rather the flow of information and material between process steps.

To understand VSM better, there are core tenets of Lean that also need to be understood, starting with the five principles of Lean. These are:
- Define value from the perspective of the end customer;
- Identify the entire (cross-functional) value stream for each product or service and eliminate waste;
- Make the remaining value-creating steps flow;
- When flow is achieved, provide what the customer wants only when the customer wants it;
- Pursue perfection.

These principles are similar to many key tenets of VeriSM, namely;
- Look at value from a perspective of the consumer;
- Look at how the entire organization contributes to providing this value (in the form of services and products);
- Do what is enough for the customer and nothing more;
- Work more effectively and efficiently.

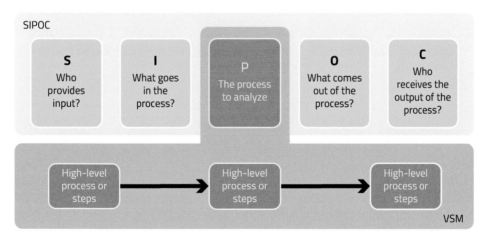

Figure 23 A SIPOC diagram

Defining a value streams also considers its broader context. This starts with the definition of a context diagram called a SIPOC (suppliers, inputs, process, outputs, and customers), as shown in Figure 23. SIPOC diagrams are also referred to as high-level process maps because they do not contain much detail. The SIPOC, however, helps to identify all role-players, including those who are not necessarily part of the process of creating value but have an influence on the process.

Table 3 provides an example of a SIPOC for baking bread.

Table 3 An example of a simple SIPOC for baking bread

Supplier	Input	Process	Output	Customer
Grocery store	Flour Yeast Salt Water Oven Pan	Mix ingredients Pour into pan Leave rise Bake in oven Leave to cool	Sandwiches Light lunches Snack	Family Visitors

It should be noted that the process is described here at a high level and generally in fewer than six steps. The purpose of the SIPOC is not to achieve deep understanding, but just enough understanding to see who is involved, how they are involved and the customers' desired outcomes. SIPOCs helps to identify the right people to be involved when conducting VSM.

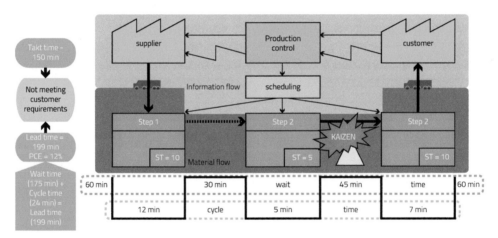

Figure 24 A typical VSM with key metrics calculated (based on Toyota material and information-flow mapping, ©Toyota)

The first step is to map the current state – do not be tempted to start redesigning the process. Then, timelines are defined to establish how much time is required to complete a task, to get something, the waiting times between steps and the total time from customer request to request fulfilment. The flow of essential information is also included in the map as shown in Figure 24.

The expected delivery time for the customer is determined. If the process takes longer than this requirement, then improvements need to be made as a matter of urgency.

Activities in the process are categorized as one of the following:

- **Non-value adding operations** (NVA): actions that should be eliminated, such as waiting;
- **Necessary but non-value adding** (NNVA): actions that are wasteful but necessary currently, such as controls;
- **Value-adding** (VA): the conversion of raw materials (data is also a raw material) and changing it into something for which the customer will pay.

The first two categories of activities are apparent candidates for improvements by eliminating waste. Lean considers the following as sources of waste:

- **The faster-than-necessary pace of work:** creating too much goods in product environments lead to stock and, in service environments, unused capacity.
- **Waiting:** any time goods are not being transported, worked on or in a service environment waiting for a dependent procedure or activity to provide the input required by the activity.
- **Conveyance:** the process by which goods are moved around. Specific attention should be given to products or service activities using back and forth between machines or role-players (double-handling and excessive movement).
- **Over-processing:** an overly complicated solution for a simple procedure or hazardous work being done. Over-processing is often the cause of communication or conveyance issues.
- **Excess stock:** requires storage and retrieval and ties up capital. In service environments, this may manifest as lost or unused capacity. The solution is not to use more but, counterintuitively, to produce less.
- **Unnecessary motion:** ergonomic waste that requires employees to use excess energy such as picking up objects, bending, or stretching.
- **Correction of mistakes:** any cost associated with defects or the resources required to correct them.

Also note that many forms of waste are interdependent, so it is essential to identify the cause of waste and not the symptom.

Once a process is mapped, and the correct time is recorded, some key calculations should be completed before any attempt is made to improve the process. The two most important are:

- To understand if the lead time (how long it takes for the customer to get what they want) matches the Takt time (the time it takes to provide products or services to customers with the current process, satisfying their needs).
- An engineering ratio called the Process Cycle Efficiency (PCE – Value-Added Time/Total Lead Time). The higher the ratio, the more efficient the process, it also serves as a good process benchmark.

Once all of this is defined and known, representatives from all functions involved in the activities mapped can see how the process can be improved, starting by eliminating obvious waste and then by streamlining the process.

How is VSM useful in a strategic context?
- It helps leaders to better understand products and services;
- Their participation in improvements using VSM signals the importance of improvement in the organization;
- When considering digital optimization, processes and ways of working should be improved first before any attempt is made to automate and digitize them;
- VSM techniques can be used to solve problems in the complicated domain;
- VSM may be a catalyst for an entirely new approach to delivering products or services because the process and the stakeholder landscape are better understood – this may lead to a case for digital transformation;
- SIPOCs may also be useful to identify new ways of interacting with stakeholders that may lead to a case for digital transformation.

> In addition to its usefulness in solving problems, eliminating waste and creating value for customers, VSM is also a very useful tool in helping executives and managers better understand business processes and value chains. Many organizations insist that leaders across the organization participate in VSM exercises and improvement initiatives like Kaizen (see Appendix D3) for this reason.

■ 8.4   MEASURING OUTCOMES

Are all outcomes truly measurable? Or are they like modern art, "I know it when I see it?"

Many organizations are excellent at measuring outputs, but poor when measuring true outcomes. To do this effectively, it is important to work back from the required value; identify the value chain, ensure that value is clearly understood and have a transparent measurement scheme that includes regular checkpoints and reviews.

Organizations, particularly in the digital world, might need to use 'output measures' as a proxy for outcomes. As the contact between service consumers and service providers can be very limited with digital products, the service provider might need to measure a range of outputs and hope this gives then an indication of the overall outcome.

Real world example

ITSM Zone

ITSM Zone is an eLearning provider based in the UK. The consumer outcomes that its delegates value will include things like getting a promotion as a result of a new certification or meeting the prerequisite for a job interview.

ITSM Zone has no face-to-face contact with its delegates, making it very difficult to measure these outcomes. A range of proxy measures (outputs rather than outcomes) must be used instead:

- Pass rates;
- Feedback;
- Tutor support enquiries;
- Technical support enquiries;
- Repeat business.

If these outputs are within acceptable limits, the organization can assume that outcomes are also being met. The range of measures will need to be regularly reviewed to assess if it is still an accurate proxy measure for the overall desired outcomes.

Real world example

Anonymous

A service provider organization had a contract to provide desktop support to a large client. The service provider met all of its contractual targets, but when the contract ended, the customer chose not to renew it. Unbeknown to the service provider, the customer was actually deeply unhappy, but the outputs the service provider was measuring did not indicate this.

This contract loss and the unhappy customer were unintended negative outcomes. The person who cancelled the contract was a stakeholder who hadn't been involved in the day to day service level measures and targets.

This situation could have been avoided or improved by mapping and talking to all stakeholders, as well as making measures more visible. If the output measures had been shared more widely, the service provider might have realized earlier that the customer was unhappy.

The outcomes (or proxy measures of outputs) that are useful to the organization need to be a shared view across all stakeholders to be most effective. IT departments in particular are often criticized for measuring outputs that are not aligned to the overall goals of the organization. Cross-functional teams should agree outcomes or proxy measure outputs and review them regularly, providing the broadest possible perspective.

Real world example

Digital design at Hippo Digital

Chapter 28 provides some examples of how organizations can apply 'digital design' and 'Design Thinking' to make sure that products and services provide the desired outcomes.

9 Transformation techniques

Introduction

This chapter looks in more detail at the transformation techniques that can help organizations meet their digital transformation objectives. This includes defining the problem or situation and reacting to it effectively.

It serves as a toolkit including techniques to help organizations understand their digital optimization and transformation requirements. The intent is not to provide a definitive list and comprehensive examples of tools and approaches, but rather to see how a select few can be used practically in an organization's transformation journey.

Although many of the techniques can be used for optimization and transformation alike, the focus is on transformation as less guidance is currently available for this area.

■ 9.1 IDENTIFYING TRANSFORMATIONAL OPPORTUNITIES

The difficulty with determining transformational needs is that no single method gives a full view of the issues that the organization faces. Humans attempt to deal with problems and complexity by framing the issue and, by doing so, they predict the answer to the question. This is natural and acceptable if the question type is aligned to the method used in the attempt to gain understanding and a solution (or solutions) for the issue or the problem is at hand.

There are thousands of 'how to' books, articles and sources of additional advice available. Critically, most of that is advice given based on experience. So, why is that a bad thing? The problem is that advice based from experience assumes that the context in which the information will be reused or applied will be the same, or at least similar. In reality, the situations are often very different. Take the examples provided in this publication. They describe organizations that are successful (or not) and can provide inspiration; but they are not prescriptive or the only way to do things well.

To understand how to approach the definition of and response to transformational needs within an organization is complex – getting it right is alchemy, not science. Fortunately, there is a set of guidance about using advice that is extremely helpful in this context.

9.1.1   Cynefin

The Cynefin framework from Dave Snowden[56] identifies five questions typically asked when trying to determine transformational needs or how an organization needs to respond to market changes. The framework describes the methods, techniques or approaches that would be most likely to work for each of these categories or domains.

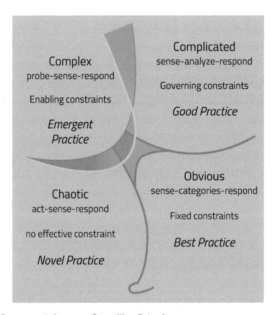

Figure 25 The Cynefin Framework (source: Cognitive Edge)

Most of the digital transformation design challenges organizations face are complicated, complex or chaotic. VeriSM suggests that from a proactive transformational design perspective, focusing on complicated and complex needs would yield more immediate and productive results, but dealing with chaos is often the source of radical innovation and digital disruptors.

---

56 http://cognitive-edge.com/videos/cynefin-framework-introduction/

Simple problems tend not to be transformational issues, but instead optimization issues. Addressing these needs, although necessary, can be done by making use of well-defined and more traditional approaches.

Most problem-solving techniques are well suited to addressing complicated questions and problems – they are specifically designed for use in this context. What's more, most consultants also operate in this domain, and they define methods based on past experiences in a very ordered environment. When these problem-solving techniques and consulting models are applied to complex questions, they fall flat or at least fall short of providing the right solution.

When compared with the different approaches organizations can apply to digitization, as described in Chapter 3, thinking patterns, methods used to address problems and the techniques used become more important. Using the wrong tools will, most probably, lead to an erroneous decision being reached.

Although not always true, the domains described in Cynefin largely map to the approaches introduced in Section 3.5 – as shown in Figure 26.

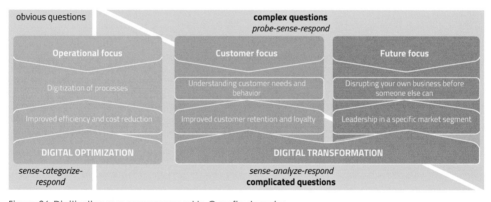

Figure 26 Digitization responses mapped to Cynefin domains

Techniques used in empirical contexts (science, for instance) may yield better results and provide better answers to complex and chaotic questions. In recent years, many of these techniques have been used more frequently and have become standard in emergent practices like Agile and DevOps. In the mid-1990s, Tom Peters was already a proponent of "fail forward fast". Today, evidence of this philosophy as an embedded management practice can be seen when organizations start experimenting in live environments with new ideas or even introduce the unexpected to see what happens. The essential message is that experimentation, observation and learning are critical elements when dealing with complexity.

To answer the question, "What's the problem?" there are two positions to consider when thinking about an organization's response to shifting and transformational needs:

- For someone who only has a hammer – every problem looks like a nail. Understand the nature of the need, trend, shift or disruption before responding.
- If the only skill known is hammering nails – screws will never be used. Organizational resources will require new skills to enable them to use different problem-solving techniques and approaches. That requires investment in training and the development of proprietary methods that work well in the organizational context.

Standard+Case

Another possible way to respond to an uncertain situation is Standard+Case[57]. In this article, author Rob England describes its use.

Standard+Case is a model that acknowledges reality: much of our service activity will always be non-standard and must be dealt with in a formalized way in order to manage, report, and improve it, as we do for the standardized part. We do that by treating non-standard responses as 'cases'.

The combination of Standard and Case concepts gives a complete description of real response handling, for any sort of activity that requires a human response.

- **Standard responses** are predefined because they deal with a known situation. They use a standardized process (and procedures) to deal with that situation. They can be modelled by BPM, controlled by workflow, and improved by the likes of Six Sigma, Lean IT, and ITIL;
- **Case responses** present an unknown or unfamiliar situation where there is no predefined process. Cases demand knowledge, skills and professionalism of the person dealing with them. They are best dealt with by Case Management, being knowledge-driven and empowering the operator to decide on suitable approaches, tools, procedures and process fragments. We can use agile thinking, swarming, and other adaptive dynamic approaches.

We look for a standard model of how to deal with a situation. If we can't find one, then we switch to dealing with it as a case. That's Standard+Case, which gives us two complementary approaches to dealing with any situation that requires a response: one or other approach will be suitable.

When we combine the generic Standard process used in most response models with Case Management, the process looks like this:

---

57 England, R. (No date). *The Standard+Case approach to response management*, (Online). http://www.basicsm.com/standard-case [2018 April].

The two approaches of Standard and Case complement and complete each other. There is either a known standard response or there isn't. When we combine conventional service management response processes and the principles of Case Management, the sum is greater than the parts. Not only do we get a more complete description of how response procedures really work, we get new opportunities that none of the approaches on their own present. This is profoundly important, because it allows our response capability to adapt to changing external circumstances such as new or changed services, new technologies in the consumer market, new customer markets, new groups of users, and so on.

Of course, the world isn't so black-and-white. Standard and Case are in fact the opposite ends of a spectrum of possible approaches. Some cases might have a certain level of process structure; some standard process models might allow flexibility. Nevertheless, the Standard+Case model is more crisply delineated than some even more blurred two-sided models that still serve us perfectly well in practice, e.g. customer vs. supplier, innocent vs. guilty, working vs. on holiday. There is no "completeness theorem" for Standard+Case. That is, we do not **prove** the assertion that the Standard approach plus the Case approach cover **all** possible situations. What is asserted without proof is that in the real world we can respond to a very high proportion of situations by one approach or the other, or a combination or hybrid of the two.

Most people who have worked in response roles will agree with this. You look for the standard, predefined way of dealing with the situation; if you can't find one you manage the situation until you can find an answer. What we are doing in the latter situation is Case Management, whether we call it that or not. Standard+Case simply recognizes that fact and formalizes it, so that our planning, resourcing, management, monitoring and improvement look at the real picture and deal with all situations we face not just the standard ones.

Standard+Case and Cynefin have been mapped together, as shown in Figure 27.

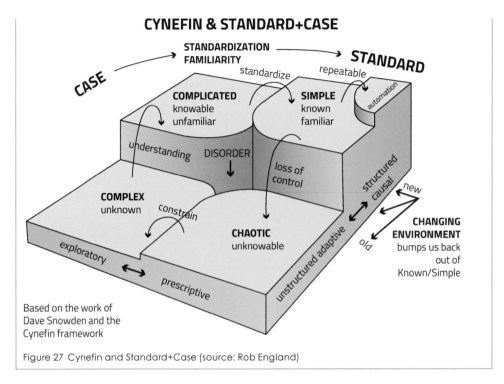

Figure 27 Cynefin and Standard+Case (source: Rob England)

Design and development teams tend to deal with complex and chaotic questions (rather than complicated questions). However, most well-known problem-solving techniques are not as effective at solving these types of problems. The rest of this chapter describes techniques that may provide additional insight in dealing with digital optimization or transformation questions. Note that few techniques deal with empirical questions directly, but many methods do help to define a hypothesis that can be used as the basis of experimentation; whether this is in response to a complex or chaotic situation or context.

■ 9.2 THE VUCA VIEW OF THE WORLD

Why VUCA? VUCA is a context tool. It should be used as a method to better understand the context in which the organization operates and help frame responses to challenges experienced.

The U.S. Army conceptualized VUCA in the 1990s. The technique is used in strategic leadership to help leaders develop better foresight and insight in dealing with their environments. VUCA was mentioned earlier in Chapter 5 from a change perspective.

VUCA is an acronym that means:
- Volatility – the nature and speed of change bring volatility;
- Uncertainty – the lack of predictability;

■ Complexity – the number of influences;
■ Ambiguity – the haziness of reality and mixed meanings of conditions.

VUCA elements provide boundaries for planning and giving direction. The current and (possible) future state of the context of the organization shape its capacity to:
■ Anticipate the issues;
■ Understand the consequences;
■ Appreciate the interdependence of variables;
■ Prepare for alternative realities;
■ Address relevant opportunities.

VUCA is about awareness and readiness to deal with the issues an organization faces. For each dimension, specific guidance is given. Bennet and Lemoine provide guidance for leadership, to help them to use VUCA to understand better the context of the organization and the issues it faces, to make more appropriate decisions and provide better direction to the organization, as shown in Figure 28.

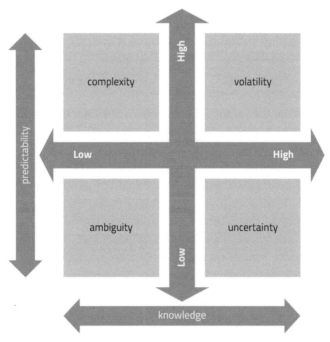

Figure 28 Knowledge and predictability are key VUCA drivers

In their article, "What VUCA Really Means for You"[58], Bennet and Lemoine describe each dimension as:

58 Bennet, N. & Lemoine, G. J. (2014). *What VUCA really means for you*, (Online). https://hbr.org/2014/01/what-vuca-really-means-for-you [2018 March].

■ Volatility:
  • *Characteristics*: The challenge is unexpected or unstable and may be of unknown duration, but it is not necessarily hard to understand. Knowledge about it is often available;
  • *Example*: Prices fluctuate after a natural disaster takes a supplier off-line;
  • *Approach*: Build in slack and devote resources to preparedness. For instance, stockpile inventory or overbuy talent. As these steps are expensive the investment should match the risk;
■ Uncertainty:
  • *Characteristics*: Despite the lack of other information, the event's basic cause and effect is known. Change is possible but not a given;
  • *Example*: A competitor's pending product launch muddies future business and the market;
  • *Approach*: Invest in information, collect, interpret and share it. This works best in conjunction with structural changes, such as adding information analysis networks, that can reduce ongoing uncertainty;
■ Complexity:
  • *Characteristics:* The situation has many interconnected parts and variables. Some information is available or can be predicted, but the volume or nature of information can be an overwhelming process;
  • *Example:* You are doing business in many countries, all with unique regulatory environments, tariffs and cultural values;
  • *Approach:* Restructure, bring on or develop specialists, and build up resources adequate to address the complexity;
■ Ambiguity
  • *Characteristics*: Causal relationships are completely unclear. No precedents exist; and unknown unknowns are faced. Little is known about the situation and the results of actions taken cannot be predicted.
  • *Example*: The organization decides to move into immature or emerging markets or to launch products outside its core competency.
  • *Approach*: Try to understand cause and effect by defining a hypothesis and testing the hypothesis by experimenting. Design experiments so that lessons learnt can be applied as broadly as possible.

■ 9.3 THE INNOVATOR'S DILEMMA

Why apply? The Innovator's Dilemma gives insight into typical behavior in organizations when the words 'improvement' or 'innovation' are used. The biggest problem is that these words can be used in many different contexts and the meaning evolves as context changes. The Innovator's Dilemma provides context and gives valuable advice for organizations embarking on a digital transformation journey – specifically when faced with disruptors and attempting to define, design or develop the 'next big thing'.

In his book "*The Innovator's Dilemma: When New Technologies Cause Great Firms to Fail*", Harvard Professor Clayton Christensen demonstrates how successful organizations seem to do everything right and still lose their market leadership when new, unexpected competitors rise and take over a market.

Christensen describes three types of innovation:
- **Disruptive innovation** – which makes products available and affordable. This type of innovation needs capital but creates jobs and growth.
- **Sustaining innovation** – which makes good products better. Most innovation is sustaining innovation. The focus is on management and produces very little growth; it does, however, create better margins and growing market share.
- **Efficiency innovation** – which helps organizations make more with less. This type of innovation can enable an organization to cope with increased growth without further capital or increases in cash flow but can destroy jobs.

Figure 29 shows how the innovation types map to the VeriSM digital transformation and optimization approaches introduced in Section 3.5.

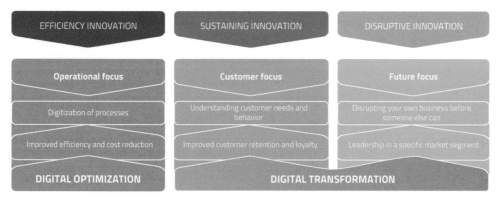

Figure 29 Christensen's Innovation Types compared with VeriSM digitization approaches

Financial management metrics used today are often skewed and motivate organizations to divert capital from disruptive and sustaining innovation to efficiency innovation. This happens because:
- Disruptive innovation is the most expensive type of innovation with the most extended period to show return on investment (ROI); it consumes cash. It will, however, enable organizations to be competitive in the long run.
- Sustaining innovation gives better ROI and ensures sustainability in the medium term, yet still does not look as promising if leaders focus on yearly or half-yearly reports and worry about stock prices and investors demanding high growth.

■ Efficiency innovation is much easier and more attractive because the ROI is quicker, easier to manage and easier to explain to investors.

The problem is that if an organization only performs efficiency innovation, it will innovate itself into oblivion. It will not be able to compete long term and will not be able to sustain itself in the medium term. Most organizations start by building products or services to do a very specific job or satisfy a very specific need. Later, they add valuable features around the core. This can lead to consumers who only want one feature being required to pay for a bundle of services they neither want or need.

Real world example

Pay television

Pay Television is good example of organizations that start with a core that customers find attractive and then build 'value adding' offerings around this core. DSTV, the leading pay-TV company in the African market has different packages but these are limited, and its prime offerings (sports) are only part of its premium service.

Many customers started resisting the packaged approach. They resented having to buy a premium product and not being allowed to build their own custom packages.

In this market, new entrants like Netflix®, were able to convince many customers to cancel their subscription to DSTV because they only want to watch series and movies, and rightly so. Netflix was a major disruptor at the time and not only affected companies like DSTV, but also companies like Blockbusters, which rented movies to consumers.

Clayton Christensen calls this the Innovator's Dilemma and defines two parts to the dilemma, namely:

■ **Value to innovation is an S-curve**: Improving a product takes time and many iterations. The first of these iterations provides minimal value to the customer but, in time, they create a broader customer base and the value increases exponentially. Once this customer base is created, each iteration provides significant additional benefits to customers, but after some time, this rate of improvement is no longer sustainable.

■ **Incumbent sized deals**: The incumbent has the luxury of a vast customer base, but expectations of high yearly sales. A new entrant with "next generation" products finds niche markets quickly, away from the incumbent customer set OR core competences OR product and builds a new product or offering in one of the non-core components that is vastly different. The new entry organizations do not require the incumbent's yearly sales volume and, therefore, have the luxury and time focus on innovation.

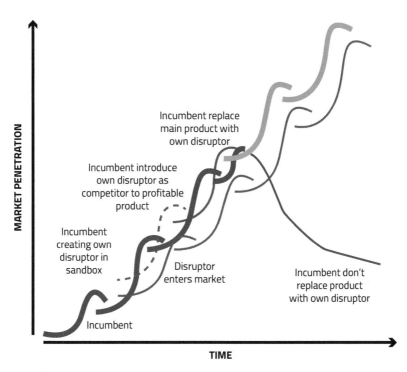

MARKET PENETRATION

Incumbent replace
main product with
own disruptor

Incumbent introduce
own disruptor as
competitor to profitable
product

Incumbent
creating own
disruptor in
sandbox

Disruptor
enters market

Incumbent don't
replace product
with own disruptor

Incumbent

TIME

Figure 30 Example of a good and bad response to the Innovator's Dilemma (based on work from Clayton Christensen)

To survive, organizations need to create disruptive innovation outside of normal business operations. Leadership must support disruptive innovation, even if the new products and services will cannibalize the organization's core products or services. The logic is that it is better to do it yourself than allow a competitor to do it. It is normally best not to build the next generation product for the larger existing customer set, who would rather keep demanding more innovation with the current product. Unfortunately, sustaining innovation – and, eventually, only efficiency innovation is possible at this late stage of the product cycle (blue in Figure 30).

A new entrant may enter the market and will be deep into its product's S-curve and providing significant value to a subset of the market with its new product [red in Figure 30]. By the time the new product becomes interesting to the organization's customers, it is too late for it to react to the new product. Innovation outside of the organization's main line of business [green on Figure 30] is the only way to ensure that new entrants and disruptors cannot use this phenomenon to their advantage, as this ensures that the organization is not too late to keep up with the new entrant's rate of improvement, which by then is on the near-vertical portion of its S-curve trajectory.

Christensen introduced his seminal theory of 'disruptive innovation' which has changed the way managers and CEOs around the world think about innovation and is substantiated by multiple case studies. He describes common principles that organizations must address to overcome the influence of market disruptors:

- Current customers drive an organization's use of resources;
- Small markets struggle to affect an incumbent's large market;
- Disruptive technologies have fluid futures, meaning it is impossible to know what they will disrupt once matured;
- Incumbent organizations' value is more than simply their workers. It includes their processes and core capabilities which drive their efforts;
- Technology supply may not equal market demand. The attributes that make disruptive technologies unattractive in established markets often are the very ones that comprised their greatest value in emerging markets.

The following strategies assist incumbents in succeeding against disruptive technology:

- Develop their own disruptive technology with targeted customers, not necessarily their current customer set;
- Place disruptive technology into an autonomous organization or unit that can be rewarded with small wins and smaller customer sets;
- Fail early and often to find the correct disruptive technology (also see Section 9.4 The Lean Start-up);
- Allow the unit developing and selling the new disruptive technology to utilize all of the organization's resources when needed, but ensure the processes and values are not those of the parent organization.

■ 9.4 THE LEAN START-UP

Why? The Lean Start-up describes a tried and tested method which organizations can use to innovate and create disruptive innovation.

Eric Ries is from a generation of Silicon Valley disruptors and in his book, *The Lean Startup*[59] gives advice to entrepreneurs that equally applies to any leader having to deal with digital transformation. Ries identifies three phases to innovation and a number of activities associated to these phases:

- Vision:
  - Start by finding scientific ways to define what customers want;
  - Define your product or service involving customers;
  - Define hypotheses and test your assumptions before you start spending money building products that no-one wants;

---

59 Ries, E. (2011). *The lean startup – how today's entrepreneurs use continuous innovation to create radically successful businesses*. New York: Random.

■ Steer:
- Use the build-measure-learn cycle (see Figure 31) for quick feedback and learning;
- Before you start building – go see for yourself and make sure – look before you leap;
- Build a minimum viable product (MVP) and get it out in the market;
- Get feedback and measure performance;
- Continue on the development path or change direction (pivot);

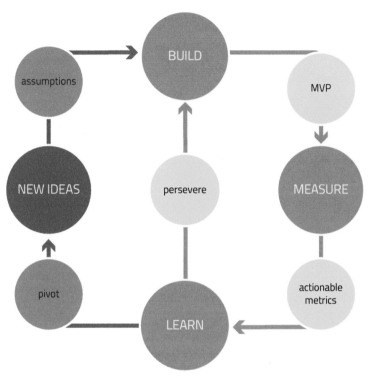

Figure 31 The Lean Start-up BML cycle (source: *The Lean Start-up* by Eric Ries ©2011)

■ Accelerate:
- Have big plans but small batches when starting to make and sell your product;
- Solve issues before you continue;
- Look for growth in existing markets but also look for new markets;
- Solve problems and become better;
- Eliminate waste;
- Innovate (in a safe environment separated from the main business).

In an article entitled "Spotting a potential Disruptor in your market & How to react?", Joce Kwong provides the following insights. Kwong postulates that there are two types of disruptors, low-end and new market disruptors.

Low end is where disruptors spot the opportunity to enter the bottom end of the market with cheaper and more affordable products, because incumbents have improved products and services beyond the needs of those customers (also see The innovator's dilemma, Section 9.3). Incumbents naturally ignore such low-end disruptors as their business model and operations are not set up to compete in the lowest end of the market and competing at the lowest end of the market will generally hurt branding and cannibalize sales. The danger is that these new low-end products or services will become the new normal and displace successful services.

New market disruptors create a new market through disruptive innovation and attract first time customers who previously did not adopt the product as it was too difficult or expensive to use, or the new product or service now allows for the use of the disruptor's product or service in ways previously not possible. Examples include supply and demand matching technology platforms where excess capacity is being matched with new demand at lower price than market price – attracting new customers who otherwise cannot afford the product or service or won't buy like Airbnb and Uber, or newly unlocked utility in the disruptor's product or service like the smartphone that provided features that was previously only available on a PC.

Incumbents in these markets generally regard these new market disruptors as amateurs and not professional enough, compared to the level of service and expertise they offer. These disruptors are usually ignored until a significant market is won over by these new entrants. Quite often it is too late for incumbents to then try and react as the adoption of the disruptor has reached a tipping point.

So how should organizations react in rapidly evolving markets led by technology and new models?

Kwong provides the following advice for incumbents as well as disruptors.
- If you are working in a profitable incumbent:
  - Continue to improve your products and services' performance to sustain your market share while competitors catch up;
  - At the same time, watch out for disruptors targeting the bottom end of the market and new market where previous non-consumers will become consumers for the right price;
  - Set-up new separate business units for disruption or invest in one – keeping them as separate operating units, while focusing your current core business and operations on sustained innovation and retained market share for as long as profitable;
- If you are a disruptor:
  - Explore opportunities in markets where premium products and services dominate and over-served customers at high prices and enter with low-end options (with less features) to attract customers with more affordable options;

- Explore new markets for non-consumers by providing easier and cheaper alternatives to existing products and services which are too complicated and/or expensive for non-consumers to justify becoming a consumer;
- Try to get disruption to work in your favor by positioning for 'low-end' and 'new-market' disruptions through new ventures – and if you are a profitable incumbent, sustain your core business to retain market share for as long as profitable in the meantime.

■ 9.5 BUSINESS INNOVATION CIRCLES (BICS)

Why? Business Innovation Circles provide a way to embark on rapid product and service innovation that can be used by start-ups or existing product and service providers. BICs provide an approach that allows for the use of different tools and techniques but defines measurable stage gates and timelines to ensure rapid and validated results. BICs are based on Lean and Agile thinking.

Chapter 3 introduced the organization-led approach to digital transformation. When described at a high level many readers would ask, "ok, so how do I do it?" Business Innovation Circles™ [60] (BIC) provide an organization-led approach with its origins in Lean concepts (such as quality circles). It is used to build high-performance cross functional teams such as those used in Agile and DevOps.

BICs are well suited for transformation projects as the constituent methods and tools frequently used (although not prescribed) deal well with complicated and complex problem solving and include experimental techniques that work well within the complex and chaotic domains. Using BICs in cross-functional teams (using techniques adapted from Tuckman's [61] group development guidance) assists with consistent delivery of quality and innovation. BICs focus on delivering demonstrable business value, iteratively and in a short period of time, but go beyond the scope of most agile approaches – BICs have a big focus on the innovation that drives incremental improvement initiatives.

---

60 Business Innovation Circles™ are used as a method to build high-performance business innovation teams by the getITright® IT consulting company.
61 Tuckman, B. W. (1965). Developmental sequence in small groups. *Psychological Bulletin*, **63**(6), 384–399.

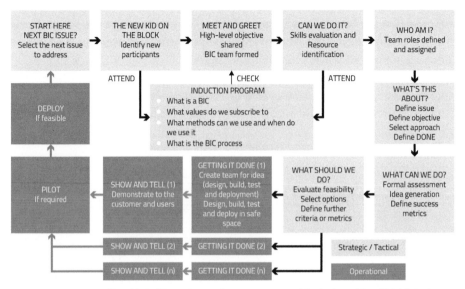

Figure 32 Business Innovation Circles™ – an innovation management technique (©getITright, Business Innovation Circles™ is a Trademark of getITright)

This section does not discuss all of the steps of the approach outlined in Figure 32 in detail. It does not discuss IT-related or operational activities. From the diagram, a few of the specific questions warrant further exploration, and the evaluation of which methods can be used to answer these questions, and under which conditions. The questions of importance to leadership are:

■ The next BIC issue (selected from the BIC list which is similar to a backlog.
  • Selection of projects needs to align with strategic initiatives or current problems in the organization. Leadership needs to play an active role in prioritization of items in the list.
■ What's this about?
  • Leadership and senior management needs to take part in activities to crystallize initiative focus and desired outcomes and ensure that we not only innovate, but also innovate for the right reasons.
■ What can we do?
  • Leadership needs to validate options, but we would prefer that they are active participants in defining options and selecting options to explore.

The list below is a brief description of the stages outlined in Figure 32, which a BIC event will follow. These stages should be followed even if many team-members work together regularly (don't skip steps or make assumptions). Before using BICs, all team members must go through basic BIC induction training – making sure everyone in the team is familiar with how BICs work and the primary methods and tools used.

■ The team and their coach meet to define the issue at hand and determine if they have all the skills required to deal with the issue. Team make-up may be re-defined and additional resources allocated as seen fit.

- If additional skills or knowledge are needed, a consensus is reached on how best this can be acquired in a speedy fashion. If required skills can be learnt quickly, a training intervention is scheduled and executed. If skills cannot be obtained in a short period of time, external resources may be sourced (note they must also go through BIC induction and preferably be interviewed by team members to determine technical and cultural suitability and fit).
- The team decides on team roles and responsibilities.
- Team meets to agree formal BIC objective and evaluate the best method(s) to evaluate the issue/problem/uncertainty. What 'success' looks like is defined as part of this activity.
- Sessions are scheduled for formal assessment and to develop a possible response to resolve the issue and reach agreement on objective, output and outcome metrics.
- Possible actions are evaluated, and the best candidate(s) for success are chosen. Success criteria for each scenario are defined and agreed.
- Joint design, build, test and deployment teams are created for each scenario. The possible solution is built. This is normally done as an agile iteration or sprint but can be run as a waterfall project also – the key here is that the project cannot be longer than two months.
- Each possible solution is demonstrated to the team and the customer (or representative).
- If required, the solution is deployed as a pilot and feedback is given to the team on customer feedback and performance metrics. If a prototype, do formal build, test and deploy activities.
- Solutions are transitioned from the BIC 'safe space' (sandbox or skunkworks) to the live environment using the organization's management practices.

Some organizations use 'sandboxes' or 'skunkworks' – these are all environments not connected to day-to-day operations, processes and controls and invaluable in creating innovative solutions or outcomes. It should be noted that there are distinctly different sandbox environments. The simplest way to describe the main difference is as follows:
- Some sandboxes are created to keep the organization safe from experimentation;
- Others (specifically used for future focused or disruptive projects) are created to keep innovators and experimenters safe from the organization.

Ideally, sandbox environments are completely free from institutional interference and organizational policies and processes do not apply in those environments. Although recommended for sandbox environments to be truly effective, complete managerial autonomy is rare.

9.5.1   Setting up BICs – the three Cs

The BIC three C's™ are[62]:

■ Commitment;
■ Conditions;
■ Confirmation.

Commitments

For Business Innovation Circles to work *management* needs to make four upfront commitments:

1. We will build temporary cross-functional teams, using the best resources from each part of the organization to dedicate time to innovate, experiment, evaluate and implement their own ideas to the live business environment.
2. We will make sure that each BIC has at least one member of the management team or senior person as a member of the BIC. Their role is a facilitator and coach and not the leader of the team.
3. If possible, we will involve consumers, failing that the manager closest to the customer/consumer (or one of their direct reports) will represent them.
4. We will create a safe space for BICs to innovate and operate free from the restrictions placed on the team by normal organizational processes and controls. We will further invest in systems to ensure that innovation can safely be deployed from a BIC to the live environment where normal processes and controls will remain in place.

Conditions

To make BICs work, some conditions also need to be met:

■ Respect is first and foremost. All are treated equally and there are no 'rock-stars' in the team;
■ The team succeeds, or the team fails – there is collective ownership, and reward for the performance of the team;
■ Failure is accepted as part of life and as an opportunity to learn – the team will most probably fail as much as it succeeds. What is important is that these lessons are quantified and lead to future actions – and maybe some form of control or guidance for future projects;
■ Feedback is open and issue-based, never personal;
■ Performance is measured and displayed visually for all to see allowing the team to quickly identify where and how to improve;
■ The BIC is a safe space and a blameless spot – managers must refrain from taking punitive action based on individual performance otherwise, not only the specific BIC but the BIC initiative as a whole will fail;
■ The prime objective of a BIC is to innovate;
■ The prime objective of BIC members is to learn.

---

62 The BIC three Cs™ is a trademark of getITright® Skills Development CC.

Confirmation

The last 'c' is confirmation – formal evaluation is continuous throughout a BIC, but confirmation is more than checking that we are on target or are focused on value creation. Confirm that everyone on the team understands that mediocrity is not an option – the team mantra is, "We unlock 100 times more value not a 100% more value". BICs normally use ROI as a measure of success and the metric is defined simply as:

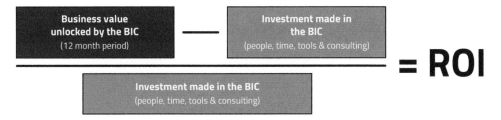

Value in this instance is defined by the consumer. If this isn't possible, value is defined by the consumer's representative or an intermediary consumer.

> Claimed business ROI for BIC projects by getITright varied from as low as 280% to in excess of 2,800% in projects using this method. This calculation could be used as part of an outcomes definition (see Chapter 8 – Outcomes).

9.5.2 Techniques used in BICs

The initial design of BICs was to facilitate rapid innovation for customer benefits in an information technology context. The use of BICs then evolved and they became a strategic tool. The approach evolved from coaching IT teams in the use of Lean and related methods (including Agile and DevOps). The intent was to create an environment where multi-disciplinary teams can design and develop new digital initiatives or make improvements to existing services to answer the question "What do we need to do to transform our business digitally?".

Selecting the next BIC issue flows from a deep understanding of consumers, organizational capabilities and market conditions. It is often prompted by a problem, an observation, a request, or a response to a market shift. Historically, BICs have often been used by organizations in conjunction with Agile and DevOps. In those management practices, requirements and opportunities form part of the backlog – in the BIC, there is a list which provides the same function.

As noted previously – the involvement of organizational leadership in the selection or prioritization of innovation cycles and also in strategic design and conceptualization is imperative for transformational BICs. This may not be necessary for more operational innovations.

Table 4 Comparing VeriSM Digitization Domains or other techniques AND common overarching techniques to define and design a response to a digital dilemma

Technique	Approach: Operational Focus	Approach: Customer Focus	Approach: Future Focus
Cynefin	Mostly obvious but sometimes chaos domain	Mostly complicated but sometimes complex domain	Mostly complex but sometimes complicated domain
Innovator's Dilemma	Efficiency innovation	Sustaining innovation	Disruptive Innovation
Standard and Case	Standard	Case	Case
Overarching methods			
Lean Start-up	×	?	✓
BIC	?	✓	✓
Waterfall PM	✓	?	×
Agile techniques	✓	✓	?
Other methods, tools and techniques			
Brainstorming, & Affinity Maps	✓	✓	?
Canvas Models (Business & Value)	?	✓	?
Cause and Effect Analysis	✓	?	×
Competitive Intelligence	?	✓	✓
Customer Journey Maps	?	✓	?
Hypothesis (A/B or Split) Tests	?	✓	✓
PDCA, Kaizen Events, A3 & DMAIC	✓	?	×
Platform Business Models	×	?	✓
Stakeholder Relationship Maps	?	✓	?
Stakeholder Value Chains	×	?	✓
Social Media & Web Analysis	?	✓	✓
Value Stream Mapping	✓	?	?
VUCA & Situational Assessment tech.	✓	✓	?
Competitive Intelligence	?	✓	?
Surveys & Focus Groups	?	✓	×

Once an issue to target has been identified, the "What's this about?" question is about understanding the need for transformation and the source of the need. The team also agrees during this step on a general approach and tools and techniques that will be used. Before "What can we do?" can be answered, organizations need to have a real understanding of the question. This allows the team to choose analysis techniques suited to the nature of the question. What type of a question is this; simple, complicated, complex, chaotic or do we just not have a clue at all? Table 4 shows some examples of when techniques are or are not appropriate (more detail on these can be found this chapter and also in Appendix D3).

As mentioned in Section 9.1.1 – Cynefin, the best results in this context will be in answering complicated or complex questions. However, organizations must also try and make sense of questions classified as 'chaos' as they often bring the biggest benefit to the organization because of their potential to be disruptive.

"What should we do?" tends to be more tactical in nature. The answer to this needs to accept that the organization has limitations and at least some form of realism is in order. Be aware that saying "we must be realistic" in many cases stifles innovation. Sometimes organizations have to dream the impossible and at least attempt to make it work.

Organizational capability and access to outside help mostly determines the boundaries when answering this question. Sometimes the team realizes that they can't do anything practically to reach the objective set. In these cases, they then change course and define what would be needed to get things done rather than they should do to solve the problem. This enables the objective to be placed back on the list with a better understanding of what is needed when selecting it as a candidate for improvement or innovation.

■ 9.6   OTHER TOOLS AND TECHNIQUES

The rest of this chapter highlights some additional helpful tools and techniques. These can be used to define a unique organizational approach to understanding digital optimization and transformation opportunities. They can also be used as tools in an existing technique like Lean Start-up or Business Innovation Circles™. Further tools and techniques for transformation can also be found in Appendix D3.
This section deals with three types of tools:
- Tools to collect information and data;
- Tools to solve problems, and better understand current environments;
- Tools to help frame a hypothesis that can be used as the basis of experimentation.

9.6.1   Collecting information and data

Market Research

Market research involves gathering and analyzing facts about a given business environment. In BICs, it is often used to:

■ Establish the soundness of a venture;
■ Determine market needs;
■ Monitor competitors;
■ Find market opportunities.

It is best if organizations engage in their own research initiatives (either conducted by their own resources or outsourced to specialists) as commercially available, pre-published research has little value in today's complex market environments.

Market research yields result if it is targeted and focused on a specific question. Many of the techniques described in this publication require some form of market research. Digital channels have vastly expanded the ways in which market research can be carried out and the speed with which organizations can get feedback from their consumers. Market research can also be done more economically (for example, using online surveys), with the organization's own resources.

Market research is a powerful approach. Internal research activities often lead to surprising and unexpected insights outside of the scope of the work that inspired the survey. Some research is challenging to conduct internally – for example, external sources will probably be able to gather better data on a competitor than internal resources. External sources can also be used where there is a risk of bias in the internal research.

Support logs and transactional data

Why? Organizations often have lots of data about customer interactions that can be used to either solve problems or develop new value propositions for customers by better understanding their support experience with the organization.

Support data (for example information from customer help desks or CRM systems and transactional data like invoices, product or service enquiries) can provide valuable insight into consumer experience, behavior, loyalty, and commitment. Looking at trends can be very illuminating. A more proactive approach to analyzing support data, especially from a customer experience perspective, proves insightful when improving services or products but also when identifying gaps in the portfolio of products and service offered by the organization.

Specific techniques to explore when looking at support data are:

■ Trends;
■ Correlation between trends;
■ Pareto analysis.

Much of this research takes place in the 'Respond' stage of the VeriSM model.

Web Analytics and Social Media

Digital products and services generate data in digital formats. Analysis of web analytics data (number of visitors, from which country, how long they stayed, what content they viewed etc.) and social media analysis (interaction with content, website visits related to social media posts, content sharing etc.) can all be a valuable source of information.

Competitive intelligence

Why apply? Gathering actionable data or information on your business's competitive environment can provide significant insights. The number of opportunities to gather competitive information is virtually limitless. As long as it is done legally, it is always good to understand competitors; but this knowledge must not distract the organization from its strategic intent.

Intelligence can be gathered from:

- **Websites** – websites provide information about products and services, competitive advantage, pricing, market segments targeted, and even customer information.
- **Print advertising and online ads** – a source on a competitor's current sales and marketing initiatives. These provide an idea about marketing spend and focus areas or where they see future market growth will come from, as ad-spend is a long-term activity. It is also interesting to see with online ads which keywords they use – a number of online tools will provide this information.
- **Industry benchmarks** – be careful that the benchmark specifically addresses the question that needs answering.
- **Industry and marketing communication** – news stories, emails, brochures and sales literature etc. can provide information about competitors, their customers, markets, market penetration, strengths and weaknesses. Competitor communication activities can act as a baseline for the researching organization's communication strategy.
- **Customer reviews** – an excellent source of competitive information (not marketing reviews like whitepapers which are seen as part of the previous category). Many platforms serve as places where customers express their views about competitors – both positive and negative. This information is a great source for understanding competitor's strengths and weaknesses. Just remember customers are more likely to talk about the bad than the good – this is not a balanced source of information. Negative reviews can show weaknesses that can be capitalized on and positive reviews provide ideas for the researching organization's own product or strategy.
- **Social media** – an excellent source to track a competitor's sales and marketing initiatives, customers, level of customer satisfaction, relationships, current targeting activities and markets. In a business environment LinkedIn and Twitter may be a better source of information than Facebook, Instagram, Pinterest etc. (market and market segment dependent).

Many other sources exist including their hiring practices, rankings, information gathered during various conversations, and (if a public company) financial and other governance reports.

The same data you gather about your competitors you should also gather about your own organization; you will be able to draw interesting comparisons.

This information should be augmented with more detailed information gathering in your own environment, for instance about your web and social media pages, trends, volumes, customer behaviors etc.

If you can find out what your competitors are up to, they can do the same to you. Lastly, what you do is more important to your success than what your competitors are doing. Be aware, but never let a competitor dictate your strategy.

Information radiators

Why apply? Information radiators are any public and visible means of communicating important information to the relevant stakeholders whether handwritten, drawn, printed or by means of electronic displays.

The world is littered with information radiators, for instance, every traffic light or road sign is an information radiator. In addition to the information communicated, information radiators convey three important messages:

- This is important and therefore everyone needs to know;
- We hope nothing goes wrong but if it does, it is better to know about it, otherwise we can't do anything about it;
- We do not hide anything from each other or our consumers.

Information radiators are sources of immediate action, and it is important to establish a culture of shared responsibility, specifically to act or enquire if some information seems out of place. They can also have a significant impact on reinforcing cultural dynamics like a culture of no-blame and collective responsibility. They often stimulate conversation and debate, which often yields innovation or improvement opportunities.

Information radiators are often used in IT teams or other operations environments but are also key management tools for progressive practices like Lean, Agile and DevOps. Probably the best know information radiator in business is a Kanban board that is often used for Agile project status tracking or Lean day or week-start meeting.

9.6.2 Tools to solve problems and understand current environments
Ishikawa (cause and effect)
Why? It is essential to understand cause and effect, especially when solving problems. If cause and effect are not properly understood, the solutions might only treat symptoms. This can perpetuate the negative effect of the cause and waste valuable resources in treating symptoms.

Kaoru Ishikawa (1915–1989), a leader in Japanese quality control, developed a method of documenting cause and effect that can be useful in helping identify where something may be going wrong, or could be improved. The main goal is represented by the trunk of the diagram, and primary factors are represented as branches. Secondary factors are then added as stems, and so on (see Figure 33). Creating the diagram stimulates discussion and often leads to increased understanding of a complex problem.

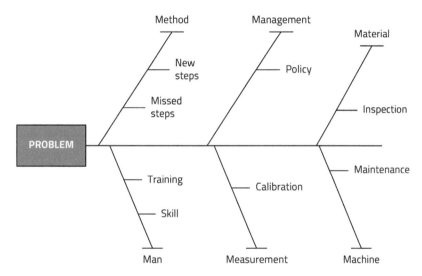

Figure 33 Ishikawa diagram

Use the Ishikawa or fishbone diagram to:
■ Organize and display theories about the root cause (or causes) of a problem;
■ Focus attention on one specific problem (make sure everyone agrees what);
■ Encourage innovative thinking (but not solutions, only possible causes);
■ Provide a graphic representation of relationships (if too many, use the 'Multivote' technique).

To construct the diagram:
■ Clearly define the effect or symptom for which the causes must be identified;
■ Place the effect or symptom being explored in an enclosed box;
■ Draw the central spine as a thick line;

- Brainstorm or construct an affinity diagram to identify the major categories of possible causes (not less than two nor, normally, more than six);
- Place each of the 'major categories' in a box and connect it to the central spine by a line drawn at about 70 degrees from the horizontal (ribs);
- Identify possible causes for each of the major categories and write them on horizontal 'bones' attached to each rib;
- For each of these ask, "Why does this happen?" (i.e., the effect or symptom being explored) or "Why does this condition exist?"
- Record the possible reasons;
- Continue to add clauses to each branch until the fishbone is completed;
- Once all the bones have been completed, identify the likely, actionable cause.

Five why's

Why? This technique forces exploration beyond the obvious. It is also a handy way to validate answers obtained using other techniques.

The 5 why's is a simple yet highly effective way to get to the underlying cause(s) of a problem. It works by starting out with a description of what event took place and then asking, 'why this occurred'. The resulting answer is given, followed by another round of 'why this occurred'. Usually by the fifth iteration, the cause or causes will have been found.

A3 problem solving

Why? A3 is a visual way to concisely define and describe improvement action taken. A3 is also a visual management technique that ensures visibility of improvements made and keeps everyone informed of progress. The goal of the A3 method is to ensure that the team solving the problem focuses on the essentials due to the limitation of the size of the paper (an A3 sheet). Information is generated throughout the improvement or problem-solving event and captured on the A3 as the event progresses, concisely and succinctly. An example of this is shown in Figure 34.

The aim is to facilitate the communication of improvements to others within the organization. A3 is a visual management technique used in Lean but also as part of other techniques like DMAIC, as shown in Figure 35.

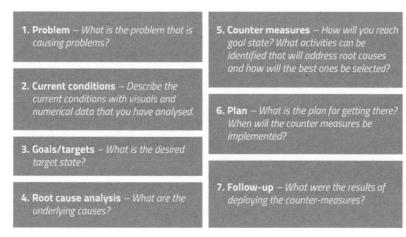

Figure 34 Using A3 as a visual tool to solve problems

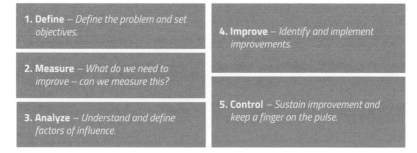

Figure 35 An A3 sheet when used as part of DMAIC

Affinity mapping

Why? Affinity mapping is an excellent analytical tool if lots of data is presented but not contextualized. It has the additional benefit of getting participants immersed in data, so they understand the context better which often leads to unrelated insights. Affinity mapping is a technique used to order data in many different situations. It creates an 'affinity diagram' a term devised by Jiro Kawakita and is referred to as the KJ method.

People have been grouping data based on natural relationships for thousands of years, and this tool provides a visual way to do so. Sort ideas or data into groups based on logical connections, relationships, dependencies, themes or some other criterion. Use affinity mapping to organize other free-form comments, such as open-ended responses, support call logs, or other qualitative data.

The process of affinity mapping organizes ideas by following these steps:
- Record each idea on a card or sticky note;
- Look for ideas that seem to be related;
- Sort cards into groups until all cards are allocated to a group;

- Once the cards have been sorted into groups, sort large clusters of data into subgroups for easier management and analysis;
- Often multiple cards seem to address the exact same issue – these cards can be stacked in a pile with the top card giving the best description;
- Once completed, the affinity diagram may be used to create a cause-and-effect diagram or any other relevant use as determined by the management practice being followed.

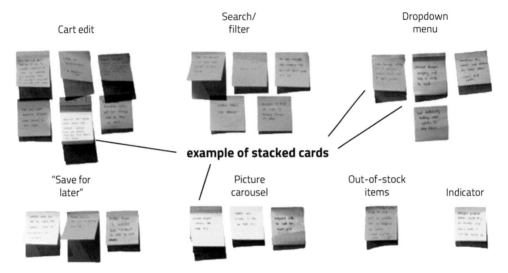

As with many other techniques, the best results are achieved if cross-functional teams use the technique – look at all stakeholders and include as many as possible or viable. A second advantage of doing cross-functional affinity mapping is that participants become deeply immersed in the data, which has benefits beyond the immediate objectives.

9.6.3   Tools to frame a hypothesis

Why? To evaluate innovative and disruptive ideas and identify those with a high probability of success.

Of all of the ideas an organization identifies, many will not be successful or will be impractical – perhaps as many as 90% will fail. The only way to improve the odds is by using experimentation and hypothesis testing, to identify as early as possible those that will fail.

The main purpose of idea generation in this context is to find digitally innovative and disruptive products. Organizations need to consider innovative and potentially disruptive ways to test these ideas too. Conventional techniques like surveys and focus groups do not yield very good results once one moves outside the conventional. See Chapter 28 – Digital Design for more information on current techniques.

Many organizations now test the market by 'releasing' information into the public domain using digital channels and seeing how their consumers or potential consumers respond. These activities are often very focused – e.g. a specific LinkedIn group, advertisements targeting online users with a specific profile on Google, Facebook and LinkedIn, tweets about the subject, vlogs on social media platforms, commercial offers on their website, etc.

Using an external organization to carry out market research can give insight but once again its value is limited for innovative ideas and for disruptive products when compared to internal research and direct results.

What level or type of response is a good indicator of success? It is helpful if organizations have some form of a baseline. For example, if an organization has a successful product for which it receives online sales/sales enquiries of 1000 units a day, it may define a measure of 800 or more sales/sales enquiries for a test product as being a success.

Some organizations now use crowd funding investment sites not only as a means of raising capital for new ideas but as a means to test the market for these ideas.

In the absence of a baseline (which often does not exist) organizations can use a form of hypothesis testing called A/B testing. Two options are provided, and the consumer's response is recorded. Just asking the consumer may not always work, Henry Ford famously said "If I asked customers what they want they would have told me faster horses!" Presenting consumers with two options or features provides more meaningful data. Quite often the features are rudimentary and not fully functional, but they work well enough to provide data about where to focus development efforts.

Real world example
Hypothesis testing
With hypothesis testing, organizations can test their assumptions and answer the elusive "why?" question.

For example, a hypothesis could be that consumers will prefer option X because of 'A' (e.g., consumers prefer to be able to save credit card details on the website, because it makes repeat purchasing simpler).

The test may confirm that the assumption made by the organization is valid either for the reason cited or for another reason. The test may also discover that consumers have a need (reason) but it is unconnected to the assumptions the organization made. It may become apparent, for example, that most consumers are uncomfortable saving their card details because they perceive the website to be insecure.

Canvas models

Why? Canvas models allow organizations to understand needs and demands compared to competitive products that already exist. They help to ensure that innovations are justified and likely to succeed.

The Business Model Canvas

The Business Model Canvas is a strategic management and Lean start-up template for developing new (or documenting existing) business models.

Its aim is help organizations to capture strategy, products, services, value proposition, infrastructure, customers, and finances and other resources in a visual manner that allows the organization to evaluate trade-offs and align activities.

The originators of the canvas are Alex Osterwalder and Yves Pigneur. On their website[63] the model is fully explained along with additional resources (many free of charge).

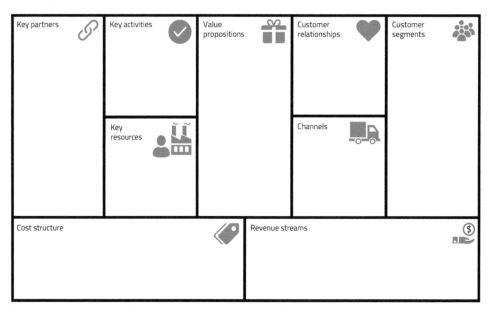

Figure 36 Osterwalder and Pigneur – Business Model Canvas (source: strategyzer.com)

The canvas is used by populating blank spaces (ideally, physically, with Post-it® notes) with the relevant information in the relevant areas.

The Value Proposition Canvas

The Value Proposition Canvas is a form of Business Model Canvas. Understanding the value proposition is essential when designing new or changed products or

---

63 Osterwalder, A. & Pigneur, Y. (No date) Business model canvas, (Online). https://strategyzer.com/canvas/business-model-canvas [2018, March].

services. The Value Proposition Canvas (VPC)[64] specifically focuses on two elements of the BMC, namely the value proposition and the customer segment. The intent of the canvas is to observe and understand customers and their requirements before starting to design products and services.

Observing starts with the customer segment of the canvas. Before customer segment analysis can be done the organization needs to define who their customer is or who the product or service would target as customers. There may be multiple customers, and if so the analysis needs to be done for each customer.

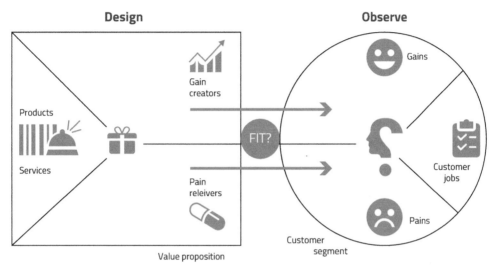

Figure 37 Value Proposition Canvas (source: strategyzer.com)

■ 'Jobs' in the customer segment does not refer to the job of the customer. It refers to the job that the service or product needs to fulfil. This 'job' may include function and/or utility and use but may also include more subtle jobs like reinforcing stature or aligning to some social construct or position or even conveying a message about the customer's values or beliefs.

■ 'Pains' are obstacles, problems or risks that the customer may want to avoid. Some of these pains may be generic, like reliability, safety, and price. Others may be directly associated with the type of product or service a consumer wants to buy. As with jobs pains may also include intangible issues like perception by others of the owners or users as the service or product.

■ 'Gains' define the customer's expectations and desires. Gains are features, capabilities, capacity, support, maintenance or other attributes of the product or service.

---

64 Osterwalder, A., Pigneur, Y., Bernarda, G., Smith, A., & Papadakos, T. (2014). *Value proposition design: How to create products and services customers want (Strategyzer)*. New York: Wiley.

Defining these areas creates a profile of the typical customer and provides the design team with valuable insights to design requirements. The defined jobs, pains, and gains are ranked and prioritized to make it easy for the design team to use the profiles. Make sure this is done from a customer's perspective and test assumptions against prospective customers.

On the value proposition side of the canvas the idea is to match customer jobs with products or services and ensure that these products and services include pain relievers (for defined customer pains) and gain creators (for customer gains) considering the relative importance of each element.

Value Propositions

A final word from Alex Osterwalder about value propositions:

- Great value propositions are embedded in great business models. (Kodak helped with the design of digital cameras and even sold digital cameras, but their business model was not aligned with the value proposition).
- Great value propositions focus on the jobs, pains and gains that matter most to customers. That implies that you understand customer priorities from the customer's view. Get out of the building and test your understanding – engage with customers.
- Focus on unresolved pains, unrealized gains, and unsatisfied jobs. Other organizations apparently got some of this right – figure out where there is most dissatisfaction and potential to create value.
- Target few jobs, pains, and gains but do so exceptionally well. Once again focus on where the most value can be created.
- Don't only address functional jobs but also tackle emotional and social jobs as well.
- Align measurements with how customers measure success and failure.
- Focus on jobs, pains or gains that either a lot of people have, or some people will pay a lot of money for.
- Differentiate by focusing on what customers care about, do not differentiate on things customers do not care that much about but that you must still offer.
- Outperform the competition substantially on at least one feature or dimension.
- Make sure your key value propositions are difficult to copy.

Brainstorming

Why? To identify innovative and disruptive ideas with a high probability of success.

Although brainstorming is frequently used as a problem-solving technique, it is included here as it is also one of the most effective ways of framing a hypothesis for empirical work. Experimentation is at the heart of any empirical problem, and in the context of innovation, very little reliable data is available to use alternative techniques. Experimentation is well suited to complex and chaotic problems that need to be solved.

Many organizations experiment to some extent but not in a structured way. They use 'gut feel' and try something out; sometimes it works, more often it does not. It is important to use a structured approach during experimentation to improve the likelihood of success. A structured approach often starts small, defining a number of things that the organization can do differently that should impact positively on their market. Here it is important to follow the brainstorming approach – generate as many as possible ideas in the time allotted to do so.

In brainstorming the rules are important and have a profound effect if followed:
- Define and describe the problem so that everyone knows why they participate. Don't look for solutions – this is a time to listen and think;
- Preferably create two or more teams. Ensure the teams are balanced, cross-functional and represent all layers of the organization. Also appoint a facilitator for the session;
- Generate ideas – do not evaluate, do not comment on them, do not judge them, just come up with ideas. It does not matter if they are good or bad. The job of the facilitator is to ensure that judgements are not made, and idea generation is focused on. Everyone should have an equal opportunity to contribute. Sometimes it works well to ask for ideas from everyone to ensure full participation;
- Swap the generated ideas between the teams;
- Sort ideas; teams will quite often find that ideas are similar. Teams can use affinity maps to group similar ideas together. If the team is unsure, send a representative to the originator to clarify if the team's understanding was correct;
- Evaluate ideas and grade the evaluation. Is this a better idea than the next one? How much better is it? The aim is to have a list of 10 or fewer good ideas;
- Teams consolidate and regrade (not re-evaluate) ideas, again creating a list of no more than 10 ideas;

Brainstorming is a very simple way of generating ideas. It's easy to learn and works well if the rules are stringently applied. According to the rules no idea is ever criticized in front of its originator – meaning no contributor is discouraged from making future contributions.

Customer journey maps and moments of truth
Why? A journey map helps an organization to explore the answers to the question "what if?" during the research, conceptualization and design of a new product or service or an improvement to an existing product or service.

Journey mapping is a tool for service design, Design Thinking, user experience design and touchpoint management. It often leads to a more detailed design like a service blueprint (which can be seen as another view of a journey map for multiple personas expanded into a detailed service design).

Mapping typically starts by defining personas. Personas are a specific role-player or group of role-players in a value stream, e.g., a particular type of consumer or a specific type of employee. Defining personas gives a better idea of who they are, what they need, what they experience and what they feel during their journey. This creates empathy and understanding and helps to create better ideas and better ways of servicing consumers who belong to a persona.

Personas are defined as the average of the person belonging to that persona group. When defining persona requirements, also consider demographics, factual information, psychographics (which characterize preferences and perceptions) and emotional experience. It's also important to be aware of the extreme limits of groups belonging to a persona, especially for testing. Personas joined by types of resources, or other stakeholders, can also be used to define a stakeholder map to analyze a specific experience of a key stakeholder (often described as a persona).

It's usual to create a journey map for each persona, outlining their journey as a sequence of steps, then map their experience during this journey and determine how it relates to things done by other stakeholders, or provided by organizational resources, capabilities, technologies, and systems. Journey maps are often combined into an overarching view of different persona's experience of a product and service and then used to understand how products and services can be built or improved by defining/designing a service blueprint.

Journey maps make intangible actions or interactions visible and actionable. Mapping customer journeys also makes it possible to create a common understanding of how a persona interacts with an organization, product or service. It is important to note that a journey map should include experiences, actions, and steps outside the reach of the organization but in some way connected with the experience of the persona when dealing with an organization or consuming products or services.

Single Persona journey maps
Single persona journey maps start by listing the steps in a customer journey.

These are then described as the persona would typically experience each step (remember, experience is emotional). This can further be enhanced with a storyboard that forms the basis of a rich dramatization of the journey.

For each step consider:
- The persona's emotional journey;
- Channels of communication;
- Customer resources;
- Front-end stakeholders (those the persona interacts with);

- Other stakeholders (not directly involved in the delivery of a product or service but who may have an influence over the experience);
- Back-end stakeholders (those the persona does not interact with but support the experience or front-end stakeholders);
- Resources required or consumed;
- Supporting systems;
- Supporting technologies.

Figure 38 is an example journey map of an early morning commuter stopping at 'Mug and Muffin' for a cup of coffee for themselves or their colleagues on the way to the office. It shows many ways in which Mug and Muffin can improve customer experience (CX) and their products and services.

The typical steps to create a customer journey map are to:
- Define the problem or question about which more insight is required;
- Perform or gather qualitative and quantitative research;
- List journey steps, customer touchpoints and channels on which these occur (e.g. pay bill, face to face, online, website etc.). List not only the planned journey to achieve a customer outcome, but also all feedback loops that keep the customer updated with progress and issue handling diversions for when the customer journey goes wrong – when thing go wrong is when the customer journey needs to be at its best;
- Sketch the journey – remember, there is no one way correct to do it;
- Create an empathy map (experience map + detailed experience for each step) that depicts various facets of a persona and related experiences in a given scenario. Hear, see, think, feel, say and do is one way to look at it, another is using pains and gains defined in canvas techniques. The goal is to get a sense of how it feels to be the person in that specific scenario;
- Brainstorm the map using different perspectives (creating a stakeholder map may help to do this – see next section);
- Define possible improvements or new innovations for different personas and viewed from the perspective of different stakeholders;
- Group ideas using affinity diagram to help find cohesive ideas – helps focus on correct solutions for specific or important stakeholders;
- Refine and digitize;
- Share with passion – make sure it makes a difference.

Every touchpoint or interaction along the customer journey becomes a 'moment of truth'; a point when the customer and the service provider come into contact, giving the customer an opportunity to either form or change their impression of the organization. Across the customer journey there may be many 'moments of truth'. A customer could spend many minutes happily engaging with a brand through a variety of touchpoints, each experience taking him/her closer to their end goal.

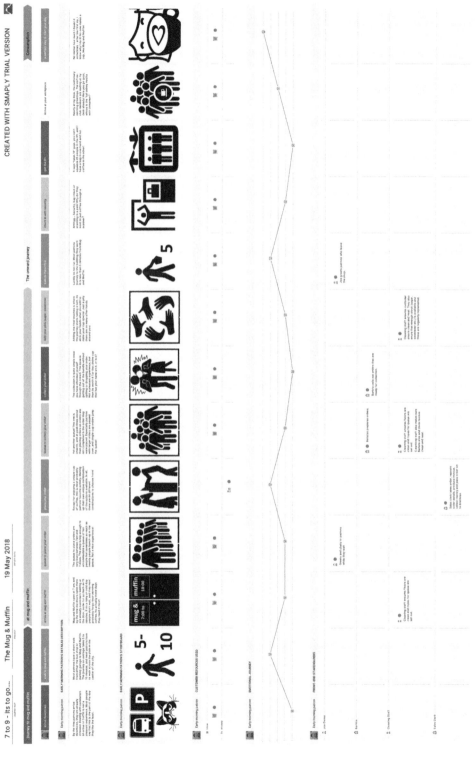

Figure 38 A Customer Journey Map of Mug and Muffin

However, all it takes is one negative experience to damage the memory of the entire experience, which ultimately leads to a disengaged customer. Foster an environment that creates positive, memorable encounters.

Remember, every action or interaction creates a personal reaction. Service providers need to understand the customer journey, customer expectations and the actual experience at each touchpoint, understanding the customer's emotional status at the end of each interaction. A customer experience is about how a customer consciously and subconsciously sees his or her experience. Conscious expectations are typically fact-based, e.g. catalogs, service levels. Subconscious expectations may be based around unwritten rules, custom and practice, preconceptions, perceptions e.g. through social media, word of mouth, marketing, competitor experiences, past experiences or urgency of immediate situation ...many of which are outside of the service provider's control. Customer expectations are not static. They will change with the world around them so will need to be continually monitored to continuously improve and even transform customer experience.

It is important to understand and focus on the 'moments' that matter most to the customer or persona, as they will not all be equal in their eyes. For example, did a delivery arrive on time to the right location is likely to be more important that how quickly the order was confirmed. Make the ending count, as the final moment of truth will carry more weight. It is the final memory carried forward into the cumulative customer experience. Finally, turn a poor experience (when something goes wrong for the customer) into a good one. Make customers feel good about the recovery experience, again this is a significant moment of truth.

Understanding the customer journey and moments of truth can be used to transform customer experience and satisfaction.

Stakeholder maps
Why? Stakeholder maps helps us to understand interactions between stakeholders and the importance of these interactions.

Stakeholder maps are drawn by creating concentric circles starting with the middle circle (the most important) and working to the outside (less important). Personas are placed on the circles and relationships between personas are defined by using arrows and icons representing a specific theme. Themes are described in more detailed in accompanying text. Figure 39 is an example of the Mug and Muffin stakeholder map.

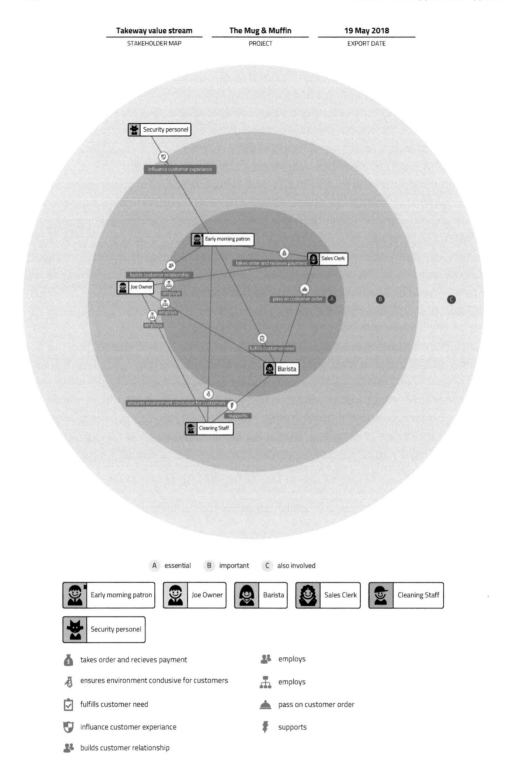

Figure 39 Mug and Muffin stakeholder map

9.6.4 Platform business model maps

Why? Platform business model maps help organizations understand the dynamics of platform-based business models and can be used to analyze competitor's platforms or to conceptualize and design a platform model for the organization itself.

Many new disruptive organizations are 'platform' businesses, who gain value from the network effect. The concept of 'network effect' is that the larger the network, the more participants there are. More participants lead to better matches between supply and demand and more data which can be used to find other matches between supply and demand. The scale of the network attracts more consumers, who create more value, which attracts more consumers. Organizations like Uber and Airbnb are good examples of this.

This type of organization dates back to earlier work from economists looking at two-sided markets, looking at situations where an organization charges different customers different prices. Most platform businesses are more complicated than this – platform businesses create value by facilitating direct interaction between two or more distinct types of customers.

Andrei Hagiu and Julian Wright define a multi-sided platform business: "...at the most fundamental level, MSPs (Multi-Sided Platforms) have two key features beyond any other requirements (such as indirect network effects or non-neutrality of fees):
- They enable direct interactions between two or more distinct sides;
- Each side is affiliated with the platform."

The word 'platform' leads most people to think about a software/web platform like Amazon, but of course Amazon was not a platform business in the beginning. It only became a platform business when it allowed other parties to list goods for resale.

Ann example of a platform business is the Android Operating System from Alphabet (Google), which can be considered using a mapping tool defined by David Rodgers of Columbia University (Table 5). Android has many customers. Some of these interact directly with each other using the Android platform by virtue of their affiliation with Android. Table 5 describes the relationship between different customers of Android and Android as the platform. For example, row 2 shows Content Providers as an Android customer. They sell videos, books and music via the platform, which provides them with a storefront and access to customers. The Content Providers' customers get access to on-demand content via Android, and Android itself gets more content and sales commission.

Table 5 Platform Business Model Map (Template source: David Rodgers)

Customer	Value received from other customers	Value received from platform	Value provided to other customers	Value provided to platform	Customers they attract	Profile
Mobile and appliance device manufacturers	Sales device	Device OS Google applications	Open platform	Platform growth License fees	Individual for business use Business users Individuals for personal use or pleasure	Primary Payer
Content providers	Sales video/book/music	Storefront More customers	On-demand content	Rich content Sales commission	Everyone	Player
Motor manufacturers	Product features	Less R&D cost	Connected / integrated driving experience	New customer type License fees	High-income, technology savvy buyers	Payer
Application Developers	Sales application	APK and tools GooglePlay Services	Platform growth Commission Hosting fee	New ideas	Everyone	Payer
Device users	Capabilities/Tools Income using app	Enhanced capabilities	Revenue for sale of apps and devices	Platform growth	Everyone	Linchpin
Car drivers	Capabilities / Tools Connected / integrated driving experience	Integrated platform	Sales vehicle features	Platform growth	High-income, technology savvy buyers	Payer

'Linchpin' customers are those without which the platform will fail – similar to an anchor tenant in a shopping mall. Transcribing the above information to a Platform Business Model Map helps an organization to understand the dynamics of a competitor/disruptor who is a platform business. It can also be used to map a proposed platform business and prioritize and sequence the development of the business over time.

Figure 40 shows an example of a map for Android.

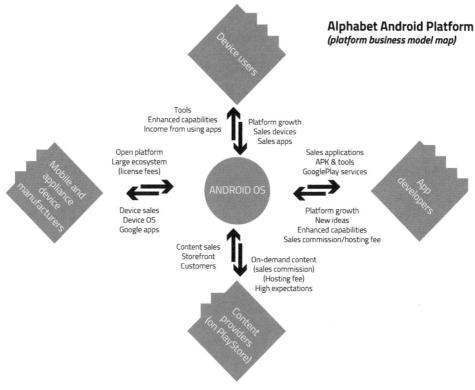

Figure 40 Platform business model map – Android (source: David L. Rogers, *The Digital Transformation Book*)

Note that in the example there are no 'sweeteners'. A sweetener can be something like news providers that publish free stories on Facebook.

Platform Business Model Map

The Platform Business Model Map is drawn in five steps, using the information filled in the chart:

- **Names**:
  - Write the name of the platform itself in the middle of the map;
  - If there is a linchpin, write its name directly above the platform;
  - If there is a primary payer, writer their name directly to the right of the platform;
  - Then, go clockwise: writing the names of other payers;
  - Finally, further clockwise: write the names of any sweeteners;
- **Shapes**: Draw a circle around the platform's name, a diamond around any payers, and a square around sweeteners;
- **Attraction**: On each customer's shape (diamond or square), add a small spike for every other customer that is attracted by them to the platform;

- **Value received**: Draw an arrow out from the platform to each customer. Next to the arrow, write the value it receives from other customers. Then, in parentheses, write the value it receives from the platform itself. (In both cases, indicate monetary value in bold);
- **Value provided**: Draw an arrow from each customer in to the platform. Next to the arrow, write the value it provides to other customers. Then, in parentheses, write the value it provides to the platform itself. (In both cases, indicate monetary value in bold).

Stakeholder value chains

Why? Stakeholder value chains helps us understand the dynamics and relationships between suppliers, the organization and its customers. They highlight opportunities to intermediate, disintermediate and better understand other business models.

When talking about value chains, it is common to focus on how value is created inside an organization. Particularly in today's complex sourcing environments, it is important to understand value chains across networks that create value for consumers.

These stakeholder value chains are the middle part of Porter's five forces, namely:

- Suppliers;
- The organization;
- Customers.

It is important to note that multiple iterations of these stakeholder chains may exist between the furthest points of the stakeholder value chain. Stakeholder value chains are important as they show two strategic opportunities. Porter called this forward and backward integration, but they are more commonly referred to as disintermediation and intermediation. Disintermediation is where one party in the stakeholder value stream has the opportunity to cut out another stakeholder, leaving more of the value created in the value chain in the disintermediating stakeholder's hands, as can be seen in Figure 41.

Figure 41 An example of disintermediation

Intermediation happens when a stakeholder (Facebook in Figure 41) with a common stakeholder (the reader in Figure 41) has the opportunity to insert itself into the value chain and therefore capture some of the value for itself, as shown in Figure 42.

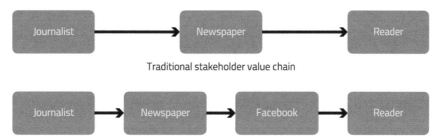

Figure 42 An example of intermediation

Drawing and understanding stakeholder value chains provides insight into how value can be unlocked in them, therefore providing strategic opportunities.

10 Governance and strategy

Introduction

An organization's leadership has a primary function – to provide strategic direction and ensure that the right resources are available to bring this strategy to fulfilment within the environment the organization operates. When risks are well understood and managed and resources are put to optimal use, then everything that is done in the organization helps it achieve its strategic intent.

This chapter introduces the organizational portfolio and looks at governance and strategy in the digital organization.

■ 10.1 SETTING THE SCENE

Preparing the organization for the digital world is a challenge almost all enterprises face today. The primary dilemma is that there is very little in the way of guidance available, and most guidance is focused on the digital (technology) aspects, not people, culture, ways of working etc. The second dilemma is that this digitally focused world requires a fundamental shift in thinking, starting with a redefinition of organizational strategy.

A digital strategy?

Please note – digital transformation requires a new strategy *for the enterprise* but NOT a 'digital transformation strategy' or even a 'strategy for digital services'. The danger of a digital transformation strategy is:

- It implies that it is a goal with an end when in fact transformation is ongoing; see Chapter 5 – Adapting to Constant Change;
- It's segmented, focusing on just one of the things an organization needs to do. That would be a fundamental flaw in thinking. Surviving in a digital age means that the strategy for the whole organization needs to be appropriate for a digital world.

Digital products and services cannot be delivered successfully through conventional structures in an organization or by traditional thinking. Transformation itself is not the ideal word to use, as it implies something that has a finish point. Effective digital transformation requires the organizational culture to change so that it can adjust now and continue to adjust and adapt in the future.

Although transformation is not the end, it is a means to an end. Unfortunately, what that end will be, no-one knows for sure. Think about Artificial Intelligence (AI) for example, who can predict what the impact of AI will be on society, much less how it will impact an organization? Strategic thinking now should be less focused on defined objectives, and more on the organization's role, position, influence or competitive position in future. The following statement encapsulates this idea.

> "The big difference between systems thinking and complexity theory is that in systems thinking you define an ideal future state and you try and close the gap, in complexity theory you describe the present and see what you can change. The only thing you define is a direction of travel and not a goal. Because if you start on a journey you would discover things that you did not know you could discover which may have high utility whereas if you have an explicit goal you may miss the very things that you may need to discover!"
>
> Professor David Snowden

■ 10.2 THE IMPORTANCE OF LEADERSHIP IN GOVERNANCE

Changes in an organization often start at the top, via leadership, governance and strategy. Successful digital transformation requires the leadership of the organization to focus on governance to provide strategic direction for managers to act upon. Organizational leaders need to grasp (with a level of urgency) that their role is to be the facilitator of the change the organization needs, to enable it to survive in future. It starts with leaders and the board of the organization. If leadership fails – the organization will fail.

Chapter 4 addresses changes in the role of leadership and Section 5.5 addresses leaders' roles in managing organizational behavior and facilitating organizational change.

Effective governance requires the leadership of an organization to focus on three primary activities, which are:

- Evaluate;
- Direct;
- Monitor.

This approach is based on a widely used governance model. From these three activities, a system of governance is created which VeriSM uses to shape a set of Service Management Principles (guardrails for behavior which are operationalized via policies).

The organizational portfolio

A tangible outcome of the governance activities is the organizational portfolio. The portfolio represents the organization's strategic decisions and how the organization has invested its resources – it represents the organization's value stream and commitment to the products and services it delivers, which form its value proposition (see Section 10.3 for more information). The organizational portfolio is the driver for the implementation of new products and services ("Will XXX support the achievement of the strategy?") and it can be used to confirm continued conformance to the enterprise strategy ("Do we need to purchase/develop XXX or is it outside the defined boundaries?").

10.2.1 VeriSM Pillars

Collectively, three elements, enterprise governance, Service Management Principles and the organizational portfolio, create the VeriSM 'Pillars'. How do these pillars work together? Enterprise governance defines the mission and vision for the organization and 'owns' the evaluate, direct, and monitor activities. The Service Management Principles are defined based on enterprise governance and those principles, along with enterprise governance, will influence the products and services the organization delivers (captured in the organizational portfolio). The Management Mesh (see Figure 43) creates an inclusive view of the organization which is based in governance, the associated principles and the current organizational portfolio.

The mesh represents how resources, environment, management practices and emerging technologies will integrate and operate together to deliver service value. Understanding what is already being delivered and its relationship to the fulfilment of defined strategy is also critical. The organizational portfolio provides this information. Without all three components, the mesh will not accurately reflect the organization and puts the organization at risk of promising something it can't (or shouldn't) deliver.

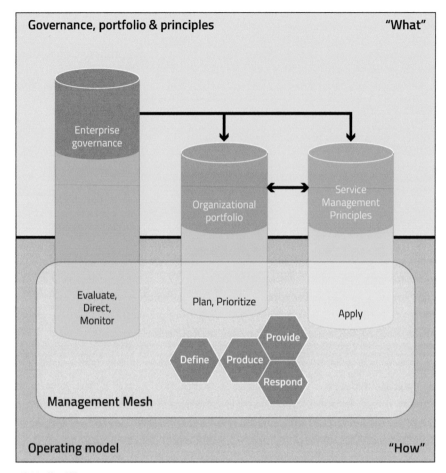

Figure 43 VeriSM Pillars

■ 10.3 THE ORGANIZATIONAL PORTFOLIO

The organizational portfolio provides the service provider with an enterprise view of its products and services and value proposition. It should not be confused with an application portfolio, supplier portfolio or financial portfolio. For VeriSM, the portfolio depicts which organizational capabilities and associated resources are involved in the delivery and support of products and services provided by the enterprise, as shown in Figure 44. Additionally, the portfolio illustrates how capabilities and associated resources enable specific value streams.

This allows the portfolio to be managed around value streams (see Section 8.3.1) rather than individual technologies, products, or services.

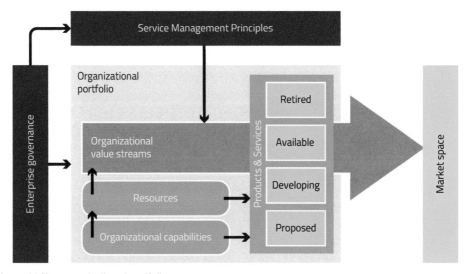

Figure 44 The organizational portfolio

Value stream

A value stream is "the sequence of activities required to … deliver a good or service to a [consumer], and it includes the dual flows of information and material. Most value streams are cross-functional; the transformation of a [consumer] request for a good or service flows through many functional [capabilities]…within an organization". (Martin and Osterling, 2013)

To illustrate the cross-functional aspect of a value stream, a value stream of "order-to-cash" in an online retail environment would involve the order management, credit, order fulfilment, shipping, and accounts receivable capabilities within the organization.

The value streams depicted within the organizational portfolio represent a high-level view of how products and services meet consumer needs within a market space. The value streams do not include the individual capability tasks or decisions, management practice processes and procedures, or the underpinning technology involved in the delivery of products and services. In other words, the value streams only depict **what** is done, not **how** it is being done.

The purpose of the organizational portfolio is to:

■ Support informed decision-making regarding investments and commitments to products and services based on enterprise strategy and governance (see Chapter 10);

■ Identify what value streams are present within the organization, and what organizational capabilities and associated resources are involved in the delivery and support of those value streams;

■ Ensure that all organizational capabilities are considered when developing or changing a product or service;

■ Understand and track the status of products and services.

■ 10.4 RELATIONSHIP OF THE ORGANIZATIONAL PORTFOLIO TO OTHER VERISM ARTIFACTS AND ACTIVITIES

■ The VeriSM stages (Define, Produce, Provide, Respond):

- Define – as business cases or approvals are developed, a record for that product or service is created with a status of 'proposed' in the portfolio. Creation of a service blueprint would result in a status of 'under development' for that product or service;

- Produce – status changes to products and services ('proposed', 'under development', 'available', or 'retired') are made as part of change control within the Produce activity;

- Provide – products or services in the Provide activity have a status of 'available' in the portfolio. In addition, products and services that have a status of 'under development' can play an important role in a service provider's marketing activities;

- Respond – responding to consumers, including resolving issues;

■ Management Mesh – resources depicted on the Management Mesh correspond with resources within the organizational portfolio;

■ Consumers – the VeriSM model starts and ends with the consumer and their needs.

■ 10.5 GOVERNANCE AND STRATEGY OVERVIEW

Governance is a system of directing and controlling. It makes sure that the organization acts on strategic intent and achieves its strategic objectives. Governance is needed to ensure decision making at lower levels of the organization is accurate and appropriate to the organization, its vision, mission and goals. This is achieved in the VeriSM model by communicating vision, mission, goals, etc. via the Service Management Principles.

Organizations often use the word 'governance' to describe direction and control activities but also the rules and customs applying to them. In this broader definition, governance should include processes, customs, policies, laws and institutions affecting the way people direct, administer or control an organization. Governance also includes strategic influence of the management of relationships among the many role-players or stakeholders and their influence on corporate goals. The management staff directed by the governing body is responsible for day to day stakeholder management. The principal players include the shareholders, customers, employees, management, and the board of directors, whilst others may include suppliers, service providers, regulators, competitors, the environment and the community at large.

The idea of viewing governance as three distinct sets of activities meant to ensure proper decision making and provide strategic direction (and the review of the effect of such direction) to an enterprise is taken from ISO/IEC 38500 (and the preceding Australian Standard for IT Governance).

10.5.1 Evaluate, Direct, Monitor (EDM)

The Evaluate, Direct, Monitor (EDM) model was first described in ISO/IEC 38500. Although originally used for the governance of IT, it is a valid enterprise governance model. VeriSM adopts EDM as the definitive reference model for governance.

The objective of the EDM model is to provide a structure for directors, owners, board members, partners, and senior executives to use for governing an organization. It provides a structure for effective governance of an enterprise of any kind by assisting those at the highest level of an enterprise to understand and fulfil their legal, regulatory and ethical obligations. At the same time, it helps to clearly define strategic direction and communicate it to management and the rest of the organization so that they can make it happen. It will include defining goals, objectives, outcomes, policy and principles for management to use when executing the strategy of the organization. Governance also needs to ensure that the intended results are achieved and intervene when things go wrong – so another element of governance is oversight and monitoring.

Using the EDM model, VeriSM proposes that governance is a process and not an event. Governance is a strategic process as it ensures direction and action – without effective governance the rest of the VeriSM model cannot be applied effectively.

The governing body of an organization has three main tasks:
- Evaluate the current and future state of the organization;
- Devise strategic direction appropriate for the organizational context and direct preparation and implementation of plans and policies to ensure that the enterprise can reach its goals and objectives;
- Monitor conformance to policies and performance against the plans.

The ISO/IEC 38500 standard sets out a number of principles for good governance. These principles express preferred behavior to guide decision making. The statement of each principle refers to what should happen, but does not prescribe how, when or by whom the principles would be implemented; these aspects are dependent on the nature of the enterprise implementing the principles. The governing body needs to describe an ideal state, and delegate the achievement of that state to managers across the enterprise.

Typical governance practices and principles include:
- Create and maintain the governance framework – define the structures, principles and practices based on the organization's goals and objectives (mission/vision);
- Define responsibilities – ensure they are understood and accepted;
- Embed the value proposition – link the outcomes of the products and services to the achievement of organizational objectives;
- Optimize risks – define organizational risk tolerance/appetite for risk and ensure it is understood, communicated and managed;
- Optimize capabilities – ensure there are sufficient resources (people, process, technology) to support the achievement of organizational objectives;
- Ensure conformance – all mandatory laws and regulations are met through organizational practices and defined policies are clear, deployed and compulsory;
- Create stakeholder transparency – ensure the outcome of all performance and conformance activities (reporting) is effectively communicated and has stakeholder approval;
- Performance – ensuring that we reach our goals and objectives;
- Ensure benefits realization.

These practices and principles define a governance process that is designed, built, executed, monitored and improved. Like most, if not all processes, the governance process is supported by:
- Policies;
- Plans;
- Metrics.

As a process, governance should be subject to all controls, checks and balances that any other process in an enterprise should be subjected to. Continual review of the performance of the process is appropriate. Governance is 'a' or even 'the' strategic process in the enterprise. It should be noted that strategic direction implies that ALL parts of the organization respond to the direction given, including organizational capabilities like HR, Finance, IT, marketing etc. Too often organizations fail to reach their strategic intent, goals and objectives because some of the organization's capabilities fail to follow the direction provided.

Real world example

Governance: anonymous

The leadership in an organization embraced the principles of Agile and mandated that executive managers actively work towards becoming an 'Agile organization'. Executive and middle managers of most core activities in the organization recognized the potential gains of this initiative and started an aggressive training and coaching program.

Staff members found the transition very difficult. 'Passage talk' was that management was just paying lip service to Agile because in practice the organization just couldn't function as an agile organization.

Upon investigation, it was found that some organizational capabilities like HR were still using outmoded thinking in terms of role definitions, performance appraisals, training and development plans. They had become the key obstacle in the move towards agility.

A few middle/line-function managers purposefully obstructed the new way of working as they feared a loss of stature in the organization.

It was also found that the sales team also didn't like 'this Agile idea'. For them, it meant that 'overpromising', 'order gorging' and selling impractical 'grand schemes' would be quickly identified and rectified. This led to some sales being cancelled by customers. A move to iterative delivery changed how sales commission was calculated. Previously, commission was based on a percentage of the deal and paid up-front – it has subsequently changed to be a higher percentage but based on invoices paid as value is unlocked for customers.

The remedy for the situation was to look again at all areas of the organization and for management to remove impediments. These included restrictive front-line decision-making capability, stopping 'grand schemes' at source, changing rigid role definitions, abandoning improper performance evaluations and replacing them with 360° reviews reflecting the new way of working. This included focusing on working in cross-functional teams, defining new role definitions and performance criteria for everyone in the organization and delegating authority as close as possible to where work is done.

Results soon improved.

From a product or service perspective the EDM process should ensure well-documented and communicated direction which reflects the organizational strategy. This could include answering the following questions:

- What is our target market, or who are our customers?
- What is our value proposition (and how does it differ from our competitors)?
- Which products and services could provide a competitive advantage?
- Which capabilities are required to enable and excel at these products and services?

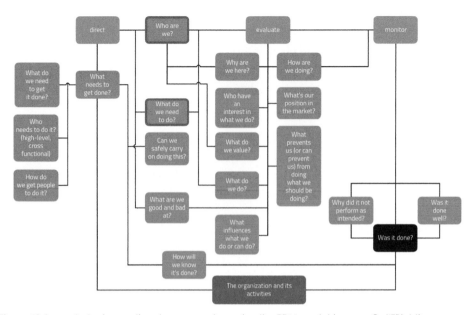

Figure 45 Some strategic questions to answer when using the EDM model (source: GetITRight)

At the outset of this section the EDM model was used as a straw-man around which an enterprise can answer a set of questions to identify and communicate strategic direction. It can also be used to evaluate the effectiveness of the direction and the effectiveness of the entire enterprise's response to the direction given. Figure 45 shows a high-level example of this straw-man. This isn't a prescriptive example but does provide meaningful insight into the 'job' of the governing body. Whilst 'governance' and 'strategy' are not new concepts in the digital age, it is worth remembering the importance of asking and answering strategic and tactical questions before the leadership of an organization attempts to define strategic goals and objectives related to digital initiatives.

Although the digital age requires a different mindset, many of the basic elements, techniques and tools used to devise a strategy remain. What is in the strategy and the way we approach the realization of the strategy will change. Some organizations choose a gradual approach and others a more radical strategic intervention. The method chosen is up to the organization and may be influenced by the competitive circumstances the organization faces.

10.5.2 Evaluate
The purpose of the 'evaluate' activities is for the leadership in the organization to have a deep understanding of the organization, its value proposition, its performance and its context before they make decisions. Part of evaluation is a more general understanding of the market in which the organization operates, competitors that the organization has, the legal, social and environmental landscape in which it finds itself, etc. Emerging technology also needs to be considered. Evaluation is also

focused on the current situation of the organization based on approved plans and directives given previously.

The outcome of the evaluate stage is a clear understanding of the action that needs to follow, and direction required to be given. Put simply – "If you do not know what you do not know, you will make bad decisions!"

Entering the digital age means that organizations need a much better understanding of their consumers and their changing needs. Organizations also need to have high visibility of competitors and how they shape consumer behavior. Evaluation may need to be carried out more frequently in the world of constant change.

10.5.3 Direct

The purpose of the 'direct' activities is to create and deploy strategies and define objectives and policies to ensure that the organization meets its goals and objectives. In a VeriSM model this will shape the Service Management Principles, support the identification of possible new products and services and the constant re-evaluation of services and products. The decisions made here are the key input into the organizational portfolio which serves as one of the three pillars of all work that management perform and the way the organization chooses to respond to direction given.

The main outputs of the direct stage are:
- Organizational principles;
- Goals and objectives;
- Policies;
- The organizational portfolio.

10.5.4 Monitor

'Monitor' aims to ensure that directives given were acted upon, policies set were followed (conformance) and to review performance against set strategies, objectives, targets and just as importantly the intended outcomes that motivated the initial direction. Monitoring is further used as a means to course-correct, ensuring continual alignment to goals, objectives, policies and plans.

There is no real change to 'what' monitoring does in a digital age. The 'how' of monitoring though needs fundamental changes. Monitoring can no longer happen at yearly or quarterly board meetings or even monthly meetings. A month in the digital age is like a year in the industrial age – by then knowing about a problem, trend, new competitor, lost customer or bad customer experience is too late.

■ 10.6 GOVERNANCE QUESTIONS

VeriSM identifies four strategic questions that leaders and members of governing bodies need to answer to ensure proper enterprise governance, but also more specifically to govern in terms of the delivery of products and services by an enterprise to its customers. The questions are:

1. Who are we?
2. What influences what we can do?
3. What do we do?
4. Who do we do it for?

10.6.1 Question one – Who are we?

"Know thyself" is a Delphic maxim and the most valuable thing any person or organization can do. Socrates said that "an unexamined life is not worth living", the reason being that self-understanding provides the basis for decision making.

One can ask questions like:

■ Why do we exist as an organization; what is our purpose?
■ What are our fundamental beliefs and values?
■ How will we make the world a better place?

These fundamental values and beliefs (wittingly or unwittingly) shape everything an organization does and are usually expressed in a number of ways. The most obvious is the organization's vision and mission statements and values and principles, but they will also be reflected in its goals, objectives and policies, the products and services it provides, the way that it becomes part of its community, the way it treats customers and just as importantly the way it treats its employees.

> An organization that knows itself is less likely to make poor strategic decisions based on fashion, or 'what everyone else is doing'. This is particularly relevant when adopting emerging technologies, which must be used to meet a strategic objective, not just because 'it is cool'.
>
> The increase in Corporate Social Responsibility (CSR) initiatives shows that organizations recognize the need to show their consumers 'who they are', as digital products and services remove face to face interaction. For example, Xerox has a Community Involvement Program. In 2013 alone, they allocated more than $1.3 million to allow 13,000 employees to participate in community causes. The benefit for Xerox comes from happier employees, community recognition and a story to share with their consumers.

Values and principles determine the boundaries within which an organization is willing and comfortable to operate. These values and principles determine organizational culture and are a guide to strategic direction, tactics, and operations.

Values become the foundation on which principles can be defined. Principles cascade into general organizational principles and more specific principles that deal with a particular area.

But what are values? How do we know what our values are? How do we communicate and share values? How do we ensure that the organization acts according to its values? The values of the organization define the identity of the organization. They are the manifestation of an organization's philosophy and beliefs. Values are made explicit by identifying and describing the core principles of an organization. The values of an organization support its vision and shape organizational culture and behavior. It would be difficult for an organization to define its principles, strategy, objectives, business models, structure, and products and services, unless its core values are determined.

The values of an organization need to be made explicit and shared with employees and customers. They can affect who will do business with the organization and its ability to attract a competent workforce.

So how can an organization identify and define its core values? Jim Collins of 'Good to Great' fame has the following to say on this topic.

"The Mars Group works like this: Imagine you've been asked to recreate the very best attributes of your organization on another planet, but you only have seats on the rocket ship for five to seven people. Who would you send?

They are the people who are likely to be exemplars of the organization's core values and purpose, have the highest level of credibility with their peers, and the highest levels of competence.

One method is to have all the people involved in the process nominate a Mars group of five to seven individuals (not all need to come from the assembled group), and those most nominated become members."

The Mars Group will be asked to answer the following questions:
• What are the core values that you hold to be fundamental regardless of whether or not they are awarded?
• If you woke up tomorrow morning with enough money to retire for the rest of your life, would you continue to hold on to these core values?
• Can you envision these values being as valid 100 years from now as they are today?
• Would you want the organization to continue to hold these values, even if at some point, they became a competitive disadvantage?
• If you were to start a new organization tomorrow in a different line of work, would you build the core values into the new organization regardless of its activities?

Collins recommends that the Mars Group does not include top management or executives. Instead, they should respond to the output of the Mars Group to create a final articulation of values.

To answer the remaining questions (how we share values and make sure people subscribe to the values), consider the following:

- The vision, mission, strategy, goals, objectives, principles, services and products and policy all need to reflect an organization's values;
- The aforementioned are also the instruments that will be used to ensure that everyone in the organization acts according to the core values of the organization.

An individual does not necessarily have to subscribe to all core values of the organization (though it is best if they do) but they do have to act according to the values to remain a member of the organization.

Ben and Jerry's ice cream: value statement
"We strive to minimize our negative impact on the environment.

We strive to show a deep respect for human beings inside and outside our company and for the communities in which they live.

We seek and support nonviolent ways to achieve peace and justice. We believe government resources are more productively used in meeting human needs than in building and maintaining weapons systems.

We strive to create economic opportunities for those who have been denied them and to advance new models of economic justice that are sustainable and replicable.

We support sustainable and safe methods of food production that reduce environmental degradation, maintain the productivity of the land over time, and support the economic viability of family farms and rural communities."

Adidas: value statement
"Performance: Sport is the foundation for all we do, and executional excellence is a core value of our Group.

Passion: Passion is at the heart of our company. We are continuously moving forward, innovating, and improving.

Integrity: We are honest, open, ethical, and fair. People trust us to adhere to our word.

> Diversity: We know it takes people with different ideas, strengths, interests, and cultural backgrounds to make our company succeed. We encourage healthy debate and differences of opinion."

Values are made explicit by identifying and describing the core principles of an organization. These principles define the boundaries in which it is willing and comfortable to operate. Values and principles determine organizational culture and guide strategic direction, tactics, and operations. Managers must cascade principles to every level in the organization. This ensures that the principles used in the workplace support practice or domain principles which in turn support organizational principles that are in line with and support the values, goals and objectives of the organization, as shown in Figure 46.

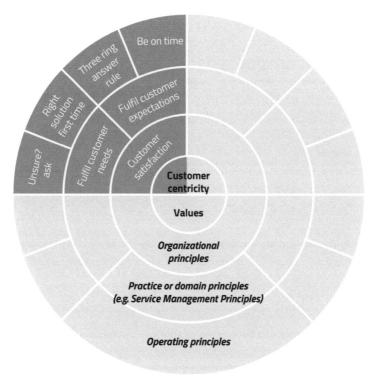

Figure 46 An example of the cascading levels of principles guiding behavior

Service Management Principles
In the VeriSM model, Service Management Principles are defined at the organizational level. These principles act as the guardrails for product and service teams, allowing them to work with progressive management practices and use emerging technologies within defined boundaries.

> **Definitions: service and Service Management Principles**
>
> **Service**: "fulfilment of a defined consumer need"
>
> **Service Management Principles:** "high level requirements that apply across all products and services, providing 'guardrails' for the Management Mesh."

Within the VeriSM model, Service Management Principles apply to all products and services. They are based on information cascaded from the strategic level and the resultant objectives of the organization, so new or changed products or services need to align with these principles.

The cascading example in Figure 46 shows how principles can be defined in organizations and made practicable at an operational level. It is essential to ensure that principles at one level are aligned to principles at superordinate levels, and at the highest level that governing, strategic or organizational principles are aligned with the values, goals, and objectives of the organization. It is for this reason that VeriSM cannot give organizations a single exemplar list of Service Management Principles. Each organization has to develop its Service Management Principles based on its governing principles – see the example below.

> **Real world example**
> **Principle in the development and design space**
> PRINCIPLE 1. Customer-centricity (Shift Left)
>
> Principle: Service queries, requests and difficulties will be handled by the "earliest team" possible
>
> Rationale: This will speed up resolution and avoid the involvement of specialist expertise where it is not necessary. This will result in greater productivity for all and reduced support costs
>
> Implications: We will have to adopt a Shift Left support model.
>
> The support model will encompass six levels of support (as defined by Gartner):
> • Level -2   Auto detection of potential issues and taking pre-emptive action. For example, in the Managed Print solution, low levels of printer toner generate an alert, more toner is ordered and installed before it runs out.
> • Level -1   Auto detection and resolution of issues before the user is aware
> • Level 0   Self-help, diagnostic tools, peer to peer support, use of the knowledge base and rich media
> • Level 1   First Line Support via a centralized Service Desk with access via multiple channels
> • Level 2   Second Line Support – the Service Desk refers the support ticket to specialists
> • Level 3   Third Line Support – more senior technical specialists or external parties

10.6.2 Question two – What influences what we can do?

There are a number of subjects that influence what we can do. These include internal capabilities, environmental constraints, legal constraints, the market in which we operate, risk, the availability of skills, suppliers, partners and our internal capability needs to be considered. Much of this is mapped in the Management Mesh, as described in Chapter 12.

PEST or PESTEL analysis

One of the simplest (and most widely used tools) for environmental analysis is PEST or PESTEL analysis. PESTEL analysis evaluates the Political, Economic, Social, Technological, Legal and Environmental factors that may influence an organizational strategy.

Organizations need to ask:

- What is the political situation of the country or countries we operate in and how can it affect our industry?
- What are the prevalent economic factors?
- How much importance does culture have in the market and what are its determinants?
- What technological innovations are likely to pop up and affect the market structure? This is particularly important for digital products and services;
- Are there any current legislations that regulate the industry, or can there be any change in the legislations for the industry?
- What are the environmental concerns for the industry?

Organizations also need a view of their internal capability and performance to be able to answer the question asked here. Good benchmarking data is always helpful in answering this question (even if it is only partially available). The problem is that in most markets and many industries good benchmarks are not readily available of just not affordable for most players. In the absence of good benchmarking information (which will be the case for most industries and markets), organizations need to find a way to make sense of their position in the market and state of the market. Many tools and techniques exist to have a view of this – some with better results than others.

Real world example

Uber

It can be challenging to understand legislation that might affect digital products and services, particularly if they are very innovative. Legislation may not exist and might be created after a product or service is launched.

For example, in South Africa, the transport department has said Uber operators need to get properly licensed and apply for operating permits after Uber started operating in the country. South African transport minister Joe Maswanganyi said licensing Uber operators means they will have a specific route or radius on which they will operate. "If you have a permit you are given a specific route, you do not operate everywhere," he said. The legal requirements set could negate the whole Uber model in South Africa.[65]

SWOT analysis

Most organizations have done SWOT (or TOWS) analysis before. This technique combines internal and external evaluation. SWOT/TOWS analysis also gives a view of an organization's position in the market. SWOT/TOWS do have a distinct risk; they are prone to bias and subjectivity from the practitioners using the method. The result of a SWOT analysis may give the leadership a view of the organization as they see it. The question is: how would this result look if one asked a competitor or customer to do the same analysis?

Porter's 5 Forces

Other techniques like Porter's 5 Forces may be better suited to make sense of an organization's position in a competitive market. The questions asked in the Porter model are more specific and allow practitioners to look for evidence to substantiate the answers given to the questions asked, as shown in Figure 47.

Figure 47 Porter's 5 Forces

Porter's 5 Forces analysis does more than look at an organization's direct competitors. It looks at multiple aspects of the industry's competitive structure and economic

---

65 K, A. (2017, July 10). *Uber operators must apply for operating licences – Transport minister*, (Online). https://www.timeslive.co.za/news/south-africa/2017-07-10-uber-operators-must-apply-for-operating-licences-transport-minister/

environment, which includes the bargaining power of buyers and suppliers, the threat of new entrants, and the threat of substitute products.

The example in Table 6 is not exhaustive – but it shows a starting point.

Table 6 Porter's 5 Forces

Force	Questions to ask
How easy it is for someone to enter your market?	How much does it cost and how long does it take to enter your market?
	What are the barriers to entry (e.g., patents, legislation, etc.)?
	Have you protected your key technologies?
How easy can customers replace your product or service with another that solves the same requirement? How likely are they to do so?	What are the differentiators between your product/service and the substitute?
	How many substitute products are available in this market?
	What is the cost of switching to a substitute product?
	How difficult would it be to make the switch?
	What products or services can you offer that might substitute a market leader?
How easily could suppliers increase their prices and thus affect your bottom line?	How many suppliers does your organization have?
	How unique is the product or service that they provide?
	How many alternative suppliers can you find?
	How do their prices compare to your current supplier? How expensive would it be to switch from one supplier to another?
Do buyers have the power to drive your prices down?	How many buyers control your sales?
	How large are the orders you receive?
	Could your buyers switch suppliers—and how much would it cost for them to switch?
	How important is your product/service to your buyers (i.e. what is the ROI of your product/service)?

Force	Questions to ask
Rivalry is influenced by all other forces. Specifically, look at the number and strength of your existing competitors.	How many competitors do you have?
	Who are your biggest competitors?
	How does the quality of their products or services compare with yours?
	What distinguishes your organization from the competition?
	What will it cost one of your customers to switch to a competitor?

Porter's 5 Forces remains a critical management tool, and in the digital age, remains valid. Being able to evaluate an organization's market position becomes even more critical now, as technology removes many traditional barriers to entry.

Whatever tools and techniques are used, even multiple sources of information or techniques do not give one hundred percent accuracy. Leaders also need to have a clear view of the organization's environment and factors outside its control. They may not have control over environmental and political factors, but they certainly need to deal with the uncertainty and associated risk they can bring.

Risk

Understanding and managing risk is one of the most complex areas executives need to deal with. Being risk adverse stifles growth; being oblivious to risk can lead to real damage.

What is risk?

ISO 31000 defines risk as follows: "the effect of uncertainty on objectives". This an extremely effective way of looking at risk. Risks are the things that will/may stand in the way of an organization reaching its goals and objectives. Risks are any and all the speed-bumps, roadblocks or road closures between where an organization is and where it wants to be in future.

Every organization need to define its own stance toward risk management by:
- Defining risk appetite
- Defining a method to analyze and manage risk

To be able to do this, executives need a thorough understanding of the environment they operate in, specifically the legal and regulatory requirements that applies to the organization. Risk appetite cannot exceed statuary and regulatory requirements.

A fundamental choice that organizations need to make is which risk management approach will best suite their environment.

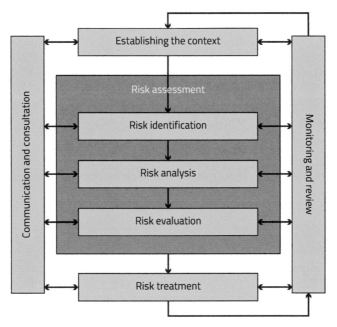

Figure 48 ISO 31000 risk management approach (source: ISO)

The choice of a risk management method is heavily influenced by the culture of the organization and specific compliance needs. ISO 31000 provides a very good approach to managing risk that is easily adapted to the specific circumstances of the organization (see Figure 48). It allows for different means of risk identification, assessment and treatment.

Some common identification methods include:
- **Objectives-based** – any event that may endanger achieving an objective is identified as risk;
- **Scenario-based** – based on different scenarios risks are identified and alternatives sought for any event that may trigger an undesired effect. This becomes a great input into strategy;
- **Taxonomy-based** – a breakdown of possible risk sources, where questionnaires are commonly used to identify risk;
- **Common-industry risk checks** – lists of known risks are available for many industries and often used. They do sometimes create a feeling of risk where there is no risk, or lead organizations to miss critical risks that are not on the checklist;
- **Risk charting** – risk charting starts by listing resources/assets at risk, threats to those resources/assets and then identifying factors which may increase or decrease the risk and consequences.

Once risks are identified they need to be evaluated based on the possible effect on the organization. Methods need to be identified to either mitigate or reduce the risk and any residual risks needs to be accepted or go through further analysis and treatment activities.

The most common approach to managing risk is to implement controls that would either lessen the effect of the risk once materialized, reduce the likelihood of the risk materializing, act as early detection or warning systems and quite often attempt to modify behavior. The implementation of effective controls is not simple, and organizations often implement excessive control regimes where simple controls would have been enough. Excessive controls are usually based on the illusion of control[66] – the tendency for people to overestimate their ability to control events by putting measure in place that in reality makes little of no difference.

There are two concepts concerning risk management that are used widely to quantify risk and the effect of risk control:
■ Risk = severity × probability
■ Residual risk = (untreated) risk – impact of risk controls

The residual risk is the amount of risk left over after untreated risks have been reduced by risk controls.

The reality is that control landscapes should heed a core tenet of VeriSM (and Lean), that **just enough** control is ideal – beyond this tipping point more controls actually makes the control landscape less effective[67].

Risk management today is mainly practiced as a quantitative fixation, maybe this came with our fixation with quantifiable evidence and our fixation with analysis and metrics. However – no matter how hard we try, effective risk management is as much an art as it is a science. We need to compliment statistical and quantitative methods with the use of heuristics to be truly effective.

Using heuristic controls

A heuristic technique is any approach to problem solving, learning, or discovery that employs a practical method not guaranteed to be optimal or perfect, but sufficient for the immediate goals. Heuristics are simple rules/methods which can be used to make decisions – they are mental shortcuts that help staff members deal with the realization of a risk for which no control was defined, or for those where the defined control failed to have the desired effect. It is often said that something is 'just common sense' – these topics are ideal candidates for heuristic controls.

---

66 Thompson, S. C. (1999). Illusions of control: How we overestimate our personal influence, *Current Directions in Psychological Science*, **8**(6): 187–190.
67 Ciborra, C. U., Braa, K., Cordella, A., Dahlbom, B., Failla, A., Hanseth, O., Hepsø, V., Ljungberg, J., Monteiro, E., & Simon, K. A. (2000). *From control to drift – dynamics of corporate information infrastructures*. New York: Oxford.

> **Heuristic control example**
>
> During the Napoleonic Wars, Doctor Dominique Jean Larrey defined the base principles of what is today known as triage. The concept was developed by French doctors during World War when treating battlefield wounded at the aid stations close to the front line. Medics who evacuate casualties wounded at the front or those who looked after the wounded at front-line aid stations would divide the wounded into three categories:
>
> - Those who are likely to live, regardless of what care they receive;
> - Those who are unlikely to live, regardless of what care they receive;
> - Those who will likely survive if they receive immediate care.
>
> Immediate effort was given to the third category as it logically is the category where medics and doctors can make the biggest difference. Common sense one would presume but emotionally and in real life this is very difficult to do.
>
> Defining a heuristic control that mandates emergency staff to act this way makes it easier for care-givers to act in a manner where the outcomes would be meaningful.
>
> With the advent of more sophisticated technology and computational capabilities scientific models emerged based on the principles defined in triage, these algorithm-based controls are still at their core heuristic controls, just more sophisticated with a higher likelihood of success.

The role of policy

Policy gives direction and provides a means for defining actions and controls. Policy is a means of giving direction to the organization and acts as a strategic tool to ensure that the organization reaches its goals and objectives. Policies can be used to give direction but also to ensure control.

Policy provides overarching guidance that is intended to influence behaviors and actions within an organization. Unlike procedures that answer the question of 'how', a policy answers the strategic questions 'what' and 'why' it is important to address the topic. (Note that policy addresses the strategic 'what' and not the tactical 'what' – that is the domain of plans.)

How does policy provide control of an organization?
- Good policies have ownership – ownership at the right level provides the authority needed to implement and enforce the terms of the policy. This results in actions such as process definition, to produce the controls required to enforce the policy.
- Good policies articulate the expected benefits from following the policy – providing insight into the positive results of compliance delivers some level of control over the behaviors and actions within the organization.
- Good policies articulate the consequences of not following or adhering to the policy – the consequences of non-compliance could be tangible, such as loss of

a job, regulation violation, or loss of revenue. Intangible consequences of non-compliance may include loss of reputation or brand damage. In either event, the negative aspects or consequences from non-compliance provide controls to the organization.

■ Good policies provide the basis for measurement – by understanding the reason for the policy, measures can be defined within resulting procedures that enable further action to be taken to enforce or comply with the policy.

■ A good policy is simple, concise, and broadly communicated – awareness of policy by individuals within the organization provides a level of control.

Governance structures

The last important element for ensuring proper control from a strategic perspective is to formally define lines of communication and opportunities for internal role players to interact. This is typically done to ensure strategic direction is appropriately communicated throughout the organization, to ensure that the right role-players are part of decision making, and to provide a means for formal feedback, status reporting and the ability to course-correct.

In more traditional settings this may include defining and scheduling meetings for these interactions to occur, and for each of these meetings to have a core group of attendees that almost always take part. Examples are:

■ Executive committee meeting;
■ Project steering board;
■ Risk committee;
■ Architecture board;
■ Operations meeting, etc.

Although many of these may still be appropriate, the means of communication change as organizations adopt principles from Lean and Agile. Commitment to these principles inevitably leads to changes in structures, communication, decision making, and control.

Using Hoshin Kanri concepts to define governance structures

One example of this change in structures is what Lean strategic planning called Hoshin Kanri (often defined as Policy Deployment or Catch Ball). For now, all we want to do is to highlight that defining a cascade for strategic intent ensures that everyone in the organization works together to the achievement of mission, values, and vision set by the organization (see Figure 49).

If this is combined with other Lean principles around management behavior, the outcome is that management spends about 50% of their time with subordinates ensuring that higher level objectives are broken down and assigned to lower levels and cascaded objectives are acted upon (as tasks or projects/sprints). Of the remaining time, managers should spend roughly 25 to 30% of their time doing day-to-day work like planning, reporting, or other standard management tasks. The rest of their time is spent with their colleagues to ensure superordinate goals and objectives are coordinated and controlled (therefore getting rid of segmented governance structures and focusing on business issues end to end).

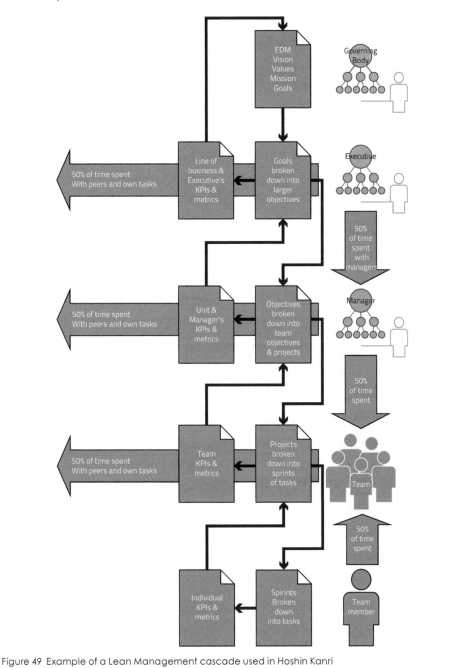

Figure 49 Example of a Lean Management cascade used in Hoshin Kanri

10.6.3 Question three – What do we do?

Once an organization has determined what it stands for, it needs to define the reason for its existence. Organizations do this by defining a vision and mission.

The main difference between these two statements is time. Although both become guiding principles, mostly at a strategic and tactical levels, vison statements define the organization wants to become, whilst mission statements define what the organization needs to do today.

Although these two terms are often used interchangeably this difference in focus means that they should be used differently; particularly the mission statement which becomes a vital starting point for organizational strategy.

Mission statements are written at a high level and need to define:
- What we do;
- Who we do it for;
- How we do that.

Vision statements are inspirational and define:
- What our hopes and dreams are;
- How we plan to make the world a better place.

Chapter 9 – Transformation techniques provided examples of how tools and techniques can be used to identify new strategies for the organization – this section focuses on product and service strategies.

Defining a vision statement is an ongoing process for any organization – remember the vision is the dream for the organization. Perhaps start by writing a simple vision statement which will evolve over time. Ask the governing body of the organization to fill in the blanks as a starting point: In XXX years from now, the organization will (be) YYY by (doing at a high level) ZZZ. The use of the Mars Group approach (see Section 10.6.1) may also be an appropriate technique to define or at least draft vision statements.

Mission statements talk about purpose and will similarly evolve over time. Mission statements are a means of communicating; they define what the organization does for its customers, employees, community, and owners.

Real world example

"We're a company of pioneers. It's our job to make bold bets, and we get our energy from inventing on behalf of customers. Success is measured against the possible, not the probable. For today's pioneers, that's exactly why there's no place on Earth they'd rather build than Amazon.com." (note the focus on who we are)

Amazon

Because mission statements are a means of informing and giving direction, they should not be written to sound impressive with a lot of buzz-words. They must convey practical and actionable meaning.

Here are some questions that will help clarify the why behind your mission statement[68]:
- Why are you in business?
- Who are your customers?
- What image of your business do you want to convey?
- What is the nature of your products and services?
- What level of service do you provide?
- What roles do you and your employees play?
- What kind of relationships will you maintain with suppliers?
- How do you differ from your competitors?

To define a basic mission statement, try the following exercise:
- We are……
- We provide (products and services) …
- We do x for our customers (repeat for all stakeholders that are to be included)
- This is what sets us apart or make us different…

Real world example

Amazon's mission statement: To be earth's most customer-centric company, where customers can find and discover anything they might want to buy online, and endeavors to offer its customers the lowest possible prices.

Based on existing strategic direction. the leadership also from time to time need to validate what the organization currently does and how well it does this. This evaluation serves two purposes:
- It provided a baseline for evaluation of previous performance;
- It gives a baseline against which to measure improvements or changes in strategy.

"What we do?" revolves around the products and services an organization provides and the customers it provides products and services to. A current baseline of products and services needs to be evaluated. This is information is then stored in the organizational portfolio.

---

68 (2003, October 30). *How to write your mission statement*, (Online). https://www.entrepreneur.com/article/65230 [2018 January].

At this early stage of evaluation, the question should not be "what should we do?" – it is merely a baseline to facilitate later formulation of strategic direction. It may also be meaningful at this time to have some measure of how well products and services perform in the market and how well the organization is selling and supporting these products and services.

Understanding internal capabilities is of vital importance but unfortunately, not a simple process. Information about the capabilities and competencies of an organization as a whole includes a complex web of individual, organizational, structural, and process capability and competencies.

> CEOs often say, "That's not our core competency". But if you ask what is, they will list their products or services. Surely our products and services are a result of competency or capabilities and not a definition of them?

There are many indicators of competency and capability, and diverse tools and techniques to help understand them. For example, carrying out a SWOT analysis will help to identify some of these at a high level. Probably the best and least complex assessment of organizational competency and capability is to simply ask our consumers, our staff and even our competitors what we do well and what do we do poorly. Organizations can assess scientifically by using a behavioral specialist to design and build the assessment instrument. This ensures minimum bias and a good understanding of the social context in which the instrument will be used. Financial analysis also contributes to an understanding of the current position. Financial trends and ratio analysis prove very insightful.

At the very least, consider the following:
- Ratio analysis (and if a listed company, comparison with competitors);
- Consumption and production metrics and ratios (especially in lean environments where many traditional financial management ratios are of less value);
- Trending;
- Correlation to current and future market predictions;
- Very importantly, correlation of past assumptions and predictions to what actually transpired.

Finance is not the only part of the business that should be evaluated here, also think HR such as staff retention, skills, management structures, performance data, education, among others.

The strategic direction of an organization is a natural outflow of stakeholder expectations and needs. All stakeholders in some way or another influence strategic direction and the products and services an organization offers. In a digitally transformed world the needs and experiences of the consumer are the most important determinant of strategy, not the desires of shareholders and owners.

A big disadvantage of a digital world is the low switch-cost between services and service providers (remember to consider this trend when carrying out Porter's 5 Forces analysis). The consumer has become the most important stakeholder, maybe they always were. There is an expression "If you look after your customers, they will look after the bank."

Defining service goals and objectives

In his book *The Practice of Management*[69], Peter Drucker declares "there is only one purpose of a business: to create a customer".

Organizations use products or services to attract consumers.

It is absolutely astounding if one looks at traditional business literature regarding strategy how little emphasis is placed on product and services. It is as if it is assumed that the organization has products or services that customers want; therefore, they have customers, and all the organization needs to do is strategize about how to get products or services to customers, on what basis will they compete, and which channels should be used. There is no denying that these things are essential but, without a product or service that a consumer needs or wants, there is no reason for the existence of the organization. Having products and services that customers want or need and knowing which customers want which product or service is at the heart of doing business in the digital age. No longer can an organization assume that "if you build it, they will come".[70]

A challenge
Go and look at your organization's strategy and see how far you need to read through the document before it defines who exactly your customers are and what your products and services are.

Similarly, pop-culture's fixation with "believing in your idea, prevailing in the face of difficulty and if you try hard enough you will succeed" is now even less true than it was before. Organizations need to learn how to innovate, test customer acceptance, and if it is not working move on to a new idea ruthlessly. Thomas H. Palmer[71], of the "If at first you do not succeed, try again" fame, was wrong. If at first

69 Drucker, P. (1954). *The Practice of Management*. New York: HarperBusiness.
70 Gordon, L., Gordon, C. (Producers) & Robinson, P. A. (Writer/Director). (1989). *Field of dreams [Motion picture]. United States: Universal Studios.*
71 Palmer, T. H. (1840). *The Teachers Manual*. Available: https://books.google.com/books/about/The_Teacher_s_Manual.html?id=hSABAAAAYAAJ

you do not succeed, understand why, and if you did not make a mistake, move on and try something else. Don't try again, that's the definition of insanity. Move on and stop justifying lousy decision making with 150-year-old literature – the world has moved on.

To redefine Drucker's words – there is only one purpose of a business: to create products or services that add value to consumers. The question now remains: do our goals and objectives define which services or products we provide OR do our products and services determine what our goals and objectives should be?

The reality (as shown in Figure 50) is that products and services reflect organizational mission and vision (and most probably values). How the organization ensures that these deliver value to customers should determine the organizational goals and objectives. This means that an organization cannot define its services unless it has defined who it is and what it does (vision and mission). Also, it cannot define its goals and objectives before it has defined how it will give credence to its vision and mission – therefore, before it has defined its products and services.

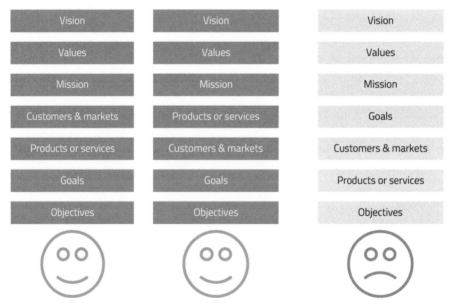

Figure 50 Products, services, customers, and markets drive strategy

Chapter 9 shared a lot of ideas on how better to understand customer/consumer needs and how best to define or improve products and services. It is at this stage of the governance cycle that all that we shared in that chapter becomes important. Note that the outcomes of the above cascade are described in the organizational portfolio.

10.6.4 Question four – Who do we do it for?

Stakeholders determine what organizations do and are the primary determinant of organizational strategy. Some stakeholders may be more important than others, and organizations are oblivious of their stakeholder landscape at their peril. It is better to define a broad stakeholder landscape and then narrow it down based on their influence on and importance to the organization. Doing a good job at defining stakeholders will also be of tremendous help when defining organizational strategy, goals and objectives and operating environment.

When identifying stakeholders, it may be helpful to create Affinity Diagrams to group stakeholders with similar requirements together, and then evaluate the importance of the stakeholder group. Only looking at individual stakeholder influence and not stakeholder group influence may lead to neglect of important groups. Most of the tools and techniques described in Chapter 9 focus on the consumer, their needs, wants, aspirations and requirements.

11 VeriSM described

Introduction

This chapter provides a high-level overview of the VeriSM approach and illustrates the evolution of the Management Mesh. Figure 51 shows this high-level approach. This diagram will be further expanded as each activity is discussed more fully in the following chapters.

As a reminder, do not skip the previous activities and discussions around enterprise governance, Service Management Principles and the Management Mesh. Jumping straight to a solution usually adds unnecessary risk and waste to the organization.

Case Studies: VeriSM applied

Chapter 19 includes case studies from three organizations who are adopting VeriSM including:
- 6point6 Cloud Gateway
- Kabu.com Securities Co., Ltd
- CITIC Tech

■ 11.1 THE HIGH-LEVEL VIEW

Governance (see Chapter 10) has been defined and the Service Management Principles outlined. Now what? The next step is to develop the enterprise view of the Management Mesh based on the organizational portfolio (see Section 10.4). Once that view has been created, adding new products or services or changing existing products or services becomes an exercise of following the four stages within the VeriSM model and evolving the Management Mesh.

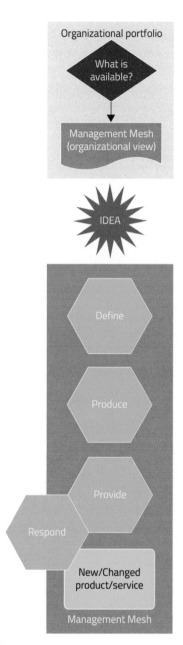

Figure 51 VeriSM – high-level view

Using Figure 51 and keeping the scenario simple, the activity starts with an idea for a new product or service. This scenario also applies to updating a product or service but for the sake of simplicity, this section illustrates a scenario based on a new product or service. Applying the VeriSM approach, these activities occur during the corresponding stages:

■ Define:
  • Approval;
  • Define the requirements;

- - Analysis and agreement;
  - Identify the gaps;
  - Source the gaps;
- ■ Produce:
  - Build, test, deploy;
- ■ Provide:
  - Protect, measure and maintain, improve;
- ■ Respond:
  - Record and manage requests, issues, and source events.

Note the ongoing interaction between the stage activities and the Management Mesh in Figure 51.

The outcome of the approach in this scenario is a new product or service. This will interact with the Management Mesh as it adds and consumes additional resources or has additional environmental, management or technological demands, thus, it will change the current view of the mesh.

Each of these steps is discussed in the next chapters. Note that additional information around the four main activities within the VeriSM approach can be found in *VeriSM™: A Service Management Approach for the Digital Age*.

Case study: readiness for VeriSM

How do you know if your organization is ready to address VeriSM? Satya Misra of HCL provides steps to assess organizational readiness in Appendix A.

Misra states, "Within the environment 'side', the service stabilizers are crucial as they include current operational processes, measurements and tools. Ensure there is an accurate understanding of the agility, effectiveness and efficiency of these elements."

■ 11.2 VERISM UNWRAPPED: THE FULL VIEW

This section, "VeriSM Unwrapped", is repeated throughout chapters 10-16 to illustrate generic examples of the outputs described within each chapter. Those outputs are then applied to a case study, FireCloud Health to provide a more detailed example (see the 'VeriSM applied' sections).

To view the full VeriSM model, refer to Figure 1. Figure 52 show a more detailed view of the activities specifically within the Define stage as well as connections to the other stages. One key takeaway at this point is this: The Define stage activities, supported by enterprise governance, the Service Management Principles and the

Management Mesh are critical elements for the build, test, deploy and support activities.

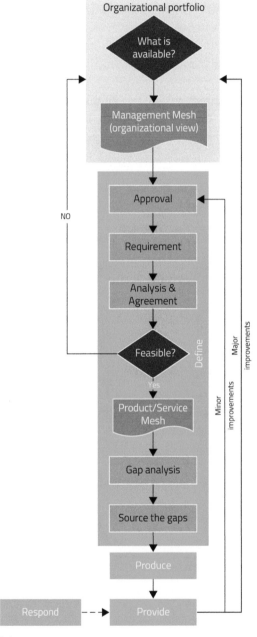

Figure 52 VeriSM – the full view

It is important to complete all steps as a new or changed product or service is delivered. Missing any steps creates a risk that something will be missing from the final output. Secondly, note the improvement cycles and their 're-entry' to the model. Services and products must improve continually.

Chapters 12 -17 describe each element.

◼ 11.3 VERISM APPLIED: FIRECLOUD HEALTH CASE STUDY

The FireCloud Health (FCH) case study (see Appendix B) is used to illustrate how a new initiative, the FCH Wearable Wellness program, would be managed using VeriSM. This case study provides background about FCH. When applied with the 'The Story', this sets up an ongoing VeriSM example. This example, the FCH Wearable Wellness program, will be used at the end of chapters 12-16 to apply the specific concepts from each chapter.

The story

Continuing with the VeriSM approach, a strategic retreat was held recently. FCH leadership defined several areas where growth could occur within the organization. Following an exercise using Porter's Five Competitive Forces (see Appendix D), the proactive community health programming was seen as a priority for FCH (a strategic initiative) that would have immediate impact across multiple FCH capabilities and consumers. The initiative includes an FCH-branded wearable device and a fitness/healthy lifestyle program. This will be developed by the FCH Wellness Center, one of the many outreach programs at FCH. The timeframe for the initial deployment (a pilot) is in the next six months.

The idea is that the wearable device will collect various vital sign measurements (heart rate (resting and during activity), respiration, blood pressure...), activity levels (land or water-based), and sleep patterns. This data would be transmitted in real time and then be available to Wellness Center staff. Using Artificial Intelligence (AI) and Big Data capabilities, each individual is automatically monitored. Within the program, a safety feature will be included to submit warnings to the individual (for example, if they exceed their maximum heart rate for longer than 3 minutes) and to the medical staff (warnings to nursing staff if unhealthy conditions are noted).

Online feedback detailing the participant's health efforts is provided with the reports focusing on four different recipient groups:
- ◼ The participant;
- ◼ Wellness program monitoring staff;
- ◼ The participants physician;
- ◼ FCH Insurance Wellness program.

Additionally, the FCH Wearable will also monitor overall health and suggest when a doctor's appointment may be necessary.

The program is to be piloted with a representative sample (adults, 35-45 years of age) taken from current FCH Health Insurance policyholders. During the pilot, a volunteer group from the FCH Wellness program will be monitoring and receiving participant data. This group includes two physicians and four other Wellness Program staff (nurses, physical therapists, fitness trainers and instructors). One member of the FCH Insurance group will be monitoring the program and assessing the impact to the insurance policy offerings.

For more information on how these decisions were made:
- Working within the retreat – see Chapter 4
- What it means to be a digital organization – See Chapter 3.1
- Digital products and services – see Chapter 3.4
- Collaboration – see Chapter 6.1
- Teamwork – see Chapter 6.4
- Defining outcomes – see Chapter 8

12 The Management Mesh

> **Introduction**
>
> The Management Mesh represents the available resources, the current environment, available management practices and emerging technologies of the organization (the enterprise view). Before developing a new or changed product or service, an accurate view of the current mesh must be available. This view will change over time due to changes to products and services, changes in the organization, the environment, and technological advances. Creating this view is not a one-time activity – effort should be made to ensure it remains up-to-date.
>
> This chapter discusses the development of the Management Mesh.

■ 12.1 WHAT IS IT?

The Management Mesh (Figure 53) represents the various elements that influence or directly contribute to product and service delivery. For digital products and services, many organizations allow (or require) their IT department to define these elements and all products and services have to conform. In today's digital environment, the organization must recognize that new technologies and practices will continue to evolve, and they must be able to exploit them, as needed. All organizational capabilities need to be involved and have input into the mesh elements. The mesh provides the means to capture these elements and integrate them into the overall operating model.

Divided into four areas, the mesh provides the flexibility to use and exploit the multitude of management practices available today as well as emerging technologies, while maintaining a close tie to the organizational environment and resources. The mesh provides the flexibility to 'mold' itself to requirements while staying true to the enterprise governance, principles and organizational portfolio. It allows the organization to continually evolve and transform, rather than being 'stuck' in one way of working.

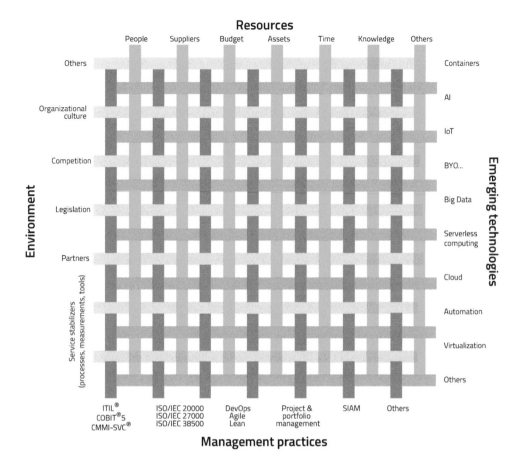

Figure 53 The Management Mesh

The mesh provides an enterprise view of the service provider. Captured artifacts include organizational-wide resources (people, budget, skills, knowledge...) and environmental operating factors (legal and regulatory requirements, competition, current operational practices...). The resources and the environment 'sides' are a direct outcome of the guardrails defined within the Service Management Principles. These two sides will influence the management practices as well as the technologies used to meet the requirements.

When discussing the Management Mesh, there is a tendency to concentrate on the more tangible sides of the mesh: the resources, management practices, tools and technologies. Remember that part of the mesh also deals with the more strategic choices of the organization and the overall guidance and direction of the organization. Thus, part of the mesh addresses practices relating to the *environment* – the way the organization operates, the methods that support how strategy is determined, and how governance is provided. While these elements are not specifically called out in the mesh, they are reflected in the organizational culture, partnerships, and how the organization defines its competition.

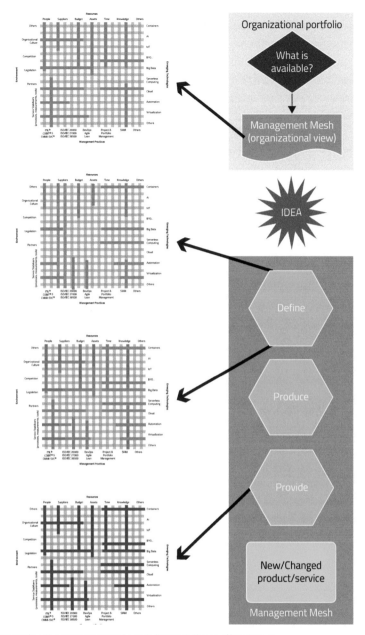

Figure 54 Progressing the Management Mesh through the VeriSM stages

◼ 12.2 HOW IS THE MANAGEMENT MESH USED?

As described in the previous section, the primary view of the mesh looks at the whole organization. That view must remain current, evolving and being updated as the organization evolves. The mesh is applied as each new (or changed) product or service progresses through the VeriSM approach (see Figure 55). However, it is important to understand that the mesh is not generically applied to each product or service (e.g., "We have these elements, this is what we must use.") but rather, choices are made to manage the new or changed product or service based on the requirements and the availability of service provider capabilities. Thus, a view of the mesh that provides an individual product or service view develops based on the requirements.

To illustrate this concept of an enterprise view and a product or service view, note the change in the mesh as indicated by the four high-level, stylized mesh illustrations in Figure 54. The length of a colored line reflects a measure of *quantity* of that element (e.g., a number or an amount of "something"). It is critical that the service provider pre-define how to interpret these lines based on their organizational need and representation. For example, in the first mesh view, review the length of the lines associated with the Service Stabilizers (processes, measurements and tools). The line for processes indicate a level of maturity, while the tools line indicates several tools. The measurements line is quite short, indicating small number of captured measurements. Interpret the four mesh views in Figure 54 as follows:

■ The first mesh picture, organizational mesh (green lines), is the illustrative view of what is current in the entire organization;
■ The second mesh (red lines) is the outcome of a review of the requirements of a new product or service (product or service mesh view). The red lines illustrate items that are needed to deliver the new product or service;
■ The third mesh (red and green lines) combines the first two (organizational mesh and the product or service mesh) and shows the 'gaps' (the gap would be the pure red line). The organization must now find a way to source those gaps. If a red and green line overlap (shown as a brown line), the service provider would need to assess if the specific element is available or if it needs to be sourced to deliver additional capacity, resources or capabilities (assessing *within* the element);
■ The fourth mesh (blue lines) illustrates the new organizational mesh (updated current enterprise view) reflecting the inclusion of elements from the new or changed product or service.

Each of these steps is discussed in the next chapters 13 through 17. Note that additional information around the four main activities within the VeriSM approach can be found in *VeriSM™: A Service Management Approach for the Digital Age.*

Visualizing the Management Mesh

For an example of how the Management Mesh might look as part of a software tool, see Chapter 28 – Sollertis Convergence.

"Whilst in many organizations and software tools, this connection to strategy and business outcomes is either presumed or inferred, within Convergence, it is placed at the heart of the design."

■ 12.3 CREATING THE CURRENT VIEW OF THE MANAGEMENT MESH – WHAT IS AVAILABLE?

Before starting any activity, it is important to know what is available. Start by defining and understanding the organizational resources and move ***counterclockwise*** around the mesh (see Figure 55). Define the elements within the environment, then management practices and end with emerging technologies. This order of activities is recommended for a digitally transforming organization. This type of organization combines organizational strategy with technology elements, so jumping straight to technology introduces the risk that something is missed, as well as delivering a technology-biased solution.

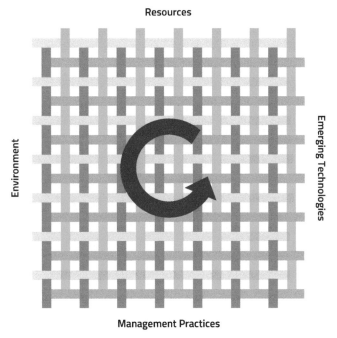

Figure 55 Applying the Management Mesh

 Real world example

An IT Managed Service Provider was looking to differentiate itself from its competitors in a market where there was very little difference in capabilities. Technical skills, service delivery, customer service and price point are the key points looked at by customers, and in a relatively small market, these are areas difficult to create a unique selling point.

The decision was made by the senior leadership team, to create a delivery and support framework focused on delivering service which was obviously different to their identified competitors. As an independent consultant, I was engaged to help design the initial framework based on the customer's requirements.

Working with key delivery staff, we walked through current working practices and identified that there were several frameworks, methodologies or approaches being referenced in various ways. These were reviewed, and a consolidated view produced.

The various frameworks, methodologies and approaches being referred to were:
- ITIL;
- DevOps;
- Kanban to visualize and prioritize workloads across all delivery teams;
- KCS as knowledge was seen to be the most critical element of their service delivery;
- Lean IT to identify and reduce waste in delivery of the managed services.

Each of the above was reviewed to understand what components were referenced and how and then a high-level design produced to demonstrate how each would interact and integrate with each other.

If equated to the VeriSM Management Mesh, the reviewed elements include:
- People and Knowledge as key Resource components;
- Competition and existing toolsets as key components of Environment;
- The Management Practices identified and reviewed were:
  - ITIL as the core of the Service Desk function;
  - DevOps to manage ongoing development of self-healing environments, automation and delivery of issue resolution;
  - Kanban to visualize and prioritize workloads across all delivery teams, including with senior customers;
  - KCS as knowledge was seen to be the most critical element of their service delivery;
  - Lean IT to identify and reduce waste in delivery of the managed services;
- Finally, Emerging Technologies were reviewed to understand where value could be added to customers and AI and automation were identified as ways to improve customer delivery.

The following sections describes the information necessary for each side of the mesh as well as where and how to gather it. The outcome is the current mesh for the organization.

12.3.1 Resources

Resource information (e.g., people, suppliers, budget, time, assets, knowledge...) is usually the easiest to gather – resources are concrete and tangible. They are managed by the various capabilities (e.g., HR, Finance, Facilities...) across the organization. While not all organizations are equal in their record keeping and documentation capability, there are some common information sources.

The main source of information is the organizational portfolio (see Section 10.4 for more information). This portfolio will be owned and managed at the strategic level of the organization and is an output of the organizational leaders and governors. The portfolio drives the implementation of strategy and is critical to the achievement of the organizational mission, vision and goals. The portfolio shows the organization's commitments and investments, thus, a view of resource consumption as well as potential future demand.

 So, what happens if the organization does not have a documented (or available) organizational portfolio? All is not lost but there are few additional steps. Meet with the executives (governing body) and ensure the mission and organizational strategy is understood. Define or confirm the activities that are currently consuming resources that support the achievement of the mission. The outcome of these activities is draft/immature organizational portfolio – make it a goal to mature this information over time and give it to the governing body for ownership and up-keep.

Consider the following areas where resource information is often captured:
- Human resources (people, skills, job descriptions);
- Financial department (accounting; budgets);
- Asset register; purchasing, procurement;
- Information technology;
- Configuration management database(s);
- Product and service catalog;
- Project Management Office (PMO);
- Steering committee;
- Facilities (physical plant).

Questions to assess resources

Some suggested questions to help with mapping Resources within a Management Mesh include:

- Competencies:
  - What skills do we have now? Within what capability(ies)? Are the skills in-house or contracted?
  - What skills are not present within the organization?
  - Do we have the necessary knowledge within the organization? If yes, within what organizational capability(ies) is that knowledge found?
  - Suppliers:
  - What do they supply now?
  - What other things could they supply?
- Budget:
  - Is the product or service adequately funded?
  - Will the product or service help with Run, Grow or Transform the Business (RTB, GTB, TTB)?
- Assets:
  - What current technologies are in place that could be used with the product or service?
  - What are the infrastructure or physical plant requirements for the product or service?
- Time:
  - What the expected timeframe for implementation of the product or service?
  - Is the timeframe adequate and appropriate for the organization to meet its goals (e.g., Run, Grow or Transform the Business – RTB, GTB, TTB)?
  - What is the expected lifespan of the service or product?

12.3.2 Environment

Defining the environmental conditions for an organization can be daunting, if only due to the breadth of potential information. Despite this, it is important not to shy away from this task – it is critical to the strategy as well as the eventual design of the product and service.

Start with the 'simple' information first – legislative and regulatory requirements. These are industry-specific and are typically known constraints to the organization and its operating practices. Check with the audit department, legal department, Human Resources, current contracts, Quality Assurance or the Compliance Officer for this information. Understand this type of requirement will change over time so there must be regular reviews to ensure currency of the mesh.

Identifying the competition might be another 'easy' task. Remember to stay within scope for this step. The goal is to define the competition and how their products/ services compete with your own, not to focus on how to overcome the competition (at this stage). Using the information from the organizational portfolio will provide context for the environment not only across the organization but also how the organization defines and interacts with its target markets. This area is addressed by some of the techniques in Chapter 9.

Looking internally and defining the organizational culture is more difficult as its elements are esoteric: how are expectations, experiences, philosophies and values expressed? These elements are typically expressed through the organizational self-image, inner workings, and interactions with the outside world. Chatman and Jehn's (1991) Organizational Culture Profile (OCP) details seven different organizational cultural dimensions. The seven cultural values are:

- Innovative – experimenting, flexible, opportunity-seeking, risk-taking, few rules, flat hierarchy;
- Aggressive – competitive, value out-performing competition, low emphasis on social responsibility;
- Outcome-oriented – action-oriented, high expectations, strong focus on results and achievements;
- Stable – predictable, secure, rule-oriented, bureaucratic;
- People-oriented – fairness, tolerance, social responsibility, treat all with respect and dignity;
- Team-oriented – collaboration, cooperation among employees;
- Detail-oriented – precise, analytic.

Understanding the cultural profile of an organization can provide some clarity around how a new or changed product or service can impact the ongoing operations of that organization. For example, if an organization is profiled as 'stable' and 'detail-oriented', consider the effect of digital transformation activities where 'innovation' and 'outcome-orientation' are necessary. How will the organization respond to the cultural changes required? Obviously, transformation efforts must include organizational change and behavior management practices to address the cultural needs. Lastly, multiple cultures can exist in a single organization in the form of subcultures and countercultures.

There are many activities and models (see Appendix D) that can help define (and then improve) organizational culture. Before choosing any model, consider the following areas. These can be used to create a set of metrics which will describe the desired organizational culture. They can also help to understand whether the culture is contributing to an engaged and effective workforce and reinforcing and promoting consumer-centric operations. The areas are:

- Communication – flow of communication from staff (thoughts and suggestions) to leadership and vice versa;
- Innovation – ability to move ideas through the organization and the openness of the organization to new ideas;
- Agility – impression from staff on adapting to internal and external changes (very different than the view from leadership);
- Wellness – mental and physical health of staff;
- Environment – support the comfort and productivity needs of staff;
- Collaboration – multi-layered – look beyond a single capability or team and measure within and between capabilities and teams (see Chapter 6 for more information);
- Support – middle managers tend to feel least supported; measure the support level not only to the organization but also managers and peers;
- Performance focus – reward/recognize successful achievement of performance factors (define what 'success' is); understand if staff feel appreciated and how they would like to be recognized;
- Responsibility – staff and leadership accountability for actions and results;
- Mission and value alignment – do staff know, understand and live by the organizational mission and values?

On-going governance activities will also measure and/or define organizational culture. The Evaluate-Direct-Monitor (EDM) governance cycle (see Section 10.5 for more information) will use common assessment tools such as a SWOT (Strength, Weakness, Opportunities, Threats) or PEST/PESTEL (political, economic, social, technology, environmental, legal) analysis – each will provide information on the organizational culture. Analyzing the results based on the organizational mission, will provide insights for improvement efforts.

A key element of the environmental side of the mesh is the service stabilizers (processes, measurements, and tools). Critically assess the operating practices:
- Are the processes and procedures accurate, documented, and up-to-date? Are they aligned across all suppliers and parties delivering the product or service?
- Are they as lean as they need to be?
- What about the supporting tools – too many? Too few? Are they effective?
- Review the currently captured metrics – are they valuable? Are they all necessary? Do they fulfill the consumer's need for information? Do they contribute to a 'death-by-data' philosophy?

Additional questions to consider when assessing the service stabilizers include:
- Are consumer and other stakeholder goals met across all capabilities in terms of delivery and support practices? Information needs?
- Are good practices applied across all capabilities?

Lastly, consider the organizational structure. While this type of assessment typically sits with the governing body, it is an assessment that is necessary. The main question is this: Does the structure support or fragment the capabilities and their performance?

Questions to assess the Environment

Some suggested questions to help with mapping the Environment within a Management Mesh include:

- Service stabilizers
  - Tools:

    What is the purpose of the tool?

    Used by which capabilities?

    What function does the tool perform / augment?
  - Processes:

    What is the purpose of the process?

    Used by which capabilities?

    What outcomes are produced by the process?
  - Measures:

    What is the purpose of the measure?

    Who captures the measure? What reports result from this capture?

    What organizational capability uses the measure?

    What decisions or actions are taken based on this measure?
- Partners:
  - Do we have / need partners we can leverage?

    Strategic

    Tactical

    Commodity

    Operational
  - Will / can a partner be used to Run, Grow or Transform the Business (RTB, GTB, or TTB)?
- Legislation:
  - Are there any country- or locality-specific regulations that could have impact on the product or service?
- Competition:
  - What products and services compete with us in the market space?
  - What is the perception or reputation of our competitors?
  - How do their products and services compare to ours?
- Organizational culture:
  - Will the current organizational culture embrace the product or service?
  - What considerations should be addressed as part of training and communications plans?

– What is the impact of the product or service on how people do their jobs? Are we prepared to deal with that impact?
- Organization portfolio:
  - Current products and services
  - Proposed products and services
  - Retired products and services
  - Resources, organizational capabilities
  - Business Plans:
  - Market Spaces
  - What is our position in the target market space?
  - Is our goal to Run, Grow or Transform the Business (RTB, GTB, or TTB)?
- Organizational structure:
  - How many levels of hierarchy exist in the organization?
  - How well does collaboration work between and across levels?

12.3.3 Management practices

Understanding current management practices across the organization may be a complex activity. The very act of choosing a management practice reflects the choices made by the governing body (e.g., how objectives are defined, motivation methods, coordination of activities, resource allocation). These choices are critical – the conscious choice by the governing body on how an organization runs impacts the quality, responsiveness and cost of the services offered.

The defined strategy, supporting principles and the current organizational portfolio will influence the chosen management model(s).

Birkinshaw and Goddard[72] (2009) define three forces that impact how one chooses a management practice. These factors include:

■ Changing expectations of employees (for example, consider the generations and their characteristics);
■ Technological change;
■ Emergence of new competitors.

While Birkinshaw and Goddard didn't specifically include consumers in their research, the changing expectations of consumers across market spaces will influence management practices. Consider the digital 'needs' that are endemic today as well as the growing consumer expectations. Due to the impact of

---

72 Birkinshaw, J. & Goddard, J. (2009). What is your management model? *MIT Sloan Management Review*, **50**(2), 81-90.

social media, customer experience remains to the forefront and therefore the management practices must meet these demands as well as those listed for the service provider.

Leadership (traits and behaviors that encourage following) and management (how to get work done through others) are distinct but most environments require both traits. Choosing a management practice will be dependent on the degree to which the practice supports the outcomes desired.

Real world perspective: not being 'sheep' …

Think about how often people choose one path or another just because someone else chooses that same path. It's the "shiny object" syndrome – choosing a management practice is not a decision to be taken lightly (definitely not the 'flavor of the day') but one that should be thoroughly reviewed and understood as to the benefits of the practice as well as the disbenefits or potential risks. The impact of change management practices is high when considering the people, the processes and cultural factors. Remember it is never the practice itself that creates the success but rather what one does with the practice.

To understand what management practices are currently deployed, check with the audit department. This team typically performs internal, compliance, financial, and operational audits. Check the various audits for their scope and results – the practices followed will be defined and measured. If there is no formal audit department, records of audit activity will most likely be found within Human Resources, the legal department, Quality Management, commercial contracts for required quality standards, or with capability leadership. Product or Service Owners will also audit the products and services for compliance and performance, which will be reflected in the management practices used.

Appendix D provides an overview of common management practices across the organization. The sheer number of management models and practices is truly overwhelming. What has been provided is a selected set, that when reviewed, provide benefit to a VeriSM initiative. These tables are not exhaustive nor are the methods to apply these management practices provided.

Note: *VeriSM™: A Service Management Approach for the Digital Age* provides extensive information on multiple progressive management practices, typically applied to Information Technology, such as Agile, DevOps, SIAM, Lean, Shift Left, Customer and User Experience (CX/UX), Continuous Delivery, as well as Kanban, Theory of Constraints, Improvement Kata/Kaizen and SWOT analysis.

Questions to assess Management Practices
- What is the objective of the practice? Does it still fit the "need" (e.g., organizational strategy, digital transformation…)?
- Used by what organizational capabilities?
- What is the desired outcome from the use of the practice?
- How well are we utilizing this practice? Could this practice be integrated with others to generate better value?

How management practices evolve

Appendix C provides more detail on how management practices evolve and move from one area or capability of an organization to another.

In this text, Lean IT expert Reni Friis explains how Lean has moved from manufacturing into IT, and Kinetic IT share a story of enterprise service management.

12.3.4 Emerging technologies

The last side of the Management Mesh looks specifically at the use of emerging technologies. Do not get confused and focus on the current infrastructure components (this information should be captured under Resources and the asset area).

What is captured on this side of the Management Mesh is the *strategic* use or exploitation of the transformational technologies (e.g., cloud, virtualization, AI, containers, Big Data…). Consider these transformation technologies classified as "Not used here…yet." What is currently presented in the Management Mesh (and discussed in *VeriSM™: A Service Management Approach for the Digital Age*) is a time-relevant list – one will have to stay up-to-date with new developments and alter the possibilities as new technologies emerge.

This may be a relatively 'simple' assessment, if the current product or service delivery is understood. Review the product or service catalog or even the organization's website – confirm the use of any transformational technology with the IT capability. Reminder: this assessment is about understanding what emerging technologies are currently used; nothing else. The re-use or the need for new or additional technologies will be handled once requirements are gathered and confirmed.

Note: *VeriSM™: A Service Management Approach for the Digital Age* provides extensive information on multiple emerging technologies including, cloud, virtualization, automation, Big Data, Internet of Things (IoT), machine learning, Robotic Process Automation(RPA), mobile computing technologies, Bring Your Own (BYOx), containerization, serverless computing, and Artificial Intelligence (AI).

Questions to assess emerging technologies
- What are the general characteristics or features of this technology? Does the organization have the necessary skills to exploit and/or support the technology?
- How might this technology have potential use/benefit to organization?
  - Be careful not to implement technology for the sake of implementing technology
- Will this technology be used to Run, Grow or Transform the Business (RTB, GTB, or TTB)?

Real world perspectives: ServiceNow, Marval, Ivanti

In Chapter 26, you'll find industry perspectives from three software vendors. They share their views about how technology is changing, and the software industry is evolving alongside to improve how organizations work and people collaborate.

"Whatever service you use in any aspect of your daily life, you have one experience of that service, you do not really care what is happening in the background or the processes involved to have reached that point.

The fundamental goal is to give one consistent experience to the end user that allows them to get work done, regardless of the downstream or systems that you may or may not be talking to."

Chris Pope, ServiceNow

"A senior manager I spoke with recently wanted an ITSM solution with all singing, all dancing AI to reduce his headcount, with little or no training to staff – but he currently fails to even have simple customer incident logging in place!"

Dr Don Page, Marval

"IT leads the championing of these practices across many organizations. The expertise for developing process, applying technology, changing human behavior and thus improving business productivity can be found in IT."

Ian Aitchison, Ivanti

■ 12.4 VERISM UNWRAPPED: THE ORGANIZATIONAL MESH

Once all four sides of the mesh have been analyzed, a 'picture' of the current state is presented (see Figure 56). The figure shows a highly stylized representation of the mesh (green lines signifying the current view of the organization). For example:

■ Under Resources, people, budget, assets, and knowledge are robust;
■ Under Environment, organizational culture, legislation, the service stabilizers are robust;
■ Under Management Practices, ITIL and SIAM are currently used.
■ Under Emerging Technologies, BYOx and Cloud are currently used

Most likely the information gathered would be stored in some 'tool' – a database, spreadsheet, a paper notebook – that would have a level of control around it. That control could be based within the purview of the change control process or under specified ownership. Defined governance and associated principles will drive those actions. The level of control is to ensure the information remains current and accurate so to support good decision-making.

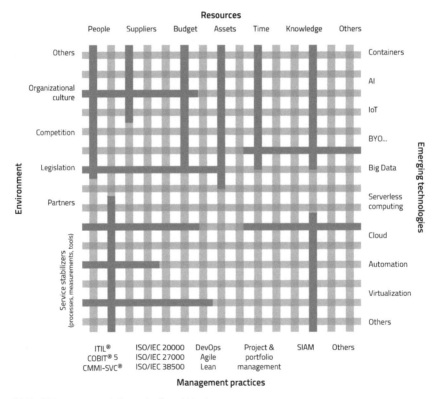

Figure 56 VeriSM unwrapped: Organizational Mesh

Remember, this current view (the organizational mesh) is only accurate for the moment it was completed. How often is an update required? When should it be updated? The easy answer is, "It depends". The guidance for updating will be based on the organizational principles (organizational risk tolerance) and accompanying policies (Change Control policies). Those principles and policies would typically call for an update after any major change to the organization (strategy change, market change, legislative change, etc.) and prior to the review and approval of a new or changed product or service. Review the organizational Management Mesh at appropriate intervals.

As the mesh is used for new or changed products or services, a specific mesh will reflect the individual product or service requirements. That specific product or service mesh will be compared to the organizational mesh to understand the gaps between what is currently held and what is the proposed need. Once the product or service is deployed, the organizational mesh will expand to include the new mesh elements.

Creating a Management Mesh must follow several logical steps, as explained in the previous pages. An organization will develop different views – the organizational mesh represents the whole organization and a product or service mesh represents an individual product or service. Comparing the organizational mesh to a product or service mesh will identify gaps where elements are needed to support the delivery of that specific product or service.

There is a second use of the Management Mesh; to critically assess the number of resources, environmental conditions, management practices, and emerging technologies and identify where there is duplication and/or redundancy. Organizations can easily become overwhelmed with too many management practices or the over-application of technology. Keep enterprise governance and the Service Management Principles to the forefront, apply Lean thinking, and consider retiring elements that are underused or not used at all.

Real world example: automating the Management Mesh

In Chapter 29, you'll find content from Sollertis. Sollertis produce a tool, Convergence, which can help to visualize or automate the Management Mesh.

"Convergence is built upon a fundamental principal that all business transformation, operational work and activity taking place within an organization must connect to strategic business objectives."

■ 12.5 VERISM APPLIED: FCH ORGANIZATIONAL MESH

In preparation of FCH Wearable Wellness program, FireCloud Health (review the full case study in Appendix B) has developed its organizational Management Mesh. It is portrayed in a high-level diagram (see Figure 57) and it is described below. (See section 12.2 to review how to interpret the lines. NOTE: The line colors have changed to distinguish the 'Unwrapped' diagrams from the 'Applied' diagrams).

As per the FCH case study, the following mesh elements are present:
■ Resources:
  • FCH's mission and vision statement provides insight into the budget, knowledge, and people elements as does the strategic enablers of people, critical thinking, innovation and finance. This organization has the people, budget, and knowledge to reach its goals;
  • Where they may be lacking (there is no direct information) is time (legislative and accreditation requirements are stated otherwise there is no additional information);
  • Assets are available, but the case indicates older technologies as well as a lot of duplication. Note that information technology is seen as a strategic enabler;

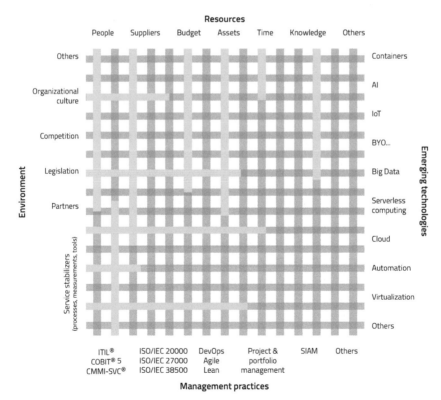

Figure 57 FireCloud Health Organizational Management Mesh – Current

- Environment:
  - The service stabilizers are fairly robust as there are several ITIL-based processes in place (but at varying levels of maturity and inconsistent use across the organization – -there is no indication there is any collaborative efforts between the healthcare and insurance divisions) and several supporting tools are available, but again duplicated (no indication that they share information);
  - Measurements are suspect as there are complaints around reporting;
  - Legislative requirements are well known and addressed (Compliance office);
  - While the culture is not specifically called out, organizational values show a culture appropriate to a healthcare organization and one that would support digital transformation efforts;
- Management Practices:
  - FCH uses ITIL practices to deliver and support services. Several processes are in place, but their level of maturity may not be at the level required. No other management practices are mentioned;
- Emerging Technologies:
  - No specific emerging technologies are named but the data center consolidation project would imply some newer technologies (potentially server virtualization, cloud, containers, automation and blockchain). The innovation and IT strategic enablers provide the possibility of exploiting emerging technologies, specifically AI, Big Data, IoT to support the current trend of using AI for diagnosing as well as IoT/Big Data to support the strategic initiative of proactive health programming (FCH Wearable Wellness Program).

13 Define: approval

Introduction

This chapter provides insights and methods for the decision-making process to create or update a product or service. Remember, the service provider has defined its governance, Service Management Principles, and has completed an organizational Management Mesh. An idea has been presented for a new or changed product or service.

Before any activity begins, there must be some form of approval (see Figure 58). This can be as simple as an 'OK' from an authorizing body to a formal business case and its approval process through an authorization structure. The route of the approval will be based on the individual organization, their governing principles, risk tolerance and managing practices. Whichever route, the outcome of this activity is the authorization to continue with the Define activities. The question that remains is: "How are the decisions made to invest?" Three options are discussed in this chapter:

- Option space;
- Opportunity portfolio;
- Run-Grow-Transform (RGT).

13.1 OPTION SPACE

From the previously defined strategy and corresponding principles, confirm the scope and guardrails. Additionally, the organizational portfolio (see Section 10.3 for more information) provides an account of how the organization has invested in the past and its commitments to future activities. It is through using the portfolio, understanding the options one has for investment and getting the necessary return on the investment that a strategy is truly executed.

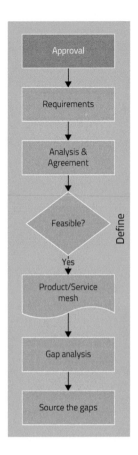

Figure 58 Approval

In the late 1990s, T. A. Luehrman wrote two seminal papers on the concept of treating strategic investments as financial options. In the second of the two articles, Luehrman (1998) wrote, "In financial terms, a business strategy is much more like a series of options than a series of static cash flows". Thus, fulfilling a business strategy requires the various options to be addressed, rather than statically providing funds without understanding the value of applied funds.

Luehrman used two metrics to measure options and plot the outcomes on a rectangular "option space" (see Figure 59). These metrics are:

- **Value-to-cost metric** – the predicted value of the asset that will be built or acquired divided by the present value of the expenditure necessary to build or buy that asset. This metric is plotted on the X-axis. When the calculated value falls between zero and one, the cost is more than the generated value (do not invest). If the number is greater than one, the value generated is greater than the cost (invest);
- **Volatility metric** – how much change can occur before an investment decision must be made. This is plotted on the Y-axis with a range of lower to higher. The lower the volatility, the less time one has to decide, the higher the volatility, the more time there is to manage the option before making a final decision.

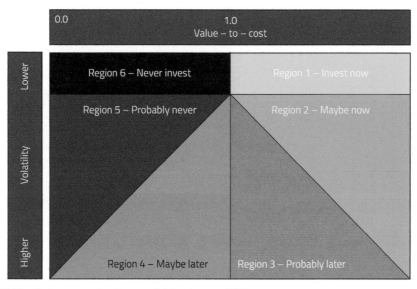

Figure 59 The Option space too (source: T.A. Luehrman, 1998)

The option space is divided into six further regions (see Figure 59), each offering a 'decision' based on the intersection of the X- and Y-axes. These regions are:

- **Region 1** – Invest now – the value-to-cost ratio is above one and the volatility is low;
- **Region 2** – Maybe now – the value-to-cost ratio is greater than one with lower volatility;
- **Region 3** – Probably later – the value-to-cost ratio is slightly greater than one with higher levels of volatility;
- **Region 4** – Maybe later – the value-to-cost ratio is slightly less than one with higher levels of volatility;
- **Region 5** – Probably never – the value-to-cost ratio is closer to zero with lower volatility;
- **Region 6** – Invest never – the value-to-cost ratio is less than one and the volatility is low (no change is expected).

Using this model, over time the natural movement of an option is 'up' (e.g. time is running out) and to the left (value-to-cost decreases over time). Options that are in regions 3 and 4 should be nurtured to increase their value or reduce their cost, moving the option to a more lucrative position. Using this tool clarifies where to focus to optimize a particular strategy.

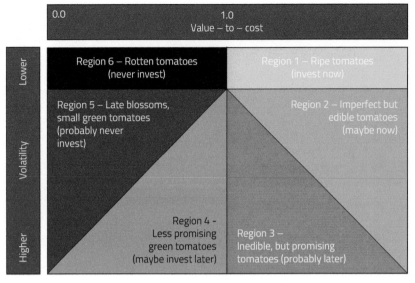

Figure 60 The Option Space Tool applied to a tomato garden (source: T.A. Luehrman, 1998)

To make these concepts a bit more realistic, Luehrman illustrated the concepts using an example of a tomato garden where the gardener needs to make some strategic decisions about the garden's production (see Figure 60). Some tomatoes are ready to pick immediately, others need a bit more time on the vine, some need a bit of care to be edible, and some are rotten and should be discarded. This method allows the organization to move beyond the 'yes/no' investment decision that traditionally has been based exclusively on a net present value (NPV) calculation. Luehrman's argument is simple – an investment with a negative NPV may still be a valuable investment. With time and information for the conditions to be 'right', the potential of abandoning a good investment is reduced (think of the gardener nurturing the plants with feed, water and fertilizer). The opposite is also true – not all investments with a positive NPV should be executed right away.

■ 13.2 OPPORTUNITY PORTFOLIOS

In McGrath and MacMillan's book (2000), *Entrepreneurial Mindset*[73], the concept of an opportunity portfolio is presented (see Figure 60). It is based on the principles of investing in stock options, where purchasing an option gives the investor the right (not obligation) to buy or sell shares at a later date. When an option is purchased, little is spent at the time of purchase, but it gives flexibility for the future. Options manage risk, allowing investors to put off investment decisions until there is more certainty. Thus, the 'real option' is represented by the small investment to create a larger or

---

73 McGrath, R. G. & MacMillan, I. (2000). *The entrepreneurial mindset: Strategies for continuously creating opportunity in an age of uncertainty*. Boston: Harvard Business Review.

full investment at a later time. The concept of 'real options' captures the value of management flexibility to adapt decisions to unexpected market developments. Exposure is limited until the opportunity potential is available. Strategists look for small bets that enable project exploration to understand what is required for success and what is the expected potential.

Reviewing a single opportunity is relatively straightforward, but rarely is that luxury a reality. Most organizations are trying to make the 'right' decision across multiple investment choices. Then, the activities become one of how to make trade-offs between the decisions with various levels of uncertainty. The opportunity portfolio allows one to think about multiple and different investments based on their varying levels of uncertainty. As the strategy is to utilize the concept of real options (small investments for flexibility), mapping in an opportunity portfolio ensures there is a right mix of projects (see Figure 61).

The opportunity portfolio is represented by a simple matrix with capability uncertainty on the vertical axis and market uncertainty on the horizontal axis. This matrix is divided into five zones, each representing a different type of investment. Opportunities in the lower left are the most certain and represent a level of standard investments (e.g. enhancements to the current delivery or expansion of current services but in new markets). Opportunities with the most uncertainty are found in the upper right (e.g., game-changing opportunities). The description of each area is:

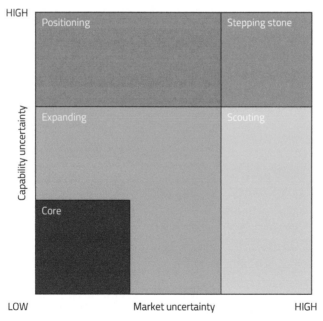

Figure 61 The opportunity portfolio (source: McGrath, R. G. & MacMillan, I. (2000))

- **Capability uncertainty** – the organization's assessment that it can take advantage of the investment (it has the correct technical and/or operational resources); the higher the uncertainty, the greater risk that the capabilities required will need to be sourced in some form:
  - This axis answers questions such as confidence in the ability to take advantage of the opportunity, the extent the opportunity utilizes the organization's strengths and abilities, the amount of change required to address the opportunity, and the level of difficulty of fulfilling the opportunity;
  - Projects that drive the organization into new areas will have higher degrees of capability uncertainty;
- **Market uncertainty** – the organization's assessment if there will be a market for the proposed opportunity:
  - This axis answers questions such as, "If we build it, will they come?", confidence the outcomes will meet the needs in a manner that is compelling, what marketing, training and other activities are necessary to gain support and interest, and does the opportunity create interest or inquiry by the users;
  - Where demand is known, market uncertainty is low;
- **Core zone** – opportunities or projects that typically represent improvements to existing products or services or the core functionality that must continue to support business operations;
- **Expanding zone** – opportunities from expanding the current products or services to a related/new market;
- **Positioning zone** – the market is known but the organization is uncertain if it has the necessary resources to deliver. Investment in a small option, developing the capability to begin learning what the full opportunity would require;
- **Scouting zone** – the organization has (or can source) the capabilities but more information around the potential market is needed before full investment. Small investments are made to test the interest or demand;
- **Stepping stones zone** – the market is uncertain, as is the capability to fulfill it. These opportunities may be worth pursuing but the environment must be right before full investment – follow the adage of fail cheaply and often (an Agile mindset).

The organization must develop an organizational portfolio – define opportunities (projects) in all zones to ensure a balanced approach. Additionally, the mapping needs to reflect the enterprise strategy. If there is not enough investment in the core area, current business will suffer. Likewise, if the strategy is to grow the existing business, there will be more emphasis in the core areas. If there are no projects in the middle areas, consumers may not trust (or want) the next item to be released. If the edges are underrepresented (idea experimentation), there is no future business. If the organizational strategy is exploration, investments will be in the edges and upper right.

Following this technique, organizations can quickly learn if they have too many projects and/or the projects in the pipeline do not fulfill current strategies. A simple fix? Allocate funding to the various areas based on the enterprise strategy and opportunities must compete for those resources before being approved.

■ 13.3 RUN-GROW-TRANSFORM (RGT)

 Quote

"Business transformations of all kinds will drive CIOs and other strategic stakeholders to better categorize the value of investments. Use 'run, grow and transform the business' views of IT spending as a catalyst for effective communication, decisions and forecasting."

Gartner

In the early 2000s, Gartner delivered an investment view of IT portfolio management with the Run-Grow-Transform (RGT) concept. Traditional budgeting practices treated IT as a cost that must be controlled tightly, creating an atmosphere of stringent cost-control with constant 'expense' justification, rather than an investment mindset. Hunter and Westerman (2009) described this situation (IT as an expense-only budget item) further – "IT investment decisions were based on a non-strategic 'process' called 'Anything Else'". The 'Anything Else' process arose from a view that IT was a cost only and not a strategic enabler. Thus, budgets were strongly influenced by politics, intuition and other non-rigorous approaches. Sounds familiar?

In the RGT concept, 'portfolio-based thinking' emphasizes investment decisions based on business value. Now, competitive advantage, innovation, market disruption and efficiency can drive or be the outcome of the decision-making process. In this model, decisions are quantified and matched to the organizational portfolio. The areas are:

- **Run** – general, day-to-day expenses of 'keeping the lights on'. Another way to think of this is the 'stay-in-business' expenses (e.g. maintenance, HR costs). These costs deliver the lowest ROI or perceived business value;
- **Grow** – expenses that support the expansion of services or overall business growth (tied directly to the organization's strategic initiatives). These expenses introduce new capabilities for established products or services or support improvement initiatives to them. These costs will positively affect the value proposition to the organization by improving operational performance or impacting the financial elements (e.g. CAPEX reductions, higher profits, reduced administrative costs);
- **Transform** – expenses that cover the cost of entering new markets with new value propositions for a new consumer base. These investments will be measured by capturing market share or new market revenues. Transformational expenses have

a potential high reward but with a high risk. Because of the risk, typically these initiatives are rejected first, but remember, these transformational initiatives are key to long-term health of the organization.

These three investment areas and how they are funded describe the expected performance levels from IT. As resources are applied to each area, the business value from IT investments is reinforced. What is the optimum split between the three areas? According to Gartner, no more than 50% of the overall budget should be applied to the Run activities, with the remaining 50% divided between Grow and Transform. This is not easy to do. Again, according to Gartner, almost 70% of the budget is spent on Run activities with little thought to the Grow and Transform activities. At a minimum, any budget should include all the Run and some Grow activities. If the budget is focused only on Run, product and services are at risk. Think of it this way, the more resources that are focused on Run, the less that can be allocated to innovation (Transform or Grow) activities. Alternatively, excessive cutting of Run budgets will introduce operational risk (e.g. security breaches or server failures). There is a definite middle ground to be found by the strategic leadership of the organization.

RGT quantifies, estimates and communicates the budget necessary to maintain the legacy products and services, as well as estimating the investment needed to drive digital transformation efforts. Understand the RGT concept is not only relevant to the IT portfolio – its principles can be applied to other capabilities and their associated decisions.

While outside the original RGT model, another investment option might be relevant – consider the innovations that disrupt the market. These innovations reflect transformational-like investments, with higher risk and longer-term or uncertain ROI. Like the transforming investments, as described above, these investments are necessary for long-term organizational viability.

■ 13.4 VERISM UNWRAPPED: TOOLS TO APPROVE DECISIONS

These three options, the Option Space tool, Opportunity portfolios and the Run-Grow-Transform technique, are financially-based decision tools. There are other modelling and analysis tools that can be used to aid in the decision process and have been presented in other sections of this volume. These tools include:
■ Canvas models (see Section 9.6);
■ SWOT analysis (see Appendix D);
■ PEST or PESTEL analysis (see Section 10.6.2).

It is of vital importance to an organization that does not have an Organizational Portfolio to start working on creating one (see section 10.3 The Organizational Portfolio) as the portfolio is the most appropriate place for approval decisions outlined here.

■ 13.5 VERISM APPLIED: FCH WEARABLE INITIATIVE APPROVAL

The FCH Wearable Wellness program was reviewed and approved following the RGT method. The wearable was classified as a 'grow the business' initiative as it is an innovative health program, capitalizing on information technology (innovation and information technology are strategic enablers) coupled with the strategic initiative of proactive health programming. The timeframe to deliver the pilot is within six months.

The intent of the program is to improve the health of the FireCloud community, thus potentially reducing the number of costly poor-health related procedures, as well as reducing the overall risk of health issues. Also, participants benefit from reduced health insurance premiums.

Corporate budgets have been adjusted to include this initiative. As the program expands in functionality as well as participants, the FCH Finance Department, in cooperation with the Office of Strategic Development, has created a 5-year plan to ensure on-going funding.

14 Define: define the requirements

Introduction

This chapter outlines the tasks of requirements gathering and their subsequent analysis and agreement. The requirements describe what the consumer is trying to achieve or overcome. The requirements, once agreed, will give rise to the product or service solution (designed and developed by the product or service team), that will identify components and their specifications. As part of the overall solution, testing and other preparation plans are defined. All information is captured in the Service Blueprint.

Requirements gathering is heavily emphasized in this publication – the success of the product or service will directly relate to how well it meets consumer needs (requirements). The ability to accurately capture the requirements depends on the ability of the service provider to understand consumer need from the perspective of the consumer.

Multiple techniques for requirement gathering are presented. Requirements are based on consumer needs (VeriSM starts and ends with the consumer), enterprise governance, Service Management Principles and the organizational portfolio. Once requirements are agreed, they are assessed against the Management Mesh (gap analysis – see Chapter 15) to identify the impact to overall product and service delivery.

Once approval has been granted, requirements are gathered to describe the outcome desired. Remember the activities within the approval process – the need was assessed for strategic fit, the ability to meet business objectives and there was clarity (and confirmation) around the goal for that new or changed product or service.

Requirement gathering, using anything from traditional methods to user stories and storyboarding, is an essential activity in developing or improving any product or service. It is also one of the most difficult activities to get right. The ability to communicate effectively is essential for developing an appropriate set of requirements.

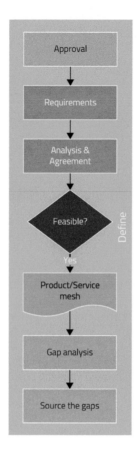

Figure 62 Define the requirements

Note there are several sub-activities within the overall requirement gathering task (see Figure 62). Not only are requirements gathered, there is:

■ Analysis and agreement – between the consumer and stakeholders with the service provider;
■ A feasibility check – even though the idea is approved, the various parameters for delivering the idea still must be considered;
■ Requirements captured in a product or service-specific mesh.

 The 'comedy' of requirement gathering
Consider this: Over 80% of errors are introduced at the requirements phase while less than 10% of errors can be traced to the design/development phases (developers are developing the things right but are they the right things?!). Additionally, more than 85% of the total project time is allocated to development and testing – a little backwards when one analyzes where the errors arise!

> In 2016, one study showed that 54% of those surveyed state that IT projects are not aligned with business goals, only 31% stated they focus on delivering business value. More than 50% state their focus is delivering on-time and on-budget.[74]
>
> The US Government lost $32 billion to failed IT projects in 2018. (Federal IT budget is $78 billion).[75]

There are many useful sources of information on requirements gathering. Appendix D includes information about the Business Analysis Body of Knowledge (BABOK), which provides extensive detail in this area.

▪ 14.1 REMEMBER THE CONSUMER

VeriSM starts and ends with the consumer (see Figure 1), therefore, it is critical to keep the consumer to the forefront when gathering requirements (and throughout the entire set of activities). As the consumer has been discussed in previous chapters (see Chapter 9), key factors that should be remembered and addressed include:

- ▪ What is the consumer profile? Understand who the consumer is, their habits, what problems they face. Learn this information (and more) through observation and discussion with the consumer.
- ▪ What does the consumer want to accomplish? What task, job or problem is the consumer trying to address?
- ▪ What are the consumer pain points? How long does it take the consumer to complete a task? Can it be quicker? What is the cost of solution? Can it be cheaper and just as effective?
- ▪ What benefits are desirable or achievable? Are savings available within time, resource and effort? Are there social implications?
- ▪ Is the consumer market clearly defined? Not all products or services can be (nor should they be) ubiquitously applied. Consider exploring the consumer market with the following techniques (see Chapter 9 and Appendix D):
  - • Maslow's Hierarchy of Needs;
  - • Roger's Diffusion of Innovation;
  - • Kotter's Five Product Levels;
  - • Business Model Canvas and the market segments.

Consumer input is critical to creating the product and services that will meet their needs and expectation. As requirements are gathered, remember that requirements are provided to remove or address a consumer pain point – ensure those pain points,

---

74 Florentine, S. (2016, May 11). More than half of IT projects still failing. https://www.cio.com/article/3068502/project-management/more-than-half-of-it-projects-still-failing.html
75 Friend, T. (2017, March 20). Agile project success and failure (The story of the FBI Sentinel program). https://resources.sei.cmu.edu/asset_files/Presentation/2017_017_001_495733.pdf

and the consumer, are well understood. Chapter 27, Digital optimization, provides some practical examples of how to meet consumer needs.

■ 14.2 INTRODUCTION TO REQUIREMENTS

Requirements are not specifications. Requirements describe problems (the 'what'); specifications describe solutions (the 'how'). To define the need clearly, first understand the 'real world' situation – **what** activities are being supported, **what** business issue is being addressed, **what** is the scope. Notice that each question begins with a 'what' and not a 'how'. Having this information will allow for a clear problem statement that then can be explored and refined through various information gathering techniques.

There are two schools of thought around definition of requirements – is it a 'gathering' activity or is it an 'eliciting' activity? Requirement gathering is simply an act of collecting – collecting from various sources (future users, process models, complaints, system reports, regulations…). Elicitation occurs when requirements are refined or drawn out via a variety of techniques (discussion, questioning…) to get to the true need. To create the most illustrative set of requirements and truly define the needs of the consumer, utilize both gathering and elicitation methods.

Case study

Context

Organization A had acquired Organization B, both active in the same highly regulated industry. Some systems were found to be redundant and some work was duplicated, along with the teams managing them. Both organizations had systems managing the existing mobile device estates, based on the same technology, but with different setups. The system used by Organization A had adequate security measures in place, mitigating potential Data Loss (Data Loss Prevention – DLP); this system had been maintained and was up to date. The system used by Organization B had a very open setup, with no restrictions in place and outdated.

Challenges

A decision was made to decommission the system used by Organization B and migrate all the users to the one used by the parent Organization A. The project team was given a mandate to complete related activities within two months, when the outdated system would be decommissioned. The project scope was established, and the team engaged an external contractor to assist the project implementation.

As the project started to communicate with the users in Organization B and a number of users were being migrated, it was identified that certain categories of users had taken advantage of the non-restrictive setup of the system. Unknown to IT and the project teams, these users had started using the features available as part of their business processes, bypassing other existing IT systems. Migrating to a more restrictive setup, although more secure, no longer allowed them to use these features, and prevented them from fulfilling their business roles in an efficient manner.

Outcome
Although most of the users were migrated successfully, the project could not complete by the deadline, as a significant number had to be retained on the old system. Consequently, the old system could not be decommissioned. Additional internal and external resources had to be engaged to find a suitable solution for the remaining users.

Lessons learned
Business practices and users will adjust device and system usage outside of the initial boundaries set by the IT teams, most often without IT's knowledge.

When gathering the requirements, the project team had focused too much on the IT aspects (reduce costs by decommissioning the obsolete system and re-organizing the teams involved) and the security aspects (DLP – mitigate risks of Data Loss), but not enough on the current business ways of working.

14.2.1 Requirements gathering techniques

To deliver a truly great product or service, there must be clarity of purpose and understanding of the intent for that product or service. A great deal of work (research, planning) is required and the information must be documented. So, how does one gather requirements? There are several well-known techniques, listed below, for gathering requirements, all of which have value in today's fast moving, digital environment. Also, review Section 9.5, Business Innovation Circles (BICs), for additional information on gathering and understanding consumer need.

- **Brainstorming** – a form of elicitation with the intent of getting as many ideas as possible from a group, but be sure to prioritize the list before acting on it;
- **Document analysis** – review existing documents for the 'AS-IS' to determine the 'TO-BE';
- **Focus group** – the purpose is to gather consumer feedback (needs, opportunities, problems) to validate current products and services;
- **Interview** – capture goals and expectations of consumers and other stakeholders in a one-on-one situation; understand their perspective to fully comprehend the requirements; practice active listening (not only hear what is being said but

understand how it is being said – notice inflections, body language… Recognize the little clues that are provided!);

- **Group interviews** – two to four similar consumers or stakeholders (same role, same level…). Greater preparation is required to keep the group involved and focused;
- **Observation** – study the habits, workflow, work patterns, bottlenecks, awkward steps and pain points, with the focus on improvements. Passive or active (ask questions while observing) observations can reveal implicit requirements;
- **Prototyping** – use when requirements cannot be articulated well, but can be understood quickly via sketches, storyboards or being shown a version of the solution. Changes are made and reviewed with the consumer or stakeholder, iteratively, until the final product or service is agreed;
- **User stories** – a short description of what the user wants from a product or service (see Section 14.3.2) captured on a card, which enables a conversation to refine the story and confirm the requirements (3Cs of User Stories – card, conversation, confirmation);
- **Use cases** – starts the same as a user story, but use cases provide a complete description of how the consumer will use the proposed product or service, including all scenarios, the processes, requirements, expected outcomes or alternatives;
- **Requirements workshop** –a type of brainstorming, but the participants are the designers/architects. The goal is to clarify the requirements and how these will be met;
- **Survey or questionnaire** – use when information is required from many consumers and stakeholders, and there are budget and time constraints. Surveys can 'force' answers through pre-defined choices or rating systems (Strongly Agree, Agree…) or they can have open-ended questions. The disadvantage of a survey is that they are hard to write objectively and without bias.

There are many templates available to assist in gathering requirements. These templates range from the very simple to truly complex and specific. A quick internet search will provide templates for functional requirements, data collection, technical requirements, user group profiles, among others. Use what is appropriate for the environment.

Requirement types

Requirements can be divided into two groups: functional and non-functional. Depending on the organization, the supporting principles and design philosophy (traditional versusiterative/adaptive), there are various requirement types. The list below, non-exhaustive, provides examples – use as needed.

- **Functional** – mandatory requirements enabling users to accomplish tasks that satisfy business requirements, defining new features or how existing features will be modified, including:
  - Legal/regulatory requirements;

- Administrative requirements;
- Reporting requirements;
- Audit tracking requirements;
- Historical data requirements;
- Authentication actions.
- **Non-functional** – requirements necessary to create or support the performance of the new or changed product or service (quality):
  - Usability – effectiveness, efficiency satisfaction, user-friendly;
  - Reliability – availability (uptime, critical processing periods), accuracy, defect rates;
  - Performance – response time, throughput, capacity, scalability, recoverability, resource utilization;
  - Supportability – on-going support requirements;
  - Maintainability – ease of maintenance (e.g. correction, expansion, modification, adaptability to new requirements);
  - Security – specific controls, confidentiality, integrity, privacy;
  - Data – types of data elements, conversion and cleansing for migration;
  - Training – end-user, documentation (manuals, FAQs ...);
  - Business rules – legal and regulatory, warranties, copyright or patent notice, trademarks, corporate policies, practices, mandates, reporting;
  - User – tasks performed by the user.

The importance of non-functional requirements cannot be stressed enough. There is a temptation to focus on functional requirements (seen as more 'tangible' and consumer focused) but non-functional requirements are just as important for delivering consumer satisfaction.

Functional or non-functional requirements can be deemed to be out of scope. This means that while the requirement might be compelling, it is not relevant for the current activities. These requirements should be logged and considered as possible future improvements.

The goal of requirements gathering is to ensure there is a clear, unambiguous and agreed set of requirements that allows the provision of what the consumer wants. However, no matter how good the process, things will be missed. Forgotten questions to ask, forgotten requirements to reveal, changes to the environment and priority shifts all play havoc with requirements. Therefore, remember the iterative flow of events:

1. Understand the strategic impact (business objectives, strategic fit, goals);
2. User stories;
3. User design and interaction;
4. Questions, clarification, scope.

Provide enough time to deal with these events (and others) to ensure the service provider is focusing on the right set of priorities that match actual requirements.

To define the requirements successfully, consider the following:
- Involve the consumer from the beginning;
- Document clear and concise requirements, that are agreed with the consumer and stakeholders before development begins;
- Don't assume anything. Validate deliverables with the consumer;
- Ensure requirements are SMART (specific, measurable, agreed, realistic, time-bound);
- Leave technology to the side until the requirements are understood;
- Prototype the solution, if possible, to confirm or refine consumer requirements.

 Practical tips

Based on the experiences of the authors, avoid these common mistakes:
- Solving the 'issue' before the issue is really understood;
- Creating a cutting-edge technical solution only to discover it can't be deployed;
- Focusing on tools rather than business requirements – even if the tool is known, it must be adapted to the consumer and not the other way around;
- Not prioritizing the requirements and 'missing' the critical element (consider a MoSCoW analysis – labeling each requirement as a 'Must have', 'Should have', 'Could have', 'Won't have' at the time of analysis);
- Not defining common terms clearly (consider 'time' – what is its exact definition (hours, weeks, days, months?));
- Making assumptions.

■ 14.3 GATHERING THE REQUIREMENTS

To gather the necessary requirements successfully for the new or changed product or service, plan first! This plan could be an Agile sprint (a strategic-based sprint), an iterative user story based on the feasibility of the idea, or a project management-based template. Whatever management practice is followed, that practice will no doubt have guidance for gathering requirements and the expected requirement artifacts. Enterprise governance will dictate the necessary controls required to stay within acceptable operational parameters. Ensure those aspects are included in all planning.

In the plan, consider addressing the following elements – use what is appropriate for the environment, product or service (this list is not exhaustive):
- Define leadership and staffing roles (who will be accountable and responsible, respectively) for the gathering activities;
- Define and/or align with relevant governing principles and policies;

- Gain commitment from the appropriate stakeholders;
- Understand the impact of various stakeholder groups via stakeholder analysis;
- Define/confirm the scope of the new or changed product or service;
- Define the gathering/elicitation approaches and outputs (see Section 14.2.1);
- Understand availability of and access to enabling technologies as well as support functionalities;
- Agree a single source of truth for all solution definitions;
- Agree a status reporting schedule, an escalation process, and an approval and signoff process;
- Define the testing strategy for the new or changed product or service;
- Plan communication, risk mitigation activities, addressing skill gaps and other key gaps.

To help formulate the plan, the following elements are useful inputs:
- Enterprise governance information and associated principles (VeriSM 'guardrails');
- Value proposition statements;
- Current problem statement, business case, or product backlog;
- Various management practices;
- Role descriptions and boundaries.

14.3.1 Traditional requirement gathering

In traditional requirement gathering methodologies, the goal and the solution are clear before work begins. Often, one starts with a pre-defined list of technical yet generic specifications. An 'interview' occurs with the customer and from that discussion, the service provider then applies or creates the technical specification. Consumer input could include anything from what they want to gain, to blindly listing or agreeing to technical specifications or solutions, to defining current pain points. Too often, consumer input has been misunderstood (or ignored) and the resulting product or service missed the mark (see Figure 63). This leads to either unexpected 'features' or, a product or service that requires multiple upgrades and improvements to achieve, eventually, the customer-intended and envisioned need, but at a much-inflated cost in terms of resources, time and reputation.

While the preceding paragraph may be overly negative, do understand that the traditional approach has value and a place in today's digital environment. What factors would dictate this approach? Consider organizational risk tolerance levels, an environment that must deliver immediate stability, or others. Remember, this method is a 'tried-refined-true' method – all stakeholders are aware of its successes as well as its shortcomings and/or misuse. Understanding those implications and addressing them upfront will create a set of requirements that have been 'done right' the first time.

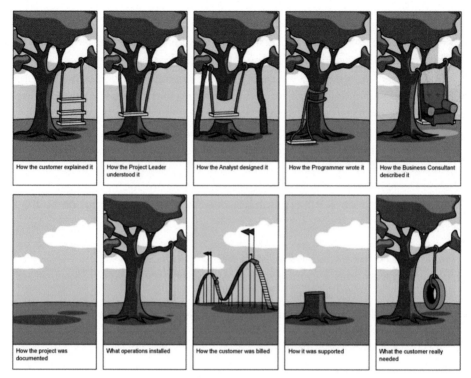

Figure 63 The famous "Project Cartoon" captures the sad reality of requirement gathering. (Source: http://www.projectcartoon.com)

 Case study

Context

An organization wanted to implement a system allowing them to manage corporate owned and Bring Your Own devices (BYOD). The project team and system architect engaged an external contractor, and together with the contractor's design team, a comprehensive High-Level Design (HLD) was established.

Once the HLD was signed-off, the implementation teams from both parties were engaged.

Challenges

Due to the desired user experience formulated by the project team, the agreed solution involved a large number of highly complex technical components. A comprehensive list of pre-requisites was provided to the organization's implementation team, highlighting the extensive infrastructure work required; these were unfamiliar technologies to the organization's implementation and support teams.

The lack of understanding of the work effort required, combined with resourcing challenges faced by the organization's implementation team, led to multiple delays and challenges between the project team and the external contractor.

Outcome

The initial technical requirements were challenged, and it was identified that most of the users would make limited use of the more advanced features (if any). When it became apparent the initial approach would not yield the desired results, the following measures were discussed, agreed and applied:

- The HLD was reviewed and simpler solution agreed – the updated solution allowed for similar end-user outcomes and business benefits, but it could be supported by the internal teams once the contractor finalized the implementation;
- The pre-requisites were split into packages that were more manageable – this allowed the organization's implementation team to be more effective and the contractor to incrementally deliver components and features for testing by the organization's teams.

Lessons learned

When designing a solution:

- The ability to implement and support the system(s) once live should not be underestimated. Communication between design, project, implementation and support teams is key;
- The best solution does not always translate into the most complex; balance what can be done with what should be done;
- User cases / stories / requirements (and not the perception technical teams have of them) should always be drivers for technical solutions not vice versa. For example, why offer someone a high-end SUV if only an economic city car is needed?
- In this case, the more agile approach to the entire implementation generated better results.

14.3.2 Iterative requirement gathering

Following an iterative or adaptive requirement gathering approach, which is a cornerstone of Agile, DevOps or Lean methodologies, the emphasis is focused on the discovery and confirmation of a consumer need (the 'what' and not the 'how') via user stories. Typically, consumers cannot articulate specific requirements and questions such as, "What does 'done' look like?" and "What business requirement is being addressed?" are much more meaningful. Following the user story concept, clarity around the 'true' consumer need is discovered first and then the 'how' is developed from a more informed perspective. Following an iterative process, both outputs (steps to get to the desired end point) and outcomes (the business objective desired) are defined (See Appendix E for more information on Agile requirements gathering).

Developing user stories – the card

The intent of the user story is **not** to provide the detail early in the process but develop it in a 'just enough', 'just-in-time' approach. The user story focuses on what the consumer wants to accomplish by documenting the need on a card (usually a 3" × 5" index card). Then, through various conversations between the consumer and the developing team, the consumer need is confirmed. These three elements – card, conversation, confirmation – make up the 3Cs of user stories. A point of emphasis here -- the final solution is unclear, but the team understands the consumer need.

The user story starts with a card that captures a single consumer need. Each card illustrates a single, stand-alone iteration of a consumer need. If multiple concepts are included on the card, it could be considered a user epic and be broken down into individual stories. The user story statement has a distinctive format:

As a <who>, I want <what> so that <why>.

Consider the three parts of the user story:
- **Who** – role (actor or user type) that is interacting with the product/service (e.g. administrator, finance director, student or tax payer);
- **What** – describes the goal or action the user wants the product/service to do (e.g. pre-screen prospective new hires, create financial reports, purchase parking pass or manage retirement payments).
  Note: This part of the statement should be action-oriented (use verbs) and be concise;
- **Why** – describes the reason or the goal/action that is important to the user/actor. These can be positive or negative statements, but they should define the value to the user (e.g. hire the 'right' candidate, speed up the report process, stop getting parking tickets or to manage a monthly budget).

This statement is a simple description of a feature that the consumer wants. It is told from the perspective of that consumer – it is NOT about the product or service but about the need to be fulfilled (desired outcome). Consider the following examples – which one illustrates a simple and concise user story?
- "I want to screen prospective candidates easily so to know their skills";
- "As the Research Manager, I want to create an online assessment for prospective researchers, so I know their skills profile."

The first user story has issues – there is no role/actor, the scope is very broad (what kind of prospective candidates?) and the word 'easily' means exactly what? The second user story is much better – the role is identified (indicating perspective – the question pool for the online assessment may be very different for the HR Manager), the goal is defined (online assessment) as well as the value statement (skills profile). Are there still questions? Of course – what exactly is an 'online assessment'? Further conversations can confirm exactly what this means, capturing the details on the back of the card or developing a new user story for assessment.

> **User cards**
>
> In Figure 64, note the front of the card has a clear need that follows the correct
> format (who, what, why). There is a management number (#49), a priority (on a
> scale of 1-10) and a MoSCoW of 'Must have'. There is also an estimate of effort
> (in days – note that effort can be categorized in multiple ways, e.g. hours, days,
> weeks). The back of the card has designer notes that have come from developers
> listening to and understanding the conversation about user need. These 'designer
> notes' are the confirmation of the need.

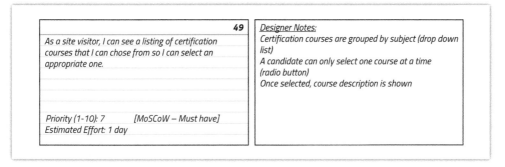

Figure 64 Front and back view of a user story card

14.4 REQUIREMENT ANALYSIS AND AGREEMENT

During requirement analysis, the requirements are assessed and refined. A key input to this analysis is the organizational portfolio. Recall that the portfolio contains not only current products and services but serves as the basis for strategic decision-making. Thus, while the new product or service may have been approved as a *concept*, individual requirements should also be confirmed (are they feasible?) with the organizational strategy, ensuring and maintaining the projected value stream.

The key output of the requirement analysis and agreement activity is the beginning of the Service Blueprint. At this step, the Service Blueprint includes documented, prioritized and validated consumer and stakeholder requirements. Validation activities can include cost/benefit analysis, impact analysis...

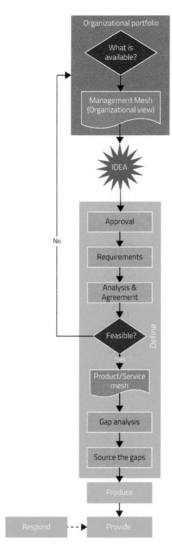

Figure 65 Rejected requirements

Consider this: what happens if one, some, or all of the requirements are outside the parameters of the organizational portfolio? Is that requirement rejected automatically, forgotten, or ignored? Or is it just tossed in with the rest of the requirements and the service provider just does 'their best' to address it? This is a defining moment for the service provider – a decision must be made, at the appropriate level, to effectively act. Consider the options:

- Accept the requirement fully;
- Accept the requirement but with conditions (accept the requirement but in an 'extreme' delivery scenario, add condition(s) based on risk tolerance, health and safety, security…);
- Reject the requirement fully;
- Modify the requirement to meet acceptance criteria.

Remember, the decision to accept or reject a requirement is based on the guardrails – the already established Service Management Principles (represented within the organizational portfolio). If the requirement is accepted and outside the previously defined parameters (e.g. a new line of business), then it would require a modification to the enterprise governance, associated strategy, and Service Management Principles. If it is rejected (See Figure 65), it is rejected with cause – it does not fit within those defined boundaries and the governing body does not envision it impacting future business direction. If the requirement is modified, be sure to capture the modification and its impact to the enterprise strategy, and ensure all documents are updated and reflect current boundaries.

Key activities in analysis and agreement are:
- Elaboration of the requirement through elicitation methods;
- Analysis of the requirements based on the organizational portfolio (feasibility);
- Agreement to the requirements, which leads to the solution design (Service Blueprint).

Multiple roles are involved at this stage – consumers, service/product owners, analysts, architects – all should have input during the various activities. These roles will be defined as per the management method the service provider chooses to follow.

User stories – conversation
The analysis and agreement of user stories is undertaken during the conversation and confirmation aspects of the 3Cs of user stories. Once the card has been completed, arrange them on walls or on a table to facilitate planning and conversation. This conversation is critical. There is a risk that it may be skipped, especially within organizations who are just learning this technique (e.g. "We have the story, let's create the solution!"). Remember, with user stories, all three elements (card, conversation, confirmation) are necessary.

Ensure the right mix of capabilities are involved in the conversation – not only should the consumer be involved (it is their story!) but also the developer and other stakeholders (keep the group reasonably sized for efficient operations). With this mix of stakeholders, a certain empathy develops – the developers understand the consumer targets (functionality and priority) and the product or service owner can concentrate on higher-level requirements as the implementation details are with the developers. The conversation aspect of the user story moves the emphasis from writing requirements to discussing (and understanding) them.

The conversation should be the primary mode of communication between and among the various stakeholders. Not only are all parties working together (maintains focus on the user story and its priorities), miscommunication opportunities are avoided or mitigated. These meetings progressively refine the final delivery with a 'just-in-time' and 'just enough' mentality. Don't make the mistake of assuming the user story is a replacement for the traditional requirement document – the user story is incomplete until conversation occurs and confirmation indicates agreement. Remember, all 3Cs are critical to the user story – card, conversation, confirmation.

 A classic example of miscommunication

In 1999, the Mars Climate Orbiter ($125 million) was designed to be the first weather observer on another planet. However, that was not to be as it burned up in the Martian atmosphere. On review, the disaster cause was miscommunication. Propulsion engineers designed the software that controlled the orbiter's thrusters, to calculate force in *pounds*. A separate piece of software used the produced data but assumed it was in *newtons*. One pound of force is about 4.45 newtons. No one bothered to check – it was assumed the conversion was made.[76]

User stories – confirmation

The outcome of the user story conversation is the confirmation and agreement of the requirements. Each user story will then be prioritized and agreed among the stakeholders (see Figure 61). The back of the user story card indicates high-level developer actions that support the intent of the user story. These actions have been developed during the various conversations and, once captured on the back of the card, confirmed. Now, the developer knows what is expected in that iteration.

Consider using a master requirements document (see Appendix E) to manage multiple requirements or user stories. These documents would certainly be an element of the Service Blueprint. Organizational principles assist in the selection and prioritization of requirements and that information is captured in the master requirement document. Follow good change control practices as well as version control to protect the master document. Using a master requirements document provides a single source of information, specifically:

■ Concise requirements, linking to user stories, and specifications;
■ Statement of key objectives;
■ A description of the working environment for the product or service;
■ Background information and references to other relevant information;
■ Design constraints.

 Requirement prioritization

How should an organization prioritize requirements? Too often, an ambiguous scale is used (consider high, medium, low or essential, conditional, operational) without a clear understanding of what each level means. Even a scale of 1-10 may be

---

76 Grossman, L. (2010, November 10). *Nov. 10, 1999: Metric math mistake muffed Mars meteorology mission*, (Online). https://www.wired.com/2010/11/1110mars-climate-observer-report/. [2018 March].

ambiguous in its meaning! To ensure no misunderstanding, clearly define how any prioritization scale is to be used and what each scale element represents.

There are also numerous illustrations available of complex semi-quantifiable prioritization matrices based on value, cost and risk. In these matrices, typically, a weighting percentage is assigned to each value and then the consumer indicates on a numerical scale the importance of an element. Then, the weighting percentage is applied to the importance value. The resulting value is the priority for that specific element.

Granularity around the scale can also be problematic – consider applying the prioritization scale at a specific level of requirement (e.g. user story, feature, functional requirement). Lastly, no matter what method is used, the method is dependent on the demand for information and control by the stakeholder.

Good requirement gathering
Context
Following an external audit, to comply with regulatory requirements, a financial organization was required to update an existing system and use a more secure email client and setup, mitigating potential data loss (DLP). The organization engaged with a long-term partner to define and implement a project to that effect.

Challenges
The project involved a series of system and configuration changes, but also establishing user clinics and updating large numbers of devices with no disruption to the business.

The updated solution involved more restrictive policies and changing from the native application present on the devices to a more secure one. User acceptance was flagged as a risk for the duration of the project and following its completion.

Although around 50% of the users were based in a coherent geographical area in the same city, the rest were dispersed across multiple locations over a wide geographic area, with many of them highly mobile and not office based.

After a successful trial, the project was approved for implementation from the end of May over the holiday season, since the organization required at least 80% compliance by beginning of Q4 that year.

Although testing during the trial had been signed-off by the organization, during the mass rollout additional use cases were identified and had to be integrated.

Outcome

An agile approach was favored from the beginning for this project:

- A combination of small and medium locations, along with key locations around the Head Office (HO) most likely to yield early positive outcomes were targeted first. This generated good momentum and confidence within the organization for the changes to come and achieving the business target;
- By high summer season, over 50% of the users had been migrated and acceptance within the community of the new solution was high, with no major set-backs;
- By Q4, the IT and Security departments were able to report that almost 90% compliance had been achieved, hence exceeding the business target.

Lessons learned

The project team was composed of well-established personnel from the organization's internal support structure and specialists from the partner. this allowed them to deliver high-quality service in confidence, whilst mitigating user acceptance challenges.

The continuous delivery approach allowed the team build momentum and gain the organization's trust.

Open communication channels allowed any issues identified during the rollout to be dealt with swiftly and effectively, with no impact to the project delivery.

User stories: conclusion

User stories have been the focus of the requirement gathering information for two reasons:

- The ability of the user story and its associated agile delivery to support digitally transforming organizations;
- It is consumer-focused.

While this method is very successful, there are potential issues. The biggest issue is the lack of detail captured on the user story card – the user story is heavily reliant on conversation and documenting those key elements can be time-consuming. Complete documentation relies on collaboration within the team that may or may not be there. Other issues to watch out for include:

- The project has a detailed list of specifications before any actual development begins;
- Updated requirements are not captured and/or communicated to the design and development team;
- The product or service owner writes the specifications without any input from the stakeholder group;
- An uncompromising sign-off from all parties is required before any work begins.

Remember, the goal of Agile requirements is to refine, evolve and mature the user stories (requirements) into a desired solution through a series of releases. Bill Wake's (2003) INVEST acronym is an excellent mnemonic for creating robust user stories. Each release further refines the product or service based on consumer need. The desired solution will probably not occur if the specifications are pre-determined or the requirements are never updated or refined.

Bill Wake's INVEST[77] acronym

To write good user stories, Bill Wake devised the acronym INVEST as a reminder of the properties of good user stories:

- **I**ndependent – stories are unique and describe single, stand-alone elements of functionality with a possibility to implement in any order;
- **N**egotiable – stories are flexible enough for a collaborative definition of success;
- **V**aluable – stories clearly describe consumer value not developer tasks;
- **E**stimable – the difficulty to fulfil the user story can be roughly (or better) estimated;
- **S**mall – the story is 'just right' – it fits the purpose and can be implemented in a single iteration;
- **T**estable – all participants (consumer, developers, testers…) agree on the meaning of the story so tests can be created.

■ 14.5 CHOOSING MANAGEMENT PRACTICES AND TECHNOLOGIES

Part of the agreement activity will be to explore all aspects of the Management Mesh. Thus, there will be a review and agreement around management practices. Questions such as "What management practice should be incorporated?" or "Are the current practices sufficient enough for the new or changed product or service?" will need to be asked and answered. Similar questions will arise from the technology choices. The following sections provide some guidance around choosing management practices and technologies.

14.5.1 Choosing an appropriate management practice

When choosing any management practice, remember the following:

- ■ There is no one best management model – there is no one set of principles that need to be replaced by another;
- ■ Organizational principles may indicate that *multiple* management practices may need to combine to support organizational capabilities and the desired outcome;

---

77 Wake, B. (2003, August). *INVEST in good stories and SMART tasks*, (Online). https://xp123.com/articles/invest-in-good-stories-and-smart-tasks/ [2018 April].

- Management models involve choices – whatever is chosen will shape practice behaviors;
- Principles are invisible and rarely explicit – one is often unaware of the management model used;
- It's never the model itself that brings success, but what is done with it;
- When choosing a management practice or elements within a specific practice, the choice depends on variety of circumstances and competitive factors – those circumstances and factors change over time and even by product or service;
- It is a conscious and distinctive choice about what principles to follow – understand what exists and their alternatives;
- There is no need to deploy new processes when simple activities will do (and then build on them). Keep in mind these axioms: "How do you eat an elephant?" or "How do you jump a chasm?" The answers? One bite at a time or one jump. The point is, there are times when many steps are necessary and there are times when it is an 'all in' situation – know the difference.

Management practices and vocabulary

One last piece of advice. When choosing a management practice, create an enterprise lexicon or glossary and make it readily available to all. Define exactly what is meant when a specific word is used. Why is this important? If more than one management practice is used, there is a risk that a term may mean one thing in a one practice and something entirely different in another. It is beyond the scope of this volume to compile all the various management model specific glossaries. There are numerous resources online that provide some compiled information (e.g. the Online Browsing Platform[78] (OBP) from ISO where specific standards, collections, publications, graphical symbols, terms and definitions can be searched).

Should it be an expectation that everyone uses the correct term all the time? Probably not. However, the resources must be available to unilaterally define (or translate) the term and then work to ensure all parties understand the term so that activities continue to move forward...in the same direction.

The importance of shared terminology
A very large global software organization was well into their 'adopt and adapt' IT Service Management initiative. A group of consultants and trainers were talking with leadership and staff trying to understand current difficulties. The phrases, "It's a problem" or "The problem is…" were used extensively. Collectively, 'problem' was used to describe incidents, continuity events and problems! It didn't make sense to the consultants and trainers as 'problem' had a very specific meaning to them. It wasn't until they specifically asked for a definition, did all the difficulties and stories

---

make sense. There was a corporate moratorium on using the word 'incident' or 'disaster', so everything was 'problem'. What a *problem*!

In another organization, different teams and departments referred to different things as 'changes' – the IT department referred to 'IT changes', the Project Management Office (PMO) referred to 'project changes', and the executive team referred to 'business changes'. When emails were sent out, no one knew what the change was and confusion ruled.

14.5.2 Choosing appropriate technology

Quote

"Technology does not provide value to a business. It never has (except for technology in products). Instead, technology's value comes from doing business differently because technology makes it possible."

George Westerman[79]

The effective use of emerging technologies has a significant influence on the success of the digital organization. It is tempting for an organization to select technology based on marketing hype or other extraneous influences. Often, it seems that the application of a technology would be an easy fix to business challenges. Selecting the wrong or inappropriate technology can be a very expensive mistake for an organization. Investing in technology is never without risk and there is rarely (if ever) a complete fit of a technology to a business need.

The progressive organization recognizes that the use of emerging technology must be based on understanding the business strategy of the organization, then finding the most appropriate technology that enables realization of that strategy. Following a technology-first approach often leads to shortsighted thinking. In a technology-first approach, often, technology is used in ways it was never intended in an attempt to meet a business need, rather than the business need driving the appropriate technology solution.

Common mistakes when choosing technologies

Do any of these sound familiar? Remember: forewarned is forearmed.
- Picking a technology first and then finding a problem it can solve;
- Overbuying ("eyes bigger than the stomach");
- Under-buying (cheap but ineffective solutions);

79 Westerman, G. (2017, October 25). Your company doesn't need a digital strategy (Online). https://sloanreview.mit.edu/article/your-company-doesnt-need-a-digital-strategy/. [2018, May].

- Not understanding of ongoing costs (for example, maintenance, license fees…);
- Will it "get in the door?" (were measurements taken for size, weight and other physical parameters…);
- Is it compatible with current investments?

Who should make technology decisions?

To have success in the digital age, all organizational capabilities must have an awareness of what technology can do to positively impact the business. Traditionally, technology decisions have been left to the IT capability to make, often with little to no involvement from other organizational capabilities (whether by design or due to lack of participation). Consider the risk or impact if capabilities are not involved in this decision – the emergence of shadow IT clearly indicates that an IT-only decision is not the way forward.

While the IT capability with its inherent technical expertise may be the most qualified to evaluate technology, technology decisions must be made with the involvement of all appropriate capabilities within the organization. Taking an approach that includes all pertinent capabilities ensures that all perspectives are considered, business needs are understood fully across the capabilities, and the evaluation criteria for using technology are defined and agreed.

Decision-making methods and techniques

Organizations must find a balance between having a sense of urgency and performing an adequate level of analysis in the decision-making process. Finding this balance ensures that decisions are not based on misinformation or are taken without exercising an appropriate level of due diligence.

To facilitate the decision-making process, there are several tools (see Table 7) that an organization can utilize to help in making decisions. There is no one decision-making tool that is superior to another; organizations may find that using a combination of tools can be helpful for reaching a final decision.

Implications of being an 'early adopter'

Being an early adopter of emerging technologies can have its benefits as well as its risks. Organizations that are 'early adopters' can have a significant influence on the continued development of the technology. Being first in the market using a new technology may provide a differentiating product or service in the organization's industry vertical.

However, there is potential business risk associated with the early adoption of an emerging technology. For example, the new technology may not be fully tested for its intended use. Additionally, there may be less formalized or completely absent

Table 7 Decision-making methods and techniques

Decision-making method	Description
Conjoint analysis	A method used to determine the value of each feature of a product or service to determine consumer preferences. Understanding what the majority of consumers prefer can be beneficial for making a decision.
Cost-benefit analysis	Used to weigh the financial ramifications of each possible alternative to come to a final decision that makes the most sense from an economic perspective.
Decision matrix	A table used to evaluate all options of a decision, with all options listed in the first column and all factors affecting the decision listed in the first row. Those participating in the decision score each option and weigh which factors are of more importance. A final score is tallied to determine the best option.
Decision tree	A model that involves contemplating each option and its outcomes. Statistical analysis is also conducted using this technique.
Multivoting	Used when multiple people are involved in making the decision. Help in narrowing down many options to a smaller set to the eventual final decision.
Pareto analysis	A technique used when numerous decisions need to be made. Helps in prioritizing which ones should be made first by determining which decisions will have the greatest overall impact.
PESTEL	Whilst PESTEL is an assessment tool, it can be used as a decision-making tool as well. PESTEL (Political, Economic, Social, Technical, Environmental and Legal) is a technique that can improve decision-making and timing through analyzing external factors and evaluating a decision from each of the six domains. This method considers present trends to help predict future ones.
SWOT	A SWOT analysis can be used as a decision-making tool. SWOT is a tool used to determine the Strengths, Weaknesses, Opportunities, and Threats (SWOT) of a particular option.
T-chart	Use of a T-Chart ensures that all positives (plusses) and negatives (minuses) are considered when making a decision.

support channels available from the supplier, which may result in higher adoption costs.

Of course, these concerns may not be considered to be risks at all depending on the culture of the organization.

14.6 CONCLUSION: MANAGING REQUIREMENTS

New products and services, defined as those that have never been delivered, are developed for various strategic reasons. For example, the organization makes the strategic decision to enter a new market space, creates an innovative solution or technology or needs to meet new demands from consumers. These new products or services will typically have a heavy assessment process, ensuring the new product or service is within the strategic direction of the organization or, if not, that the strategic implications are fully considered, including a potential change in strategic direction.

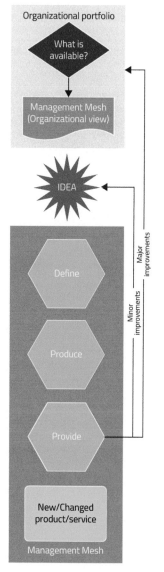

Figure 66 VeriSM and Improvements

Products or services that are already in place will fall within a continual improvement cycle and will change as need demands. That need may rise from an organizational strategic review, change in consumer need, change in technology, development of new features or others. In an Agile environment, these requirements may come from the product backlog. In a traditional environment, the changes may come from original requirements that were not included in the delivered product or service (consider the 'could' and 'won't' requirements from a MoSCoW analysis).

Most management practices provide guidance on managing unmet requirements – follow that guidance. Any collected information should be managed via an organizational change control process and associated policies. The impact to the organization and the consumer should be assessed and managed following the principles of organizational change management (OCM). As shown in in Figure 66, the improvement cycle is managed easily within VeriSM: minor improvements cycle through the Define-Produce activities, while major improvements need to begin with the review of the organizational portfolio.

Whatever the situation – minor or major improvements – the requirements will be assessed against the organizational strategic plan, governing factors, principles, and the organizational portfolio. The requirement lifecycle has begun again.

Real world example: Hippo Digital/Kidz Klub Leeds

Chapter 27 shows how Hippo Digital worked with charity Kidz Klub Leeds using a design sprint/hack day to understand their requirements and redesign the charity's system for working with volunteers.

"Design sprints can help when there is a shortage of resources (time, money…) or if there are a number of ideas that need to be tested quickly. With Kidz Klub, the challenge was mainly a lack of time for planning/change as the charity spends the majority of its time helping kids."

■ 14.7 VERISM UNWRAPPED: REQUIREMENTS

Once requirements have been agreed, a Management Mesh for the specific product or service can be produced. Following the generic example started in Section 12.4, a new product or service has been proposed and the gathered requirements have confirmed some new elements. As a result of several clarifying discussions, there are some new requirements that are not currently within the organizational Management Mesh, including:

■ Suppliers – new suppliers have been included and potentially managed via SIAM. While not confirmed, there is a possibility of outsourcing the technologies needed for the new product or service;

■ ISO/IEC 20000 – a new customer for whom the new service is specifically designed, requires ISO/IEC 20000 certification;

■ To meet the demands of the new market, DevOps practices are crucial. The service provider must incorporate those practices into the delivery of the new product or service;

■ Several emerging technologies will be exploited in the design and delivery of the new product or service. While the requirements are known, the 'how' to get it done, is not known. There is a possibility of outsourcing the technologies. This will be decided after a gap analysis during the sourcing plans.

In Figure 67, all requirements have been mapped to the mesh. The red lines signify the requirements for the new or changed product or service.

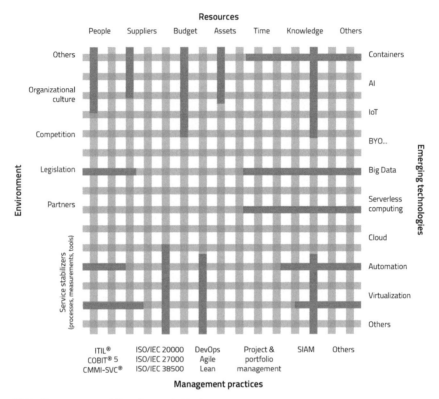

Figure 67 VeriSM unwrapped: Requirements Mesh

14.8 VERISM APPLIED: FCH REQUIREMENTS

As the next step in developing the FCH Wearable Wellness program, user stories were collected from a sample of stakeholders, now called the 'Wearable Team' or WT for short. The team includes:

■ A sample from the consumer group representing the target audience (adults between 35-45 years old holding FCH insurance policies);

■ A sample group from the Wellness program of physicians, nurses and fitness staff;

■ A representative from the Insurance group;

■ The product owner (the physical wearable) and service owner (program functionality, data management, reporting...);

■ Designers and developers.

The WT created numerous user stories. The user stories are not all perfect, but they do represent the consumer and stakeholder needs. Some of them include:

- As a participant in the Wearable Wellness program, I want the FCH wearable to maintain a charge for at least a week and can be recharged within two hours, so I do not lose any potential exercise data;
- As a participant in the Wearable Wellness program, I want feedback during my exercise time, so I know when I'm not performing in my target heartrate range;
- As a participant in the Wearable Wellness program, I want the FCH wearable to count the number of laps I swim, so I can concentrate on my performance;
- As a Wellness program physician, I want consolidated reports for each patient, so I can review their performance/participation at their semi-annual physicals;
- As a Wellness program physician, I want real-time emergency communication, so I can prevent or mitigate a critical health issue (heart attack, stroke…) proactively;
- As a Wellness program nurse, I want real-time warnings if a participant exceeds maximum performance levels (indicated by heart rate, respiration, blood pressure) for longer than 3 minutes, so I can send an emergency signal to the participant to stop;
- As the Insurance program manager, I want concise reports on participant performance (exercise time/day, distance covered…), so the appropriate discounts on personal medical insurance can be applied.

Multiple conversations within the WT occurred and the design/development team clarified the requests so that the appropriate functionality could be delivered. The group then prioritized the requests and the initial iteration of the FCH wearable included the following features:

- The physical wearable is waterproof and sweat-proof. It can capture vital sign data during all types of activity;
- Each individual wearable is individually programmable by the FCH Wellness staff to reflect the prescribed exercise parameters;
- The initial reporting features are by participant as a bi-weekly summary (ability to drill down to daily performance, if necessary);
- An emergency signal (loud 'whistle') occurs if the participant exceeds maximum performance levels for longer than 3 minutes.

Additional features, based on priority, were confirmed.

As a result of the confirmation, a specific mesh for the FCH Wearable Wellness program was created (see Figure 68). Note the need for several emerging technologies and new management practices:

- Suppliers- several new suppliers are proposed to support the physical wearable, as well as consultants to support the ISO/IEC 27001 certification process and the SIAM implementations;

- Competition – due the innovative nature of the new product or service, the service provider's Sales and Marketing capability must actively promote and market to existing and new market spaces;
- ISO/IEC 27001 – as the new product or service has interactions with personal data, the service provider has engaged consultancy to assist in their efforts to achieve and maintain the ISO/IEC 27001 certificate;
- Agile – due to the required timeframe for this initiative, it was agreed the use of Agile methodologies were necessary to deliver the pilot within the six-month timeframe;
- SIAM – the new product and service has many components from supplier organizations, thus an initiative to deploy SIAM principles for managing those relationships is required;
- Big Data, IoT and AI – in the design of the new product or service, the service provider is exploiting these technologies to reach new market spaces as well as maintain current consumers with cutting edge innovation and technology.

An initial Service Blueprint is created to reflect the activities to this point. Elements that may be included are the cost-benefit analysis, service impact analysis, potential changes to management processes and initial procedures for report production (data management and manipulation).

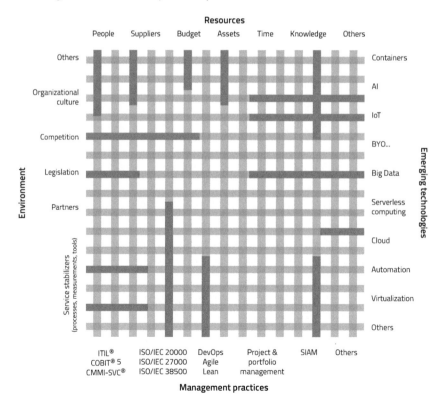

Figure 68 FCH requirements – needs for the Wearable Wellness program

15 Define: analyzing gaps

Introduction

A gap analysis exercise has a simple purpose: compare the current state with a desired state, determine the 'gaps' and then devise a plan to overcome those gaps. This activity has the outcome of defining the elements necessary for the solution.

Many techniques and tools exist to discover why gaps exist and how to overcome them. These tools include simple spreadsheets, surveys, Fishbone analysis, SWOT analysis, PEST or PESTEL analysis, McKinsey 7S framework, the Burke-Litwin model or the Nadler-Tushman model. Each has its own benefits and application conditions.

This chapter specifically focuses on a basic gap analysis, the McKinsey 7S framework, the Burke-Litwin model, and the Nadler-Tushman model.

■ 15.1 PERFORM A GAP ANALYSIS

Organizations undergo a gap analysis for many reasons and the most common reason is to raise performance levels. The concept of a gap analysis is found in Figure 70. Note there is a pre-defined desired state and once the current state is known, several steps delineating the necessary actions are defined. This type of analysis has numerous granularity levels from organization-wide to a specific project or even for strategic development. The key to success for a gap analysis is to define clearly the scope of the analysis and the desired state. The desired state is based on business position and direction, competition, skill requirements or any other measurable condition.

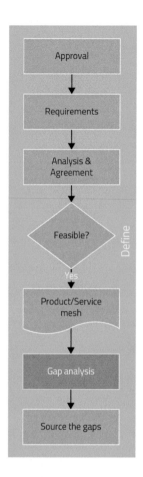

Figure 69 Analyze the gaps

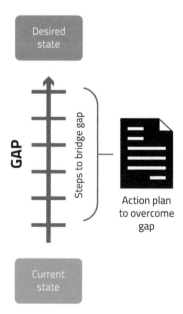

Figure 70 A simple gap analysis

■ 15.2 STEPS TO PERFORM A GAP ANALYSIS

The high-level steps are:

- Describe the AS-IS state:
  - List the attributes that require improvement. This list could be narrow or broad, quantitative or qualitative such as current skill sets, organizational objectives, performance levels (50 orders per day) or cultural observations (lack of organizational diversity) respectively;
  - Ensure specific and factual – the point is to be able to identify and measure weaknesses (and eventual improvement);
- Describe the TO-BE state:
  - This list is the 'ideal' state, which can be very specific (increasing orders from 50 to 100 orders per day) or more generic (improve the work environment focusing on inclusivity). Generic lists will need to have more detail added as the analysis progresses;
- Define the measures and metrics that define the performance and quality criteria that monitor gap reduction activities;
- Analyze the difference between the AS-IS and TO-BE, and recommend methods to overcome the gaps:
- Consider the factors responsible for the gap (be specific, objective, and relevant);
- Methods of analysis include spreadsheets, surveys, Fishbone analysis, SWOT analysis, PEST or PESTEL analysis, McKinsey 7S framework or the Nadler-Tushman model;
- Define possible solutions to overcome the gaps. The solutions should be action-oriented, specific and measurable;
- Define a strategy to improve the processes, procedures, technologies, systems, staff, infrastructure and organizational structures that will reduce/remove the gaps;
- Gain stakeholder agreement and deploy the strategy.

■ 15.3 TECHNIQUES FOR ANALYZING AND MANAGING GAPS

Several techniques for analyzing and managing gaps have been discussed already throughout this book, specifically SWOT analysis, PEST or PESTLE analysis, Ishikawa or Fishbone analysis. The remainder of this chapter will concentrate on organizationally focused methods, specifically the McKinsey 7S, the Burke-Litwin and the Nadler-Tushman.

15.3.1 McKinsey 7S framework

The McKinsey 7S framework is a useful technique to understand if the organization is positioned to achieve its objectives or to review underperformance of a single capability, team or project. The outcome of this analysis is a statement of alignment. The model consists of seven elements, categorized as either 'hard' or 'soft'. Hard elements are easy to define and influence, such as:

- Strategy – how to maintain and build competitive advantage (elements include a mission and vision statement, principles and policies);
- Structure – how the organization is organized (organization charts, lines of reporting);
- Systems – day-to-day activities and procedures used to complete work (formal processes, IT).

Soft elements are more difficult to define, less tangible and influenced by culture. These elements are:

- Shared values – the core values of the organization reflected in the corporate culture and work ethic;
- Skills – general capabilities of employees (strongest skills, skill gaps, what does the organization do well…);
- Style – leadership style(s);
- Staff – actual skills and competences of the workforce (positions or specializations, competency gaps…).

Superordinate goals or shared values are at the core of the model and they are key to the development of the other elements. These goals reflect why the organization was created and for what it stands (see Figure 71; from Waterman, Peters and Philips[80] (1980)). As the goals change, so will the other elements.

This model operates on the principle that all seven factors interact equally and each must be present and aligned for effective operations. Therefore, this model will identify the elements that require realignment as a result of change (e.g. restructuring, new service, merger/acquisition, leadership change and others). As each element is interrelated, the wider impact of a seemingly small change can be assessed. Once the AS-IS and TO-BE situations are defined, assess the seven elements and adjust/tune them so the organization remains effective. This is neither simple nor quick – the 'right' leadership, sponsorship, knowledge, skills and experience are still necessary.

---

80 Waterman, Jr., R. H., Peters, T. J., & Philips, J. R. (1980). Structure is not organization. *Business Horizons*, **23**(3), 14-26.

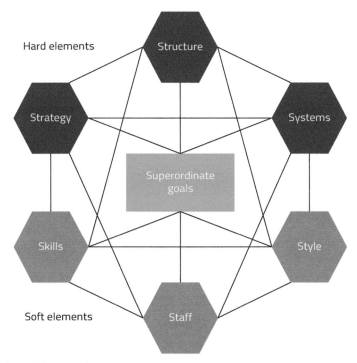

Figure 71 McKinsey 7s framework

15.3.2 Burke-Litwin model

An alternative model to the McKinsey 7S is the Burke-Litwin model[81] (see Figure 72). Burke-Litwin utilizes twelve variables (it includes all seven from McKinsey) but posits the external environment (e.g. markets, legislation, competition, economy) is the most powerful driver for organizational change. All factors interact, and a change in one can eventually impact the others.

The external environment factor influences the strategy, leadership and organizational culture. These are considered long-term, transformational influences (a change in one of these factors will impact the entire organization and staff). These transformational factors will drive organizational change.

Collectively, these transformational factors influence the structure, work climate, management practices, and systems (policies and procedures). This set is more transactional and operational in nature (may or may not impact the entire organization). These factors are more relevant when refining or modifying the performance of an organization. Together, the transformational and transactional factors affect motivation, which in turn impacts performance (individual and organizational). For change to be sustainable, the transformational and transactional factors must be consistent with each other.

---

81 Burke, W. W., & Litwin, G. H. (1992). A causal model of organization performance and change. *Journal of Management*, **18**(3), 523–545.

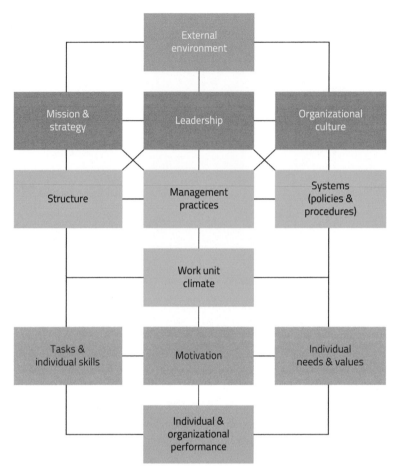

Figure 72 A stylized view of the Burke-Litwin model

To use this model, data is collected from surveys, organizational reviews or interviews. Data is then structured to reflect corporate, departmental and individual levels, thus providing insight into the functionality of the organizational structure. Correlations of data can provide insights into employee satisfaction and motivation, customer satisfaction, and profitability to name a few.

15.3.3 Nadler-Tushman model

An alternative to the 7S or the Burke-Litwin models is the Nadler-Tushman model[82]. This model looks at how the entire organization works together. Sometimes known as the Congruence model, the organization is viewed as a social system that is made up of four elements (people, work, structure, and culture) that transform inputs into outputs. These elements collectively define organizational performance. Note how strategy provides the input and direction to the four elements. The more

---

82 Nadler, D. A., & Tushman, M. L. (1980). A model for diagnosing organizational behavior. *Organizational Dynamics*, **9**(2) 35-51.

congruence between these four elements, the better the performance (see Figure 73). For example, if there are brilliant people within the organization but the culture hinders their performance, their brilliance will not be exploited. The same can be true if there is great technology and great decision-making processes but if the culture is heavily bureaucratic, no benefit will be gained.

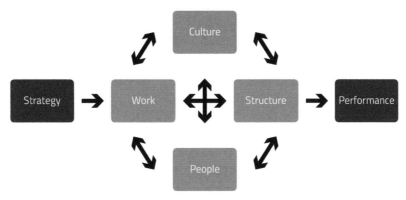

Figure 73 Nadler-Tushman model

To use this model, analyze each element (culture, work, structure, people) separately then analyze how they relate to each other. Consider the following:

■ Work – what work is done and how it is processed;
■ People – what types of people are currently performing the critical tasks;
■ Structure – what are the structure, systems and processes that support the organization;
■ Culture – what are the attitudes, beliefs, commitment, and motivations evident (these are unwritten and typically hard to define).

As each element is compared to the others, look for areas of congruence (works well) or incongruence (ineffective outcomes). The last step is to resolve the major incongruences, prioritized within organizational strategy, and reinforce the congruent efforts.

■ 15.4 CONCLUSION: GAP ANALYSIS

The purpose of the gap analysis is to not only identify the gaps but to also create a strategy and eventual plan to overcome those gaps. Many of the management models and practices presented in Appendix D can assist in those efforts, especially in leadership, strategy, culture, and skills. Removing the more tangible gaps (assets, technologies, and the like), are usually handled via sourcing strategies, which are discussed in the next chapter.

A final word: do not forget as gaps are assessed to include the impact on skills and capabilities in the scope of the assessment. The models presented include these elements – they are critical to the overall success of the new or changed product or service. View this gap not only from the view of the service provider but also the consumer, thus have appropriate training, communication and marketing plans. These plans would be included in the Service Blueprint to be operationalized in later stages.

■ 15.5 VERISM UNWRAPPED: INTERPRETING GAPS

In Figure 74, the impact to the current mesh is now known – what the organization currently has (green) and what is needed (red). Brown indicates existing elements that may need additional capacity or resources to support the new product or service.

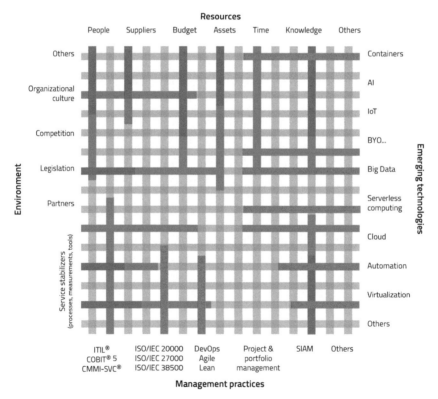

Figure 74 VeriSM unwrapped: interpreting the gaps

Looking at the high-level view of the mesh, several new capabilities are needed: AI, IoT and Big Data, and security measures from the ISO/IEC 27000 series. There are several areas where the 'available' and 'need' overlap (shown as brown lines). These areas should be assessed to see if **new** or additional resources are needed to effectively address the new product or service. For example, consider the following questions:

■ Will new legislative expertise/information be necessary?
■ Does the current marketing and promotion plan (and staff) have the ability to address and overcome the competition?
■ Will additional people be required with expertise in the new technology areas or will a concentrated training plan fulfill the need?
■ Are additional technology assets required or can current assets fulfill the proposed solution?
■ Are the appropriate knowledge articles available or can they be developed or gained?

In the service stabilizer areas, an assessment of the processes showed they could integrate the new product or service without difficulty, but the measurement area requires the development of additional measurements, metrics and reports. The impact to service integration (SIAM) was minimal – it was determined the current service integrator could handle the requirements for the new product or service.

■ 15.6 VERISM APPLIED: FCH GAPS

Looking at Figure 75, several different gap analysis activities will occur around the FCH Wearable Wellness program. Using a similar structure as in Section 15.5, the overlapping lines show what is available (yellow) and what is needed but currently unavailable (red). Where elements are already available and new requirements overlap those areas, that overlap is shown in orange. Review Figure 75 and note the following gaps.

■ Resources:
The four areas that have been noted (knowledge, assets, budget, people) are quite robust at this point. From the strategic initiative, budget has already been allocated, thus included. What will be necessary is to ascertain the gaps in knowledge and people. Use any of the previous models (McKinsey 7S, Burke-Litwin...) to discover skill and associated knowledge gaps. Also, consider the impact of this new service and include potential organizational change management initiatives to help people to incorporate the new service into their support and delivery protocols. For assets, a careful look is required due the heavy duplication, but also because of the data center consolidation initiative;

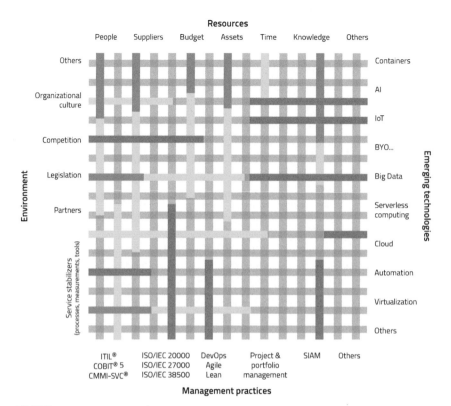

Figure 75 FCH gaps

■ Environment:

The clear gap on this side of the mesh is the competition aspect. As wearables are popular, especially across Gen Y and Gen Z, an effective promotion and marketing campaign is necessary. The direct impact is to the Insurance Marketing capability. The second gap may be in the service stabilizer area around measurements. A key element of this new service is the reporting and tracking of performance. Currently, reporting is questionable in FCH. Therefore, this new service is a perfect opportunity to clarify and improve the reporting activities. Additional skills to fulfil the new requirements of the new service may be required;

■ Management practices:

Three new management practices are required: ISO/IEC 27001, Agile, and SIAM. ISO/IEC 27001 is required to address the additional controls for data security (the decision was made to gain this certificate as it would also satisfy many of the requirements around patient confidentiality). To meet the stakeholder expectations for delivery within the six months, Agile practices are to be introduced to the established ITIL processes to expedite service delivery. SIAM is being addressed to bring an integrated approach to the many suppliers to FCH. All three areas are totally new to FCH and will require expertise, thus a key element within the sourcing plan;

- Emerging technologies:
  Multiple new technologies are possible for the FCH Wearable Wellness initiative, including AI, IoT, Big Data, Cloud, Blockchain and others. As there is no specific information in the case study other than the events around a data center consolidation, it might be presumed these technologies and others may be deployed. This gap may be addressed in the sourcing activities. Additionally, there must be a concerted effort within the IT capability for cooperation between the designers and developers.

16 Define: source the gaps

Introduction

This chapter focuses on the methods that allow the organization to source the identified gaps. A key element within sourcing is the definition of a sourcing policy based on the Service Management principles. This policy will provide guidance to the capabilities responsible for sourcing the needed elements to produce the agreed product or service.

Once the requirements for the new or changed product or service have been agreed, the plan for getting from concept to the outcome is defined. The current mesh is vital at this stage, as it states what is currently available in terms of resources, environment, emerging technologies and management practices. A key consideration here is what is to be done to address the requirements for which solutions are not readily available?

Within VeriSM, the enterprise governance and the supporting Service Management Principles will guide the development a sourcing plan. This plan will consider the options and define the operating policies and practices for the sourcing activities. This plan should be a part of an overall project plan and managed accordingly.

A relevant organizational capability for sourcing is procurement. Many organizations have procurement departments with responsibilities for specifications development, value analysis, supplier research, negotiation, buying activities, contract development and administration, inventory control, receiving and stores.

The purchase of products and services, in the context of sourcing the gaps in the Management Mesh, is an important aspect of procurement. All procurement activities will be guided by defined Service Management Principles and accompanying policies. Another important capability is contract management, which ensures that contracts initially meet the needs of the organization and that they continue to do so throughout the contract period.

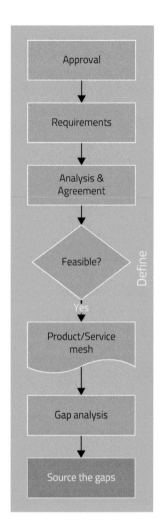

Figure 76 Source the gaps

Contract management is the process of systematically and efficiently managing contract creation with external parties, up to and including execution and analyzing the execution. The aim is to maximize operational and financial supplier performance and reduce risks. Therefore, contract management includes the broad spectrum of:

- All types of sourcing;
- Purchasing process;
- Implementation and performance of agreements;
- Performance of suppliers;
- Management of appointments and dates;
- Relationship management with all relevant stakeholders.

Procurement and contract management capabilities are important elements in resource and management practice areas of the Management Mesh if sourcing is to be considered.

◼ 16.1 SOURCING OPTIONS

Based on organizational strategy, source the gaps. There are many sourcing options to consider, including:
- **Insourcing** – work completed in-house rather than contracted externally;
- **Outsourcing** – one organization provides services for another:
  - **Onshore** (domestic outsourcing) – an external outside organization based within same country;
  - **Offshore**– an organization based in another country, typically working at a much cheaper rate;
  - **Global Sourcing** – source across geopolitical boundaries; exploit the efficiencies;
- **Co-sourcing** – combine insourcing and outsourcing to fill gaps in internal expertise;
- **Partnership** – pool resources and share profit and loss in accordance with terms;
- **Multi-sourcing** – strategy that treats a given function, such as IT, as a portfolio of activities, some of which should be outsourced and others of which should be performed by internal staff; requires strong governance and oversight to ensure overall successful delivery (also known as multi-vendor sourcing). In response to the challenges organizations face when using multiple service providers as part of their supply network, a service integration approach such as service integration and management (SIAM) is often used. SIAM provides a standardized methodology for integrating and managing multiple service providers and their services. It enhances the management of the end to end supply chain, and provides governance, management, integration, assurance and coordination to maximize the value received.
- **Business Process Outsourcing** (BPO) – contracting a business function to an outside organization in order to reduce costs (can be done on- or offshore):
- **Knowledge Process Outsourcing** (KPO) (a type of high-end BPO) – knowledge and information related work carried out by a different organization or subsidiary within the same organization (the intent is to save costs/resources);
- **Public cloud** – task solved using multiple technologies including the internet.

Importance of understanding the contract

Whichever sourcing option is chosen, do not forget to clearly define contract terms, vocabulary and intentions – too many times poor relationships are the outcome of loosely defined contracts leading to inconsistent interpretation of the agreed terms.

16.1.1 Strategic sourcing

Strategic sourcing is an organization-wide, collaborative activity that goes beyond traditional supply chain management. The purpose is to leverage consolidated purchasing power across all capabilities to find the best possible value from services and service providers in the marketplace. The silo mentality of purchasing is transformed into a cross-functional, cross-location team through developing long-term relationships with service providers that are capable of providing quality products and services at lower costs.

Strategic sourcing is a systematic, fact-based approach that optimizes the supply base, as well as improving the value proposition. It has a total cost of ownership (TCO) focus where consumer needs, organizational goals and market conditions are drivers for choice and decisions. The scope of strategic sourcing goes well beyond negotiating the purchase price (amount paid to the supplier) and extends to the total acquisition and ongoing transactional costs associated with managing the service provider relationships and delivered services.

Strategic sourcing is about engaging the best product/service at the optimal value rather than the cheapest. The approach is rigorous (see Appendix F – Steps for strategic sourcing) and collaborative, as the strategic sourcing team consists of representatives from across the organization. Procurement teams take a leading role in actively managing the supply chain through ongoing collaboration with internal stakeholders and external service providers, whilst critically analyzing organizational spend and managing supplier risks. This is not a one-and-done activity, but a continuous process that is based on the objectives of:

- Improving the value-to-price relationship;
- Leveraging the entire organizational spend;
- Understanding category buying and identifying improvement opportunities;
- Agreeing multi-year contracts with standardized terms and conditions.

Advantages of strategic sourcing are:
- Best practice sharing;
- Cost savings;
- Increase quality;
- Create partnerships with suppliers;
- Standardized pricing;
- Improve operational efficiency;
- Access to new suppliers.

A word of caution here: do not forget to include the possibility of niche suppliers. Efficiencies are gained from the key suppliers delivering commodity items or items that a have a variety of sources. However, this might stifle innovation if niche suppliers are not considered, simply because they do not fit within the sourcing strategy.

■ 16.2 VERISM UNWRAPPED: SOURCING PROTOCOLS

Enterprise governance and the supporting Service Management Principles will define the operating policies and practices for the sourcing activities. Ensure the connection between procurement, purchasing, finance and the product or service team.

■ 16.3 VERISM APPLIED: FCH SOURCING

As sourcing is one of the Service Management Principles, it is important to define a sourcing policy. The sourcing policy is a code of conduct defined in a set of associated policies covering each of the elements of the approach to sourcing services and service providers. FCH has defined the following policy statement:

> "It is the sourcing policy of FireCloud Health to obtain all supplies, equipment and services at the lowest cost to the hospital that meet or exceed the consumer's specifications for performance, quality and availability at the time of purchase. The decision process will be based on the capability, capacity and historical performance of the supplier. Supplier diversity and environmental impact will be considered in the decision process. Competitive bids will be solicited whenever possible and practical, and in compliance with all applicable federal regulations and hospital policies."

As such, several requests were prepared and posted for the various elements of the FCH Wearable, including (not a full list):
- The physical device;
- Design/product management staff;
- Web and mobile engineering staff;
- Firmware engineer;
- An ISO/IEC 27001 consultant;
- A SIAM consultant.

Additionally, a search was initiated to look for organizations who could take on the entire service as an outsourced delivery.

Once all necessary elements were commercially engaged, the Service Blueprint was updated and presented to the design and development teams for the build, test and eventual deployment (Produce stage).

17 VeriSM Produce, Provide and Respond stages

Introduction

This chapter provides a brief insight into the remaining stages, specifically, Produce, Provide and Respond. As a quick reminder, these activities tend to be more mature in the overall scheme of things. Organizations have invested in frameworks and methodologies to support the design, build, test, deploy and support activities. VeriSM clearly states, those processes and procedures should be retained as long as they are providing value. Requirements will dictate what management method or technology are used. It is up to the organization to choose the method or technology based on their mesh and enterprise governance.

Therefore, this chapter will focus on how management practices can be merged and how to ensure in-place processes are as efficient and as effective as they need to be.

The output of the Define stage is the Service Blueprint. Within the Blueprint, there are several elements, including, among others:
- Master requirements;
- Design solution;
- Sourcing and procurement plans;
- Build and testing instructions;
- Performance requirements;
- Preparation plans (training, communication, marketing...)

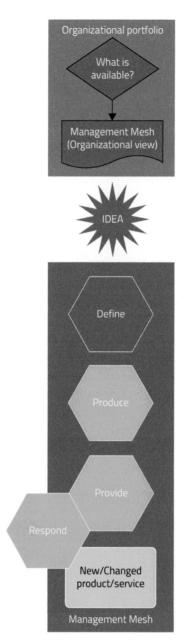

Figure 77 Produce, Provide & Respond

This Blueprint contains critical information for the next three stages: Produce, Provide and Respond (see Figure 77). *These stages will follow the activities from the management practice or practices chosen by the service provider.* It is never the intent of VeriSM to replace *any* management practice but rather provide an integrated enterprise view of service management. What VeriSM does recommend is this: critically assess in-place processes with a focus on lean and agile practices – do any steps create waste (time, resource, skills)? Are there any steps that could become more efficient without increasing organizational risk? Does the process meet the needs of the organization in terms of the defined enterprise governance and Service Management Principles?

■ 17.1 PRODUCE

The main activities within the Produce stage are build, test and deploy within the guidelines of defined change controls. Follow the chosen management practice protocols, ensuring all elements of the Service Blueprint are addressed. Remember, VeriSM exploits what is already in place and provides the option of including other management practices based on consumer requirements. Therefore, the key elements that must be addressed and/or reviewed in this stage, from a VeriSM perspective, are:

■ Service Management Principles (guardrails):
  • Ensure the development of the new or changed product or service accurately reflect the defined principles. Update as necessary;
■ Service stabilizers:
  • Define the necessary measurements with the consumer and begin collecting that data (to show improvement or performance once the service or product goes 'live'- see Chapter 8 Outcomes);
  • Consider the impact of the new or changed product or service to the various management processes or functions – will more capacity be required? Additional continuity measures? A change in security measures?
  • Evaluate support tools and ensure they can support the new or changed product or service. If there is a need to update or add a new tool, follow the necessary change control protocols.

17.1.1 Merging management practices

Often in the delivery of a product or service, more than one management practice is necessary. Are the practices operated separately or are they merged? Currently, one such dilemma is around IT service management practices such as ITIL or COBIT and the emergence of the progressive practices such as Agile, DevOps and Lean.

If an organization experiences 'conflict' between management practices or how teams are working, the VeriSM model can help. Guided by the organization's enterprise governance and Service Management Principles, the key elements (what is actually important) for each management practice are clearly evident. Teams have direction. This allows all staff to focus on what they are trying to achieve, namely, meeting the needs of the consumer, not achieving a perfect process or way of working. This guidance (governance and supporting principles) can cut through the unnecessary tribalism (e.g., waterfall versus Agile) and a misguided focus on management practice artifacts, theatrics and power-plays (e.g. mandatory form-filling, inflated role titles).

Where there is a 'clash' between different management practices, step back and critically assess – is it really the management practice itself or the level of familiarity and comfort with one practice over another that is creating the difficulty? In reality, the core activities within any management practice are similar (see "Conflicting management practices" below). Rather than wasting resources debating the merits of one management practice over another, define and embrace the elements that meet consumer needs and best support the organization's enterprise governance and Service Management Principles. Then, collaborate to build an integrated way of working. A culture that supports collaboration (see Chapter 6) and embraces change (see Chapter 5) creates teams that are willing to learn from each other and try new things. Don't forget: management practices that work well in one area of the organization may be adapted more broadly. See Appendix C – How management practices evolve – for some examples.

Conflicting management practices

For an example in this area, consider one of the greatest misconceptions or misunderstandings in today's IT community: the lack of change control within an Agile environment. Too often the focus is on the speed of delivery (interpreted as 'out of control') and the multiple iterations of delivering a product or service (interpreted as 'too disruptive'). Understand that the controls of a change process are still included and necessary – Agile principles are not and were not developed to increase risk to the consumer or service provider. Therefore, the question is, "How does Agile reflect and embrace change controls?".

Figure 78 illustrates the basic activities in a waterfall change management process and the basic steps in an Agile Scrum flow. Both sets of activities are aligned by similarities as illustrated with the dotted line dividers. For example, both will start with some sort of a request process – change control activities may begin with a request for change (RFC), change proposal, or a business case; Agile is no different, but would depend on the organization. The record and assess activities are very similar to Agile's product backlog. Both sets of activities do have an authorization point – within waterfall, this occurs with a change authority (Change Advisory Board – CAB) prior to the built, test and deploy activities. At the same level, the product owner will be determining the next iteration based on the user story and team prioritization. Within Agile, the Sprint Review is similar to a CAB – a review is completed around the current increment (or Sprint), its success (or not) and whether or not that increment is 'approved' and will be deployed. Both activities are managed with a defined role (change manager and product owner) and each role is accountable for the operation of process or product.

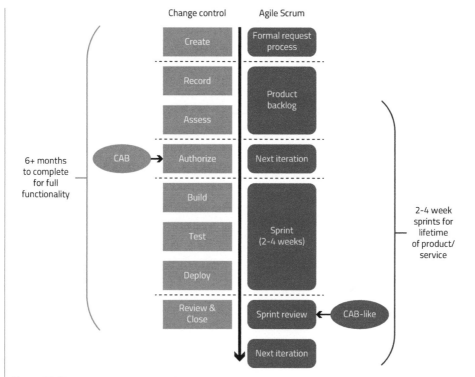

Figure 78 Change control versus Agile Scrum change control

The difference between the linear/waterfall approach and the Agile sprint is obviously time. The waterfall approach tends to deliver the full product or service in one iteration (typically, minor improvements are pending), hence the longer delivery times. Within Agile, there are multiple iterations of delivery, with each iteration being completed within a 2-4 week timebox. Thus, small viable elements (standalone requirements – review the discussion around user stories in Section 14.3.2) of the product or service are delivered in short iterations.

Both methods have value in the digitally transforming organization. Remember the guidance on choosing a management practice (see Section 14.5) – know what is needed then pick a practice to fit the need rather than choosing a practice because other organizations use it.

17.1.2 VeriSM unwrapped

In the generic example presented thus far, there were four areas that 'changed' – additional suppliers, the need for ISO/IEC 20000 certification, DevOps practices, and several emerging technologies. All have been addressed within the sourcing plan, procured and deployed. Following the Service Blueprint specifications, the new or changed product or service is deployed, adopting the chosen management practice protocols (in this case DevOps practices) and defined release models.

17.1.3 VeriSM applied: FCH Produce

Due to the size of the FCH Wearable initiative, several project managers have been assigned to coordinate the various components – specifically the physical wearable, the application functionality, the ISO/IEC 27001 initiative, the new management practices and the updating of the in-place processes, and the potential technology updates. There is overall coordination via the Office of Strategic Development. The Service Blueprint provides the overall specifications and various outputs that will deliver the outcome desired: the FCH Wearable device and accompanying service functionality.

The Wearable Team continues to work together ensuring the requirements maintain appropriate priority, the iterations meet the expectations, and the promotion and marketing of the program accurately reflects the intent of the program. Communication remains to the forefront for this initiative, if only due to the many 'moving parts'. Organizational Change Management (OCM) programs have been initiated, as well as training programs for the consumer (use of the wearable), Help Desk staff (preparation for issues and requests), and IT staff (maintain new technologies and reporting protocols).

■ 17.2 PROVIDE

The main activities within the Provide stage are protect, measure and maintain, and improve. These activities will be fulfilled via the chosen management practice. From a VeriSM perspective, consider the following areas to address:

- Service Blueprint – ensure the information is accurate and current so that it can be a reference for the service as well as guidance for future updates or projects;
- Operating within the defined security, risk and continuity policies;
- Ongoing training needs – consider cross training from a support perspective or user training;
- Continue professional development activities – the importance of a lifelong learner cannot be stressed enough;
- Marketing and promotion activities to maintain position in the market space or to develop new market spaces;
- Continual improvement, as required, of the delivered products and services; capturing new requirements to re-start the cycle of Define, Produce and Provide activities;
- Communication with consumers ensuring services continue to meet expectations;
- Reporting to stakeholders and consumers, as agreed. Reports should be tailored to the requirements of the stakeholder and delivered in an agreed manner and timeframe;

- Review efficacy of current measures, metrics and associated reports;
- Cross-capability reporting and sharing of information for staffing, finance, procurement, facilities planning;
- Produce necessary regulatory or legislative documentation (for example test results, copyright, patents...).

17.2.1 VeriSM unwrapped

Once the new product or service is operational, review the organizational Management Mesh to ensure it reflects current conditions. Figure 79 provides an illustration of the updated mesh. Note the changes from the original mesh where the new elements from the product or service are now included.

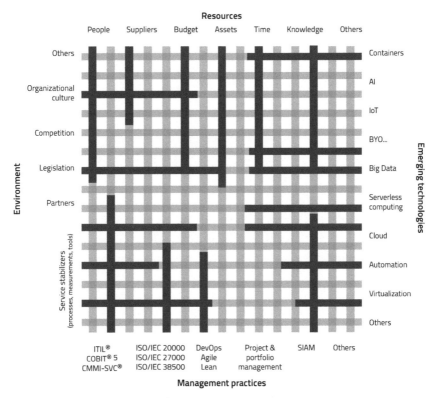

Figure 79 Unwrapped – "new" Organizational Mesh

17.2.2 VeriSM applied: FCH new Management Mesh

As a result of the new FCH Wearable, the organizational mesh has changed (see Figure 80). It now incorporates the new elements (e.g., marketing and promotion campaigns, new emerging technologies, progressive practices, new suppliers...).

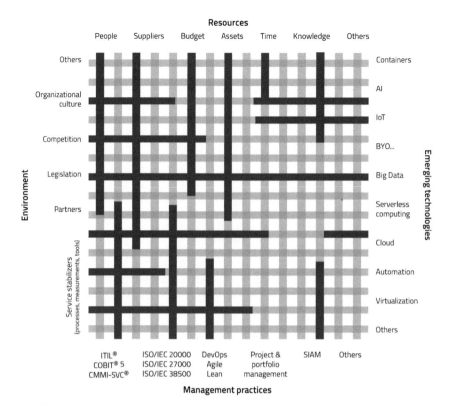

Figure 80 FCH Organizational Mesh – includes FCH Wearable

Additional considerations for FCH during the Provide stage include:

- Reporting issues – utilize the FCH Wearable initiative as a hook, to not only produce the necessary and agreed reports, but to apply the same updated processes to other services;

- Ongoing review and update of security controls – security controls must be actively reviewed and tested to ensure viability to prevent security breaches in the ever-changing security environment (plus security is a dominating element in healthcare accreditation);

- Continuing the data center consolidation activities – the new FCH Wearable and its technology should 'easily' incorporate into the infrastructure and be appropriately managed;

- Update/maintain the organizational portfolio – ensure the portfolio accurately reflects not only the FCH Wearable but also all products and services;

- Maintain the Service Blueprint for information about the service (e.g. historical records, assist in issue resolution, support improvements) as well as using it as a template for future new services.

■ 17.3 RESPOND

The main activities within the Respond stage are record and manage requests, issues, and source events. These activities will be fulfilled via the chosen management practice. From a VeriSM perspective, consider the following areas to address:

■ Ensure current processes are efficient and effective to reflect the needs of consumer:

- Are requests, issues and source events documented as needed? Is there a single point of ownership for these events? Is the owner known and easily contacted?
- Can elements from other management practice be incorporated to create efficiencies?

■ Consider automation or self-service to support both requests and issue resolution:

- Look for efficiency but retain control – a person will always be welcome (and needed) when support is required;
- Consider exploiting emerging technologies (AI, Big Data, IoT, Machine Learning) to anticipate need (requests) or to minimize the impact or eliminate issues and source events.

Lastly, review the information in Chapter 8 (Outcomes) for additional views and possible improvements. Sometimes, it just takes a change in perspective (truly looking at outcomes and not outputs) to understand where an improvement can take place.

18 Making a case for VeriSM

The world is changing, the market is changing, and competition is becoming fiercer. The world is a digital one and organizations that embrace the digital world win, regardless of what is done or sold. Those who don't embrace the digital world run the risk of becoming obsolete. VeriSM helps organizations to transform. Even the most traditional 'brick and mortar' organizations can learn to outperform competitors by becoming more digital, in a practical and pragmatic way.

The adaptation of VeriSM *may* begin with middle managers. Why? Middle managers are often 'beaten up' by events and responsibilities outside of their control. As a consequence, they look for ways to make their life easier. Is change successful starting in the middle of the organization? Rarely. Remember the analogy of burning a candle – lighting it from the middle is difficult but eventually, enough wax burns away from the wick and the candle is lit. But, at what cost? To be successful, an enterprise-changing approach must follow a top-down approach, thus VeriSM must become an initiative within the C-suite, with appropriate transparency and agreement among organizational owners and stakeholders (e.g. board of directors).

VeriSM and the board of directors

The owners and stakeholders define the direction for the organization (mission and vision) and empower organizational leadership (the C-suite) to create the plans to achieve organizational objectives. It is essential that owners and stakeholders understand the VeriSM initiative and the subsequent benefits. As with any major initiative, cost is always a factor. It should be explained that VeriSM preserves existing investments in frameworks (such as ITIL and COBIT). This is a key point as it confirms that the previous decisions to embrace various management practices, technologies or resources moved the organization in the correct direction. VeriSM will improve the organization's digital strategy but not at the expense of previous investments.

Who exactly are the C-suite? Common C-suite roles include:

■ CEO – Chief Executive Officer – leads the entire organization and, typically, is the public figure; answers to, is a member of, and can be replaced by the Board of Directors;

■ CFO – Chief Financial Officer – right-hand to the CEO and oversees the financial aspects of the organization (venture capital, profits, acquisitions, mergers…);

■ COO – Chief Operating Officer – runs operations; works closely with the CEO and CTO;

■ CTO – Chief Technology Officer – designs and recommends appropriate technology solutions to support the policies and directives of the CIO;

■ CIO – Chief Information Officer – works with the CTO; ensures the organization's information technology and computer investments are aligned with strategic business objectives;

■ CMO – Chief Marketing Officer – guides and directs all things related to communication, branding and sales.

Some organizations are adding a new C-suite role, namely, the Chief Digital Officer (CDO). The main responsibility of the CDO is to transform the technical future of the organization as well as envision and evangelize digital transformation to the other members of the C-suite and the stakeholders. If this role exists in the organization, the holder of the position could be an important supporter for VeriSM. They could be a good person to approach individually before speaking to the entire C-suite. See Chapter 25 for more information on how digital transformation is affecting C-suite roles and salary expectations.

What does the VeriSM champion need to do to gain C-suite support? The list below includes suggestions that have been developed by the author team over their years of working with executives – review and tailor these to fit the needs of your organization and situation:

■ Key factors for the VeriSM champion include a strategic mindset (understand the organizational mission and vision and its risk tolerance levels), exceptional soft-skills (e.g. Emotional Intelligence, listening skills, understanding body language – yours and the executives), great preparation, and succinct and credible arguments.

■ Know the industry – what is the competition doing? What is their strategy and initiatives? How does this affect your organization?

■ Keep the message clear – three to five key elements that are compelling to the C-suite. Don't get lost in the details. Remember, the C-suite is not so concerned with the 'how' – tell them what they need to know to make a decision – what, why and how much. Provide the solution. Be able to articulate how the executive defines success. Answer the question: What are the CEO and the board trying to drive with respect to the mission, vision and objectives of the organization?

- Tailor the message for the audience – CEOs/COOs want the big picture; CMOs are concerned with the brand; CFOs focus on the bottom line. Know the individuals – look online, magazine interviews, executive profiles or other biographic information. Know the strategic initiatives, recent successes or failures, interests and peculiarities. Research everything.

- Don't use technical language and acronyms – remember, VeriSM is a service management approach for the digital age. Why does the C-suite need to know about the digital age? What is the likely impact to their plans and intentions? VeriSM is not about technology, though it is a key element of a digital transformation.

- Know the 'gatekeepers' – the executive administrative assistant and direct reports all have influence within the C-suite – know them and develop a good rapport. Ask them for an introduction to the executive. Many executives accept meetings only when suggested by a trusted colleague.

- Define the role and value of VeriSM – what is the value that VeriSM brings to the entire organization? The 'value' discussion needs to focus on the consumer – it is about their 'buying' behaviors. Today's consumer is tied to digital and mobile services – what is the organization doing to help the consumer achieve their goals?

- Once the strategic role and value of VeriSM is understood, be able to educate the C-suite and other stakeholders to overcome their fear of the unknown, of change and of failure. Organizational change management is key. Consider the following:

  - Empathy is key (understand the executive's point of view). Fear of change is rational. Prepare the message that VeriSM reduces the risk of change and provides well-tested methods to contain and manage change.

  - Articulate urgency – what is the impact if the organization doesn't address digital transformation?

  - Be the champion and guide (without you, nothing will go forward), and have demonstrable support from key managers and staff (for example, Kotter's (2014) volunteer army).

  - VeriSM is not a one-off, one-time activity – digital capabilities and initiatives will continuously be built, optimized and refined. The changes that VeriSM proposes must be institutionalized.

  - Take time to the job right – quick wins are good and necessary, but ensure those wins move the organization forward and demonstrate tangible business results. Agile has the underlying philosophy of 'fail fast' – be sure to learn from each achievement in order to sustain change and velocity at which the organization moves.

What are the characteristics of the C-suite message? Most executives have their entire day filled with back-to-back meetings. Therefore, any meeting demands efficiency. The message needs to:

■ Be direct, simple and relevant (e.g. what is the business benefit or business problem that is being addressed?) – focus on real business problems.

■ Be iterative – big ideas get lost in middle management – great ideas use 'guided learning' to get traction – show progression from what is 'now' to the eventual 'to be'. Iterative messages are not 'pushy'.

■ Speak in the language of the C-suite – what initiative is at the forefront for the executive and how does VeriSM support its achievement? Make the message personal – understand what motivates the C-suite to approve decisions.

■ Resonate with the C-suite objectives. Every executive understands and is driven by two factors: customer satisfaction and loyalty. Be sure those factors are addressed, tailored to the organizational objectives, and in the forefront of any message.

  • Risk mitigation is another key factor – in the C-suite, the executives focus their effort enterprise-wide. Digital transformation is a strategic issue, not an 'IT issue' and the risk of NOT addressing digitization, is high, real and relevant. Include it.

■ Be efficient. Close the meeting with a one-page summary of bullet points – if the summary is beyond a single page or 5-minutes, reduce the message until it is a single page or 5-minutes or less. Distribute concise back-up documentation (executive summary, financial projections, compelling articles and research, key performance indicators) tailored to the recipient.

Throughout both VeriSM volumes, many arguments have been presented showing why organizations should move service management to the enterprise level as well as why industry and the global community are embracing the digital world. What benefits does VeriSM help an organization realize? Consider the following benefits:

■ Articulated direction and plans to address and embrace the digital age;
■ Integrates disparate management practices;
■ Unifies governing and managing organizations end-to-end;
■ Facilitates organizational transformation, successfully in the interest of all stakeholders;
■ Improves market understanding to develop better products and services;
■ Improves stakeholder and customer engagement and loyalty;
■ Products and services are on-target and focused;
■ Enables an adaptable way of delivering products and services;
■ Flexible management approach that evolves as organizations change and morph within their respective markets;
■ Improves governance, management, financial, and operational effectiveness and efficiency;
■ Better understanding of future demands and consumer requirements;
■ Better understanding of risk and methods to mitigate and reduce risk;
■ Better resource planning and utilization;
■ Enterprise-wide collaboration with efficient communication;

- Organizational transformation to a learning organization, which ensures relevancy in the market space today and in the future.

Bottom line, the VeriSM message is about creating value – but look beyond quantifiable value and return on investment. How does a change in a service approach impact the overall performance of the organization? Consider also the impact to the consumer...and staff. Before going to the C-suite, understand their top-level requirements as well as the consumer and the staff. What are the pain points and current high points with the services currently being delivered? What are the operational aspects (marketing, sales, finance, technical...) behind each product or service? Based on this information, ensure an inclusive message.

And do not forget, the more things change...the more they stay the same. While the pace of change is increasing, there has always been pressure on organizations to do more, faster – as the quote below from a 1999 article shows. What will differentiate you and your organization is how you respond.

> "Who has time for decision trees and five-year plans anymore? Unlike the market place of 20 years ago, today's information and service-led economy is all about instantaneous decision making."[83]

---

83 https://www.bloomberg.com/news/articles/1999-10-31/religion-in-the-workplace

PART B

Part B of this publication builds on Part A with practical examples, case studies, interviews and industry perspectives. It includes a wide range of material from around the world that will be a source of inspiration and advice for your own digital journey. This section includes:

Case studies: from early adopters of VeriSM and organizations who have carried out a digital transformation

Real world perspectives: interviews with industry experts, vendors and innovative organizations

19 Case studies: early adopters of VeriSM

■ 19.1 6POINT6 CLOUD GATEWAY

In this case study, VeriSM early adopter, Steve Leach from 6point6 Cloud Gateway, talks about why they chose to work with the VeriSM approach, how they got started, and the results they've seen on their journey so far.

Steve Leach is the Head of Service at 6point6 Cloud Gateway. His first IT Service Management role was in the late 1990s with the Ministry of Defense (MoD) and required the ITIL® Red Badge (Manager's) qualification. He has been an ITIL practitioner, trainer and evangelist, implementing support models in the MoD, Norfolk County Council, Cable&Wireless, Vodafone and Serco. His current role, as Head of Service for a Cloud start-up, requires the development of a modern, responsive service management model.

About 6point6 Cloud Gateway
Founded in 2012, 6point6 is a challenger technology consultancy focused on delivering business value-driven solutions, underpinned by cutting edge technology and agile delivery methods. 6point6 enjoys a strong reputation across the government, financial services and media sectors, not only for high quality strategic IT advice but also for its program delivery.

"Since 2018, 6point6 Cloud Gateway has existed as a separate entity within 6point6. This is essentially a startup company offering "Cloud Gateway" as a portfolio of solutions that turns into reality the (much talked about but rarely delivered) 'agile network'. It provides a secure gateway that is entirely vendor- and technology-neutral, connecting organizations to any cloud service provider or legacy infrastructure using any carrier medium, enabling transformation at the pace of change that suits the consumer. Already prized by two major public-sector entities, its solutions put organizations back in control of their IT, their data assets and their business, enabling agile transformation without contractual lock-in.

Getting started with VeriSM

Coming from an ITIL background, the Cloud Gateway team recognized that ITIL alone would not provide the holistic Service Management capability required – where the support aspects were aligned with all the 'best' elements of DevOps, Agile and Continuous Integration/Continuous Delivery (CI/CD). Therefore, something different was required and a start was made on an approach to deliver precisely this.

The Cloud Gateway team soon discovered that VeriSM had already formalized the required approach. Despite VeriSM being new and, therefore, immature in a market sense, Cloud Gateway confirmed that there existed a mutually beneficial opportunity to adopt the VeriSM methodology:

- VeriSM's pragmatic, up-to-date approach is well-suited to development in the cloud computing environment, vital to 6point6 Cloud Gateway's line of business;
- VeriSM recognizes the need for the design and development teams to get updates and enhancements to market very quickly, while applying the necessary level of transition governance through change management. It also enables user support via Respond activities, incident management and related processes – also important to 6point6 Cloud Gateway and its customers.

VeriSM provides an integrated service management approach, allowing elements of ITIL-based service management to be adopted alongside DevOps, Agile, etc.

The Relationship Now

For the Cloud Gateway team, the relationship with VeriSM has developed well, with benefits typical of those enjoyed by an early adopter. Specifically, the VeriSM authors listened to early adopters, and VeriSM has evolved and continues to develop in a way that exactly mirrors Cloud Gateway's original ambitions for its service management.

In just six months, Cloud Gateway has:

- Recruited new support staff and trained them to ITIL Foundation level;
- Put key staff through the VeriSM Plus exam to build on their existing ITIL knowledge;
- Purchased ServiceNow as its service management tool;
- Recruited a trained ServiceNow administrator;
- Agreed new SLAs with its public-sector customers;
- Adopted and started to implement VeriSM:
  - Built a draft VeriSM model for the organization (see Figure 81);
  - Flowcharted, documented and agreed support processes;
  - Adopted new Service Management Principles.

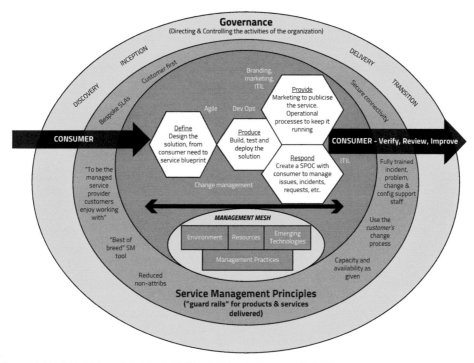

Figure 81 Draft VeriSM model at 6point6 Cloud Gateway (source: 6Point6)

An interim support model is currently in place, depicted in Figure 82, as the company continues to work towards its vision where the VeriSM stages of *Define*, *Produce*, *Provide* and *Respond* seamlessly work together. Customer feedback to date indicates that this support model already delivers exactly what they require, while also enabling Cloud Gateway to demonstrate how it is different from its competition – an equally important aspect.

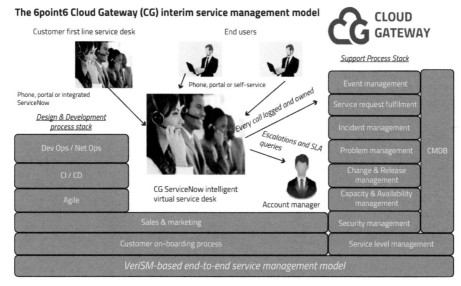

Figure 82 Interim service management model at 6point6 Cloud Gateway (source: 6Point6)

Benefits

VeriSM has enabled 6point6 Cloud Gateway, as an early adopter, to enjoy the following benefits:

- **People**: an organization-wide understanding of the approach, with previous 'silos' eliminated;
- **Process**: confirmation that rapid, Agile releases of new functionality can still be deployed with sufficient governance. Establishing Service Management Principles has helped Cloud Gateway to focus on its unique selling proposition (USP), and its service agreements and support processes have been written to reflect these principles;
- **Technology**: Cloud Gateway needs to be capable of rapid development to meet changing demands for cloud computing, and at the same time, it needs latitude to explore automation, AI and Machine Learning. The VeriSM Management Mesh facilitates this, while imparting a certain level of governance. As a result, Cloud Gateway is not forced into a risk-averse approach by its Service Management Principles, and in fact, embracing new technology is actively encouraged.

Next Steps

In the near term, 6point6 Cloud Gateway:

- Plans to evolve its Service Management model to align even more closely with VeriSM's guidance. Management techniques and support processes will be grouped by the VeriSM stage where they add best value to continue improvements to cross-team working and communication;
- Is also working on a more detailed breakdown and description of how the onboarding elements of Sales and Marketing, Design and Support will all work together up to the 'Respond' stage, with the objective of creating a highly repeatable customer onboarding process;
- Is contributing to the ongoing evolution of VeriSM as lessons are learned about implementing it as an early adopter in a start-up company.

■ 19.2 CITIC TECH: USING VERISM TO SUPPORT DIGITAL TRANSFORMATION

In this case study, Song Xiang and Deng Hong describe how CITIC Technology Co., Ltd. (CITIC Tech) used the VeriSM Management Mesh as a practical managerial instrument to guide top-notch design of digital service management, and to summarize and accumulate best practice for digital transformation and management like a 'vessel'.

About CITIC Group

As China's biggest conglomerate, CITIC Group operates in financial services, resources and energy, manufacturing, engineering contracting, real estate and others. According to the latest Global Fortune 500 rankings released by *Fortune Magazine*, CITIC Group is ranked 172nd with an approximate operating income of $64,720.56 million USD and a net profit of $8,823.73 million USD.

CITIC Tech was founded in 2016 to boost the digital transformation of the conglomerate and to act as the main player for technological empowerment and business ecological transformation.

Digital strategies

CITIC Group has taken the initiative to put into force digital transformation strategies. On August 29, 2016, it launched the 'internet + transformation' strategy and proclaimed that it would adopt the principle of openness and sharing. Additionally, CITIC Group would employ internet technologies, such as cloud computing, big data and the Internet of Things. This would change its previous point-to-point and project-to-project business communication and collaboration model, which put capital as the bond, so that new cross-border applications and collaborative scenarios could occur. With its year-long ample offline industrial resources, the Group is no longer a simple corporate island but an organically-melded industrial ecology with valuable online data assets piling up that further elevate its platform values and associated effects.

In this case study, CITIC Group explains how the Management Mesh is used to summarize and state how it implements digital strategies. They started from the generic Management Mesh shown in Figure 83.

Environment

According to an analysis report by IDC, a respected organization on marketing surveys, digital transformation has become the major strategy for all organizations to meet today's challenges. In 2018, half of the top 1000 domestic organizations have incorporated digital transformation as their strategic core. CIOs agree that the integration of digitalization with real economy and the promotion of digital transformation are inevitable for central government enterprises.

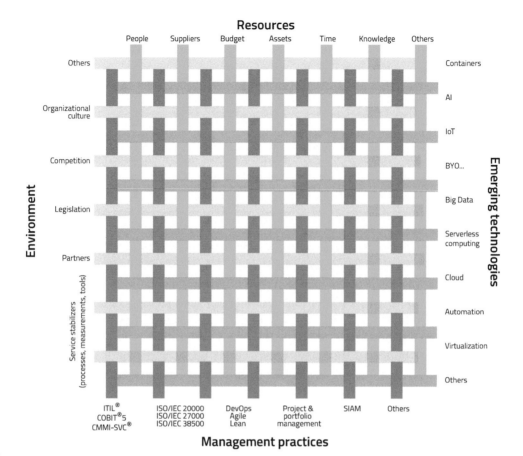

Figure 83 Generic Management Mesh

Resources

Since launching CITIC Group's 'internet + transformation' strategies, CITIC Group has adopted the following procedures to implement the strategic transformation:

a) Set-up of the 'internet + transformation' supervisory team and execution teams;

■ Guided by the management of the Group, the provision of science and technology is to be forged into a new core capacity alongside asset and brand. Through internal and external collaboration, the organization promotes innovation and entrepreneurship, defining a number of projects for business development in the Group and its branch companies;

b) Set-up of the management organization;

■ Regarding organizational resources, the Group established CITIC Cloud, a service-oriented organization. The president of CITIC Group is the new organization's president. CITIC Cloud is undertaking the task of 'internet + transformation' in the conglomerate;

c) Set-up of technology organization;

■ CITIC Tech was established under CITIC Cloud. Using a market-based operational model, it has recruited and cultivated over 200 talented staff members on internet technologies. It is dedicated to three core missions of 'connectivity, congregation of users and production of data'. With scientific and technological innovation as the bond:

- It forges the internet empowerment platform in CITIC Group;
- It propels the collaboration and aggregation of superior resources in CITIC Group, its subsidiary companies and its partners;
- It facilitates the formation of an industrial ecosphere of 'co-production, co-building, co-existence, and co-winning' with CITIC features;
- It boosts its holistic values.

New technology

'Internet + transformation' can't do without advanced technologies. CITIC Cloud is a technology empowerment platform built by CITIC Tech to drive the horizontal interconnectivity of industrial resources and to attract new cross-field applications and collaborative environments, and a concentrated embodiment of advanced technologies. A hybrid cloud-computing platform, based on cloud intermediary model, CITIC Cloud platform fuses cutting edge technologies, such as leading cloud computing, big data, the Internet of Things, mobile internet, blockchain, and artificial intelligence technology. It has developed three platforms namely IaaS, PaaS and SaaS that provide 'front-edge, secured, good quality and low-priced' cloud services and solutions for subsidiary organizations under CITIC Group.

Practice of management

The implementation of an ISO/IEC 20000 service management system and an ISO27001 information security management system supports CITIC Tech in management, operation, information management and other areas. The development team adopts Agile software development methods to deliver a quick response from IT to the business. Construction of a DevOps (development and operations) integration platform achieves automation of development, testing and deployment of software. An ITIL-based IT service management platform helps service operation and maintenance.

Digital transformation

Empowerment transformation model

Drawing reference from VeriSM's Management Mesh led to the design of the CITIC Cloud empowerment transformation model (see Figure 84) for client organizations. It translates business values from four levels: 'capacity building', 'capacity output', 'capacity transformation' and 'business values'.

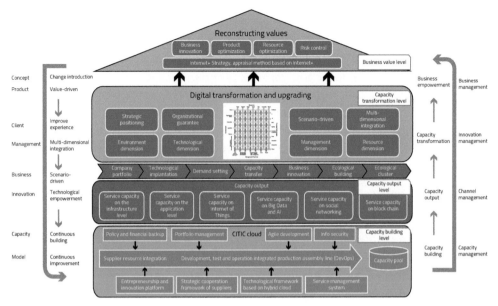

Figure 84 CITIC Cloud Empowerment Transformation model (source: CITIC)

Capacity output

With a vision of building an ecological cloud alliance, CITIC Tech co-mingles four models (business, technology, management and service) with the model of building a cloud platform. Its output is six emerging technological competences – cloud computing, Big Data, Internet of Things, mobile networking, artificial intelligence and blockchain – to its internal subsidiary organizations and other conglomerates via the cloud platform.

■ Output of service capacity on the infrastructure level:
  This covers IaaS cloud service, PaaS cloud service, cloud framework building, private cloud and output of Oracle product capacity. It covers such core cloud resource services as computing, storage, internet, safety and database. It includes four sectors namely consultancy, implementation, backup, and proxy.
■ Output of service capacity on the application level:
  This covers tax receipt cloud service, videoconferencing system, unified OA portal, cloud platform for unified files, solution for corporate collaborative office-running, application/networking/terminal performance surveillance platform, secured upgrading and transformation, cloud platform for financial management, cloud platform for data recording, cloud platform for concentrated analysis, analysis and display platform of big data, secured plan of SaaS model etc.
■ Output of service capacity on the Internet of Things:
  This covers the universal internet development platform, safe and stable maintenance of the Internet of Things platform, solutions for Internet of Things for specific industries and application and development.
■ Output of service capacity of Big Data and artificial intelligence:

This includes the Big Data basic service, data analysis and visualization, data application, and artificial intelligence etc. that can help companies glean and excavate data resources and accumulate Big Data advantages.

■ Output of service capacity on mobile networking:

By referring to such internet technologies as cloud computing, Big Data and mobile networking, this area delivers a business collaboration platform and industrial ecological platform for the Group, its subsidiary organizations and its external partners. CITIC Cloud, the platform organization, can be combined with the CITIC industrial ecology to share resources and risks. With ecological strength, this boosts the organization's comprehensive competitiveness. It links its internal and external resources with other CITIC organizations and provides services for office-running, collaboration, life, culture etc.

■ Output of service capacity on blockchain:

Blockchain is a new applied model of computing technologies such as distributed data storage, point-to-point transmission, consensus mechanism, and encryption algorithm.

Practice of digital business

Successful cases on CITIC Cloud's replacement of traditional businesses through transformation with its six technological capacities are many. This section shows 'smart warehouse logistics' as an example to explain how to link the upstream and downstream through digitalization.

Warehouse logistics is a common challenge for many organizations. Its core flow is shown in Figure 85. As a major document of title and audit trail for commodity circulation, it also carries strong financial features. However, it doesn't have an acceptable management and approval system when it comes to authorizing and crediting warehouse receipts. This means that warehouse receipts are held back in terms of stock levels, payments and logistics. They fail to satisfy the needs of stakeholders such as traders, banks, stock markets, insurance organizations and so on.

While tackling these challenges, CITIC Cloud deployed the Internet of Things and blockchain technologies to the cloud platform for warehousing supervision, the cloud platform for warehouse receipt management, an offline warehousing supervision mesh and a reliable ecosystem of warehouse receipts to address the issues of authorizing and crediting warehouse receipts. Establishing reliable warehouse receipts called for the backup of sensors, the Internet of Things and blockchain technologies. The financial ecosystem of the supply chain that covered producers, traders, warehouse staff, stock markets, banks, insurance organizations, security, and so forth was set up by linking the upstream activities with those downstream and financial services through credible warehouse receipts.

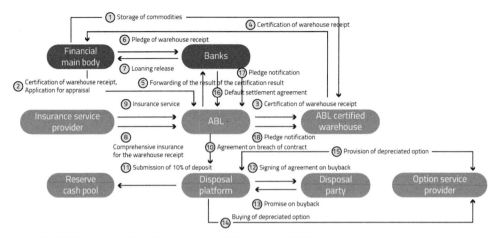

Figure 85 CITIC – Business flow of warehouse logistics (source: CITIC)

With nonferrous metal as the pilot in the early stages, and CITIC Wutong Port Supply Chain Management Company as the main operational organization, it provided an individual solution to the supply chain for the subsidiary organizations and external clients. Integration of upstream and downstream trade, logistics, capital flow and information flow helped to generate highly-correlated business data in a bid to achieve dynamic risk control, before improving the upstream / downstream supply chain efficiency, reducing operational costs and realizing the values of digital transformation.

Summary

By May 2018, CITIC Tech had assisted 150 subsidiaries in digital transformation. CITIC Tech is exploring breakthroughs on multiple fronts including organization, business, technology, management and culture. The key factors of successful digital transformation are listed as below.

Policy and organization

Digital transformation is restructuring at the organizational level. Business innovation, technology upgrades, financial backing and organizational restructures all call for vigorous support by the executive managers in the organization. During the process of digital transformation, CITIC Group provided support for digital transformation on the following three levels:

- A special guidance committee namely 'internet + transformation' supervisory team, under direct leadership of the top executive of the Group to address financial backing;
- The platform service organization, CITIC Cloud, to address issues on business orientation, innovative incubation and investment;
- A scientific and technological organization, CITIC Tech, to address the issues on scientific and technological output and commercial transformation.

Building of infrastructures for digital transformation (hybrid cloud)
Regarding infrastructure utilities, CITIC Group involved multiple industries and its subsidiary organizations in varying sectors – all with disparate demands. Both a private cloud and singular public cloud fell short of fully satisfying all demands. In response to this challenge, CITIC Cloud adopted the strategy of building a hybrid cloud. While building its private cloud, it released the public cloud and introduced an advanced Oracle database cloud service to satisfy the demands on the infrastructure level in its subsidiary organizations. Upon completion, various workloads and business activities under CITIC can trace their resources through CITIC Cloud.

Agile development assembly line
For the software development stages, it introduced an Agile development project and achieved its goal through the use of sprints. During the whole development process, timely responses were provided to changes in business demands so that innovative technology could quickly deliver business benefits, under the controls of a systematic methodology.

To deliver software products and services on time, the development, IT operations and quality assurance departments worked together, constructing an automated assembly line for development and maintenance, by implementing DevOps. They also established key performance indicators based on five dimensions: speed, quality, security, staff satisfaction, and the input-output ratio of return on investment (ROI).

Data interconnectivity
Issues such as data integrity, difficulty during implementation, low input-output ratio and the integration between industries create barriers to realizing the value of data in an enterprise. The biggest challenge lies in the combination of data and production experience, as well as gathering, integration and analysis of basic data.

Through data application, positioning of label imaging, cross-system correlation of data and data source integration, CITIC Tech delivered business benefit to China CITIC Bank, CITIC Securities, CITIC Prudential, CITIC Press Group, CITIC Holding, China Asset Management and more. This was in terms of credit integration, membership management, smart forwarding, joint marketing and offline integration. At present, CITIC Cloud has realized data interconnectivity on three levels, namely user, payment and connector, leading to better visibility of business and data resources in its subsidiary organizations.

■ 19.3 KABU.COM SECURITIES CO. LTD.

This case study examines how VeriSM is being used at Kabu.com, a financial organization from Japan. This case study, based on an interview with mr. Toda, the project leader, explains some additional steps including Inception and Reflection that may be of interest to readers.

About Kabu.com

Kabu.com Securities Co. Ltd is an online stock trading and foreign exchange (FX) trading organization, part of the Mitsubishi UFJ Financial Group (MUFG). It was founded in November 1999, employs 120 people and had a revenue of $217 million USD (profit $54.86 million USD) in 2018.

Context

The organization's aim is to enter a new market for virtual currency (Crypto-Currency) such as Bit Coin. They are targeting new customers and want to attract a new customer segment of 20-30 year olds. The majority of the existing customer base is aged 40 to 50.

They also plan to develop 'MUFG Coin' in the future. (Mitsubishi UFJ Financial Group had announced the "MUFG Coin Crypto-Currency" will launch in 2018.)

Figure 86 Kabu.com staff

Preparing for digital transformation

The team followed a process that included these steps:

- Summarize the existing business model and create plan;
- Carry out a SWOT analysis;
- Redefine the business model and IT services;
- Carry out a planning session;
- Create a minimum viable process and value stream map;
- Create user stories;
- Continue to deliver via DevOps.

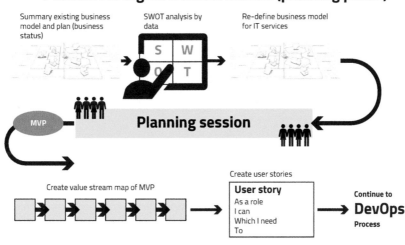

Figure 87 Kabu.com VeriSM and DevOps

VeriSM and DevOps

Figure 87 shows the relationship between DevOps and VeriSM in this model. Combined with VeriSM, DevOps 2.0.creates various PDCA cycles in the process and support Define, Produce, Provide, and Respond in the VeriSM model.

Planning phase

During the planning phase, the Management Mesh needed to be defined. The Management Mesh is a key factor to manage quality and EOL (End of Life) of the service. To manage the Management Mesh effectively, the team set up Obeya. Obeya (large room) is a concept from the Toyota Production System (TPS). It is aimed at gathering all required information/data and visualizing it in one place to make decisions quickly. This way, every stakeholder can easily access related information. Usually Obeya displays information/data posts on a wall and then updates information/data every day. This is truly decision making by Genchi-Genbutsu (existing facts).

The team set two levels of Obeya, one at the strategic level for the business and another one at the operational level to visualize all the activities within the VeriSM model.

"We recommend holding a planning session for developing a plan and gaining consensus among stakeholders."

The planning session should involve business staff, the product owner, development(Agile) team, operations team, DevOps engineer team (infrastructure), technology advisor(s) and governance and security specialist(s). The outputs from the planning session are the definition of the Management Mesh, a value stream map for the minimum viable product (MVP), user stories, criteria for EOL, and service levels. The team applied 'Customer Planning Session' (defined by IBM) practices for the planning session. This was a controlled discussion facilitated by the session leader.

This was a key activity for this project. Since we hadn't had enough time to deploy the new service, we needed to ensure a good understanding of the business, project and new IT service across the stakeholders. We needed to achieve complete consensus for moving quickly and avoid rework. OBEYA helped to visualize all existing information, enabling us to make decisions promptly. Another benefit of OBEYA, was it provided a good approach for managing the Management Mesh in VeriSM and monitoring the status (progress and problems) of each stage all at the same time (Define, Produce, Provide, and Respond).

Project timeline
The project progressed well. These major activities in each month are shown below:
- April 2018:
  - Project kick-off April 1st;
  - Generate new business model;
  - Define business model for new business (Bit-Coin);
  - Approve the project budget;
  - Review and define governance;
  - Review and define Service Management Principles;
  - Plan for planning session;
  - Prepare for the planning session;
  - Gather data;
  - Collate documents;
- May 2018:
  - Hold two-day planning session on May 11 and 12;
  - Share and ensure a clear understanding of the business environment, business strategy and business model;
  - Define personas (2 types);

- Arrange requirements from users;
- Define architecture drivers;
- Define the four factors of the Management Mesh;
- Define the value stream map and user stories;
- Define core process for new system;
- Define the criteria for EOL;
- Create and agree the service levels;
- Set up Obeya;
- Develop;
■ June 2018:
- Develop;
- Test and deploy;
- Release of phase 1 on July 1st.

Aligning the project to the VeriSM model
Planning phase (VeriSM: Define) April 2018
■ Create business model and strategy:
- Establish market status and position;
- Define target business model and story;
- Identify targeted customers or users;
- Undertake SWOT analysis of the business;
- Determine required total budget or resources;
- Determine required release date and estimated EOL;
■ Define requirements for IT services:
- Define target user journey;
- Develop target business process (value stream map);
- Define personas for two typical users.

2-day planning session
■ Design IT services;
■ Define architecture drivers:
- High-level functionality;
- Technical constraints;
- Business constraints;
- Quality attribute requirements.

Design rough sketch of the IT service
■ Define the Management Mesh for VeriSM;
■ Re-define value stream map;
■ Create user stories.

Development phase (Produce and Provide in VeriSM) May, June 2018

'Produce' and 'Provide' processes are really the same as the DevOps process. We added one more process before the 'Produce' process, which is 'Inception'. The goal of this additional process is to prepare development work faster and quicker. The 'Produce' process strictly applies the basics of Scrum and extreme programming (XP) practices, and all tasks should be small and equally sized. This is the key success factor for faster and quicker development work.

The main workflow for the 'Provide' process is really the deployment pipeline. It should operate as single steady stream, aligned to the Toyota Production System (TPS). Again, smaller and equally sized tasks are a key success factor for smooth operation of the deployment pipeline as well.

Inception stage

- Review and arrange product backlogs;
  - Finalize user stories;
  - Set priority;
- Breakdown into small tasks;
  - Create sprint backlogs;
  - Define 1 hour-tasks;
- Final set up for DevOps infrastructure.

Roles include the service master (product owner), development (Scrum) team and DevOps engineers, working together collaboratively.

Produce stage

- 2 weeks (10 days) a sprint, with 4 engineers per team;
- Develop the core process for the services (MVP) in 3 sprints.

Provide stage

- Operate deployment pipeline manually, as a tentative plan;
- Integrate into existing proof of concept (POC) and enhance POC capability (support social networking service);
- Enhancement or Adjustment Phase (Respond in VeriSM) operates from July 2018 onwards.

Respond stage

- POC communicates with customers by SMS, not phone;
- Record customer feedback, sort and organize by week;
- Share failure information;
- Update POC's KPT (Keep [good things], Problem [bad things], and Try [countermeasure]) board daily;
- Analyze customer experience;

- Review value of the service provided to consumers (consumer satisfaction);
- Create any changes required based on the product backlog and give them to the service master.

Reflection stage
- Update KPT board in Obeya weekly and undertake countermeasures defined by daily activities;
- Hold weekly Obeya meetings and share all status changes, supported by facts, making decisions quickly;
- Review Management Mesh to identify EOL.

In the Respond process, KPT is an important practice, using feedback from customers to drive staff to think about effective actions to adapt to their needs. KPT is easy and a powerful tool for reflection which was taken from Japanese Agile engineers.

We added one more process after the 'Respond' stage, which is a 'Reflection' process. The goals for this process are to manage EOL for the service and to review each element of the Management Mesh. We added one more process after the 'Respond' stage, which is a 'Reflection' process. The goals for this process are to manage EOL for the service and to review each element of the Management Mesh.

From my experience, the Management Mesh should be operated via Obeya, because it makes it easy to review each element of the Management Mesh and adapt to the existing situation. I think Produce, Provide and Respond are small PDCA cycles within VeriSM, keeping services effective. On other hand, the goal of the 'Reflection' process is to build a larger PDCA cycle in the VeriSM model to manage the Management Mesh and the whole project/business. Therefore, Obeya provides a best practice to manage the Management Mesh in VeriSM.

The Management Mesh
We've defined our Management Mesh for the project as shown in Figure 88.

The defined elements of the Management Mesh include:
- The business environment and emerging technologies, these two factors affect EOL decisions – watch their status carefully;
- Resources, which are easy to manage, because when you implement Agile concepts in your organization, resources are already addressed;
- Management practices, which address speed-to-delivery or faster operations.

Management Mesh (defined)

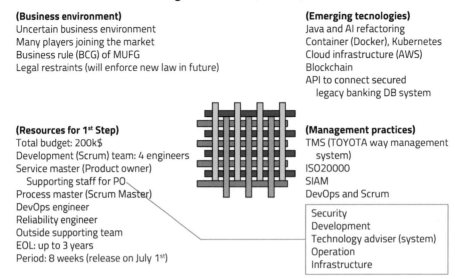

(Business environment)
Uncertain business environment
Many players joining the market
Business rule (BCG) of MUFG
Legal restraints (will enforce new law in future)

(Emerging tecnologies)
Java and AI refactoring
Container (Docker), Kubernetes
Cloud infrastructure (AWS)
Blockchain
API to connect secured
    legacy banking DB system

(Resources for 1st Step)
Total budget: 200k$
Development (Scrum) team: 4 engineers
Service master (Product owner)
    Supporting staff for PO
Process master (Scrum Master)
DevOps engineer
Reliability engineer
Outside supporting team
EOL: up to 3 years
Period: 8 weeks (release on July 1st)

(Management practices)
TMS (TOYOTA way management
    system)
ISO20000
SIAM
DevOps and Scrum

Security
Development
Technology adviser (system)
Operation
Infrastructure

Figure 88 Kabu.com Management Mesh

Figures 89 and 90 shows how the project was organized.

Agile organization (1)   May ~ June 2018

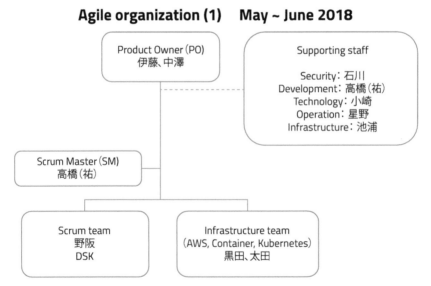

Product Owner (PO)
伊藤、中澤

Supporting staff

Security：石川
Development：高橋（祐）
Technology：小崎
Operation：星野
Infrastructure：池浦

Scrum Master (SM)
高橋（祐）

Scrum team
野阪
DSK

Infrastructure team
(AWS, Container, Kubernetes)
黒田、太田

Figure 89 Kabu.com – Agile organization

DevOps organization (2)   Beyond July 2018

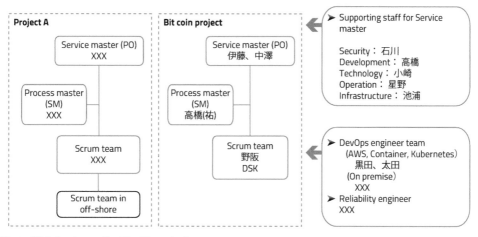

Figure 90 Kabu.com – DevOps Organization

20 Case studies: digital transformation – WuXi AppTec and ANONCORP

■ 20.1 WUXI APPTEC

This case study illustrates how the Chinese organization WuXi AppTec used technology to transform its business processes.

Since launching in December 2000, WuXi AppTec has been devoted to accelerating the research and development (R&D) of drug and medical devices, with lower cost, higher efficiency and quality, through its leading global capability and technology platform. As a research and client-oriented company, WuXi AppTec offers a variety of comprehensive laboratory services to its global partners and consumers, from research to development to clinical trial and manufacturing. The services cover all stages, from drug discovery to commercialization.

Small-molecule drug discovery has been the foundation of WuXi AppTec's platform since the beginning of its business, with more than 5,000 chemists providing pharmaceutical services for consumers globally. More than 500,000 compounds are purchased, synthesized and delivered through WuXi's state-of-the-art platform.

20.1.1 Procurement's challenges

With the rapid growth of the business, many leading suppliers are attracted to WuXi's platform and its direct competitive advantages, such as low-cost purchasing, fast delivery, and high efficiency. On the other hand, however, the need to source more building blocks and reagents became a big challenge for the procurement departments. Alongside the growth in volume, the ongoing demand to source more diverse compounds creates additional challenges.

The problem is clear, but solutions are very limited in the context of a growing business. The whole procurement team was struggling with the manual maintenance of suppliers, quotations, and order follow-up. Simply adding more employees was becoming more difficult due to cost pressures and low efficiency in cross-collaboration between staff and teams.

WuXi AppTec decided an all-new model, with digitally disruptive innovation, was needed. LabNetwork (www.labnetwork.com), a research-based e-commence platform, started in 2015 to connect compound buyers and suppliers, and eliminate offline manual processes and 'brokers'. The e-commence platform also provides a digital way to streamline the online procurement process between WuXi chemists and external suppliers to improve procurement process efficiency.

Some of the key development milestones were:
- 'All-in' to Digital Procurement:
  - Q1 of 2016: Requisition module is open to WuXi R&D users;
  - Q3 of 2016: online Quote module is released to all users;
  - Q4 of 2016: Internal Requisition module is released to WuXi R&D users;
  - Q1 of 2017: Lab Consumables category is online;
  - Q2 of 2017: Bio Reagents category is online.

For a procurement team, most of the routine work has been simplified and redefined by the digital platform. 90% of quotations and order follow-ups are accomplished directly between the R&D users and suppliers (including online approval and budget control). The team just needs to handle the 10% of exception cases. They can devote the rest of their time to more high value activities, including:
- Managing supplier relationships;
- Supporting internal users using LabNetwork;
- Listening to and collecting feedback from end users;
- Working with the technical team to improve system iteratively;
- Sustaining strategic suppliers;
- Coordinating with suppliers / logistics to maintain inventories (physical and virtual).

The process is now simple and creates more value for WuXi and the whole industry, as shown in Figure 91.

LabNetwork is an innovative digital business model from WuXi AppTec. With the internal usage and continuous improvement, the platform has gradually boosted the level of online and offline digital operations. It also provides the compounds for global chemists and pharmaceutical researchers by connecting the manufacturers and suppliers.

For years, consumers had to pay high prices to purchase the compounds they needed. Many good suppliers (manufacturers) in China were unable to reach global clients because of challenges such as channel, language and cost. They had to rely

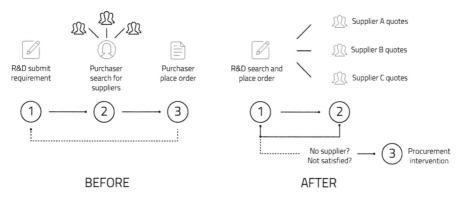

Figure 91 WuXi AppTec before and after E-commerce model (source: WuXi AppTec)

on traders to sell their compounds and lost the opportunity to develop their own brands. LabNetwork's global e-commence platform directly connects buyers and suppliers and so helps to alleviate these challenges. Steps in LabNetwork's global reach included:

■ Q1 of 2015: went live in North America;
■ Q1 of 2016: focused on the Chinese market;
■ Q3 and Q4 of 2016: entered Japanese and Korean markets;
■ Q1 of 2018: consumables and bio-reagents were open to all users.

As well as an e-commence portal for buyers, LabNetwork provides a supplier portal, a dashboard center and a backend administrative user interface. These front-end applications call mid-tier services and surrounding system APIs to support the frequent changes from the business as shown in Figure 92.

Figure 92 LabNetwork features and micro-services (source: WuXi AppTec)

By October 2018, LabNetwork's website achieved its business goals.

20.1.2 Looking ahead

LabNetwork continues to enhance its platform and its business practices. It improves the level of operational excellence for the entire organization across many aspects, which is important in helping WuXi maintain its leading position with fast growth year on year. Through the iterations of LabNetwork, many surrounding systems have also evolved, such as compound inventory management, as well as SaaS applications, which have formed a powerful industry solution for all the stakeholders in the supply chain.

Looking forward, besides accelerating the business digitalization, LabNetwork is also expanding its field – from traditional enterprise or e-commence functions, such as procurement, logistics, inventory and operation, to new business models, such as community, O2O (online to offline) and new retailing – from molecules, building blocks and library compounds, to antibodies, bio-reagents, genome sequencing products and clinical tests. The platform has grown to provide more and more capabilities to global healthcare leaders.

The IT team has also laid out a long-term plan to develop the 'mid-tier shared services' strategy by injecting successful business values and has achieved the goal of 'quick response to market' in order to fuel the digital transformation of the entire organization.

■ 20.2 ANONCORP

ANONCORP is an equipment supplier for the semiconductor industry, located in Europe. It has over 15,000 employees worldwide, and a turnover of more than 10 million Euros.

20.2.1 Past approach

Until recently, the realization of new digital services was primarily governed by ANONCORP's IT department. This was done via a set of very strictly governed processes to initiate, specify, define, realize and enhance its digital service solutions. One of the core artifacts was the IT Project Start Architecture document, specifying which each IT project needed to deliver and have approved before the project was allowed to proceed with the realization of new digital service solutions. The review and approval of the IT Project Start Architecture document was done in a very formal way via these IT focused boards and teams:

■ Multiple lower-level IT domain architecture control boards reviewed all (even minor) changes to the existing solution architecture regarding IT technical aspects;

■ An overarching top-level IT architecture control board reviewed all major changes to the solution target architecture;

■ Multiple project and program boards approved changes to the existing architecture for feasibility regarding constraints, such as available time, resources and budget.

While this approach ensured that the new digital service solutions were being documented and approved, in detail, as early as possible, the business was often not able to provide proper feedback on the design. Usually the business was only really asked for real feedback after a lot of the design and build effort had been completed. Typically, they provided feedback just before the start of user acceptance testing. Another challenge was that not everyone involved in the realization of new digital services was working as one team to achieve a common goal. For example, IT project teams tended to work separately from both the various IT boards and their business stakeholders.

As a result, most people involved in developing new digital services tended to be more focused on achieving near perfect documentation first, before asking for feedback from their stakeholders.

This meant that many of the new digital service solutions introduced did not produce the expected benefits because:

■ The new solutions implemented were not making use of the latest business knowledge and practices;

■ The tactical and strategic business needs had already changed. ANONCORP operates in a very dynamic consumer environment, trying to achieve the impossible within the laws of physics and technology available.

In the past IT projects only succeeded in successfully realizing new digital service solutions due to close informal contact between individual IT architects, project/ program leads and other IT experts with the business and vice versa.

20.2.2 New approach

The new approach implemented is based around business needs leading the new digital service development. As a first step, an enormous effort has been undertaken to properly define all the primary business processes in a single business process management (BPM) framework, and to assign business process owners that are responsible for the proper functioning and support of the processes they own. This includes defining all of the resources required to ensure a business process is able to be properly executed. Nowadays, these resources are often made available as digital services. This way it is clear to everyone involved:

■ What the impact will be, on which digital services, when business processes need to be enhanced;

■ Which business process owners to involve from the start when designing a new digital service.

As a next step, a new way of working is being introduced to ensure that the IT department is not solely in the lead for what needs to change in the digital service portfolio. A new artifact has been introduced – the Business Information Plan.

The Business Information Plan

The Business Information Plan primarily defines the required business capabilities / services that are needed in the next months and years. The digital service's IT solution principles are not defined in these plans. That is still done in the IT Project Start Architecture document, when an IT project is initiated to realize the IT elements of the digital service solution. This integrated plan is prepared by the business architects, with support of IT, and owned by the business process owners. It is updated on a regular basis.

Based on the Business Information Plan, priorities are set, and resources are arranged via the portfolio governance boards, where both business and IT are involved to realize the required capabilities/competences within the timing and resource constraints provided. As these boards only give approval on what capabilities need to be achieved in the next months and years, the technical and business project/program teams now have much more freedom to:

1. Determine what E2E digital service solutions are needed to achieve a certain capability within the constraints given. Previously the IT Project Start Architecture document was leading while now the business requirements documented in the Business Information Plan are leading;
2. Adapt the IT solutions to new technologies, knowledge and needs, as long as the capability is still delivered within the time and money constraints given. In the past, less than perfect 'compromising' IT solutions would often be implemented, as it was too costly to radically change the IT architecture already built to incorporate all of the business requirements.

20.2.3 Recent example

An example of what has be achieved via this new approach is the project to realize a new platform to deliver facility documentation/information collaboration services.

The new platform enables fast but controlled management and sharing of all ANONCORP facility and asset management documentation, and other information both within ANONCORP and between all of its suppliers. The new approach ensured that both the ANONCORP business end user teams, the facility management supplier teams, the ANONCORP IT organization and its suppliers were communicating effectively from the start of the project about exactly what was needed to properly enable the digitization of the facility management processes.

As a result, the design, principles, digital service architecture, platform software selection, build and implementation of the platform were completed in a couple of months, with ANONCORP's facility management suppliers being very enthusiastic about the service solutions delivered. In the past, it would have taken many years to deliver the same result, as a lot of redesign and major changes to the platform would have been needed to deliver an acceptable result.

21 Case study: digital transformation in the public sector – Aylesbury Vale District Council

■ 21.1 INTRODUCTION

This case study tells the story of Aylesbury Vale District Council's (AVDC) digital transformation journey, and shares what worked for them along the way. It shows that digital transformation is just as applicable in the public sector as it is in the private sector. We interviewed Maryvonne Hasssall, Digital Programme Director at AVDC and the main driver behind their 'Right Here Right Now' digital program.

"AVDC is an ambitious council with a strong culture, based on clearly defined values and underpinned by a new commercial behavioral framework."

Andrew Grant, Chief Executive, AVDC

■ 21.2 HISTORY AND CONTEXT

AVDC is a district council in the United Kingdom, providing services to approximately 190,000 residents in 80,000 households, businesses and other service users. AVDC has approximately 400 permanent staff. The strategic trends for AVDC include:
■ Financial challenges/grant reduction from central government;
■ Increasing demands and expectations from residents in respect of services.

In this situation, many organizations would focus on cost-cutting. AVDC, however, made a bold decision to stop focusing on cost-cutting and staff cuts, seeing this as a race to the bottom that would inhibit innovation. Instead, they implemented a 'New Business Model' that takes a more commercial approach to service provision.

■ 21.3 TRANSFORMATION

The decision was made to transform as an organization, rather than continue to cut costs and services. AVDC identified some strategic areas to focus on:

■ Growing their services, not shrinking them;
■ Identifying and reaching customers that weren't being served;
■ Offering services based on data profiles and marketing services more proactively;
■ Generating revenue to fund services (thinking like a social enterprise).

> Connecting data, information and knowledge across departments using agile technology and a digital mindset would lead to innovation and new opportunities.

How challenging (how different) was this initiative for the current mindset in the council?

"For AVDC, this was a long journey – taking more than five years and involving many changes. AVDC recognized that it wasn't possible to carry on in the same way, so had to create a culture that was comfortable with pushing boundaries.

The strategic driver for change came from the top of the organization with the full support of its counselors. They believed it was very apparent that:

■ The current financial situation was not sustainable;
■ A new model was needed.

However, this message hadn't fully filtered through the organization. For example, there was a lot of innovation in the IT department leading to initiatives like a move to cloud based services, but the wider reason for this technical change hadn't been fully communicated."

> AVDC recognized that to move beyond local optimization a major culture change was essential, and a cultural transformation/program needed to take place. As it embarked on a restructure, the council needed to recruit enthusiastic, motivated and commercially-minded people. A behavior framework was implemented that identified how staff would need to work in order to deliver commercially-viable products and profitable services valued by customers.
>
> This included:
> • Outlining the behaviors that were needed;
> • Describing what good would looked like in the new culture;
> • Carrying out behavioral assessments of all staff;
> • Appointing staff to new roles based on assessments.

What was the impact on staff?

"This program led to a significant level of staff change; some people decided that they didn't want to be with AVDC anymore. AVDC focused on helping these people to find new roles and leave the organization. Some staff found potential they didn't know they had and were encouraged to apply for roles they may not have previously felt capable of doing."

> There was a large influx of new people into the organization, about 30% overall, leading to new ideas and perspectives.

"The changed mindset and model in the organization started to generate innovation. The IT department was an early adopter, identifying technical changes that then drove organizational improvements. These IT projects enabled other changes to happen. For example, the IT department embraced the idea of change from the top level and, working in partnership with a strategic digital development partner, Arcus Global, created the award winning 'My Account'. My Account is a self-service online customer account. On My Account residents can access a range of transactional features such as managing council tax, waste collections, and others. These are available 24/7 on any device with no need for a phone call. However, this led to recognition that the departments within AVDC weren't necessarily structured to take advantage of it, and as such, acted as a trigger for wider change.

> AVDC turned its attention to becoming less hierarchical, with staff focused on:
> - Solving problems at their own level;
> - Sharing horizontally with their peers;
> - Finding development partners that were invested in finding solutions;
> - Problem solving across the council (not just in their own area).

The new behaviors that staff were assessed against also allowed staff to be challenged – if they aren't enacting the behaviors, why not?

There wasn't much change at the senior leadership level. Instead, the change came more at the next level down, where 'champions of change' led the business reviews that drove the transformation and organizational change."

> One key innovation was the separation of 'digital' from operational IT. Operational IT sits within Operations and is run by a business support function, where it fits with other support services like Finance, Payroll, etc.
>
> Digital has been separated out and sits at Assistant Director level, working horizontally across the organization. This helped the digital transformation to become embedded. 'Digital' can't be isolated in a department, it must work across the whole organization.

What was the impact to AVDC's products and services?

"The digital transformation program led to new initiatives such as targeted marketing of existing services, development of transactional services, innovation, and a focus on prevention and early intervention (for example, in debt management).

Joined up data

AVDC is focusing on new products and services such as the use of historical data for fraud detection. Still in its early stages, this service is focused on connecting data sources together (rather than creating a data warehouse/big data). Connected Knowledge is a digital strategy, turning data into information and knowledge. Joined up data provides much more insight, for example tying data together using the Salesforce platform to show all attributes associated with a person (waste collection, single person discount etc.). AVDC is migrating customers over one service at a time, with about half of all households now online. The use of this data will only grow over time.

Artificial intelligence

Another innovation is the use of artificial intelligence (AI) across inbound webchat and emails. AVDC merged six call centers into one so all agents are required to multi-task and deal with a wide range of queries. Technology supports them to help them to deal with a huge range of issues. This means they spend less time on training and can provide support for many services (rather than having different call centers and departments for each type of query). At AVDC, AI reads webchat, codifies it, checks to see if it is something that has been seen before and suggests a response, with a % estimated accuracy (e.g. "this answer is 85% likely to be correct"). The agent can then just click send. The AI learns and amends the accuracy rating, getting better the more it is used, as it recognizes the questions and matches them to a response. It works alongside the agents; like an expert on their shoulder.

AVDC has also gone live with some automated responses directly to customers. The AI response is identified as such but offers the customer an option to access information rather than waiting until the call center is open.

> AI has reduced call times even when compared with a database of templates (which do not improve). AI learns and changes all the time, so it has improved consistency and reliability, as well as quality.

AI was initially 'hidden' from residents to allow it to be tested internally before being used with customers. AVDC have not had any negative feedback, as it is an additional offering, not a replacement."

What does a new product or service journey look like at AVDC?

"AVDC uses a business canvas (see Chapter 9 for more information) to map out any new idea on a page, including:

- The proposition;
- Cost;
- Benefits.

If accepted, this will lead to a business case, for either an exploratory test or full execution. The process is as systematic as possible, using data-based decisions, evidence, and whether the idea is aligned with the AVDC strategy. The level of funding needed defines the level of approval required."

■ 21.4 ORGANIZATION AND PEOPLE TRANSFORMATION

How did the organization change?

"AVDC moved from 'stovepipe' service delivery which required customers to interact with multiple departments to an integrated online service. In 'stovepipe' organizations, information mainly flows vertically through lines of control and horizontal communication and collaboration is poor. They transformed their traditional 'department' model to put the customer at the heart, which led to changes to the structure.

> The new structure is built around the 'cornerstones' of sales, finance and the customer.

The team at AVDC considered how a wide range of technologies could enhance the quality of its service delivery by producing a set of clear short-term and long-term objectives. The resulting plan was more ambitious than had been originally envisaged. However, AVDC established a clear set of criteria for how they would invest in IT, focusing on value and flexibility rather than short-term cost. As a result, they have been able to deliver business change and save money by working more flexibly and with new technology, such as the use of AI, to improve services and reduce costs to respond to customer enquiries.

AVDC reimagined their structure, with the question, "What would we choose if we started from nothing?" They wanted to ensure the new model is customer-centric and gives the customer what they want (customer fulfilment). Some areas were related to customers but not directly (e.g. strategic planning, community safety, place shaping). These were moved to 'community fulfilment'. Customer and community fulfilment are customer facing, as well as areas like property management, town center improvement, building a theatre, etc. All these are underpinned by the organization's internal capabilities: IT, HR etc. Over the top of the organization are the strategic elements, which differ from day-to-day operations and plan for the future.

Business processes also had to change at the administrative level, because departments had changed. 'Keeping the lights on' was a massive challenge. Staff were doing skills and behavioral assessments whilst also doing their day job. Additionally, the HR department was renamed People and Culture to recognize that it is not just about people. People are important, but maintaining a focus on culture is also essential, so the name was changed to reflect this significance."

> AVDC started to use the word 'customer', not 'resident', 'business', etc. It was felt that thinking about the 'customer' gives employees a different mindset.

How did people change?
"AVDC wanted to change staff behavior – for example, if there is a problem, do not just fix it, think about how to improve service overall. The council used an organizational assessment center and a restructure, putting customer facing staff into one team, with merged call centers and a focus on enabling self-service. There was a large amount of churn, some staff decided to move on, some staff moved within the organization, and external recruitment brought new ideas, experience and skills."

How did this affect morale?
"The staff in the organization definitely went through the change curve. Everyone goes through it at different times and in different ways. Morale did drop, and some staff got concerned about the assessments, so AVDC focused on providing support, for example, allowing them to have practice sessions. Some staff came out with incredible new roles, which encouraged others to be aspirational. The whole process was anonymized so there were no preconceptions. Recruiters didn't know who the applicants were until they came for interview.

> The key to successful organizational change management is to emphasize that this isn't being done to you, but with you, so we will shape this together.

AVDC has moved away from an annual appraisal system to focus on more regular support to help individuals grow. They are still recruiting – and are prepared to wait for the right people. There were no formal complaints during the process and the unions supported it."

> The council was transformed, refreshed and invigorated while keeping the lights on as they continued to run projects.

What is the role of technology in all of this?

"AVDC uses architectural principles to ensure all decisions fit with their longer-term strategy. They have done work on their procurement process, so everything bought is in line with these principles. As part of the transformation, they talked to existing suppliers to see who would go on the journey with them and made decisions about the suppliers with whom they might need to end their relationships.

They have an ongoing review process for technology. For example, they currently use MS Office 365, which is doing a good job so there is no reason to change, but this will be reviewed in two years as the world and the market will have changed.

Some systems can't be changed immediately. For example, their 'revenues and benefits' system, which is a big monolithic system, does not have a good modern competitor. AVDC will keep their existing system and move it into the cloud, using APIs to access data directly. Salesforce has been used to create a single customer record, implemented across the top of 'stovepipe' systems to join them together. Rather than changing everything at once, this allows residents to log in and access their data. The council have a principle of only buying SaaS products."

■ 21.5 FUTURE PLANS

"AVDC is now focusing on sharing knowledge with other councils, including its 'council of the future' concept. They have and continue to create reusable solutions underpinned by Agile technology. AVDC have gone through an extensive digital transformation, with technology being just a small part of this. The people and culture changes have been critical in their success."

22 Case study: digital organization – Sky Betting and Gaming

To get some more examples of how 'digital first' organizations are innovative in their ways of working, including collaboration (Chapter 6), we spoke to Rachel Watson, Head of Service Operations at Sky Betting and Gaming. Rachel shared how Sky Betting and Gaming blends a range of ways of working including DevOps, Agile and Lean, as well as a range of tools and technologies.

Sky Betting and Gaming is a British-based organization with offices in the UK (Hammersmith), Italy (Rome) and Germany.

What's different about how you work at Sky Betting and Gaming?

Rachel joined the organization from a more traditional service management background. When she started her role, she started by exploring the service management processes in place. Rachel quickly realized that while some rigor was needed, strict processes and service level agreements would not deliver the results the organization wanted.

One building block was putting trust in people, making sure that service management wasn't seen as a blocker (for example, not creating the 'change management police').

People and culture

Rachel told us there is a strong focus on allowing staff to progress internally at Sky Betting and Gaming, so support staff and junior TechOps staff can move into DevOps teams. There is an initiative called Tech Ninja, where every technology member of staff gets £1000 a year to spend on training, attending a conference or piece of technology, if it is connected to their role. For example, Rachel is considering buying a robot this year to look at how it could answer FAQs. Tech Ninja is in addition to the training and development budget for each member of staff.

Every Friday afternoon from 1pm is allocated as learning and development and collaboration time; where BAU work stops. This investment in staff has led to some ideas that have been of real benefit to the organization.

The role of the service manager

There are 1400 staff at Sky Betting and Gaming, organized into tribes. The organization wants to keep a 'startup' feeling, so continually looks for more agile ways of working.

Service managers in the organization sometime struggle to keep up with the requirements from the development teams. Newly hired service managers may require a period of adjustment to adapt to the organization's ways of working.

Rachel told us the key skills she feels a service manager needs:
- To be open to risk;
- To be flexible, particularly around processes;
- To understand that no single process fits every situation;
- To collaborate;
- To adapt and learn;
- To be technically aware;
- To think 'automation first' – for example with service reports.

Each tribe has a PeopleOps Manager; these are 'agile human resources'. Their role is to think about people, not just policies and processes. How can they make things better? Staff are trained in service management and Agile, and also have customized training, for example incident response training from ex-emergency services staff.

Ways of working

The management practices and ways of working that are integrated with Sky Betting and Gaming include:
- DevOps;
- Agile;
- SecOps;
- PeopleOps;
- Agile principles;
- Lead principles;
- Some service management;
- Site Reliability Engineering (SRE)/error budgets.

Most tribes follow the ethos of "you build it, you ship it, you run it, the product is yours, end-to-end."

Transition plans are one area where Sky Betting and Gaming have created a more flexible approach to product and service management. Rachel described a service transition plan with gold, silver, bronze, and copper levels. For example, copper could be a minimum viable product being used to trial something, so the transition does not need to be as in-depth. The transition plan is seen as a guide, which is adapted depending on the situation, rather than a set of restrictive rules.

For major incidents (MI), the MI manager will be a technical resource called 'Incident Commander', guiding the staff working to resolve the issue and providing updates to the associated Service Manager. Statuspage allows people to subscribe to get outage information via email or SMS, and there will be a real time service blog in Slack. Tools like Pager Duty have improved the mean time to response (MTTR) by using 'response plays' that contact the people who need to be involved. This has saved approximately 20 minutes of time at the start of an MI, where staff are being contacted.

Change management at Sky Betting and Gaming

All changes, except those that are defined as non-standard/high risk, go through an agile pipeline e.g. Jenkins. Changes are peer reviewed in the tribes within the organization. When a change launches, it automatically raises a change record in their service management tool, Cherwell, so that the service desk is aware of what has happened.

The focus for all changes (whether automated or not) is on technical approval and peer review. Service management carry out spot checks and increase their involvement if there is any pain related to a change.

The amount of notice required for changes has been kept as brief as possible and is flexible based on business priorities – if a change is ready to go then they won't hold it back due to an SLA; 18 hours for a high-risk change with no downtime and 3 days for a high-risk change with associated downtime. This allows product owners and traders to plan around the outage.

The change advisory board runs daily, but is focused on scheduling, not approval. The changes reviewed at the board have already been technically reviewed. The board is held via Slack, with a conference call if required. This way of working was introduced when attendance at the face-to-face boards dropped, and allows staff to participate around their day job, as well as providing an ongoing conversation and audit trail. Occasionally, things can take a little longer to discuss digitally if people misunderstand what's being asked.

Sky Betting and Gaming has 200+ changes/week. There are no change freezes, because halting changes increases the risk of failures.

Tools and technology

Rachel has found that traditional service management tools do not fully support digital business, so a suite of tools is necessary. In addition to Cherwell, DevOps teams use slack, which has then been integrated into Cherwell.

Cherwell is useful for providing an audit trail and reporting, but at Sky Betting and Gaming teams aren't forced to use it if it does not suit their working practices.

For example, if there is a major incident then a record will be raised in Cherwell to get a record number, then Pager Duty and Statuspage are used for communications to the business. They are continually looking to innovate, for example thinking about allowing the team to tell a Bot/AI that there is a major incident, with automated actions from there.

The organization's managing director interacts in the major incident Slack channel, leading to collaboration and improved communication within the organization's hierarchy. Rachel sees the use of digital tools for collaboration and integration as essential for the organization's success, particularly as the number of staff grows and Sky Betting and Gaming tries to keep the 'startup' feel.

23 Real world perspective: interview with Jack Bischof from Technology Business Management

Technology Business Management (TBM) seeks to drive and instrument how the business and business customers are receiving value from technology services, and to understand and impact those value chains and their corresponding demand behavior. We spoke to Jack Bischof from TBM to learn more about how they see the world changing and get their perspective on digital transformation. This includes more information about how digital transformation affects the whole organization, so business processes and ways of working need to evolve.

What did the world used to look like? Why do we need to look at the world a different way?
"The 'old world' was very waterfall, very technology and technologist-centric. People focused on becoming technology specialists and services were often technology components or devices. There was little concern for, or visibility of, efficiency, impact, performance, optionality, demand or value. The business would place an order with IT and eventually something would come back at some point.

There was great, often unknown or invisible, variability. Perhaps there would be a charge for all or some of what was received. What was generating demand or why, or whether an order was covered by preferred contracted pricing or expensive time and materials, was unclear. Nor was there visibility into consumption behavior, cost drivers, delivery performance, resource capacity etc.

There was huge potential for consumption abuse and delivery lapses because there was almost zero visibility, and this extended to the ability to determine how consumption tied back to business priorities, total costs, budgets and variance of separate consuming entities. There were huge blind spots in terms of understanding impact and optionality: impact on next year's budgets, on business efficiency, innovation or speed to market, or whether better capital allocation options or request alternatives existed. The ability to shape demand was virtually unheard of.

Not only was the relationship between technology and business competitiveness opaque, other aspects were simply out of reach, such as the ability to support mature use cases around the optimization of business value chains, mergers and acquisitions, or transfer pricing and thus tax position. Historically, this has been extraordinarily difficult for technologists to conceptualize, let alone implement.

As a result, the relevance of many IT organizations has been declining, reduced to a set of repetitive commodity tasks and services, as the business takes greater ownership of funding and technical innovation.

Now, TBM is spreading to IT organizations across the globe, providing a narrative of hope that we can change as an organization and as a strategic capability. This includes not just how IT is structured and run, but how it engages the business and supports these mature value cases. This capability is even propelling individuals in their careers, and CIOs are earning a 'seat at the table'.

IT organizations are establishing foundational capabilities for demonstrable control, planning for value, and having a consumption dialogue reflecting the interrelationships between consumption volumes and demand patterns back to IT budgets, spend and business priority. In some cases, they're recognizing that practitioner success in driving down unit costs are offset by subsequent increases in demand or poor consumption choice. This extends to cloud, digital platforms, personal devices and so on.

Worldwide, organizations are acknowledging that demonstrable cost efficiency and service availability are here to stay as 'table stakes' capabilities. These capabilities begin to change the business dialogue and its perception of IT, but to make IT relevant and get the CIO a seat at the table, so that IT can do real business transformation work, TBM practitioners are taking it to the next level.

Mature TBM practitioners become true business partners and can demonstrate IT's contribution to innovation or speed to market and can accelerate and/or mature IT transformation in areas like service-oriented operations, intelligent cloud migration and service integration and management (SIAM). They can also demonstrate contribution to business actions and outcomes, like every time a plane leaves a gate, every time an outpatient service is completed, or to the cost of a hospital bed, or a customer channel."

What's changed? Why is this becoming more pressing?
"It is the increasing speed of change and complexity. The speed of technological and business change we're living right now is something nobody alive has ever seen. We're witnessing an era where only 12% of today's Fortune 500 companies existed on that list just 50 years ago, and half of the companies on that list have

vanished since 2000[84]. The pace is staggering, and it requires new solutions, skills and capabilities.

It began with technologists – people who learned to work with storage, or compute or code. Those that failed to keep pace with next generations of technology saw their skills become less relevant. Then the advent of AI and cloud, and next generation outsourcing occurred – suddenly someone…or something…different is now doing that work for us. We have brand new interfaces and languages that remove the need to know the bits and bytes of programming. Machine learning is taking over more sysadmin activities and speeding development work. Suddenly the technologist skills people were originally employed to provide are no longer the skills that organizations actually need.

Today it is more important than ever to get your demand and resource planning correct, and to achieve financial and operational agility. Understanding how financials and resources align to your agile story-points, how those story-points are transacted across locations, the consumer base and the service portfolio, can mean the difference between strategic advantage or slow decline.

We must show that our actions and outcomes actually create business value and highlight where our outcomes are perhaps not in the best interest of the organization. For instance, demonstrating where portfolio investment is creating increasing technical debt, or where investment continues in things that were strategically agreed for disinvest. It is irrelevant whether you're heavily outsourced or insourced, or running a hybrid cloud operation, or whatever architecture you care to name, the value in the ability to manage this complexity is beginning to outweigh many of the technology specializations that have existed in the past that were so valuable. This newly valued skill set is in short supply.

The big question is: how do you bring it all together, expose it, and use it to your advantage?"

What are the major shortages in skills areas? What are the key skills this new world requires?

"Recently I was on the phone with the CIO for a global manufacturer and he was talking about a massive shortage that they have in areas specific to Agile development, building a blended team between on-shore, near-shore and off-shore locations. He needed skilled individuals that understand Agile and DevOps and could drive development as an integrated, mature team working alongside business and product leadership.

---

84 Arbesman, S. and Stangler, D. (2012, June). What does Fortune 500 turnover mean? (Online). https://www.kauffman.org/what-we-do/research/2012/06/what-does-fortune-500-turnover-mean [2018 June].

He also needed to find finance people that know how to deal with this complex resourcing and funding scenario. This is where the TBM community is coming into play – the number one topic that some of our member Working Groups want to address is best practices around supporting the movements in Agile and DevOps. It changes the way you plan, fund, and resource, it can alter your transfer pricing strategies, and can have massive impact on financial processes, let alone the potential for runaway spend and technical debt. All of these issues need to be addressed or guarded against. People that understand these nuances and can begin to address it are in very short supply. Other skill shortages are ones we hear about all the time – cloud security, cloud integration etc."

What do you say to architects who claim that cloud will be the answer to all business problems?
"We just conducted a large session with global leadership on the TBM Council. It was our annual board retreat and we had dozens of CIOs with Fortune 500 backgrounds. It took us less than 10 minutes to list out half a dozen different forms of hybrid 'cloud' operations just looking at Infrastructure as a Service (IaaS) alone. Include this with other forms of cloud, and things like edge computing across geographies and the permutations get really crazy. This does not even begin to address how cloud is actually consumed. We've found poor IaaS consumption behaviors that were costing practitioners millions.

But that's just the technology and the consumers. How are you able to intelligently adopt cloud and create the right workload strategy for yourself, if you do not know the total cost of ownership, cost drivers, performance and capacity aspects of your own internal options? Capacity is an important player here, few companies have a good handle on the cost of peak or spare capacity (in all its forms), and the adoption and utilization related to those services. This causes expensive issues in the deployment of private cloud, and/or migrating customers away from legacy technology.

You also need to instrument and analyze vendors in terms of performance, unit rates, volumes, total spend, cost drivers, geographic coverage, service accountability and switching costs. You need to understand how embedded you are with solutions or managed service providers. Very few companies are doing this well today, so TBM is helping to address these vendor aspects, which are very, very important.

The part of the community that are not early adopters have a lot to learn from practitioners who are."

How are Agile, cloud and transparency impacting business processes, decisions and outcomes?

"A former CFO and later CEO for two of Europe's largest financial firms told me once, "I've had CIOs reporting to me the major part of my career, mostly poorly, because they are incapable of showing up ready to talk about value, risk, performance, business or customer impact...and options for changing that formula". Successful CIOs are resolving this issue, often leveraging TBM as part of their arsenal.

In mature TBM practitioners we see a cultural shift happening toward what I refer to as 'value by design', where IT can no longer just 'take orders', and Finance can no longer just 'report costs and volumes'. Both must proactively contribute, working with the business to understand and shape demand, plan for value creation, then execute, instrument and communicate that value and learn from both their mistakes and their successes.

Changes in dialogue, focus, facts and stakeholders inherent in TBM forces the business and IT to speak the same language, and also brings them together around common notions of 'what value is'.

Agile was a topic at our TBM Board retreat. On one side it affords the business the ability to accelerate innovation, and also to change its mind as it learns during development. Better choices are made based on information as they progress through story points or epics, which is very valuable. But on the other side it is counter-balanced by a related phenomenon. In most organizations, few business people are highly engaged with IT, but now they're coming together in ways they never have before. As that happens, many business professionals find they're unprepared to make those kinds of decisions at that kind of pace. There is a massive learning curve where suddenly they find themselves in the driver's seat making rapid-fire decisions to fix, create or enhance things, and realize the decision point volume and speed is more difficult and/or complex than anticipated.

This problem is exacerbated by an important aspect of Agile: the need for accountable engagement of business resources. You can't pull the entire business into development, so if you've got a multi-functional omni-channel platform development in flight, who do you pull in to represent 'the business'? What is the one person per function, per feature? What is the right resource mix?

One example is the global CIO of a Financial Services multi-national that is highly regulated, who pointed out that you may have many different kinds of lawyers practicing different types and scopes of law in different geographies around a single product (local vs. international, liability vs. corporate etc..). If you're developing a new product platform for your business, who is the right legal person to pull into the development cycle, and when? Suddenly, you find you need to engage with 20+ lawyers in order to trust that the right decisions are made.

Many TBM concepts focus on how adoption, fact-based decisions, and value generation should work alongside control mechanisms and risk mitigation. Practitioners find that TBM supports the planning, analysis, instrumentation and communication of value, while affording new paths for risk mitigation and control, and driving superior Return on Investment (ROI) and Return on Assets (ROA). From the perspective of Agile, Cloud and other investment and resource decision-making, it can often be helpful to think of a metaphor:

How you would drive a Formula 1 racecar if it didn't have any brakes, your windshield was filthy (opaque), and your entire crew was just two people. You would creep along slowly, selecting only the narrowest of risk free paths that you could see, right? You would have limited support, guidance or ability to navigate. TBM gives you the freedom to perform at full speed, with controls, and actionable insight that better alternatives to be chosen, and valued outcomes improved across a much broader stakeholder base.

Value perceptions vary wildly between organizations, even in the same sector. What constitutes strategic advantage, and the decisions and bets being placed in terms of funding, labor, assets and vendor resources, differs radically from organization to organization. Fixing this requires a more mature demand intake and value realization management capability. In most companies, the demand intake and value realization processes are badly broken, impacting investment decisions and outcomes, consumption choice, portfolio and value chain optimization.

At the same time, there is a growing awareness that "what works for you may not work, or may work differently, for me". We're seeing this materialize in cloud adoption where strategies that work for an organization in one country may not work as well in a different region, or for a different organization in the same country. Without transparency, linked to the ability to 'plan for value', and to ensure supply / demand equilibrium, many business and IT decisions and actions are impaired...full stop.

People and organizations with legacy skills and a pure 'cost controlling' mindset, are realizing they're failing to keep up with the market – those skills create less value. This is another unfortunate result."

How do companies adapt to doing all this at speed?
"There are lots of anchor points that correspond to your organization's chosen priorities that allow you to accelerate as an organization. You shouldn't try to do too much, too soon. Attend to the things that you need to work faster, better, now. Then grow the rest later.

For some organizations, that means a focus on intelligent cloud adoption so that they optimize their workload strategies. Others will focus on their vendor strategy and management capabilities. Many organizations are amazed to discover the extent to which their strategic vendor programs are being circumvented, or how much they're investing in small agile organizations, some of which are acquired by huge players they've not selected as strategic vendors. Also, 'vendor lock' is real.... especially in Europe, and many organizations need to manage the vendor portfolio so much better than they are.

Other organizations need more speed and clarity around investment priorities, budgets and spend variance, run cost optimization, consumption trends, or value creation from their programs.

However, if you try doing all these simultaneously it becomes a very heavy lift. If you focus on things that are top priority today they become achievable. Remember, not all of these things are managed by the same resources. So, while everybody is generally resource constrained, you can pick and choose your focus and be able to achieve a lot more than you think. Another key aspect of this is to ensure you have a technology platform that accelerates your efforts, rather than one that requires you to build something from scratch or use legacy data techniques that really slow things down.

The automation inherent in purpose-built TBM systems makes it possible to do much more with same – or even more with less – and provide a larger stakeholder base with more actionable information."

Is this a 'fail fast' strategy?

"Actually, it is very much a fail fast type of strategy, combined with critical path thinking. You begin incrementally, where you can have the biggest desired impact. Then, you establish a 'minimum viable product' for your needs, realizing that the 80/20 rule is always in effect – that there are some things (data, relationships, stakeholders, use cases...) that may just have to wait or are not worth pursuit time. Once you've established a great foundation, you move on to the next area and repeat, but ensure that the capability you just left continues to mature, that user adoption is trending properly, and that those users are receiving continuously better insight that enables action.

You measure value along the way, expand the instrumentation and utilization of information that matters, to an ever-widening stakeholder base. The virtuous cycle begins to snowball."

How do you do this with large legacy estates?

"IT organizations routinely forget that the language of business – whether we like it or not – is money. If you can't defensibly discuss the total cost of a system, platform, or service, broken into Run, Grow, Transform (and sometimes 'Defend'), or articulate risk appropriately, the business often isn't willing to make a decision. Knowing what is fixed and variable, or what addressable cost drivers may exist, or what the Run cost impact is from planned investment – all this can help you move forward. Exploring options and scenarios and exposing these levers to the business has great impact.

Too many IT and Finance organizations see 'P (price) x Q (quantity)' as the height of success, only realizing the truth too late.

Often the business simply does not possess fact-based information regarding opportunities it might capitalize on, or the impact it could make from changes in its consumption behavior, or the role its demand plays in the total IT budget. All too often their eyes glaze over at simplistic allocation schemes that do not reflect actual costs, real consumption or demand. Sometimes the transactional unit cost of an output from a system, or its total cost of ownership (TCO), or its cost per user, represents information the business didn't have, and the moment it becomes visible across leadership, they act differently.

We've seen this multiple times, where the TCO of a system, or the cost of the output or per person, resulted in an immediate reaction by the business to turn things off or migrate. It makes sense, because once you begin exposing these cost drivers and potential efficiency opportunities – for instance by moving to modernized platforms, adopting a different strategy or altering consumption behavior – how could you ever expect your business partner NOT to begin making better choices with you? Of course, there is an aspect related to the art of "shining light" within your organization.

Many of our practitioners want to stop having the legacy conversation and are taking steps to blow up their legacy systems. Some are literally building and buying an entirely new stack, following a strategy for creating new products, features, customer capabilities and even markets once they turn off their legacy. In other instances, they're in vendor lock with their legacy and have agreed a strategy where every new platform is built outside the vendor, and they are carving their way out, so they're ultimately left with a next generation capability that they own and operate. In both instances, the ability to assess cost (transactional, capacity, total cost of ownership, support, etc.) of old and new and compare that against options so they can be sure when the value of the new outweighs the old, and when a new course of investment becomes justified, is a must-have.

Without your finger on cost, risk, value, volume, demand, and consumption of resources, services, products, and vendors, by consumer, operating or legal entity, you're not making intelligent choices.

Top recommendations to successfully adapt to these challenges

1. Don't boil the ocean. Find a pragmatic incremental starting point or on-ramp;
2. Change the dialogue: be able to answer fundamental questions mentioned here, drop the simplistic cost control mindset, leverage practices, principles and a framework that help you accelerate insight and adoption – and watch your conversation with the business transform;
3. Organizations are way too afraid to bring in a broad base of stakeholders that all have skin in the game. Don't be afraid of growing your stakeholder base broadly. Get all the right stakeholders involved so that they perceive this as low-risk and educate them by bringing them along to the point where they are comfortable with the next big thing that really is a big thing. Now you've got your buy-in established and your support in place for growth;
4. It's extremely beneficial to start small and incrementally. If you look at how you're going to manage all of this through a legacy business intelligence (BI) lens, you've already failed. The community and tools that are out there today are not the same as those of decades ago. When you're moving into the next generation areas we've been talking about, you need a next generation purpose-built kit that accelerates time to value;
5. Don't be afraid to adopt new processes, procedures or products – the opportunity for massive improvement outweighs the rest by a long shot. Think of the early days of ITSM, or TQM, Lean, etc.;
6. Drive cultural change across your critical stakeholders early, the rest will become easier if you stick to a pragmatic roadmap for value creation and stakeholder onboarding;
7. Don't be afraid to depart from what you've always done. If you're afraid then maybe you should be following somebody else."

24 Real world perspective: Interview with Karen Ferris, OCM Expert

"It's all OCM...and OCM is the bit everyone gets wrong."

Organizational change management (OCM) is a discipline with decades of history. We interviewed OCM thought leader Karen Ferris to hear how OCM practices need a shake-up in the digital age.

How did you get interested in OCM?
"I started my career in IT service management in 1995, when the range of qualifications was very limited and mainly restricted to ITIL. I realized early on that the people side of service management was a really interesting area. In 2009/10, while researching sustainability, I discovered a framework that could be used to embed change into an organization. Albeit designed for sustainability, I realized that it could be used for service management (and pretty much anything else). As a result, I wrote my first book, *Balanced Diversity*, focusing on organizational change management for service management. For the last 8 years, I have been focused on OCM, attracted to it because of its criticality and the fact it is often neglected."

Is OCM an essential precursor to effective service management?
"There's a famous quote *"organizations do not change, people do[85]"*.

Organizations can only change by getting people to adopt change and drive a change forward. Many organizations have projects that fail because of lack of adoption or not getting people ready for change. In the past, overcoming resistance to change has been a key OCM activity, viewing resistance as a negative to be overcome. We need to see that resistance isn't necessarily a bad thing, the change itself could be wrong.

Resistance informs you. It tells you what you need to do for successful change."

---

85 Source unknown

> What is OCM?
>
> OCM is an approach or an activity, to manage the people side of change.
>
> There are lots of different methodologies and frameworks, like PROSCI, ADKAR, PCI, AIM, etc. Change could be to processes, technology, structure, but it all involves people.

Why is OCM more important than ever?

"In the past, organizations struggled and OCM was viewed as 'fluffy' or inessential. Organizations have now woken up to the fact that projects are failing or have not delivered the desired outcomes. We are now living in a VUCA world (volatile, uncertain, complex and ambiguous). Change is happening faster and faster. We can't foresee what's coming and we could be dealing with something very different tomorrow than we are today. We operate in a very different world, where the speed of transformation and disruption is challenging us all – and OCM is needed more than ever before."

> We must treat our staff like adults. Everyone has been transforming since they were born, learning new skills every day, adapting to new environments, overcoming challenges etc. So why should it be any different in the workplace.
>
> People resist change only if we've not shared the reason for change and done it 'with' people as opposed to 'to' people.
>
> Constant change is being driven by our consumers, competition, environments, shareholders, stakeholders and technology, and the direction can change at the drop of a hat. If our staff can understand this, they are better able to survive in that world.
>
> If our staff aren't change ready, we have:
> - Disengaged staff;
> - High attrition;
> - High costs related to attrition;
> - Inability to attract talent;
> - Inability to retain talent;
> - Likelihood of becoming irrelevant.
>
> For the digital organization, talent attraction and retention are of utmost importance.

Change resilience versus change resistance

According to Karen, change management is broken. That does not mean it is not necessary. In fact, it is more important than ever, but most of the current frameworks and methodologies for OCM are not appropriate in a world of constant and complex change.

Most OCM approaches focus on a 1947 change management model attributed to Kurt Lewin: *unfreeze* (prepare for change), *transition* (move to new state), *refreeze* (embed the change), and *establish stability*. This approach does not reflect the current situation. There is no stability anymore. If change is constant and organizations must respond (and have an agile mindset), then OCM must be able to do the same. OCM can't spend copious amounts of time on communication plans, training plans, the change management strategy etc. – by the time we've written them the project's moved on. We need 'plans on a page', and a focus on simplicity and speed (see Figures 93 and 94). The need for OCM hasn't gone away, the tools and approaches need to shift.

> Think about using new techniques such as:
> * Change on a page (see Figure 93);
> * Commitment canvases;
> * Strategic change canvases;
> * Lean Coffee – a meeting with no agenda, where the attendees decide what to discuss, for example, how do they feel about the change being proposed?
> * Kanban – use simple columns: to be discussed, discussing, done;
> * Collaboration – leverage technology and collaboration channels, encourage two-way collaboration. Find tools that suit the organization;
> * Change scorecard.

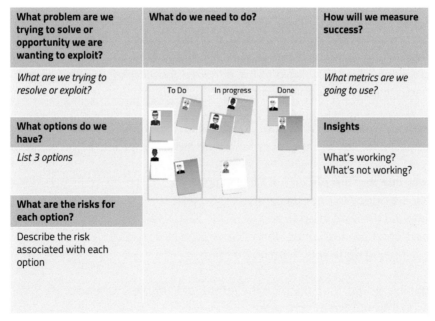

Figure 93 Change Plan on a page

Change name:		Product owner:		Change coach:	
Problem / Opportunity (What)		Stakeholders (Who)		Value proposition (Why)	
How will we measure success?			How will we demonstrate progress?		
Risks	Timing		Enablers		Resources
How will we support people? What actions will we take?					
What is our plan?					
1	2	3	4	5	6

Figure 94 Strategic Change canvas

There may not be as much time for OCM activities, for example huge surveys, because the change itself may have changed (or been scrapped) by the time the results are in. This is a very different world for OCM practitioners who are struggling with an out of date toolkit.

Is this new approach to OCM at odds with wider business processes?
"Areas like business cases, project planning, 5-year plans etc. might also need to change. Some organizations are still in a waterfall world and it is working ok, but the new world is just around the corner. Some organizations are already immersed in the new world, are ahead of the competition and change ready.

Rapid, iterative delivery does not work with a 50-page project plan. Yes, we still need business cases, but they need to be fluid, short and to the point. Many organizations also need to rethink the approval process. If artifacts like communications plans are changing daily, it is not feasible to have them signed-off by 10 people each time. We need a fluid, changeable approach.

The methods we use for OCM need to be linked to how the projects are working. If the business priorities change, our plans need to be adaptable in the same way."

Is it really true that people do not like change?
"People are happy to change if they:
■ Believe it is the right thing to do;
■ Understand how it will affect them;
■ Feel it is being done *with* them not *to* them.

If we get these right, then bring on the resistance! People can learn:
■ Why do they not like this change?
■ Were they not told the right things?
■ Is it the wrong thing to do?

> Listen to the frontline! What do you want, what would make your job better? You are the people who hear what the consumers are saying? What do they need? What do you need?

Effective OCM now needs to build communities of change agents, who are:
- Creative;
- Questioning;
- Curious;
- Brave;
- Experimental;
- Having meaningful conversations;
- Driving change.

This is our *change network*. OCM can also leverage data much more than it does currently. For example, if OCM sends out an email with a link, we can get instant feedback through data analysis. Who's opening? Who's clicking? Who's reading stuff? If people aren't, we need to find out why.

> Why not split test (A/B test) communications? Draft two communication copies. Send out to two small segments. Use the data to determine which communications is most successful. Who opened the email? Who clicked on the link? Send out the most successful to the wider community after the test.

OCM can leverage more feedback and faster feedback. Communication must be two ways. It always needs to provide the opportunity for feedback and questions."

What might a new approach to OCM look like?
"There's a myth that OCM is just communication and training. Communication and training is part of it, but not all of it. OCM needs to prepare for change even more than ever and we need to do it in a different way. If we have an agile mindset and are using a scrum methodology, we need to focus on the backlog and be prepared for what might be prioritized and included in the next iteration.

Think about preparing building blocks for all the scenarios that could be played out. We might ask, if we are delivering a prototype to end users, what do we need to provide to do that? If we do A, what will we need to deploy? If we do B, what will we need to do? Then we can deploy our building blocks quickly when they are needed.

OCM is now more about co-design, collaboration, and working with staff to prepare them for constant change. It's not necessarily such a structured procedure anymore. It's certainly not linear – it is cyclic and iterative with continual feedback loops."

Who does OCM?

Traditionally, there are lots of OCM roles:

- OCM subject matter experts – Change Leads, Change Practitioners, Change Managers, Change Analysts;
- Sponsors – executive, primary, reinforcing;
- Stakeholders;
- Targets;
- Change champions;
- Change agents;
- Change advocates.

The list goes on!

But, we do not need to overcomplicate it. Karen talks to people about simplifying the roles, using the soccer analogy.

Think about a soccer team (or any team sport!)

Consider these roles:
- The players (staff) – each week, everything changes for them – they play a new team, on a new pitch, new tactics, with a new crowd, different weather, new position etc. They can change position mid-game. They do not get upset about that, they get on with it;
- Coaches – change agents – make sure the players have everything they need to be resilient to those changes – they make sure they are game ready;
- Managers – change practitioners and leads – determine what needs to be done to keep on moving/improving (game strategy).

A strong team can cope, but if we have a weak team or an incompetent manager, we might not be able to cope with changes.

What are your OCM top tips?

"For anyone driving change (leaders, managers practitioners), be brave! Our current tools are not working as intended and need to be adapted. Change practitioners must be adaptable and open to change.

Keep it simple. Ask, is what you're doing relevant? Look at what other people are doing, and share communication plans, change plans etc. and be ready for feedback. Don't throw away what you do now but think about how it could be simpler. Can you do it on a page?

OCM must look to the Agile world and be visible and transparent. For example, use Kanban boards for OCM to start the conversations. Think of them as information radiators, so that people stop and look, and start to talk. How can you be faster, more visible, make your information accessible? Don't make people ask, show them.

If you work globally, use collaboration tools. Get collaboration going however you can (see Chapter 6 – Collaboration). By being visible and transparent, you will start conversations.

Get better at sharing results – if it does fail, why? People will tell you – and it might not be for the reason that you think.

Consider using scorecards for change readiness – and again, make them visible (Figure 95). You can assess regions against measures, like awareness, understanding and active collaboration. This will also start up conversations – someone who's ranked as 'green' might feel they aren't quite there yet, or someone who's ranked as 'red' might want to know how to improve."

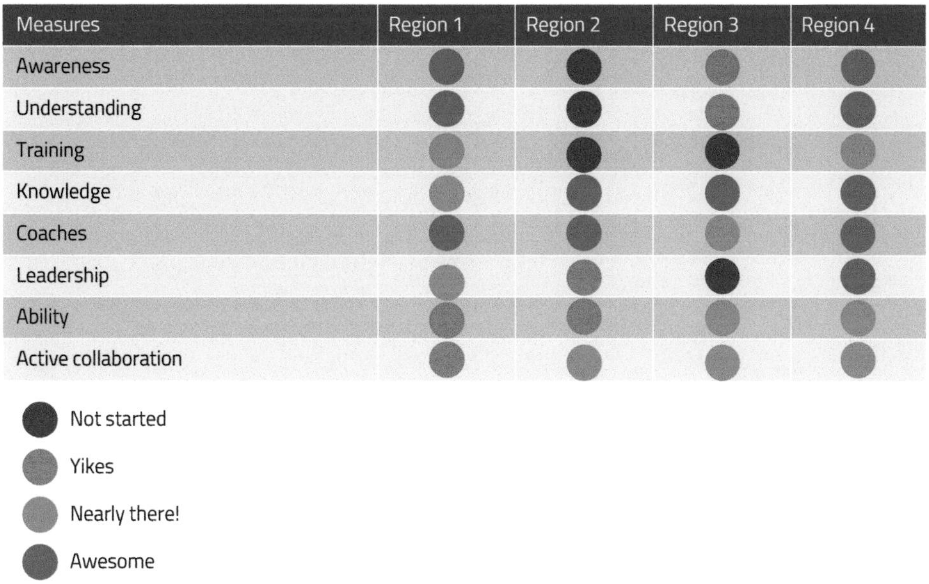

Measures	Region 1	Region 2	Region 3	Region 4
Awareness	●	●	●	●
Understanding	●	●	●	●
Training	●	●	●	●
Knowledge	●	●	●	●
Coaches	●	●	●	●
Leadership	●	●	●	●
Ability	●	●	●	●
Active collaboration	●	●	●	●

● Not started

● Yikes

● Nearly there!

● Awesome

Figure 95 Change scorecard (source: OCM)

Where do 'old style' organizations start?
"It starts with the mindset – get ready for change – because things could change pretty quickly. For many organizations, change is IT-led, such as the move to Agile development. This then requires changes in other areas of the organization. It does not matter if you're a waterfall organization – being faster and better at collaboration is good anyway, so it is still a good idea to take a fresh look at OCM. Plan 'on a page' – is anyone going to read your 50-page change management strategy?"

25 Real world perspective: digital transformation and the jobs market

Cranford Group are a specialized executive sourcing organization operating throughout the UK and in Europe. They have a strong focus on placing C level candidates, cloud architecture roles and service management professionals, and work with clients in both the public and private sector. In this section, they share the C-level trends they are observing as a result of digital transformation.

■ 25.1 EMPLOYMENT MARKET OVERVIEW

It's no wonder that organizations are keen to become a digital enterprise. Recent statistics have illustrated that companies at the forefront of digital transformation are 26% more profitable than their peer group[86]. We see that the majority of businesses are now wholly dependent on technology and the ability to deploy it quickly. Each business process is segmented, measurable and optimized, for the best delivery and outcome, for a demanding consumer who is used to expecting and getting more. This business functionality must delight the consumer and provide employee autonomy in equal measure.

We have seen first-hand that the right people within organizations have never had such an important role to play. Who else will be discovering and sourcing this new technology, learning how to deploy it, managing this change effectively, and having the vision and the direction to plan and align a digital strategy in the first place?

A hierarchical shift is occurring in the traditional organizational structure, starting with the 'digital workplace' (Gartner's definition: the ability to work from anywhere at any time), along with:

---

86 Source: https://www.bmc.com/it-solutions/digital-transformation.html

- Outsourcing to multiple suppliers, especially in the technology industry – with this distribution model comes higher risk if not properly managed;
- An increase in demand for contract/temporary staff allowing companies to grow their workforce and reduce it when demand lessens, which Cranford can clearly track;
- Cloud storage is an area of exponential growth. There are no servers to worry about, reduced infrastructure costs, no issues with scalability and the cloud model gives organizations much needed flexibility in their evolving business strategy. This is fueling a strong demand for personnel with cloud architecture and software experience, like AWS, Microsoft Azure and ServiceNow;
- Management structure is changing, as more and more work is automated, outsourced and streamlined. Traditional roles are changing as teams become more self-managing and less reliant on middle management. This automation translates into the need for DevOps talent within the workforce (see Chapter 5.1 on flatter structures);
- The rate of technology development means leaders must have vision to spot trends and stay ahead of the competition;
- Intelligent automation in every department is revolutionizing services, with HR and administration particularly benefitting, making onboarding and communication smoother and more proactive;
- More Agile working strategies are apparent through organizations, including management structure, workplace locations, resource flexibility and technology considerations;
- Employee expectations are at an all-time high. Demand for the right people is high and employer branding is essential to attract the best talent to your workforce.

An organization embracing a true digital strategy certainly has a lot to think about, so let's look at these components in more depth from a personnel and recruitment perspective.

▓ 25.2 DIGITAL STRATEGY

In a recent survey of CIO's[87] 88% of leaders said they had yet to benefit from their digital strategy, so what is the way forward and how does this equate into the global job market?

People
Change and transformation need to be running through the DNA of an organization. There are many new capabilities to master, and this puts a new set of pressures

---

87 Harvey Nash, & KPMG. (2017). *2017 CIO Survey*, (online). https://assets.kpmg.com/xx/en/home/insights/2017/05/harvey-nash-kpmg-cio-survey-2017.html

on to both leadership roles and staff. Technology is inevitably a huge focus but change management (especially from the personnel perspective) cannot be underestimated and CIOs report this as one of their largest challenges. Coupled with this, the dynamics have shifted in organizational hierarchy, a more Agile working structure means teams have more responsibility, workers more autonomy and greater freedom to make critical decisions. High caliber staff (T-shaped staff persona) have never been more important for organizations.

We are seeing a constant demand for these high caliber people, but with attractive remuneration comes exacting standards from an employer. Data analytics, business analysis and enterprise architecture skills are a shortage reported by CIO's globally, and one that is reflected in the contract roles we are requested to source at Cranford.

CDO versus CIO versus CTO demand

Almost a quarter of all organizations surveyed by Harvey Nash have a Chief Digital Officer in post, with three times as many CDOs as there were three years ago. More than half of large organizations adopt the CDO role as they recognize that digital transformation is a primary focus.

C suite roles have become harder to differentiate between due to the increasingly technical nature of all of their responsibilities but there are clear distinctions in those roles as illustrated in Figure 96[88].

Digital strategy in enterprises

Ensuring communication and alignment among an organization's C-Suite is imperative when implementing a digital strategy. More importantly, roles and responsibilities should be defined from the start to enable the right executive or executives to drive the company toward digital transformation.

Trend attribute key:

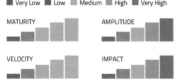

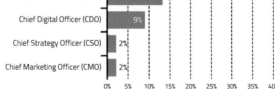

Figure 96 Digital strategy in enterprises (source: Centric Digital LLC and Emarketer 2017)

The CIO has responsibility for the overall technology strategy, covering the wider enterprise, and ensuring that the digital and business strategies are aligned towards the organizational goals. They understand the technology, but do not necessarily need to understand every element, in detail, aside from the cost, delivery and

—

88 https://centricdigital.com/blog/digital-strategy/cdos-cio-cto-cmo/

service implications. They must steer the organization to its destination skillfully, whilst respecting budgetary constraints and the difficulty of recruiting in the technology sector due to a global skills shortage.

The CDO must ensure that the organization has a continually evolving strategy, with an eye on sourcing and delivery of the latest technology to maintain continuous competitive advantage. They are expected to innovate, be agile, predict potential issues before they escalate, and align and implement change management strategies within the organizational structure to minimize disruption.

The CTO is the external face of IT for the business; operationally they are responsible for delivering the best technology for the benefit and delight of the consumer. This role requires a full understanding of how the technology works, why it is needed and how it will deliver to the needs of the consumer.

◼ 25.3 SALARY EXPECTATIONS CDO/CTO/CIO[89]

The average salary for a Chief Digital Officer is $175,303 worldwide. CTO average salary is $144,057. CIO's earn a slightly higher average salary of $169,296.

◼ 25.4 LEADERSHIP AND SKILLSET REQUIRED IN DIGITAL TRANSFORMATION

Who are our leaders?
A strong leadership team is the catalyst for success. Dynamic organizations recognize the need for technology savvy individuals in the boardroom to maintain their competitiveness in their industry sector and move them forward into the future.

Against this evolution in the workplace, we see a strong rise in demand for C-suite hires that have a more technology focused background than in recent years, as well as having well-rounded professional skills. Organizations desire strong leaders with passion, vision, great communication skills, and resilience, who can immerse themselves in their role to lead the organization through digital disruption effectively and with a strong conviction to the brand values and culture of the business.

Leaders need the ability to implement digital practices strategically, source the latest technology, and focus on digital design and output to deliver the very best customer experience.

---

89 Harvey Nash, & KPMG. (2017). *2017 CIO Survey*, (online). https://home.kpmg.com/xx/en/home/insights/2017/05/harvey-nash-kpmg-cio-survey-2017.html

The CIO and the CTO/CDO need strong collaboration skills and to understand how their decisions and roles impact the organization.

■ 25.5 WHAT DO STAFF NEED?

The people within the business need leaders who will provide autonomy and motivate them, but they must also possess the right skills to thrive in the shifting sands of the modern organization. Staff need to be change-resilient, understand the need to foster an agile mindset, be adaptive, self-motivating, self-managing, and have softer skills like communication, empathy and the ability to listen. They need to be analytical, a fast learner, and have user research skills which allow them to see the bigger picture and how their tasks and responsibilities affect the consumer experience.

Desirable service management qualifications we see frequent requests for are SIAM, DevOps, ITIL and increasingly Change Management, with specific cloud IT experience of the major cloud providers, like AWS and Azure, as well as ITSM tool providers.

■ 25.6 THE ROLE OF THE CDO AND TEAM

The role of the CDO is to innovate and evolve a continual strategy to maintain and deliver a competitive advantage. How does the CDO and their team accomplish their role? They must:
- Take a whole enterprise view, they can't work in silos;
- Ensure the team and its leader have a real technology focus to deliver at speed and deliver the best outcome for the business,
- Be able to recognize opportunities and potential issues before everyone else;
- Completely understand that intelligent technology and automation go hand in hand with human-centered design and user focus, and its impact on service delivery;
- Create a full and varied portfolio of data driven technology solutions that maximize performance in the organization, whilst reporting and analyzing this data back to the CIO, so they can maintain a cost-effective infrastructure that fits into budgetary requirements across the whole organization.

■ 25.7 DIGITAL TRANSFORMATION AND THE IMPACT ON THE JOBS MARKET

Over 50% of organizations report they are dedicating staff members to innovation purposes and projects[90].

Automation and intelligent management systems are increasing with an incredible momentum. This will streamline and remove many repetitive and mundane tasks from workers and allow machines to learn about and assess data and patterns to spot trends which could cause issues. This will have a huge effect on service and help desks, healthcare, HR and admin (for example, the growth of AIOps).

The World Economic Forum report supports steady growth in job roles associated with technology and mathematical algorithms including processing power, big data, automation, cloud technology and the Internet of Things. Their report suggests that the advancement of these technologies and the 4th industrial revolution will have the biggest impact on traditional office and administrative roles within an organization.

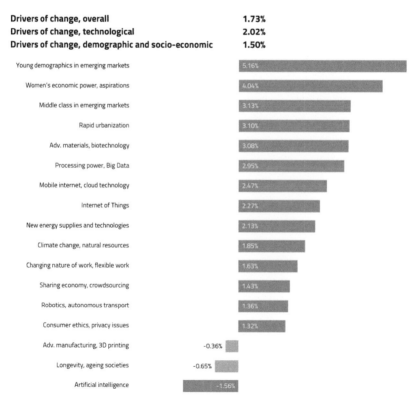

Drivers of change, overall	1.73%
Drivers of change, technological	2.02%
Drivers of change, demographic and socio-economic	1.50%

Young demographics in emerging markets	5.16%
Women's economic power, aspirations	4.04%
Middle class in emerging markets	3.13%
Rapid urbanization	3.10%
Adv. materials, biotechnology	3.08%
Processing power, Big Data	2.95%
Mobile internet, cloud technology	2.47%
Internet of Things	2.27%
New energy supplies and technologies	2.13%
Climate change, natural resources	1.85%
Changing nature of work, flexible work	1.63%
Sharing economy, crowdsourcing	1.43%
Robotics, autonomous transport	1.36%
Consumer ethics, privacy issues	1.32%
Adv. manufacturing, 3D printing	-0.36%
Longevity, ageing societies	-0.65%
Artificial intelligence	-1.56%

Figure 97 Employment effect of drivers of change (source: World Economic Forum)

—

90 Harvey Nash, & KPMG. (2017). *2017 CIO Survey*, (online). https://home.kpmg.com/xx/en/home/insights/2017/05/harvey-nash-kpmg-cio-survey-2017.html

Figure 97 from the World Economic Forum[91] illustrates these trends, and also highlights younger demographics in the job market, women's economic power, the middle class in emerging markets and rapid urbanization around the world as other key factors effecting change.

■ 25.8 SUMMARY

With organizations unable to plan too far ahead due to the volatility and speed of change, there is still a high demand for traditional service management skills like ITIL, DevOps, Agile, SIAM, Cybersecurity and Data Protection, alongside multi-modal IT and SaaS.

The visible trend is that these roles are more likely to be on a contract rather than a fixed basis as organizations do not wish to commit their budgets to an expensive permanent workforce if their business needs change quickly. Expenditure is on the increase, but organizations are spending wisely and carefully.

Cloud architecture and tools experience is a huge area of growth, as the demand soars as more and more organizations move their IT to the cloud and automate their workplace processes. Our experience is that there is also an escalation of pressure on employees to be exceptional. Employees must have the desired attributes for this digitized modern workplace and must adopt an open and positive mindset towards professional development, both inside and outside of their workplace. Employees that want to succeed need a lifelong learning approach.

—

91 http://reports.weforum.org/future-of-jobs-2016/employment-trends/

26 Real world perspectives: Ivanti, ServiceNow and Marval

■ 26.1 IVANTI

We asked Ian Aitchison, Senior Director of service management at Ivanti to share Ivanti's experiences of the service management market, how digital transformation is affecting their customers, and why they see VeriSM as relevant.

About Ivanti

"Ivanti is the result from the 2018 the merger of LANDESK and HEAT into one service-centric technology provider. Both organizations had strong credibility in the service management space for many decades and were also well recognized for their endpoint management, security and asset technologies.

As a vendor, we see numerous frameworks, methodologies, best practices and bodies of knowledge swing in and out of focus in the service management space. In some ways this is reflective of the healthy nature of the service management space – based around a combination of process, governance and technology, the provision of good working practices has naturally come from the IT community.

IT leads the championing of these practices across many organizations. The expertise for developing process, applying technology, changing human behavior and thus improving business productivity can be found in IT.

Enterprise Service Management

In recent years, the growth in the concept of 'Enterprise Service Management' is continuing that transition. In addition, the commercial need for organizations to evolve from a traditional model to a 'digital' operation is increasingly an imperative. VeriSM provides a new approach as these two converge, combining the transformational capabilities of technology that only recently would have seemed like magic, with the application of good governance and a service-centric approach across a compete organization.

Ivanti has contributed to the VeriSM body of content. The relationship between service providers and technology vendors is a close one. Just as good service provision requires a good fit between culture and people, the selection of a technology vendor – especially in the service management space – requires a good fit of culture, vision and personality between the vendor and the customer/ service provider. (And yes, of course, the vendor is also a service provider).

Tech-balance

Another reason we are pleased to contribute is: tech-balance. There are many (many) well-respected consultative industry experts and thought leaders involved in this work and great wisdom comes also with some small risk. New operating frameworks that are group-authored can sometimes exclude the technology perspective favoring a process-only theoretical bias. Yet technology is transforming our world all around us at a dramatic and startling rate. Everything we do today is enhanced and improved through technology, all businesses are IT businesses now, and technology is fundamental to modern business. You can't have any new recommendations for business improvement without the consideration and application of beneficial technology.

Unified IT

At Ivanti, we have responded to this need for tech-balance with our vision: Unified IT. The future is about more than just individual separate tech products. We see our customers challenged by rigid processes, departmental silos and manual (repetitive) work, and often, conflicting work. VeriSM rightly talks about how a partner model breaks down barriers and silos. We have the same goal. These barriers hold organizations back from the sort of transformation that VeriSM talks about. We firmly believe that innovative digital transformational changes in an organization can only come about through dramatic improvements in *speed* and *accuracy*. Unified IT means that service management, asset management, endpoint management, security management and identity management are very tightly integrated and increasingly automated to make this possible.

Process

Process (or workflow) is the definition of what steps are required to achieve an objective. That might be fulfilling a request, requesting HR services, releasing a website update, completing a satisfaction survey, responding to a security event, providing a knowledge bot or deploying software, all orchestrated and automated.

For digital transformation to happen, organizations need to understand and optimize their workflows, across the whole of the business.

Service automation

As mentioned, speed is an essential part of any digital transformation. When Ivanti talks about automation, we are referring specifically to the two-way flow of activity between multiple systems. The removal of 'wait time' can lead to remarkable improvements in user experience. Our Automation Platform (Ivanti Automation) provides the sequencing between all our technology and many other third parties. It's probably best described with some examples.

Some of our customers use our technology to transform employee on- and off-boarding. When an employee leaves the organization all the accounts and services are disabled automatically, all software is automatically uninstalled, and the employee is guided to return all hardware assets that they have been allocated over time. Literally, as they step out of the door for the last time, everything is shutdown, returned and accounted for. Automatically. All following service management processes, but only after waiting for people to perform the very important approvals and confirmations.

Another example is around request fulfilment. Our Request Catalogue experience for our customers often feels like a mobile app-store to a user. Click to request something and often see it appear in real time. The service management workflow provides automated delivery across desktop, mobile and cloud resources, driven by a user request.

Artificial Intelligence

The vital third component is Artificial Intelligence. Ivanti's application of machine learning and conversational interfaces is providing exciting changes even to the above examples. We see the impact of AI coming in two waves. The first is here now and is enhancing the individual business user through a redefinition of what we think of as self-service.

We recently introduced a new type of Virtual Support Agent (The Hub) offering interaction, searching, requesting and information from any business service provider to their business users. It's a totally different take on the traditional self-service. Contextually, it knows who you are and moves away from form-filling and navigating websites. And it introduces the Ivanti Bot – a conversational AI – a chat bot – that creates tickets, provides answers, and drives automation. Ask the Bot for a document, a link or access to an application and see it arrive in real-time through automation. This is a combination of virtual support agents that is sometimes referred to as robotic process automation. And this is just the start.

The second wave of AI is starting to appear- that is the use of machine recommendation and conclusions from large and complex data sets. Patterns, trends, and suggested next-actions from historical behavior and large data sets.

Ivanti's data scope for this is fantastic. We have almost 30,000 customer organizations, many millions of supported individuals, close to 50 million devices (servers, desktops, laptops and mobile devices) around the world directly using Ivanti management technology. It's an unparalleled understanding and insight into our customers' requirements. There will be exciting announcements this year from Ivanti around the application of AI for pattern and peer recommendation from massive data sets.

Looking ahead, through combining these concepts, we're excited about the application of AI decision-making directly into high-speed automation, yet also very mindful of the need for control, safety and security. The future will be faster, more intelligent, yet also safer."

■ 26.2 SERVICENOW

Chris Pope is the global vice president of innovation for ServiceNow, who have been recently named by Forbes as number 1 in the leader board of the world's most innovative company ahead of such household names as Amazon, Facebook, Tesla and Netflix. We spoke to Chris about the trends that he is seeing with their customer organizations.

"ServiceNow (registered at New York Stock Exchange as: NOW) makes work, work better for people. Our cloud-based platform and solutions deliver digital experiences that help people do their best work.

Digital services trends
More than ever we feel you can't just go about using technology for technology's sake, if I look at many examples from meeting global customers, time and time again, it is evident that to really add value, it is about getting outside of IT and into the rest of the business. This is where the push of innovation will be driven from. It is undeniable that yes, you will need new markets, new channels, new ways of serving your customers but in the same way how do you reinvent the core of your business delivery?

You are still doing things today that you've probably done historically but there are just better ways of doing them now. There aren't new problems to solve, there are just better ways to solve them and that means the likelihood of using automation or other technology to fix those fundamental and high-volume problems.

The future is not that automation will remove jobs, but it is freeing people up to do more meaningful work.

Historically, we have gone from forms on paper to a pdf, a process in the past would be to send a pdf that I print, fill in, scan and send back. We may have believed this was forward thinking at the time, but this is not digital. We are now immersed in the next step, the fourth industrial revolution. That piece of paper or pdf is now information that is recorded interactively, captured online and processed via humans or machines.

We see a vast discrepancy between the stages of digitization globally. An example of this is digital identity, in Asia-Pacific you can obtain a passport and driving license using your profile through the social network WeChat, but in many other countries paper documentation still needs verification. These initiatives have to have the right processes and security behind them to operate cohesively. There is a huge movement across the world around verification of identity and how, as we carry out more transactions online, we can prove who we are.

New demands

Against this background of changing expectations, we are seeing a push from businesses to embrace being truly digital much more quickly.

Using the example of financial services, the number one problem as a consumer is around the ability to apply for a new account online. It is still a dream for many organizations. Regulators demand paper documentation, especially for established providers with traditional processes. There is a stark contrast with fintechs like Starling bank and Atom bank, younger organizations that do not have legacy IT. They can work in a modern way from the outset unlike more established financial institutions who are finding themselves digitally disadvantaged through infrastructure, processes and culture.

It could be a generational impact and certainly ServiceNow customers want to know how they can relate digitally to the younger generation either as a workforce or as customers.

The danger to a business weighed down by legacy is that the customer experience falls short of expectation and that customer then becomes somebody else's customer. Many organizations have generalized the things that they know in service management and IT service management and are using that as a framework to try and solve business problems that actually really relate to workflow.

The real question is "How do we connect everything but also reduce the overhead of more systems, more people and more dedicated resources? That really is just a generic workflow problem."

Service Now manages this via 'forms-based-workflow'. Uber is a good example, their whole business is based on a clever analytical workflow, which consumers do not see as it is hidden behind a user facing app. That digital experience has been presented in such a way that customers don't feel like they are 'filling in a form'. The customer's information is captured, Uber know where they went from and to, payment details and driver ratings. From an IT perspective that feels like a request, a chargeback and a survey, but this isn't how the consumer would describe their experience. In transportation, digitalization with apps has changed the face of that industry in comparison to many other sectors.

In the banking sector there is still a need for physical presence, with customers still looking for social interaction and the reassurance of a human relationship. There is a danger that it becomes so disintermediated that you lose that personal touch.

The other alternative I see is that the personal touch point is reserved for those high-end luxury purchases versus the everyday commodity type of services.

"Customers still want a high level of interaction personalized for them to feel that they are valued. That is a key factor in the success of organizations using digital services effectively – to distinguish the right balance between technology and humans."

As an organization that is involved with every industry sector, it is truly interesting to see the variation in how businesses are transforming digitally. There are organizations that do one thing really well, so why not transact for those services and focus on the last 20% that's meaningful to your customers? Services like Office 365 and Microsoft Azure are doing what IT departments have done for years; they just do it better and at scale. There is a tipping point in digital services where it makes sense to utilize the technology fully and for that type of task, we are turning into a task-based economy.

It would be incorrect to state that digital is always the most efficient option. A business could be fully automated and not be as efficient as an organization that isn't. There will always be exception cases where humans need to make a decision. The key factor is recognizing that the right infrastructure for an organization is an amalgamation of technology, processes and people that presents the vision and understanding of the true meaning of digitization that will drive an organization to successful achievement of its strategic goals.

Even innovators have to innovate
ServiceNow are keen not to be seen as a 'pixel perfect' organization, you can make a product look great but if it does not solve the underlying issue then you haven't achieved the true objective.

We evaluate the needs of our customer demographic and break them down to two fundamental questions:

■ What is it that's trying to be achieved?
■ What is the outcome that we are trying to design for?

If that design works from a process of functional standpoint then you can make it look beautiful but at the same time create a leaner version to deliver a perfect straight through process. It can then be automated to increase efficiency or integrated with another application. There is no point prettying up a problem, it is better to look at a way to automate for self-service where you are not creating all that work of UX and UI design unless you can make that transaction seamless for the end user.

The launch of virtual agent by ServiceNow is a good example of this. The design process was centered around it not just being able to answer questions but reacting and responding intelligently to add value and help the user to solve the problem themselves. The design means that the company can analyze the data coming through from their virtual agent, and if they recognize something as an issue within their product it can then automatically provision change."

Chris comments that in this process "our role has become more like a broker of services."

"Everything lives and breathes on the platform and knowledge and experience of the platform is important but on the other side if they are handing off to another software platform, for example a human resources information system (HRIS) platform, the experience is easy. It's a one stop shop for the customer or the user. The workflow is integrated with another platform and it all happens within the automation and there is less concern about experience.

Whatever service you use in any aspect of your daily life, you have one experience of that service, you do not really care what is happening in the background or the processes involved to have reached that point. The fundamental goal is to give one consistent experience to the consumer that allows them to get work done, regardless of the downstream systems that you may or may not be talking to. ServiceNow is building more and more integrations and we have changed our own business parameters in order to respond and react to our customer's needs."

Changing to meet the needs of customers

Historically, ServiceNow released updates twice a year. This format will remain the same, but as part of their continual development and innovation, future updates will be segregated down into content and code. Code has to go through all the normal testing and development on a larger scale. Content is a workflow or integration into another application, the idea is that those will be released 'off cycle' through their user and customer community. These changes rely on the same fundamental code that was in the release and is already signed off, but the use of platforms to configure it to talk to something else.

ServiceNow have found that by managing changes in this way their customers are adopting them more quickly, more of them are engaging with new functionalities sooner and they are also doing more configuration rather than customization. They've improved their delivery model to meet the customers' demands of speed, pace and frequency of change which ultimately delivers a better experience and outcome.

A large part of being able to change in this way is through the focus on DevOps.

Using Agile teams at ServiceNow
"We have over 100 Scrum teams worldwide with 10 delivery/development sectors. These teams are working continuously to initiate and develop new ideas. Structurally they have designated responsibilities day to day and within our locations we have site reliability engineers (SREs). SREs are responsible for end to end delivery, from the infrastructure to the network. As a result of that they are highly connected to support, engineering and development teams so that if an issue comes in they can troubleshoot it immediately. These are hugely focused centers, and from the code through to the infrastructure control, those teams will increase as we innovate for our customers and work on product alignment and delivery of releases.

We have introduced 'shift left' from a testing perspective. There may exist a huge amount of automation in a design but at the end of a release cycle, our teams are switching roles from the product they have built to one they haven't. This allows us to have a completely separate view of testing where a fresh perspective is used to internally audit that product. The ultimate outcome is to drive down defects, speed up upgrade times and minimize patches."

One size can fit all
"Our customers are a mesh of sectors, industries and demands on our product, the ServiceNow platform has to support many and all. Customers will have their own desire to use certain approaches, frameworks and methodologies like VeriSM, ITIL or IT4IT. We have provided positioning documents to which components of the platform align with their own organizational structure and how they can leverage those for their own internal processes.

This is aided by a new ServiceNow initiative to share their own internal processes suites used for testing with their customers. This will help customers complete testing themselves and understand when an "out of the box" option can deliver what they need and when customization is required.

Community in a digital world

The ServiceNow community is a hugely successful and valuable part of the platform for many customers. The community runs directly on the platform and receives 4,500 questions a month from users. There are 165,000 registered users and 70% of questions have a response in 6 hours or less. It was originally run separately on a third-party platform before moving internally to align with the company message that everything lives and breathes on the platform. It has evolved significantly over recent years and is fully integrated with the internal DevOps teams.

A customer can raise a question or report a behavior through the community. If this is outside of the expected parameters, professionals from the 100 Scrum teams at ServiceNow will be informed. A conversation can start immediately around how to solve the problem or answer the query.

The DevOps teams use the community aspect of the product to identify defects and bring those straight into the release cycle, or into a sprint. This proactive approach of putting the developers on the frontline to respond to customers has a dual benefit:

- Developers understand customer impact in their own words and can analyze where else an issue might be having a negative impact;
- It breaks down the walls to the ServiceNow organization. Customers can access the company easily and it provides a really useful mechanism for real time feedback.

This focus on customer feedback, experience and accessibility of the people behind the product means issues and queries are dealt with in a timely manner.

For all the spotlight on technology and machines, this community service aligns itself back perfectly with the need for personal and human touchpoints, as essential elements of business in the digital era. It allows our customers to maintain strong relationships and trust with us at ServiceNow, for continued mutual achievement, whilst allowing us to listen and evolve to ensure we continue to be their platform of choice into the future."

26.3 MARVAL

Dr. Don Page is the Strategic Director of Service Management at Marval UK. Marval provides IT service management training, consultancy and software tools. Marval is ITIL, ISO/IEC 20000 and ISO/IEC 27001 accredited.

Market changes

"The service management market is in an exciting phase, with more developments and hype than ever before. While many parts of the industry are moving forward, others are still struggling with the basics, some of which continue due to the global economic recession.

In the area of frameworks and ways of working I am keen to see the ongoing developments in ITIL, ISO/IEC 20000, and VeriSM. If these developments yield benefits to Marval customers and the ITSM industry, I am a happy man.

One of the most interesting developments and areas of customer interest is that of AI and Machine Learning. I think this is fantastic, and it is being constantly reviewed by the Marval Tech folks. It may provide numerous opportunities in many areas such as Healthcare, but I do not expect **true** ITSM AI or Machine Learning to be here any time soon. The reasons for this include:

- It will be too **expensive** for most organizations;
- Being **service aligned** is still your best option and one to keep;
- People with **passion** and good **training**, will, for the next few years, remain your '**killer application**';
- Don't expect the **hype or clever marketing** to solve all your problems…

For many of our customers, Marval provides what I refer to as '**Little AI**', which is based on only a few simple elements such as username, service and symptom of the request. With this, Marval MSM automatically assigns activities based on the skills matrix, experience rating and availability. This allows the activity to the assigned to the most appropriate skilled resource, person or team.

MSM will also present important information about the user (e.g. seniority level, last experience rating, call history), previous interactions and feedback along with knowledge sorted by relevance. With an ever-increasing customer usage of self-service, '**Little AI**' allows us to solve problems faster.

How do you think service management will continue to evolve?

This statement is working on the premise that most organizations are mature and ready to evolve – unfortunately many are not and struggle with people, culture and limited budgets. We are still struggling to solve the original problem, having already changed technology platforms several times but with the same required outcomes not being fully realized. Even today this requires a nudge theory approach which has taken many years, for example the driverless car.

Warning: several senior managers I have spoken with have unfortunately unrealistic expectations of what they and the business want to achieve and the budgets they have to do it with.

A senior manager I spoke with recently wanted an ITSM solution with all singing, all dancing AI to reduce his headcount, with little or no training to staff – but he currently fails to even have simple customer incident logging in place!"

27 Real world example: digital optimization- Hippo Digital/Kidz Klub Leeds

Kidz Klub Leeds is a UK-based charity that works in the inner city and outer estates of the city of Leeds. The charity works with over two thousand children each school term week, facilitating fun activities that help them to discover positive aspirations for themselves and their communities.

Hippo Digital (a Leeds-based design agency) was looking to support the local community. It decided that, instead of applying some of the traditional fundraising methods for charity donations, it could help a charity by drawing on the expertise of in-house user researchers and designers, as well as the wider digital community. Meeting with Kidz Klub Leeds leadership, their passion and vision resonated with Hippo Digital, who chose to partner with them to support growth in the city by working with its children.

This interview explains how Hippo used digital techniques and practices to support Kidz Klub Leeds.

■ 27.1 THE PROBLEM TO BE SOLVED

Kidz Klub Leeds[92] depends on volunteers to accomplish its mission. The charity's existing volunteer onboarding process is a huge time drain for the administrative staff and trainers because it relied on face-to-face interaction and paperwork. A design sprint/hack day was held, involving 30 digital user experience (UX) specialists, such as researchers and designers. These experts were divided into design sprint teams, with Kidz Klub Leeds staff members providing input and real-life experiences of working for the charity and the processes in place.

---

92 http://www.kidzklubleeds.org.uk/

■ 27.2 DESIGN SPRINT PREPARATION

The Hippo team had several pre-meetings with the Kids Klub Leeds team to identify the charity's key problem areas, and the opportunities for improvement that would give the most value and benefit to the charity. These areas were then the focus during the design sprint.

Design sprints can help when there is a shortage of resources or if there are a number of ideas that need to be tested quickly. With Kidz Klub, the challenge was mainly a lack of time for planning/change as the charity spends the majority of its time helping kids. In this scenario, it is not feasible to give up time to be part of a traditional 5-day design sprint. For Kidz Klub, Hippo Digital had to do things differently.

Because of the time shortage, we did some preparation to ensure the day ran smoothly. These included developing the user journey and a problem statement, both of which were agreed with the charity in advance. Having both elements prior to the one-day sprint provided a foundation to focus the conversation immediately.

The two key areas that emerged from preparation as priorities were:
1. Volunteer recruitment process:
   ■ Opportunity – increase new volunteer experience/engagement and streamline the application process, reducing processing time;
   > Every new volunteer has to complete an application form including two references of their character. Kidz Klub Leeds completes a security check online (visual proof of ID documents also needs to be provided) and contacts the two references via email. Any delay in confirming application information or character references delays volunteer onboarding activities.
2. Volunteer onboarding and training:
   ■ Problem – onerous and time-consuming manual back-office processes for Kidz Klub trainers;
   > Administration of manual tasks to support onboarding consumes the valuable time and effort of the Kidz Klub trainers. Easing this burden will allow the trainers to focus on more valuable activities, such as face-to-face training. As there are multiple training pathways for volunteers, we decided to concentrate on the two main programs – 'Home Visits' and 'Large Gatherings' – for the design sprint.

An additional output of the discussions between both parties was a journey map that captured the pathway a prospective Kidz Klub volunteer would take, from point of interest in volunteering to joining the charity. The journey map highlighted some pain points in the process for the prospective volunteers, Kidz Klub administrative staff (who processed the volunteering paperwork) and the Kidz Klub trainers (who conducted the training).

The journey map (see Figure 98) was created using Post-it® notes. This artifact was created for the sprint event because it allowed the design sprint teams who were unfamiliar with Kidz Klub to visualize the prospective volunteer's journey. A Kidz Klub senior official presented this journey map to the design sprint teams and provided context about the timeline. The design sprint team needed this information to be able to tackle the charity's key challenges/problems.

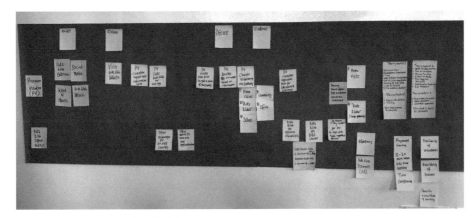

Figure 98 Journey map with Post-it® Notes

Lastly, to run this event, everyone who registered was assigned to a design sprint team based on their work experience. This meant that each design sprint team was balanced; each team had a user researcher, designer, business analyst, etc. Each team had a work table with marker pens, Post-it® notes, blank paper, a document containing the two Kidz Klub challenges, persona templates, service design blueprint templates, etc. Every team had at least one laptop to conduct secondary research, which included doing online competitor analyses of how other charities had addressed Kidz Klub's challenges. The laptops were also used to create digital prototypes that addressed these challenges.

■ 27.3 DESIGN SPRINT COMMUNITY APPROACH

Together with volunteers from other design companies and members of Kidz Klub, we hosted a one-day design sprint. The purpose was to understand a problem, think about how we could solve the problem (from a high-level view), validate it with the subject matter experts from Kidz Klub, prototype the idea and then test it in the real world.

The day consisted of 45-minute sessions with 10 – 15 minute breaks every hour:

1pm: Forming
We welcomed everyone and explained the purpose of the event and the agenda. Teams were formed, ensuring spread of skills/roles in each team and team names created. The session also included an ice breaker to help people get to know each other.

2pm: Understanding the problem
Kidz Klub Leeds members ran through the user journey and the problem statement, allowing the teams to ask questions. This developed an understanding around the Kidz Klub Leeds objectives for fixing the presented issue. Teams were asked to pick and focus on a specific problem.

3pm: How might we?
The teams explored, at a high level, how they could solve these problems innovatively and strategically. Teams created end-to-end storyboards to understand what 'good' would look like.

4pm: What can we do quickly?
To ensure solutions stayed within scope, we asked the teams to focus on what could be delivered tactically and quickly. The parameter of the solutions was to solve the issue in two weeks. We reminded teams to include their "How might we" thoughts from the previous session and make sure it was possible to move, from what we can do tactically, to a more strategic view, developing a service design roadmap.

5pm: Delivering the design
We asked teams to prototype their designs, using whatever tools/skills they had within their teams (paper models, HTML prototypes, code/functions, open source software...).

6pm: Research
During this session, teams asked questions about their ideas and solutions. Other people in the room were asked for their opinions. Additionally, teams left the building and spoke to the general public to gain feedback from potential real users.

7.15pm – 7.45pm: Show and tell preparation
Team members prepared a presentation of their solutions and prototypes for the other groups, and the volunteers and staff from the charity. Each team chose how to present their ideas.

7.45pm – 8pm: Break

The participants had a break to get ready to present their ideas.

8pm – 9pm: Show and Tell

A group of 50 volunteers from Kidz Klub Leeds was invited to watch the presentations from the individual teams. The ideas ranged from self-populating forms, improvements to the website, online training portals, and many other time-saving and innovative ideas. The audience was visibly excited about the real difference that the digital solutions could make to the running of the charity in the future.

■ 27.4 ONGOING WORK WITH KIDZ KLUB

Hippo Digital is currently working with Kidz Klub Leeds to implement some of the ideas that emerged from the one-day design sprint. The event was a success for all concerned. The digital teams got to use their skills to help a charity address its challenges, which was socially rewarding and meaningful. The charity team, who are self-confessed technophobes, got the opportunity to collaborate with digital specialists who helped them overcome some of their digital fears.

28 Real world example: digital design – Hippo Digital

◼ 28.1 HIPPO DIGITAL: BUILD THE RIGHT THING

Hippo Digital is a design consultancy based in the city of Leeds in the UK. Since their inception, they have established themselves as a leading supplier of large scale digital transformation programs to public and private sector organizations.

Hippo Digital has several objectives:
- ◼ To add value and leave a lasting benefit within their clients;
- ◼ To ensure the user is at the core of everything they do from research to design and delivery;
- ◼ Combine a 'digital first' strategy with a 'people first' design to create lasting change and a positive impact.

◼ 28.2 WHAT IS DIGITAL DESIGN?

When addressing digital transformation efforts, design goes beyond designing artifacts and extends from strategy to the outcomes experienced by consumers (see Chapter 8, Outcomes). Design is multi-dimensional and goes beyond designing a feature for a product, a service or a space. Design provides organization and structure to user experiences. Design supports user-made decisions by understanding what is important and what is less important. Design ensures interactions with a product or service are positive experiences based on efficiency and effectiveness. Good design reflects organizational policy and strategy. Done well, design expresses philosophy or even ideology.

Design requires context and it must incorporate the coherent whole of the product or service, not just functionality. Design strategy defines the overall vision for a service, which is then devolved to designing user journeys at a high level. Journeys are enabled by developing user stories that articulate the features required to meet user needs and deliver outcomes. As the design moves forward, user stories are refined, sliced and detailed.

This approach maintains a coherent service design without wasting time designing elements that may never reach delivery. It also means the design intent is shared immediately with the delivery team, is visible and available to all stakeholders ahead of delivery, lowering design communication barriers.

28.3 WHAT IS DESIGN THINKING?

Public and private organizations worldwide are under pressure to deliver improved services, at pace, for less. Applying 'Design Thinking' provides an approach that adds significant value when faced with these pressures.

The core of Design Thinking is **the people** who need or want to use the products or services being provided and recognizing how they interact and relate to those products or services. Understanding the people helps you design, build and deliver the most value, as quickly and cost effectively as possible. Combining a 'people first' approach with a skilled collaborative team with a 'digital first' mindset shifts the approach and outcomes.

For success:
- **People-first design**: evidence-based and user-centered delivery of services places users and service operatives at the center of service innovation. It helps design and delivery teams understand the needs, behaviors and expectations of users interacting with services, as well as the operational needs of the service. People-first is an iterative and hypotheses-driven discovery process.
- **Digital-first strategy**: a mindset and approach to service transformation that acknowledges that the digital landscape and the expectations of users change constantly. It offers a way to evaluate strategy, develop capabilities and to support these activities through the process of 'continuous discovery' and the innovative application of technology.

28.4 ABOUT THE USER AND MEETING THEIR NEEDS

Most organizations care about what they design, build and deliver and what they put in front of users. However, it is all too common for an organization to fail to put user need at the heart of what they do, leading to poor design and architecture choices that can be costly.

The 'we' in these organizations can be any number of people – ministers, officials, the chief executive, the owner, senior managers, policy makers and the delivery team, including designers, technical architects, developers... the list is endless. The 'we' is critical to delivery; it includes the wider stakeholders that support, challenge and assure and the team that delivers.

In reality, how 'we' view the solution and design should not matter. People will do whatever works for them to get the outcome they want. In Design Thinking, we refer to people as **users**, but they can be citizens, administrators, patients, customers, claimants.

It's what these users do when they interact with your product or service that matters, not what you expect them to do. All too often, we hear "but we told them what to do...".

A great way to understand this is to consider the 'desire path', seen in every park, in grass verges and in woods. This is the path that is trodden to get to a destination across the neatly groomed lawns, ignoring the concrete pathways, which were designed to look aesthetically pleasing. In digital design, a user will create a desire path by knowing what button to press or what to say to get to an agent in a call center; knowing that if they go into a specific branch they will get a response quicker.

For example

In a UK public sector delivery, over 4.5 million pieces of medical evidence provided by users needed to be processed so they could receive financial support. This is a major operational challenge, as the evidence could not be actioned quickly enough before the user was chasing payments and progress, which led to bottlenecks and over half a million duplicated efforts. Users soon discovered, that if they walked into the face-to-face outlet, they could be assured the evidence was received and it would speed up the process. The consumer did what they needed to do and what worked for them. The effects were costly, delaying the delivery of high-value interactions at the face-to-face outlets.

An analysis of the current user journey was carried out to identify the pain points. Users wanted to trust the service, know the document had been received and was being actioned. This lead to a redesign of the service, including the ability to upload and submit documents directly through a mobile app. The new app eased the operational burden and reduced unnecessary footfall. User research must be an embedded feature within any design and delivery – and it has to be a team sport that everyone engages in. Therefore:

- At the start, use research to understand the problem, motivations and behaviors to inform thinking;
- During design, develop prototypes and validate hypotheses (use the information gathered from users and give this to the delivery team).

■ 28.5 WHAT IS A USER JOURNEY?

If understanding the user is at the heart of Design Thinking, journey mapping is one of the best tools to use; no matter what stage of the design you're at. A user journey is not about the processes, integrations or data flows. Whilst they are important and build the overall service blueprint (you cannot deliver without them), they do not capture the user journey.

A user journey map is a visualization of the process that a person goes through. It builds a step-by-step view of what the user is doing when they interact with your service or product, not what you expect them to do. It is used to understand and address customer needs and pain points. Starting with the **as-is** (or present) journey, map what actually happens. This can be carried out with users and experts. This is a process that is great to do with your team, at the start of a design. It will be iterated as you move through the design process, identifying types of user personas and validating assumptions made.

A user journey helps achieve some key information – identify the pain points of any journey, the elements that frustrate, slow down and confuse. These points are often why a user drops out, gets annoyed, phones, calls in to the office or decides not to buy, and it is exactly where you want to focus your effort. With this level of understanding, a user journey is a great tool to create understanding and empathy from the whole team and stakeholders.

As you start to develop and evidence solutions, the **to-be** (or future) journey provides a view that drives the vision for your service, priorities and roadmap. You can develop this as soon as you want, but you need to accept it will be assumption based. The to-be view must be validated as the product or service moves through the phases. It will change as it progresses – understand you may never need to build out the whole journey.

■ 28.6 DELIVERING DESIGN THINKING

Embedding Agile practices into Design Thinking allows you to iterate, deliver value and learn continuously. The more quickly you can get something in front of a real user, the more quickly you start to learn.

FUEL

Hippo Digital has developed a simple framework that supports all levels of service transformation. The **FUEL framework** is a Design Thinking feedback loop that ensures a disciplined approach to the discovery process and the validation of requirements. Simply, the FUEL framework is:

- **Frame the opportunity** – the opportunity is explored, at a high level, from several perspectives. Answer the questions: "Who are the users?", "What problems do they have?", "What are the current solutions?", "What value will the users get from the proposed opportunity?";
- **Understand users and options** – building on the understanding gained when framing the opportunity, a more comprehensive picture of the users and their specific needs is explored and a detailed picture of the options available to address the opportunity is developed;
- **Envision possible solutions** – the most promising options are developed into testable journeys and prototypes. During this phase, define the Minimum Viable Product (MVP) – an estimate the cost of delivery versus the expected value to be delivered – through the collaborative design process;
- **Learn and validate findings** – the possible solutions are tested with target users and feedback is incorporated into designs (even back to framing if needed). The MVP is established, the value of the opportunity is validated, and the expected cost of delivery determined.

Each design also needs to be *accessible* and have the necessary *assistance* to support the users. Accessibility is the responsibility of the whole team and includes the design, the software and standards, the devices and the context in which users operate.

■ 28.7 DESIGN TECHNIQUES

These techniques can be used throughout service development to understand, validate and meet user needs and organizational goals:

- Elevator pitch/problem statements – one of many techniques to set a shared business vision within the team and stakeholders;
- User journey mapping – to create a shared understanding of the user experience, needs and journey pain points for prioritization. This also allows us to understand the technology, policy, architecture and data including commercial, legacy, vendor and policy constraints;
- Stakeholder mapping – to understand who they are, including power and influence, as a method to prioritize engagement and identify legal and policy owners;
- Research – including a combination of desk research and contextual enquiry drawing upon the research gathered by other government and public bodies, focusing on key areas with one-to-ones and co-design workshops. Lab-based user research is helpful to explore prototypes. Where appropriate use proto-personas and personas to validate insights, shape the to-be journey/solution options and prioritize use cases;

- Service prototyping – a powerful approach to visualizing success, discounting options and forming the plan for building out a service;
- Design sprint/ tailored hack events – collaborative and immersive events and activities to address specific design challenges and develop shared understanding.

■ 28.8 ABOUT THE TEAM

VeriSM provides a service management approach specifically tailored to help an organization succeed in the world of digital services. To succeed in service design, embed Design Thinking throughout delivery. This requires a collaborative relationship between the service provider and consumer as well as clarity around all elements of the proposed product or service.

At Hippo Digital, we use a customer team model. The team supports the product owner in defining and refining stakeholder requirements and delivering these into the delivery and service team through the process of continuous discovery. As a team, they are responsible for designing testable hypotheses which then determine the minimum viable product (MVP), the proposed iterations, and the delivery roadmap.

Within the customer team, multi-skilled people drive a collaborative approach. The team will change to meet organizational needs (do not blindly follow so-called 'best practice', – it is about building a model that works for your organization). This approach is similar to the VeriSM model.

Stakeholders drive the need and demand for the service as they are the policy experts, suppliers, senior managers and fund holders. They are also the users. They can also be potential blockers to delivery. They need to be actively managed, so the team can be empowered to deliver. We often place an engagement lead alongside the delivery team to manage these relationships.

The customer team includes highly skilled roles including:
- Product owner/manager who represents the customer and user;
- Service and experience designers who map interactions, design and build prototypes;
- Researchers and analysis who drive evidenced-based approaches.

These roles are critical as they ensure the delivery team has a pipeline of user stories to take into build, as shown in Figure 99. The delivery team is where the 'magic' happens as this group builds, iterates, tests, deploys and manages the new product.

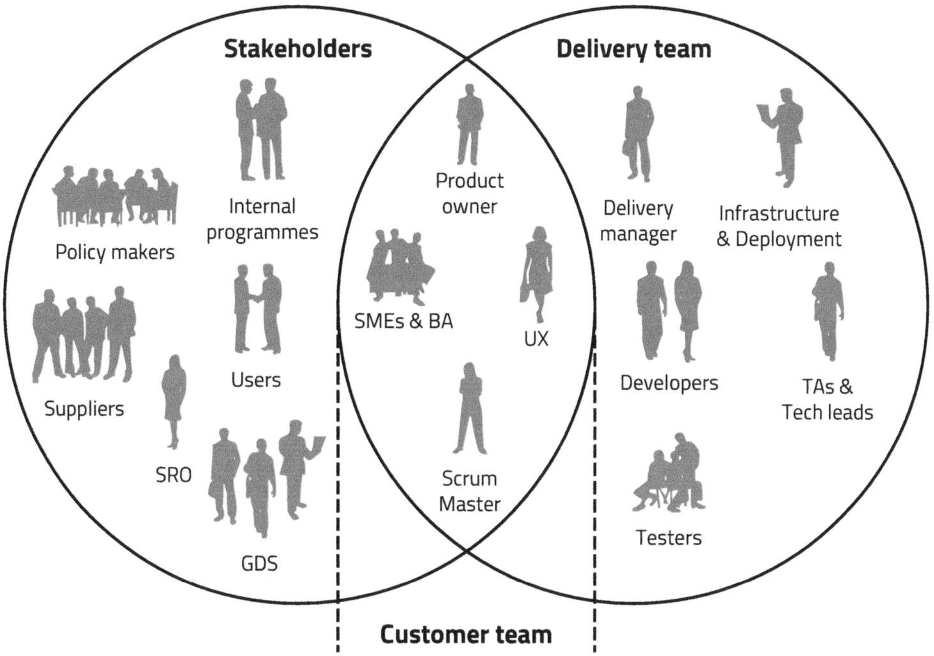

Figure 99 Hippo Digital Teams

Silos are not tolerated. The teams collaborate throughout, sharing insights from research, creating inputs to early Design Thinking and creating technical solutions that are feasible based on joint planning, appropriate prioritization and story writing. These are all critical elements, so a product owner can effectively prioritize design activities to avoid technical debt and a developer can identify solutions to an issue that has been drawn out in research sessions.

■ 28.9 TOOLS

The team must be supported with the tools they need to deliver. These will differ depending on the service or organization. Ideally the teams should be empowered to introduce the tools or disciplines that are necessary. Regardless of team type (face-to-face, virtual or a combination of both), progress tracking and visual displays (e.g., user journeys, risks and dependencies, blockers, journeys) are vital. These tools need to be readily available and support collaborative work and Agile practices.

■ 28.10 APPLYING DESIGN THINKING ACROSS THE ORGANIZATION

Hippo Digital supports the view that Design Thinking can help in any situation. Before pursuing this philosophy, be clear about your motives and commitments. Ask (and answer) these key questions:

■ Do we want to do it?

- Senior management support is absolutely critical as well as a desire to change. Known or potential blockers to the success of the initiative must be managed. Mitigation will come from within the current structures and teams demonstrating the success of this method, as well as the value delivered to the customer.

■ Have we got the skills and where do we start?

- Bring in the skills and experience to augment the team already in place. Ideally, start small, build the skills and prove value. The number one requirement is to work through the phases. Not every organization has the time or funds to adopt these methods fully, but these techniques can be applied in many settings. They are not limited to time-bound or costly projects (see the Kidz Klub, our partner charity, case study in Chapter 27).

29 Real world example: Sollertis Convergence - automating the Management Mesh

After the first VeriSM publication, the author team were asked about what tools could be used to support the VeriSM approach. Because VeriSM is so new, there is no specific VeriSM tool as of yet, but there are toolsets that can be used to support it. One example is Sollertis Convergence. This chapter and the screenshots within it provide some illustrations of how the Management Mesh might be integrated into a tool. There are other tools available, and no doubt in future there will be dedicated VeriSM functionality in some tools. This chapter merely provides some illustrations to help answer "what does VeriSM look like within a tool?".

When considering the VeriSM Management Mesh within Sollertis Convergence, we must understand and interpret what the mesh is representing throughout the VeriSM model and relate that to areas of the product that support or represent that concept. In taking this approach, it is possible to see the interpretation of the Management Mesh throughout key areas of Sollertis Convergence.

■ 29.1 WHAT IS SOLLERTIS CONVERGENCE?

Sollertis Convergence is a software product that has been designed and created using the same philosophy as VeriSM. That is, Convergence is a blend of best practices, frameworks and Sollertis intellectual property into an integrated, single holistic system. Convergence is an enabler of organizational order and alignment. It provides capabilities that are used by the complete range of strategic planning, business relationship management, project and portfolio management and service management functions. It is designed to be used as a unifying system of record and engagement across the entire service business spectrum.

It is built upon a fundamental principal that all business transformation, operational work and activity taking place within an organization must connect to strategic business objectives.

Whilst in many organizations and software tools, this connection to strategy and business outcomes is either presumed or inferred, within Convergence, it is placed at the heart of the design. It reflects 'The Golden Circle' model from Simon Sinek's (2009) book and associated business model, *Start with Why*. Convergence considers the 'why' and 'how' of the organizational direction as fundamental to the definition of business value. This is represented through various modules under the 'Value Framework' section of the tool (Figure 100).

Figure 100 Sollertis Convergence – Value Framework (source: Sollertis)

■ 29.2 OUTCOMES AND ORGANIZATIONAL PORTFOLIO

In Convergence, Strategic Objectives are placed at the top of the Value Framework hierarchy. Outcomes underpin (or cascade from) Strategic Objectives, are SMART, and represent what specific business areas are targeted. The final two elements, Key Performance Indicators and Capabilities, complete the value framework and organizational portfolio. In this structure, Outcomes are enabled by the organizational Capabilities (Figure 101). Capabilities represent the organizations' competences, resources, skills, processes, technologies, business conduct, etc.

It is within the Capabilities area that the Management Mesh elements first appear.

Figure 101 Sollertis Convergence – Management Mesh Capabilities (source: Sollertis)

■ 29.3 THE MANAGEMENT MESH FOR THE CURRENT STATE

Capabilities are defined generically, but when connected or linked to Outcomes, they are linked via mesh strands. Thereby, the mesh strands form the unique need of the Capability required to enable the specific Outcome.

The example (Figure 102) below shows an Outcome of the Sales function (increase of sales) and the Mesh Strands show the Capabilities which are required for that Outcome. Note the Capabilities are further defined with a Mesh Category and an Attainment Level. The Attainment Level represents the quantity of the element -- either in hand or needed (depending on the scenario). This value will be represented graphically in upcoming screen views. Various options and tools are available to view this data relationship in different visual formats (Management Mesh, Analysis Dashboard...).

Figure 103 looks at the Outcome (Increase Average Order Value) via the Analysis Dashboard, we can see the Mesh Capabilities in the context of other related data points, including business performance (KPI), Service Delivery, Project Intake, CSI, Linked Services and Suppliers, etc.

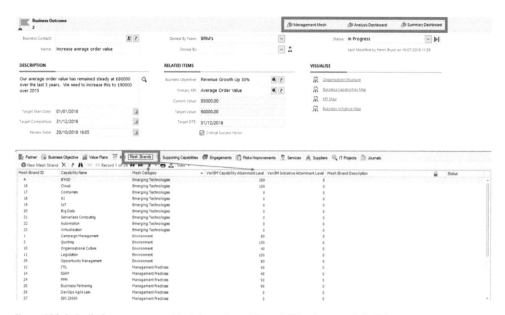

Figure 102 Sollertis Convergence – Mesh Strands and Capabilities (source: Sollertis)

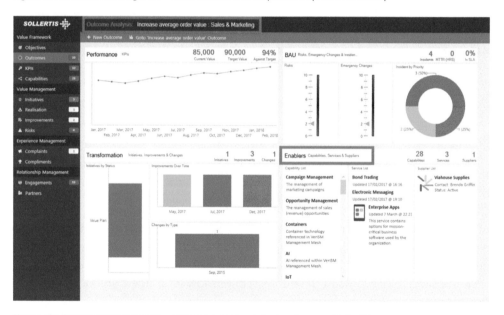

Figure 103 Sollertis Convergence – Mesh and data points view (source: Sollertis)

When we look at the data via the Management Mesh dashboard, it is visually representing the Capabilities needed to achieve the current state of the Outcome. The length of the lines link back to the Attainment Levels, again, representing quantity (Figure 104).

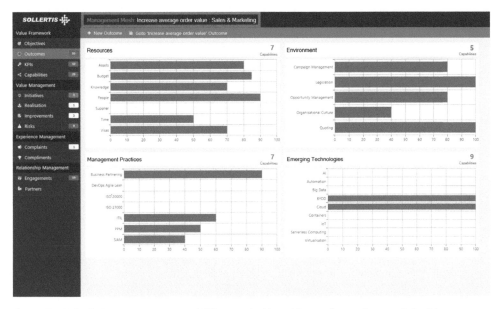

Figure 104 Sollertis Convergence – capabilities needed to achieve outcome (source: Sollertis)

■ 29.4 THE MANAGEMENT MESH FOR IDEAS AND TRANSFORMATION

Through a strong business relationship management capability, the project intake (demand shaping) takes place via the Initiative process. Demand shaping is the use of tactics such as price incentives or cost modifications to increase the purchase of a product or service (e.g., sale prices, new product launches, etc.).

Using the Convergence process, initiatives progress through the key stages of:
- Idea;
- Value plan;
- Change plan;
- Business case;
- Approval;
- Implement;
- Monitor values.

Once the Idea is captured, the Initiative progresses to the Value Plan stage (Figure 105). At this stage, the Initiative is linked to a primary Related Strategic Objective and Related (or primary benefiting) Strategic Outcome.

Figure 105 Sollertis Convergence – Value Plan stage (source: Sollertis)

Upon linking the Related Strategic Outcome, it is possible to auto-create all Mesh Strands for the Initiative. These are generated for the Initiative based upon the Mesh Strands against the Outcome (previously defined above). The default Capability values required for the Outcome are also pre-populated into the Initiative Mesh Strands.

With the Mesh Strands in place, it is now possible to determine the specific requirement for each specific capability within each strand. With the Capability requirements defined, we can run the Requirements Management Mesh dashboard, which is accessed from the top of the Initiative form (see Figure 106).

At the top right of the Requirements Management Mesh dashboard is a link to the Gap analysis Mesh dashboard. Running the Gap analysis Mesh results in the following representation (Figure 107):

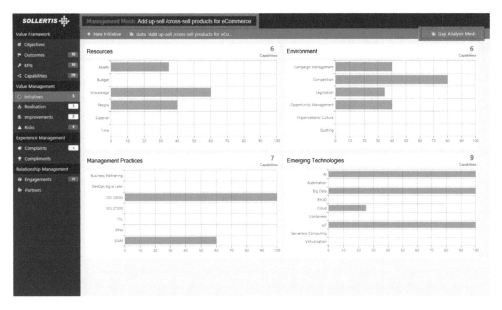

Figure 106 Sollertis Convergence – Requirements Management Mesh dashboard (source: Sollertis)

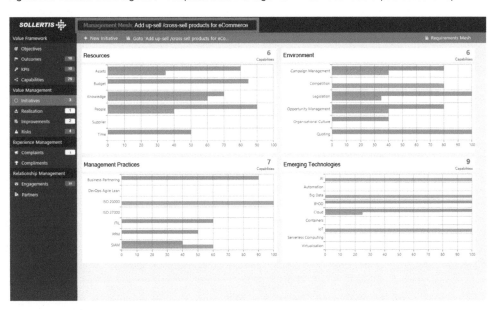

Figure 107 Sollertis Convergence – Gap analysis Mesh dashboard (source: Sollertis)

These graphs tell us which capabilities (defined within the mesh strands) are in place and we do not need to change (green), which capabilities are in place and may require change (red and green) and which capabilities we do not have (red), and we need to develop.

■ 29.5 CONNECTING TO PROJECT PORTFOLIO, PROJECTS AND DEVELOP

As the Initiative is progressed through to the Implement stage (passing through business case and/or approval, if appropriate), we are then able to link the Mesh Strands to Project Portfolio, Projects and Development effort (Figure 108).

We see this via the linked Projects against each Mesh strand:

Figure 108 Sollertis Convergence – linked projects per Mesh strand (source: Sollertis)

As projects and development work are completed and delivered, the business relationship management capability takes responsibility, to make sure that value realization is actively pursued. This is to ensure that the intended planned value is attained.

Appendix A:
Readiness for VeriSM

How do you know if your organization is ready to address VeriSM? Satya Misra of HCL provides steps to assess organizational readiness.

1. Kick-off meeting – understand business strategy and objectives, identify key stakeholders, finalize the project plan, and clarify expectations and deliverables.
2. Review current operating model – review the current operating model and all associated documentation to gain an overview of the organizational capabilities.
3. Review basic conditions – is it clear who the consumers are? Does the current leadership support VeriSM? Are staff motivated to change, and do they support the view of the organization as a service provider? Is the organization ready to involve all capabilities?
4. Interview impacted stakeholders – multi-layered interviews at strategic, tactical and operational levels to get a detailed understanding of the current state and future initiatives.
5. Analyze available management tools – evaluate the capabilities, functionality and configuration of in-place management tools and autonomics (e.g. AI, cognitive intelligence, ITSM processes and other technology tools).
6. Consolidate assessment findings – consolidate all the information gathered through analysis, documentation review, interviews and other mechanisms.
7. Compare to the VeriSM's model – review the current capabilities against the VeriSM components (defined enterprise governance, Service Management Principles, Management Mesh elements and current management processes) to understand the delta.
8. Identify gaps and opportunities – identify specific gaps and improvement opportunities that will bridge the gap between the as-is state and the to-be state.
9. Produce assessment report – consolidate all findings and produce a formal assessment report, recommendations tracker and solution roadmap.
10. Present assessment findings – present the findings, recommendations and solution roadmap to stakeholders, and gain buy-in.

11. Adopt VeriSM – embark on a formal project to execute the agreed recommendations, initiate an organizational change management program, and schedule and complete necessary training.

The assessment of the Management Mesh from an enterprise view will be most informative (Step 7). Ensure a full view of all mesh elements: resources, environment, emerging technologies and progressive technologies. Within the environment 'side', the service stabilizers are crucial as they include current operational processes, measurements and tools. Ensure there is an accurate understanding of the agility, effectiveness and efficiency of these elements.

Appendix B:
FireCloud Health case study

Company background

FireCloud Health (FCH), currently rebranded from Midwest Regional Health, is a $4B 'integrated health care system' that was founded 15 years ago as a merger between two competing regional hospitals – one for-profit and one non-profit. The hospitals and supporting facilities are non-profit; other services are for-profit. Located in the midwestern United States, FCH currently is characterized by the following:

- Two (2) Level 1 Trauma Centers;
- Air ambulance service;
- Six (6) general hospitals (Emergency Departments, Operating Rooms, Intensive Care Units [ICUs], Progressive Care Units [PCUs], Maternity, Pathology laboratories, full diagnostic services with various hospital-based outpatient clinics);
- Five (5) specialty hospitals: Children's Hospital, Cardiac Care Hospital, Women's Health, long-term critical care and rehabilitative facility;
- 15 rural critical access hospitals;
- 2,300 licensed in-patient 'beds';
- 350 Ambulatory Outpatient clinics;
- 1,500 physicians, 500 medical providers (i.e., any person providing health services, who are typically reimbursed directly by the 'payer' [insurance, government programs such as Medicare/Medicaid, etc.]);
- Health insurance plan with 700,000+ plan members (and growing);
- 20,000 staff and 2,500 volunteers;
- Partnered with a privately funded regional medical research group and a major state university-sponsored medical school.

FCH has become aware of the VeriSM approach and is applying the concepts to support its digital transformation efforts. As part of the governance activities, FCH has defined its **mission** (purpose and reason for being). The mission is to improve the health of the communities they serve. Additionally, the **vision** (what they aspire to be) is to be a national leader for health by 2025. The strategic enablers (the capabilities that facilitate strategic execution to meet the vision) and values include:

- Strategic Enablers:
  - People;
  - Critical thinking;
  - Innovation;
  - Agility;
  - Information Technology;
  - Finance.
- Values:
  - Excellence;
  - Integrity;
  - Compassion;
  - Teamwork;
  - Respect.

Note: the values listed will help to define the Service Management Principles.

This complex, sophisticated and vital health system is accredited through the Joint Commission on Accreditation of Healthcare Organizations (JCAHO). However, one of FCH's hospitals is in jeopardy of losing the accreditation and is to be audited within the next 30 days. Additionally, FCH (the non-profit portion) maintains an Aa3 credit-rating from Moody's Investors Service and an AA rating from Standard & Poor's (S&P). Health premiums for medical insurance from the health plan rank in the lowest quartile when benchmarked against regional competition.

The strategic direction of the organization, in order to fulfill the health care system's vision, is to ensure that all services (e.g., hospital functionality, insurance programs, etc.) are streamlined, secure and take full advantage of technology enablers. There are currently several system-wide strategic initiatives, including:

- Continue to meet the criteria for Accountable Care Organizations as defined by the Patient Protection and Affordable Care Act of 2010 (the 2018 repeal efforts are not highlighted in this case).
- Continue to grow – the success of FCH has created ever-increasing use of the clinics and hospitals as well as the health insurance program. As such, there is an opportunity to merge 1-3 new hospitals into the current organization.
- Expand proactive health programming to the communities through partnership with various public and private sector businesses (e.g., after school programs for all grades, prison healthcare, Senior and Assisted Living programming, etc.).
- Upgrade their Electronic Medical Record (EMR) system to comply with Meaningful Use Stages 1 and 2 requirements stemming from the Health Information Technology for Economic and Clinical Health (HITECH) Act of 2009.
- Upgrade their inpatient revenue systems to comply with the Department of Health and Human Services (DHHS) latest round of Electronic Data Interchange

(EDI) standards ("ICD-10") stemming from the Health Insurance Portability and Accountability Act of 1996 (HIPPA).

■ Create an Enterprise Compliance Office headed by a Chief Compliance Officer (CCO) responsible for ensuring compliance with U.S. Federal regulations, JCAHO requirements, and corporate policies (e.g., HIPPA, EMR, patient information security, and enterprise information security).

FCH is structured as shown in Figure 109.

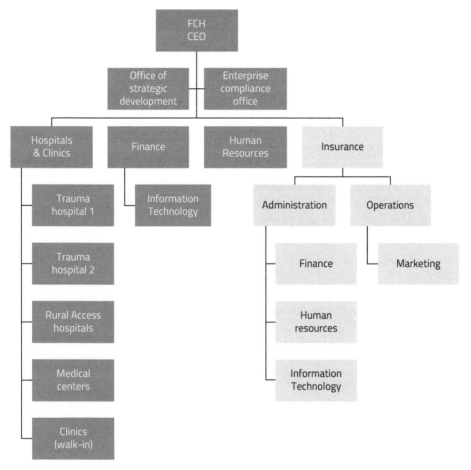

Figure 109 FCH structure (source: FCH)

Office of Strategic Development (OSD)

The OSD ensures that the corporate strategy is reflected in a corporate plan and in departmental planning. This office conducts market research and competitive analysis to ensure FCH remains on target to achieving national recognition as a health leader by 2025. OSD is responsible for the development of annual goals and objectives and assesses their achievement on a quarterly basis. This office works closely with the CEO and shareholders ensuring their vision and values are reflected appropriately. This office oversees all strategic initiatives.

Organizational capabilities
Human Resources (HR)
The Human Resource departments are key areas within FCH. Separate departments support the medical and the insurance areas. Each group utilizes a different software platform to provide the necessary knowledge, tools, training (e.g., onboarding, new skills), administrative services (e.g., tracking vacations/time off, shift management, performance measures), coaching, legal and management advice, and talent management oversight (e.g., recruiting, promotions, benefits). As each capability functions independently, these two HR groups do not share any functionality or recordkeeping. The only cross-over between the HR capabilities is during the onboarding process when the two divisions present a unified view of FCH.

Their main function is to manage the scheduling of approximately 22,500 staff members and volunteers as well as ensure each has the appropriate training and skills. There is a robust training and refresh program to ensure compliance with various regulatory and accreditation requirements. Additionally, on the medical side, there is a critical training initiative for the upgrades to the EMR system. Ongoing training occurs for all volunteers to ensure the FCH's values and processes are fully embedded within all volunteers.

Finance
Within FCH, there are two separate financial departments supporting the medical and insurance divisions. The Chief Financial Officer (CFO) sits within the medical division and, with the financial team, is accountable for the performance of both divisions. Planning and auditing (internal and external) are performed by the CFO and the financial team. Day-to-day financial activities, including monthly consolidation is performed within each division. The CFO and team in the medical financial division are responsible for producing FCH's consolidated financial statements as well as the strategic forecasting activities. The medical division's financial functions are further broken into sub-departments: accounts payable, accounts receivable, procurement, collections and reimbursements. The insurance division has a similar financial structure but also manages premium payments and awards claims against policies. A centralized corporate payroll group sits in the medical division.

Payroll works closely with the HR departments in both divisions to calculate accurately staff working hours, set salary or hourly rates, manage vacation and sick leave time, ensure adherence to the appropriate tax laws, and dispersal of paychecks. As both divisions are heavily regulated, there is a strict internal and external auditing program to ensure compliance.

Currently, the medical Information Technology (IT) department is a direct report to the CFO. There is growing internal support to restructure and hire a CIO to send a message to the entire organization that IT is responsible for innovation and developing solutions to fit today's digital environment.

Marketing

FCH's Marketing department is very active and quite successful in its internal and external campaigns. This group was critical in the initial success of the insurance programs as well as the success of online capabilities supporting patients and the insurance clients. Continued growth of FCH is clearly dependent on the creative planning and delivery of critical information. There is an initiative to expand the current insurance offerings catalog with specialty plans to supplement current offerings.

Marketing also depends on the IT teams to provide the necessary technologies to deliver their developed communications. FCH is depending on Marketing to put together a campaign to communicate and promote the proactive health programs.

IT organization

There are two main IT departments in FCH: one under the 'corporate' banner, covering the CEO, HR, Finance (which includes IT) and the second under the insurance administration, which also has its own Finance and HR departments. Both IT departments have a primary data center as do several of the hospitals. This system was created during the original merger with the management philosophy of "just keep things running – give them whatever they want". As such, uncontrolled growth in applications and technology solutions is the norm. That practice has now stopped through tough and non-flexible corporate policies, but the impact is still felt – there are over 1,500 distinct applications and over half of them are duplicate instances of applications. There are multiple systems available to complete most clinical tasks. Fortunately, there is only one ERP solution, but there is little automation. There are several initiatives at varying stages of maturity to improve processes – both business and IT.

There is a WAN connecting all the various hospitals and clinics via several overlapping SONET rings. Outlying clinics and physician offices use multiple connectivity methods to connect to the hospital systems network. The strategic leadership recognizes the higher costs associated with redundant organizations and data centers. The efforts to integrate/consolidate the redundancies have had mixed success.

Storage is not an issue in any data center. The storage architecture and equipment are the same in all data centers. Between all systems, there are 14 Petabytes of data (and rapidly growing) being managed.

There is a total of 12 data centers supporting FCH. These data centers are all within a 120-mile area, and a new data center is being built that will be centrally located to the two main trauma hospitals. This new data center will allow the shutdown of six (6) of the outlying data centers. To ensure security and compliance-regulated "separation of (staff) duties," physical access to the new data center will be granted only two days per week, and only to a very short list of IT operations staff members. One of the main Level One data centers which is 22 miles away will be the redundant site for the new data center (specified data only). This data center will be expanded as part of the new data center build.

The print architecture is antiquated and has daily service disruptions. Availability of the printing services averages 93.2%. Printing is a critical service, even with 'green' initiatives. While staff within the system can enter and/or access any necessary information online, any discharge instructions, copies of patient medical records, etc. are still provided to the patient on paper.

IT service management

The Help Desk is the centrally known aspect of the IT department for FCH. There is a staff of 16 to cover the 7×24 operation. The number of calls to the Help Desk has doubled over the past two years while the staff supporting the Help Desk has not increased. Call wait times and call abandonment rate are unacceptable. Customer satisfaction is at an all-time low. A self-service portal has been deployed but has had limited success – it is not well-utilized by the customers and no attempt to understand why has occurred.

Financial management is under increasing scrutiny, as customer groups and Executive Management are demanding accurate costs and billing, by customer group. Currently costs are estimated for each line of business manually by each IT manager – though that practice may have served well in the past, the current economic climate will no longer tolerate the inaccuracies. Additionally, as customers must pay for services, they are also demanding better reporting on usage and expected performance. No longer is the "shoot from the hip" or "fly by the seat of one's pants" style of management or reporting tolerated.

There are four (4) service management tools in use within FCH. These tools support several ITIL-based processes – not all tools support all processes nor do all tools share information. Processes deployed across the FCH are incident management, event management, problem management, change management, capacity management, supplier management, and configuration management. Access management, request fulfillment, IT service continuity management and knowledge management are used in some areas but there is no coordination or consistency across the organization.

Appendix C:
How management practices evolve

This section looks at how management practices can 'travel' from one area of an organization to another as ways of working evolve. The first section looks at how Lean has been applied outside of manufacturing, and the second part looks at how a corporate team adopted 'service thinking' to help manage its workload.

■ 29.6 LEAN APPLIED OUTSIDE OF MANUFACTURING

The emergence of Lean

The Toyoda family had been active in Japanese industry a long time before they founded Toyota Motor Corporation (TMC) in 1933. Before founding TMC they produced manual and automatic looms for textile production. They made some of the most advanced looms in the world and looking back you can see some of the cornerstone principles of Lean emerging already back then.

The Toyota Production System was developed over decades in TMC, and rests mainly on two principles: Just-In-Time and Jidoka, in a constant strive to reduce waste. Both principles had emerged already at the time of loom-making. Where Just-In-Time focuses on minimizing stock, Jidoka focuses on making machine cycles and processes that cannot be completed incorrectly. After WWII, TMC had to rebuild itself, as did the rest of Japan, so it was critical to work in a way that did not require large investments in stock, new technology, etc. It was imperative for the survival of TMC that they came up with a way to develop and produce cars that resulted in short production times, minimal defects and rework, minimal stock, and minimal work-in-progress in general. They knew that their staff were the experts in what worked best in production. So, in relentless pursuit of waste reduction, staff and managers alike would stop and prevent defects on the factory floor, instead of fixing defects in final assembly as was the custom in the rest of the automotive industry. Other principles developed in TPS were 'Single Piece Flow' as opposed to mass production, Kanban as opposed to push production based on forecasts, as well as principles of multi-skilled workers in work cells as opposed to the division of work. All these principles in TPS were different from the prevailing way to orchestrate production work in general and in the automotive industry in particular.

TPS has evolved into the Toyota Way, which encompasses disciplines and ways that go above and beyond the focus of the production line. Not that an improved production line is still not the primary focus of Toyota Way, but TMC has reached a size of well over 350,000 employees[93], which means that management and coordination disciplines must also be in scope to operate in a Lean way. Strategy deployment, formalized approaches to leadership and management, as well as to product development and engineering have evolved. Both principles from the improvement of the production line, as well as principles to improve the rest of the Toyota Corporation, have been adopted by both the automotive industry as well as other industries. And although an organization may not be in the automotive industry, there is a lot to learn and much to be gained by studying and seeking to adapt the principles developed over time in Toyota.

Lean transcending to other contexts (service and IT)
In the late 90s, the service industry (banks, insurance, real estate management ...) started to apply Lean principles in their value streams. Most had great success, and soon it was a well-establish approach. The adoption of the Lean approach mostly centered around reducing waste, increasing flow, applying pull and leveling in a value stream setting, and less about strategy deployment, culture and enterprise-wide adoption of the principles. Lean is a great approach for improving a value stream but taken out of the Toyota and Japanese context in which it evolved, may pose challenges for long time retention of results. Western culture and Japanese culture are very different, as is the corporate culture of Toyota to that of other organizations.

Many times, the application of Lean Manufacturing and Lean Service/Office left IT out of scope. It was considered by many too complex to draw into the future state design of new processes, as changes in IT were and are, in many places, expensive and have a longer lead time than is preferred in Lean projects (90 days from start to finish). However, once initial improvements have been made, it is important to dare to bring IT back into scope. The successful application of Lean in Manufacturing and Service/Office is exactly what has initiated the application of Lean in the IT domain in many large industrial organizations. In many places, Lean specialists from the Manufacturing and/or Service/Office domains have led this application. This has been a success in some places and challenging in others. Lean in the IT domain is based on the exact same principles as in Manufacturing and Service/Office, but

---

some Lean approaches and tools, which are very appropriate in a Manufacturing context, may be less effective in an IT context.

The software development industry had long been working in a way that was not that different to the fundamental Lean principles. Agile, SCRUM, Continuous Delivery, and later Kanban and DevOps, all believe in giving staff ownership, breaking down deliveries to smaller viable products, learning from mistakes, and reducing interdependencies between code releases and the infrastructure in general.

Mary and Tom Poppendieck defined Lean Software Development in their book *'Implementing Lean Software Development'* from 2007. In this book, they defined seven+ principles of Lean Software Development. Many of which highly resemble statements and principles in the more recent software development approaches. The key focus in Lean Software Development is how to apply an approach, originally created for processes where mistakes and waste is unwanted, and pull is not the prevalent way of working, to a development domain. In the development domain, you create new features or configurations, and mistakes are as unwanted as in traditional Lean, but they are inevitable in the creative process. The focus must then be on ensuring that as much knowledge is gained as possible from the mistakes made. Waste is sometimes created on purpose, in order to defer commitment to a particular design. Pull is generally the way work is initiated, as most software is developed when required and, as such, is not initiated by forecasts.

Another important contributor to the application of Lean within the IT domain is David Anderson, who published his take on implementing Kanban in a software development content in 2010. The approach and specific techniques from the book were widely adopted as good practice.

Several valuable contributions to the understanding of how Lean can be applied and bring value in a general IT context have been made[94]. The contributions each show how different parts of the IT organization can benefit from applying Lean. There are cases showing:
- How queue management and Jidoka have been applied to improve the flow and quality of work in a Service Desk environment;
- How heijunka has been used to level work in operations departments;
- How gemba walks and mapping competences, matching them to what is needed, improves levelling of work flows.

---

94 For additional resources, see Cunningham & Jones (2007) *Easier, simpler, faster*; Ghavami (2008) *Lean, Agile & Six Sigma Information Technology Management*; Orzen & Bell (2011), *Lean IT*; Plenert (2012) *Lean Management Principles for Information Technology*; William & Duray (2013) *Making IT Lean*; Bell (2013) *Run Grow Transform*.

It has been well-established that Lean can be applied successfully in most domains within IT: software development, managing platforms, IT Project Management, as well as IT Service Management.

Adoption of elements such as strategy deployment and culture, and enterprise wide adoption of the principles, is still less evolved than the adoption of tools and approaches to improve specific value streams. However, it is sure to happen.

Lean in a digital context

Applying Lean in the management and integration of business and IT continues, as such, Lean is a natural component in the VeriSM mesh of practices.

The digitalization of products and services, as well as a growing dependency on IT in general, means that the back office processes may become more invisible as they are 'put into or carried out' by computers.

Applications of Lean in the digital domain include:

■ Improving the processes in the VeriSM operating model:
   Lean originally emerged to eliminate waste, while ensuring a flexible and responsive production line. These principles have been applied to many of the different business domains, including IT, over the past decades. In this regard, IT must be seen as only one of the areas contributing to the outcomes that the organization produces and delivers to consumers. The task of improving and integrating the operating model across all contributing areas is thus even more complex – but even more important – than in the traditional operating model, where often the IT department views itself as somewhat isolated from the rest of the business.

   With increased application of RPA (Robotic Process Automation), AI (Artificial Intelligence) and ML (Machine Learning), it is even more important to ensure that the operating model and processes are improved and fit for purpose. Applying these technologies on top of dysfunctional or overly complex process will only make them more dysfunctional and complex. Once they are "digitalized" it may be more difficult to 'see' them, not to mention analyze and change them.

■ The strategic approach in the organization:
   Lean also originally emerged as a method to ensure that customer value was known and guided all activities in the organization. Today, consumer demand, emergence of new technology, and market actors and offerings change faster than ever, so it is imperative to know what is going on. With the evolution of the Toyota Production System to The Toyota Way, it is described in a way that allow a wider and more strategic application of the principles.

■ Lean culture and leadership:
The service areas (legal, finance, HR, IT, facility management, etc.) of an organization are very often characterized by being intangible, complex and people dependent. Culture and leadership are what holds standards in place, as well as high quality and structure. It is key that errors and non-optimal setups are detected and corrected. Lean offers a strong culture of continuous improvement to remove waste and barriers for flow, employee autonomy, as well as standardization to give room for creativity, where it is needed.

■ 29.7 ENTERPRISE SERVICE MANAGEMENT AT KINETIC IT

Kinetic IT profile
Kinetic IT is an Australian owned and operated IT managed services company that has enjoyed significant growth in a number of regions and sectors across Australia since commencing operations in 1995. Through a dedicated resourcing model, we have people working on the various accounts/sites across Australia that deliver IT and consulting services to customers and end users.

We spoke to the Stakeholder Engagement leader about how service management principles and processes are being used across the organization at Kinetic IT, to provide another example of management practices being shared between different organizational capabilities.

Current situation
As with any large organization there are important corporate services supporting the staff (Finance, HR, Facilities, Payroll, Communications, Recruitment etc.) The Stakeholder Engagement team is centrally based and has evolved over the history of the company. The functions it fulfils and the services it delivers include consumer surveys, feedback management, relationship management, corporate events organization, charity management, graphic design and brand promotion.

Here, I define the problem that enterprise service management has started to address. The eclectic and ever-growing range of services supporting the delivery teams has led to the Stakeholder Engagement Team being a victim of its own success. Company growth and high-quality deliverables have contributed to an increase in demand for the services. As a small organization, people would call through to the team and request support or help. Now, with well over 1,000 staff, many of whom are onsite with customers, located nationally in several time zones, there is a need to have an engagement methodology that is accessible and scalable. Furthermore, with increasing demands for services, a system is needed to prioritize and manage requests.

For example, our graphic design specialist has well recognized skills often requested by managers on accounts to assist with the development of annual reports and infographics. The CEO also requests support with compiling presentations and financial reports. Furthermore, the graphic designer is responsible for creating event invitations and communication templates. How should people request her skills and how do we prioritize the urgency of the work over importance? Apart from word of mouth, how do people know about accessing this valuable corporate service? As a manager, how do I ensure good resource management?

Another example revolves around measuring customer satisfaction and the growing need to manage customer surveys. This is a key function of the Stakeholder Engagement team that has evolved to a sophisticated methodology, and set of tools/reports to help track, trend and influence strategic and operational objectives. As the organization has grown in both size and the types of services it delivers, there is a greater reliance on data from the surveys. The suite of surveys has increased, and scheduling and prioritizing them is becoming more complex. Having a mechanism for senior managers in the business to request this service, specify the type of survey and with whom it is to be conducted, will hopefully enable more targeted, timely survey implementation and therefore better insight.

The final example relates to events. The organization is renowned in the industry for the quality of staff and customer events. However, additional requests for support to enhance the quality of corporate and site-based events (e.g. product launches, seminars, briefing sessions) has led to the team being overwhelmed. Qualifying the effort required and quantifying resources needed to maintain the very high standards set is a key issue.

Thinking service
Within Kinetic IT there is a strong service culture and focus. All staff are taught that through word and deed they should maintain clarity and balance in acknowledging the needs of 'Customer', 'Crew' and 'Company'. To support this, all staff, as a minimum, receive a Foundation level of training in ITIL and our Kinetic IT specific approach to service management. This learning, and the subsequent knowledge they build 'on the job', helped the Stakeholder Engagement team to recognize that, as a service provider, it was important to put some clarity around service offerings, quantify the efforts associated with the services provided and also ensure that we had a way to sell and manage these services. The 'sell', is not a reference to a financial transaction but simply an acknowledgment that it is vital that we ensure our services are accessible to our customers. In terms of management, this means creating standardized working approaches across the team, and ensuring that the services delivered are both timely and to the required quality, thus creating value.

Actions taken

As a team building activity and to define our offerings, I organized a team planning day. From my background as a primary school teacher, I recognize the importance, when introducing a new concept, to be able to relate to already known ideas and concepts. With this in mind and considering we had just returned from the Christmas period, I used the analogy of planning a holiday. I purchased a number of travel magazines and resources from which each person chose a location they'd like to go to for their dream holiday. We worked through a process to plan this trip. Ironically, there were quite a few common elements even though the locations varied hugely – as did the budgets and who they would take. I had devised a template to assist the planning of budget, transport, accommodation, clothing and entertainment. As with the range of holiday locations chosen, as a team, we offer a wide range of corporate support services.

To help with the next phase of the process, I engaged a service management expert to help the team to define our services and then to create request forms. I engaged an expert for her subject knowledge, but also to enable me to also be a participant in the process too. We ran a series of workshops to define the services and came up with a 'service wheel' (Figure 110).

The next step was to work out how we wanted people to be able to request services and what information we needed to process this request (including prioritizing and scheduling activities). While some commonalities across the requests were necessary, there was also some individualization needed to ensure the requests were capturing the right information. These request forms were paper based at first and trialed across a number of use cases.

Over the following weeks, some trials of the paper-based systems were implemented, and the forms were fine-tuned. We were then able to work with a service management architect and application developers, through a range of both group and individual workshops, to map processes and start creating the online request systems and service catalogue. We were also able to incorporate a knowledge base into our system too.

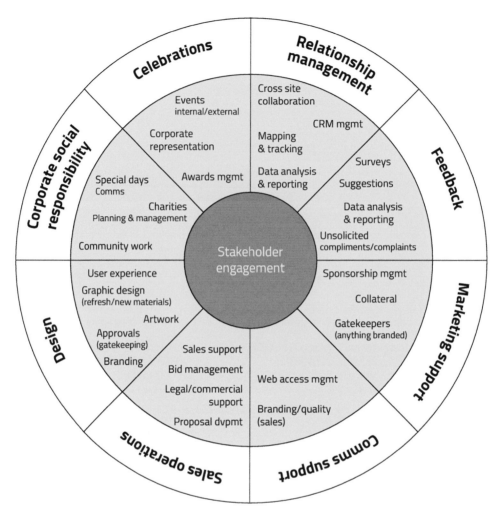

Figure 110 Kinetic IT – Service Wheel (source: Kinetic IT)

We are now at a stage where we have a fully functioning web-based service request system with some items in our growing service catalogue (see Figure 111). A 'soft launch' has happened and we will look to publicize via formal organizational communication channels to the senior management team and the wider staff once a few bugs have been fixed. There is a 'generic request' form in operation that will be used for a wider range of requests while we define and document the other services. So far, we have a fairly empty knowledge system that we have great plans for. Some examples include that many FAQs associated with events management. We would also like to use the system as a repository for corporate images and documents like the corporate style guide.

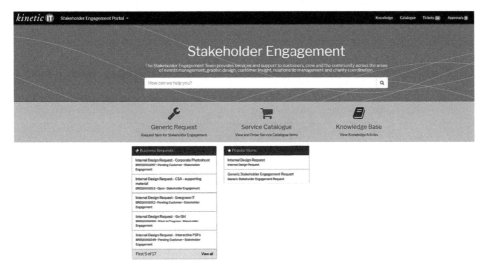

Figure 111 Kinetic IT – request system (source: Kinetic IT)

There have been some challenges along the way and I would caution those about to embark on the journey to have a rudimentary plan in place for both the overall digitization process and what services should be targeted first. Knowing an approximate destination for your journey is also critical. Along the way, we came across some organizationally challenging questions, such as internal charge back and some technical limitations like using the knowledge base to store the corporate image library. However, the close working relationship and proximity we had with the technical staff, architect and the process experts ensured we were collectively working towards a common goal and held each other accountable. The commitment of my team and the access to resources, such as those mentioned and a graphic designer, were also key factors in the success to date. Importantly, we are still learning, making improvements and adding to the system.

Benefits

As a team, we now have a consolidated list of activities that we can collectively visualize, prioritize and allocate in our team meetings. We have a consistent engagement methodology through a web-based portal accessible to people across the organization – even on sites and their networks. We have a defined list of services we provide to support the business that we review and advertise. We can now also report on deliverables and provide a more consistent service to the organization.

We realized that when you offer services, they need to be managed. Service management, therefore, must be a focus for all departments, as we are all service providers. If there are existing management practices that can give us what we need, why start with a blank piece of paper?

Appendix D: Management practices information

This Appendix provides an overview of common management practices across the organization. The sheer number of management models and practices is truly overwhelming. What is provided is a selected set, which when reviewed, provide benefit to a VeriSM initiative. These tables are not exhaustive nor are the methods to deploy necessarily these management practices provided.

Note: The first book, *VeriSM™: A Service Management Approach for the Digital Age*, provides extensive information on Organizational Change Management (OCM), Organizational Behavior Management (OBM), as well as multiple progressive management practices. Typically, these are applied to Information Technology, such as Agile, DevOps, SIAM, Lean, Shift Left, Customer and User Experience (CX/UX), Continuous Delivery, as well as Kanban, Theory of Constraints, Improvement Kata/Kaizen and SWOT analysis. This information is not repeated here.

Note: The 'Apply to…' column reflects the areas where these models best 'fit' or can be used. For example, Maslow's Hierarchy of Needs is a model that could be utilized by leadership and management, or personnel management, to improve interactions and performance of staff. Additionally, it could be applied by the Marketing and Sales capability to understand or exploit these concepts to impact uptake of the organization's products or services.

Note: The table has been sorted by the 'Apply to…' column and then by 'Model' name.

Table 8 Management practices

Model (Author)	Description	When to Use	Apply to...
Disruptive Innovation (Christensen, C. M.)	Explains the inability of well-managed, industry-leading organizations to stay on top of their industry when confronted with disruptive technologies. Two types of technology changes: • Sustaining (improve product performance) • Disruptive (disrupt [new market] or redefine performance [attacks the least-profitable and over-served customer]).	• Use to understand why different value networks need different management decisions (different consumers and competition) • Understand reasons for failure (bureaucracy, arrogance, poor planning, inadequate skills) • Defines (in) capabilities of the organization	• Innovation & Risk • Strategic Management • Technology & Operations
Management by Objectives (Drucker, P.)	A manager's primary task is to achieve results by translating corporate objectives into departmental, group and individual performance measures. Drucker's cycle is: strategic plan to tactical plan to unit objectives to individual managers to a review and control activity which returns to the strategic plan. This method allows the manager to focus on innovation and new ideas and not be stuck in the day-to-day activities.	Use to... • Clarify priorities in supporting the initiatives of the organization • Gain agreement between the manager and employee (which leads to better participation and commitment by the employee)	• Innovation & Risk • Technology & Operations
5S System	Originating from Lean Manufacturing, the 5S system focuses on improving workplace efficiency, organization, and standardization. 5S is a derivative of Just-in-Time (JIT) production. The 5Ss are: • Sort (Seiri) – remove rubbish and unrelated materials • Set in Order (Seiton) – put everything in its proper place	Use when there is a need to increase efficiency and reduce costs	• Leadership & Management • Technology & Operations • Organization Design & Development

Model (Author)	Description	When to Use	Apply to...
	• Shine (Seiso) – clean the workplace • Standardize (Seiketsu) – standardized how to maintain cleanliness • Sustain (Shitsuke) – embed 5S into culture; maintain commitment While it is easy to see the benefits for a factory floor, these same steps can be applied to any office environment.		
Five Functions of Management (Fayol, H.)	Fayol was most well-known for his definition of the six general activities within an organization (technical, commercial, financial, security, accounting, managerial). Seeing a deficiency within management information, Fayol further defined managerial into the Five Functions of Management: 1. Planning 2. Organizing 3. Commanding 4. Coordinating 5. Controlling These five functions focus on the relationship between management and staff with the goal of creative problem-solving. NOTE: underpinning the five activities is a sixth – overall management function supporting the original five.	Use to solve problems by starting with an environmental analysis and ending with an evaluation of the implemented solution	• Leadership & Management • Organizational Design & Development
Hierarchy of Needs (Maslow, A.)	Human motivation is based on five different and escalating needs: physiological, safety, belongingness and love, esteem, and self-actualization.	Use to... • To improve employee satisfaction • To understand consumer purchasing patterns	• Leadership & Management • Marketing & Sales • Personnel Management

Model (Author)	Description	When to Use	Apply to...
	As one need is met, others in the hierarchy become stronger. A limiting factor to this model is that culture is not considered. It is wise to be cautious in interpreting Maslow's Hierarchy of needs. Remember that all levels apply to all individuals.		
Leadership Pipeline (Drotter, S., Noel, J. & Charan, R.)	This model operates under the premise that management should develop and maintain a pipeline of skilled and prepared leaders from within. The six "passages" describes the necessary skills that need to be developed to progress through the defined stages. Beginning with the base level of managing self, the stages are: • Managing others • Managing managers • Functional manager • Business manager • Group manager • Enterprise manager	• Use to develop leaders internally and understand how the leadership and management roles differ across levels within the organization • Facilitates succession planning and leadership development	• Leadership & Management • Organizational Design & Development • Strategic Management
Stages of Team Development (Tuckman, B.)	Tuckman's stages can be used to identify factors that influence team development. The five stages are: • Forming • Storming • Norming • Performing • Adjourning This model has limitations as it was developed with small groups in mind and team development may not be linear. Regardless, this model is still the seminal model for understanding team development.	Use to build, manage and/or analyze teams	• Leadership & Management • Organizational Design & Development

Model (Author)	Description	When to Use	Apply to...
Theory X & Y (McGregor, D.)	Based on Maslow's Hierarchy of Needs, McGregor theorized two separate and contrasting portraits of managers. Theory X managers (authoritarian and centralized) assume people are intrinsically lazy, not responsible, lack self-discipline and only want security. Theory X managers have a very hands-on style. Theory Y managers (participatory) have opposite assumptions – they believe people take pride in their work and are intrinsically motivated. These managers have a more decentralized approach encouraging trust and collaborative between the manager and staff. Understand a blend of both styles are found to be the most effective in today's environment.	Use these motivation and management theories to help in organizational development. Understand a "pure" deployment of X & Y represents unrealistic extremes.	• Leadership & Management • Organizational Change Management • Personnel Management
Two-Factor Theory (Motivation-Hygiene Theory) (Herzberg, F., Mausner, B. & Shyderman, B.)	To understand employee motivation and satisfaction, a set of extrinsic hygiene factors which prevent dissatisfaction (company policies, quality of supervision, working conditions, interpersonal relations, salary, status, job security) and intrinsic motivation factors which leads to job satisfaction and higher levels of motivation (achievement, recognition, the work itself, responsibility, advancement) are measured. Minimize the impact of hygiene factors and maximize the motivational factors to increase positive job attitudes.	Use to develop motivation programs or understand what motivates staff. To successfully apply this theory, first eliminate dissatisfaction and then help the employee find satisfaction.	• Leadership & Management • Personnel Management

Model (Author)	Description	When to Use	Apply to...
Diffusion of Innovations (Rogers, E. M.)	This theory attempts to explain the rate which new ideas or products spread through a culture. Known today as the "tipping point" (the point when a trend catches fire), this theory confirms the importance of differentiating customer segments. Clearly defining adopter group types (shown as a bell-shaped curve) – innovators, early adopters, early majority, late majority, laggards – marketing strategies can be adopted to appeal to the various types and gain approval. The premise of this model is if the product/service convinces the innovators and early adopters, it will be successful as the appeal of the product spreads to the early majority and beyond. Where this model has difficulties is around technology and disruptive technologies as consumers will adapt those based on their own needs. Where this model exceeds is the ideal types and percentages of those types can be used to create a focused communication plan.	To understand the appeal of the product to the adopter group types and plan the communication and/or marketing to meet those needs (e.g., early adopters – they are opinion leaders, aware of the change, comfortable with new idea – appeal to them with instruction manuals or implementation steps – there is no need to convince this group to change).	• Marketing & Sales • Communication • Innovation & Risk

Model (Author)	Description	When to Use	Apply to...
Five Product Levels (Kotler, P.)	Defined, a product is anything that can be offered to a market for attention, acquisition, or use or something that can satisfy a need or want. Thus, customers will choose a product based on their perceived value of it based on need, want or demand. Satisfaction will only occur if the value is the same or exceeds the perceived value of the product. Additionally, Kotler redefined marketing as a "social process by which individuals and groups obtain what they need and want through creating and exchanging products and value with others". The five product levels (from a base level to a proposed future) are: 1. Core benefit of the product 2. Generic product 3. Expected product 4. Augmented product 5. Potential product	When there is a need to understand the value of a product or service from the eyes of the consumer. Understanding this information directly influences the marketing strategy and activities.	• Marketing & Sales • Technology & Operations
Change Equation (Gleicher, D., Beckhard, R., & Harris, R.)	To gain positive staff involvement in change initiatives, three components must be present. These components create an equation which will, when all are present, overcome resistance to change.	Use to overcome resistance to change	• Organizational Change Management • Organizational Design & Development

Model (Author)	Description	When to Use	Apply to...
	The components are: • Dissatisfaction with the present situation • Vision of what is possible • Achievable first steps to reaching the vision If any element is zero or near zero, there will be resistance to change. The formula is: Dissatisfaction (D) × Vision (V) × First steps (F) > Resistance (R) to change.		
Change Phases (Kotter, J.)	Kotter's *Leading Change* (1996) describes eight steps, that when deployed, would facilitate a change. The original eight steps were linear, finite, sequential and rigid. Recognizing a need for the model to reflect current environments (speed of change, globalized economy, revolutionary change, adapt as you go), Kotter released an updated model (2014). This has Eight Accelerators, which better reflected the nonlinear and complex environment (self-organizing networks, multi-initiatives that are small to reduce risk...).	Use the 1996 model when change is necessary in an environment that is stable predictable and repeatable. Use the 2014 model when change impacts an environment that can be characterized as a complex adaptive environment.	• Organizational Change Management • Leadership & Management
Double Loop Learning (Argyris, C. & Schön, D. A.)	Double-loop learning occurs when feedback from past actions is used to question current underlying assumptions (take nothing at face value). The argument is that for change to occur, not only does the change need to be completed but the 'why' behind the change must be understood and accepted.	To facilitate change through communication and feedback loops	• Organizational Change Management • Innovation & Risk • Organizational Design & Development

Model (Author)	Description	When to Use	Apply to...
	For organizational change to be effective, top management cannot rely on memos, orders, and directives to change behavior. This will only lead to defensiveness, cynicism, evasion and the like. With double-loop learning techniques, the 'take-for-granted' mentality is replaced by a detect-and-solve problems mentality.		
Force Field analysis (Lewin, K.)	The premise of Force Field analysis is that opposing forces (driving and resisting) create an equilibrium of sorts that maintain situations. For change to occur, the driving forces must be strengthened (or the resisting forces weakened). This 5-step analysis looks at the forces that are for and against a specific change. The outcome is the communication of the decision and the reasoning behind the decision.	To understand the pressures for and against a change or a decision.	• Organizational Change Management
Situational leadership (Hersey, P. & Blanchard, K.)	Situational leadership refers to the adjustment in leadership style to fit the development level of the followers. The leader/manager must change their preferred style rather than the follower adapt to the leader/manager. This model defines four types of leaders based on the ability and willingness of the followers: 1. Directing (low ability/ low willingness) 2. Coaching (low ability/ high willingness) 3. Supporting (high ability/ low willingness) 4. Delegating (high ability/high willingness).	• Use to address staff resistance due to new initiatives or changes • Use to manage a diverse workforce and/or when working in the global marketplace	• Organizational Change Management • Leadership & Management • Personnel Management

Model (Author)	Description	When to Use	Apply to...
The 4 Disciplines of Execution (4DX) (McChesney, C., Covey, S., & Huling, J.)	4DX is purposely NOT defined as a theory, but rather a set of simple, repeatable and proven activities for executing strategic priorities during the daily 'whirlwind'. 4DX focuses on four activities... 1. What is wildly important 2. Acting on lead measures 3. Keep a compelling scorecard 4. Create a cadence of accountability ...that when properly executed, creates a team that performs consistently with excellence within the daily myriad of distractions.	Use these activities to ensure execution of the necessary activities to accomplish a strategic initiative or to improve any given situation	• Organizational Change Management • Leadership & Management • Strategic Management
Three levels of culture (Schein, E.)	Schein defines organizational culture as "the basic tacit assumptions about how the world is and ought to be that a group of people share and that determines their perceptions, thoughts, feelings, and, their overt behavior". Thus, there are three levels: • Artifacts (surface, easily characterized but hard to understand) • Espoused values (below artifacts – conscious strategies, goals, philosophies) • Basic assumptions and values (the core or essence of culture – hard to discern as they exist at an unconscious level).	• Use to define the three layers of culture (artifacts – what we see; norms & values – what they say; underlying assumptions – what is deeply believed) • Provides leadership and management insight into the organization which can impact the development and deployment of strategy	• Organizational Change Management • Organizational Design & Development • Personnel Management

Model (Author)	Description	When to Use	Apply to...
Five configurations (Mintzberg, H.)	Organizational structures are "the sum total of the ways in which it divides its labor into distinct tasks and then achieves coordination among them". The model provides a framework to analyze organizational structures in relation to the five defined ideal types: 1. Entrepreneurial 2. Machine (bureaucratic) 3. Professional 4. Divisional 5. Innovative (adhocracy) This is not a 'one and-done' analysis – understand organizations change over time and powers shift; each will affect the structure.	Use to review current organizational structure and determine the best structure (based on organizational strategy, environmental forces and the structure itself).	• Organizational Design & Development
Five Star model (Galbraith, J. R.)	This model stresses that strategy drives organizational structure. Five interrelated categories provide the base for organizational design: 1. Strategy; 2. Structure; 3. Processes; 4. Reward systems; 5. People. These five factors must be internally consistent to enable effective behavior.	Use this model to overcome the "negatives" of any structural design	• Organizational Design & Development • Information Technology
Business Analysis Body of Knowledge (BABOK) (International Institute of Business Analysis)	Referenced in Chapter 14 Define the requirements, and includes requirements lifecycle management, requirements gathering and requirements classification.	Use this model to support requirements gathering, management and classification	• Business Analysis

Model (Author)	Description	When to Use	Apply to...
Five Competitive Forces (Porter, M.)	Porter's Five Forces not only shape any industry, they can also determine an organization's strengths and weaknesses. A typical use of the model is to measure competition intensity, profitability, and attractiveness. The Five Forces are: • Competition in the industry • Potential of new entrants into the industry • Power of suppliers • Power of customers • Threat of substitute products	Use to understand the five forces which then allows an organization to adjust its strategy and more effectively use its resources	• Strategic Management
Operating Model Canvas (Campbell, A., Gutierrez, M. & Lancelott, M.)	An operating model is a "visual representation... that shows the elements of the organization...that is important for delivering the organization's value proposition and how these elements combine to successfully deliver the value proposition". The operating model uses a simple six section 'canvas' to describe and design the link between a defined strategy and operational activities. The six sections are: • Management system • Organization • Information • Value delivery chains • Suppliers • Locations Note: The Operating Model Canvas links to the Business Model Canvas which describes how an organization "creates, delivers and captures value, what value is being delivered and to whom".	There is a need for a high-level understanding of the organizational elements that deliver the value proposition	• Strategic Management • Technology & Operations

Model (Author)	Description	When to Use	Apply to...
Three generic strategies (Porter, M.)	The three strategies – cost leadership, differentiation, or focus – for product/service delivery are critical in how a service provider presents its products and services. None of the strategies are 'best' – time and circumstance drive the position. For example, if the market is commodity driven, the strategy should focus on lower costs. In a "specialist" market, the focus is on differentiation as price will not matter to the consumer. The last strategy, focus, has the service provider pursuing a lowest cost or differentiate product to a niche market. The Three Generic Strategies are part of the Porter's Three Stage Analysis: Five Forces, Generic strategies, Value Chain Analysis.	Use to determine a strategy based on what is attractive for the organization – be if profitability or position in the industry.	• Strategic Management
Value Chain analysis (Porter, M.)	To identify primary, secondary or support activities that add value to a product. These activities are then analyzed to reduce costs, optimize efforts, eliminate waste, increase profitability, or increase product differentiation.	Use when: • There is a need to create a cost advantage (identify and reduce costs of the primary and support activities) • There is a need to create a competitive differentiation advantage (identify the activities that create the greatest value to the consumer).	• Strategic Management • Finance & Accounting • Marketing & Sales • Organizational Design & Development

Appendix D2: Knowledge management specific practices

Knowledge systems become more robust, efficient and sustainable when the knowledge gap between the experts is narrowed. Table 9 shows several approaches, methods and techniques that have proven practical application for an adaptive Knowledge management approach.

Table 9 Knowledge management Practices

Name	Type	Description	Ownership / Links
Knowledge Centered Service (KCS®)	Principles Based Methodology	"KCS is a proven methodology for integrating the use, validation, improvement, and creation of knowledge into the workflow."	The KCS® methodology is a registered service mark of the Consortium for Service Innovation. http://www.thekcsacademy. net/kcs/kcs-resources/
OBASHI	Framework and Method	The OBASHI methodology provides a framework and method for capturing, illustrating and modeling the relationships, dependencies and data flows between business and Information technology (IT) assets and resources in a business context.	OBASHI – http://obashi.co.uk
Cynefin	Framework	Cynefin allows executives to see things from new viewpoints, assimilate complex concepts, and address real-world problems and opportunities. Using the Cynefin framework can help executives sense which context they are in so that they can not only make better decisions but also avoid the problems that arise when their preferred management style causes them to make mistakes	http://cognitive-edge.com/ videos/cynefin-framework-introduction/
Knowledge Café	Conceptual Practice	Knowledge Café adheres to several conversational principles that help create a relaxed, informal environment conducive to open dialogue and to learning.	David Gurteen http://knowledge.cafe/ knowledge-cafe-concept/

Name	Type	Description	Ownership / Links
DIKW	Model	Representing purported structural and/or functional relationships between data, information, knowledge, and wisdom. "Typically, information is defined in terms of data, knowledge in terms of information, and wisdom in terms of knowledge"	https://en.wikipedia.org/wiki/DIKW_pyramid
Johari window	Model	There are several adaptions that exist in using the Johari Window. Examples: Strategic use as a solid basis for a map to guide leaders on selecting knowledge management practices to contribute to a holistic knowledge sharing strategy. Blindside: The premise is to disclose and discover unknown information that can impact organizational and group success in any area of the company—management, planning, team performance, and so forth.	• https://en.wikipedia.org/wiki/Johari_window • http://knowledgebird.com/a-model-for-knowledge-management-strategy/ • http://gamestorming.com/the-blind-side/
Knowledge ecosystem	Approach	The idea of a knowledge ecosystem is an approach to knowledge management that claims to foster the dynamic evolution of knowledge interactions between entities to improve decision-making and innovation through improved evolutionary networks of collaboration	https://en.wikipedia.org/wiki/Knowledge_ecosystem

Appendix D3: Transformation techniques

This section provides some additional information on transformation techniques that can be used to support Business Innovation Circles and to help organizations understand their current position and how to address it.

Kaizen events

Techniques like Kaizen are used to help drive the culture change that is an essential part of digital transformation. The concept of making continuous improvement in small increments is called Kaizen in Japanese and translates into English as "change for the better". In effect, Kaizen means continuous improvement involving everyone

– managers and workers alike – every day, providing structure for processing improvement.

There are two types of Kaizen:
- Daily Kaizen – focuses on carrying out small improvements on a daily basis that are aimed at making work better, simpler, faster or more pleasant;
- Kaizen Events – which deals with more significant problems for which more research needs to be done.

Kaizen Events are intensive (normally short) and focused improvement projects where employees are taken away from their regular jobs for a focused improvement initiative, but also to learn from the experience. Kaizen teams are a vital part of any Lean initiative, where there are engaged in a Kaizen event or rapid improvement workshop.

The best one-line description is that "a Kaizen event is a cross-functional learning event that leads to improvement". Using cross-functional teams of people with deep and distinct process knowledge in a highly focused environment to analyze issues and processes yields remarkable improvements.

Kaizen events may also be used as an action-oriented method to deploy the organization's strategy systematically. They have the most significant impact when they are linked to an organization's overall strategic direction.

The Kaizen team is a cross-functional group typically comprising between five and 10 people, including a Kaizen Lead (facilitator or expert in the methods used) and Kaizen Sponsor (who acts as both sponsor and enabler). Teams work together to implement meaningful improvements to a specific value stream.

The Kaizen team uses the creativity of people working in the value stream, independent of place in the organization, to take a fresh, objective look at current performance and the value desired by customers. Kaizen teams tend to use visual observations and simple data gathering tools to identify and eliminate waste out from processes.

With the advent of Six Sigma, it has become popular to use DMAIC (see Figure 112) to deliver Kaizen events. As Six Sigma is a disciplined, data-driven approach for eliminating variability, defects and waste that undermine customer value, the technique seems to work well in this setting. The DMAIC cycle needs to be expanded if used in a Kaizen Event. After the Kaizen Event, the improvements that were made during the Kaizen need to be sustained and further cycles of improvement need to be initiated.

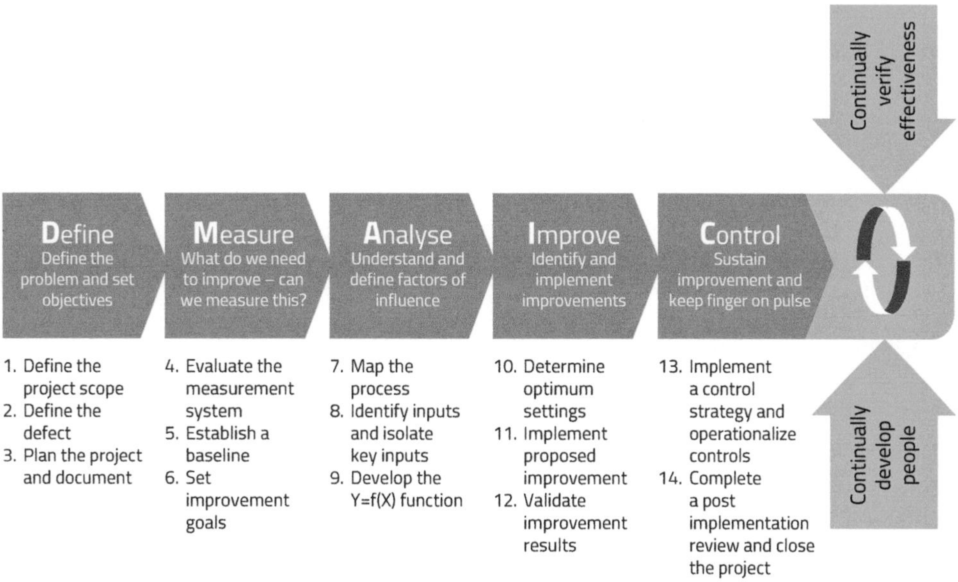

Figure 112 Using DMAIC in Kaizen events

A verification that the claimed cost savings are real may be a key success factor for future Kaizen events. Just as important as the actual physical results is the way in which people have developed and grown as leaders because of their participation in a Kaizen event.

Questionnaires, surveys, interviews and focus groups

Why? Gathering data or information directly from customers can provide significant insights.

"Why not ask the customer?" seems like an obvious question, yet very few organizations do this in a meaningful, repeatable fashion that provides longer-term insights and also give insights into the emotional states that customers often experience when dealing with the company.

Three common methods of formally gathering information from customers are:
- Questionnaires and surveys;
- Interviews;
- Focus groups.

The most common of these seems to be customer satisfaction surveys – which on rare occasions yields meaningful results (more on this below).

The biggest problem with most of these techniques is that people assume this it is a simple process to develop a list of questions. This is not true – questioning is fraught with problems like bias, regency, and groupthink amongst others. Although all of these techniques are very useful and helpful – great care should be given to how these instruments are designed. If possible, consider involving a behavioral specialist.

Common survey problems

Here are some common problems to avoid when using any form of questioning technique:

- Inadequate response options – response ranges do not cover all scenarios, or have overlaps which create confusion;
- Rating level inconsistencies – keep to one format and one direction, do not mix negative and positive responses (5 is good on one answer but bad on another);
- Assuming prior knowledge or understanding – it is common to think someone else will know what you are talking about – not true. Examine the question to ensure that it includes all the required information to allow it to be answered;
- Leading questions – if the question suggests a response it is inappropriate (for example – how good is this question? A) excellent B) brilliant C) fantastic);
- Compound questions – words like 'and' or 'or' are a good indication that the question asked is actually two questions. This usually happens when the number of questions in the survey has been limited, forcing designers to combine questions. The answers are hard to interpret and do not provide meaningful data;
- The question is ambiguous or unintelligible – negative wording for instance quite often confuses the issue – if you see the word 'not' in a question you know you should NOT use this question;
- Unnecessary questions – if the question cannot be answered, it should not be asked;
- Questions that do not relate to the topic at hand – once again an attempt to use the form of inquiry for another purpose creates ambiguity and should be avoided;
- Excessive open-ended questions – sometimes open-ended questions are asked on purpose (for instance during focus groups), but generally, this should be avoided;
- Over-long surveys and questionnaires – studies have shown that the longer the survey, the less helpful the information gathered, and the less likely respondents are to complete. Keep it short and straightforward.

An alternative/supplementary approach, used more commonly in business than IT, is the 'Mystery Shopper' approach. This offers a more holistic view than "How was it for you?" Whilst the "How was it for you" surveys reach wider audiences, only 3% of recipients typically complete them, so they are not representative of the typical customer experience. Survey responses are often skewed by motivation, incentives to respond and previous experiences. Mystery shoppers are better able to capture the true experience. Walt Disney, for example, spent time in his theme parks undercover, listening and interacting with to identify possible improvements.

Kepner-Tregoe

Charles Kepner and Benjamin Tregoe developed a useful way of problem analysis that can be used to investigate deeper-rooted problems formally. They defined the following stages:

- Defining the problem;
- Describing the problem in terms of identity, location, time and size;
- Establishing possible causes;
- Testing the most probable cause;
- Verifying the true cause.

Pareto analysis

This is a technique for separating the most important potential causes of failures from more trivial issues. An example is shown in Figure 113.

To use:

- Have an 'ideas generating' session – five or six most likely causes (do not discard the others though);
- Decide on the best way to measure their relative significance and collect the data;
- Plot the data in descending order of importance;

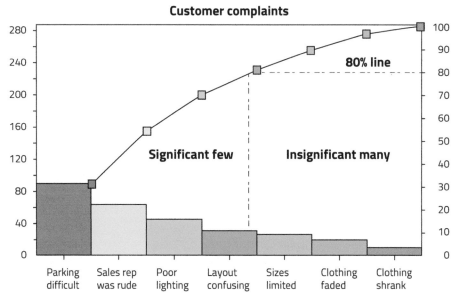

Figure 113 Pareto analysis

- Use the histogram to discuss the validity of the findings and how to pursue the issues involved; for example, "Why do customers experience delays in the delivery of goods from the time a picking slip is generated in the warehouse?":

- Picking errors, missing stock, sent to wrong address, part-supply refused, refused at delivery address, goods returned, goods mislaid by carrier, etc.;
- Reduced to – goods returned/incorrect items, goods returned/defective, goods returned/wrong address, goods not found in warehouse;
- Data collection found how much time was taken to correct these problems for the customer;
- The Pareto Chart indicated that the problem causing the most delay was incorrect goods being sent; next major cause was goods not in warehouse.

PDCA

> "You must focus on the process if you are to continually improve your ability to meet your customers' needs and expectations. There is no substitute for knowing (defining) your processes and improving on them."
>
> W. E. Deming

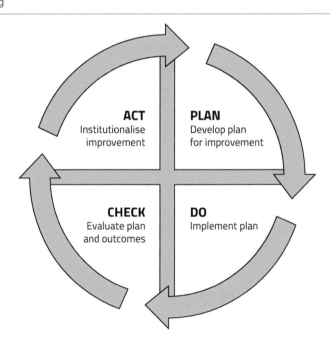

Figure 114 PDCA

Figure 114 illustrates the PDCA cycle.

Planning for improvement (Plan):
- Establish goals and measures for success;
- Do a gap analysis;
- Identify and define action steps to close the gap;
- Define measures to ensure the gap was closed;

Implementation of improvement initiative (Do):
- Develop a project to close the identified gaps;
- Implement the improvement;
- Establish the operation of the process;

Monitor, measure and review services (Check):
- Compare the implemented improvements with the measures of success established in the Plan phase;

Continual service and service management process improvement (Act):
- If gaps were found during check, take remedial or corrective action and correct the situation;
- Also, at this stage evaluate the effectiveness of the original plan.

DMAIC

Initially developed in the 1980s at Motorola and further developed at General Electric, Six Sigma is widely used in many industries as a "disciplined, data-driven approach for eliminating variability, defects and waste that undermine customer value and loyalty".

Using the method helps organizations to increase performance and decrease process and product defects, usually leading to improvements in profits, employee morale and the quality of the organization's services and products.

Six Sigma is often mentioned as a synonym to Lean as the two concepts have some considerable overlap. However, there are distinct differences in the approach and focus of these two techniques. Six Sigma focuses on eliminating variations while Lean focus on consistency (flow) and the elimination of waste.

One of the Six Sigma techniques is the DMAIC problem-solving approach which is often used in Lean IT.

DMAIC is an acronym standing for:
- **Define**: clarify the problem and break it down if needed, define requirements, set target and objective;
- **Measure**: validate the process, refine the problem, measure inputs, key steps and outcomes;
- **Analyze**: develop cause and effect relationships, identify the vital few root causes, validate hypotheses;
- **Improve**: develop ideas to remove root causes, test solutions, standardize solutions and measure results;
- **Control**: establish standard operating procedures to communicate the way of working, maintain performance and correct problems as needed.

Appendix E:
Agile requirements

The benefits of Agile requirements

The challenge most organizations face with Agile is integrating it into the strategic business delivery cycle. Agile methods and courses frequently focus on the 'last mile' of a solution. People involved in requirements gathering, modelling, design and architecture live in a world of confusion, denial or even active resistance to the adoption of Agile methods in the enterprise.

The challenge associated with the traditional roles that are usually involved in requirements gathering and specification is that there is often a huge gap between business requirements (strategically driven and present in some form of a portfolio) and what developers are doing in an iteration or sprint.

Often the frustration among business and systems analyst and architects is quite distinct when they are faced with this new approach: "they just do not see the big picture and can't conceive work long term. And what's worse, they have no controls". The sad reality is that in many environments, these objections from analysts and architects will ring true to some extent. These organizations will most probably be delivering sub-optimal benefits, and often even fail, because requirements gathering and design in an Agile environment is neither understood nor well thought through.

The Agile way of requirements definition is often much more effective.

Business sponsors, business process owners and analysts often get caught up with trying to define the minute specifications, due to fear of missing something important. The result is over-specification and many times this may even nullify the predefined business case made for project funding.

Conversely, Agile requirements gathering depends on a shared understanding of the customer, users, product owners, and those who design, develop and deliver the new or changed service. This shared understanding often leads to unlocking hidden requirements and benefits that may otherwise have been overlooked. It also ensures that the focus remains on the practical and the utility/value to be unlocked. Leaving low-level and implementation details to the development team is a much more effective practice. The ability to do this is based on close collaboration with users when (and where) products and services are built. Additionally, many functional and technical requirements are often only fleshed out 'as-it-happens' or sometimes, only defined during an iteration, thus keeping the focus on the practical.

How Agile requirement gathering works
The first level of requirements starts with a strategic business requirement being defined in the business portfolio (see Figure 115). For this step, the only difference from the traditional approach is that the level of detail found in support of the entry in the portfolio is very high-level and includes just enough detail to make a rudimentary decision on its approval and inclusion in the portfolio.

The moment an entry is made in the portfolio–ownership is assigned to a business sponsor, who, in most cases, would also fulfil the role of product owner. Remember every product owner owns a product backlog.

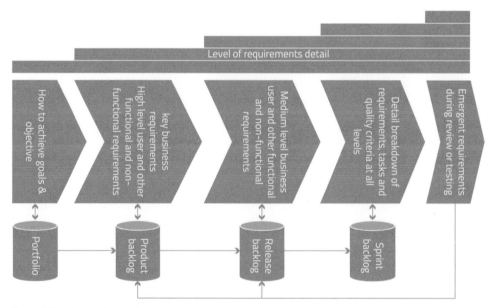

Figure 115 Agile requirement gathering

This is the point where architects and analysts become involved with product owners to contextualize entries in the portfolio, seeing conceptually how it will fit into the architectural landscape considering the dependencies and interdependencies. Once this is understood, the entry will now become part of a program (a product backlog of things that belong together). In instances where a user story does not have enough detail, attach use cases, traditional requirements or decision tables, etc. In some situations, a consumer may demand more documentation, especially while dealing with organizations that are audited for process compliance purposes.

Note: some organization have one 'super' product backlog that represents "the single truth of an organization". However, there is a strong belief that breaking product backlogs into what traditionally would have been seen as a program, is a more sensible approach.

At a product backlog/program level, stakeholder identification is determined, and Agile requirements are recorded in the form of stories (most often epics) in a product backlog. Stakeholders at this stage will not only include business process owners and users but also others who may contribute to defining technical and other non-functional stories (e.g., a technical, security or a support story).

Product owners then use numerous techniques to prioritize stories for assignment to either 'mini projects' run as releases or just plain iterations or sprints. It may be a good idea to create Affinity diagrams to identify stories that are similar or interdependent. System analysis may also help to create dependencies between user stories and some of the non-functional stories defining governance/control and technical requirements (as these are often seen as not important by the business but other important user stories may have dependencies on these). At this level, various modelling and prototyping techniques may also be valuable as long as they do not attempt to define finite requirements. Be sure to involve users when undertaking modelling. This is the first level of grooming applied to the backlog.

It is vital to create governance structures where product owners of different product backlogs can interact, have visibility of what is happening in other areas, and identify dependencies or even areas of overlap.

At a release level, stories are further evaluated and broken down (epics broken down into their constituent stories and dependencies are validated). This will most probably be the level at which resources for sprints will be assigned. These resources may in turn ask that some stories are further fleshed out with the business, business process owners and users, architects or owners of technology. It is quite common to identify new dependencies and requirements at this level now that needs are added to the release backlog. Constituent parts of the release (possible sprints or iterations) may also be identified at this stage. This is the second level of grooming completed within the backlog and the second time that requirements are refined (or new requirements defined).

Iterations that belongs to the same release may run in parallel and frequently have areas of interdependencies or even areas of overlap. A governance structure sometimes called a 'scrum of scrums' should be constituted to ensure visibility of all active iterations, their progress, issues, dependencies and the possible effect progress in one iteration may impact on another.

At an iteration level, the process will be similar to that of a release level, just more granular. It is highly advisable to include users and other stakeholders whose stories are included in the specific iteration or sprint. The absolute minimal participation would occur during sprint planning where final acceptance criterial will be defined (e.g., capturing the definition of 'done'). It is during the iteration or sprint planning that the final level of detailed requirements definition is handled and that the backlog is groomed.

Upon conclusion of an iteration or a release, all detailed requirements can be validated for quality in two ways:
- The output required;
- The required outcome.

The ability to evaluate BOTH quality criteria is locked up in the magic of how user stories are written:

> *"As a ROLE, I would like to be able to ACTIVITY/*
> *OUTPUT so that OUTCOME/RESULT."*

Feedback on both output and outcome metrics should be kept and periodically assessed as they quite often show areas where improvements can be made in requirements gathering and definition.

Mendix[95] offers some helpful pointers for Agile requirement gathering (with some additional input from us):
- Focus on the business problem, not the user's envisioned solution – because users are often limited by prior experience, their envisioned solution isn't necessarily the optimal way of doing something. (Note that user stories never ask what we should do for you – we only ask what you need to be able to do);
- Divide work based on user stories, instead of developer specialties – rather than focusing on specific technical areas (database, UI, etc.), developers should build a full working piece of functionality each sprint based on user stories. When developers focus on solving business problems, not completing tasks, the outcome is better software and happier users. (Sprint teams must be cross functional and be able to deliver something useable);

---

95 https://www.mendix.com/blog/7-keys-deliver-better-applications-faster-effective-itbusiness-collaboration/

- Provide working demos or prototypes every sprint – systems design can be abstract. That's why it is crucial to regularly show working demos to validate requirements and assumptions, as well as to discuss modifications because needs have changed. The longer you wait, the greater the potential disconnect and the more time you'll need to fix it. (Sprint reviews are great places to catch final requirement not defined before, make sure these are recorded and added to the backlog);
- Implement 'walk-in' hours to validate assumptions and synchronize with the business – no matter how precise requirements are, there are always points where developers have questions or need clarification. By providing them with an opportunity each day to interact with the business, developers won't be forced to make assumptions that lead to rework. (If at all possible have some users attend daily stand-ups – they will quickly tell you if you make the wrong assumptions.);
- Model complex business rules and interfaces together with the business – sitting developers and business users together to build applications facilitates continuous collaboration. Each has a unique perspective that helps ensure the solution is sound from a functional and technical perspective. In addition, any issues can be identified on the spot versus waiting months until the app is built;
- Collaborate closely with end user testers – traditional user acceptance testing (UAT) is a formal, time-consuming procedure: creating tickets, planning them for release, etc. It's much better to make UAT assessments on the spot. By collaborating closely with the end user test team, developers can identify and fix issues immediately. This enhances the bug fixing process and ensures a better user experience. (Some organizations define UAT as an iteration/sprint with members of the spring being users, testers and developers that can fix small issues on the fly. It's also much easier for users to show developers what the issue is than to try and document it);
- Implement a feedback loop to capture end user feedback – complex ticketing systems or spreadsheets stifle user feedback. Moreover, it can be difficult for users to explain what they were doing or expected to happen. In-app feedback loops make the process easier, allowing end users to submit feedback with all the context (user, browser, form, etc.) captured automatically and fed to the development team.

Appendix E2:
Master requirements document

Consider the following elements to create an overall requirements document based on Lean/Agile principles. This has been adapted from Radigan's article, *Product Requirements, Downsized*[96].

- Project specifics;
- Participants (product/service owner, designer, developer, consumer, stakeholders…);
- Status (on target, at risk, delayed, cancelled, deferred…);
  - Release date;
- Goals and business objectives – concise and simple statements for each:
  - What is the goal for the product/service?
  - What business objective is it fulfilling?
- Background and strategic fit – provide context for the project:
  - Why this is being done?
  - How it fits within the corporate strategy?
- Assumptions – document any assumptions:
- Business;
- User;
- Technical;
- User stories:
  - Link to the "cards" – ensure each story has a priority;
  - User interaction and design – potential solutions for each user story/prototypes:
  - Link to the iterative solutions based on user stories;
- Questions – items that require an answer at the next conversation:
  - What is not happening, what is out of scope?

---

96 Radigan, D. (No date). *Product requirements documents, downsized*, (Online). https://www.atlassian.com/agile/product-management/requirements [2018 April].

Appendix F:
Steps for strategic sourcing

The activities to deploy a strategic sourcing model (summarized and adapted from Engle[97] (2004)) include:

1. Identify specific spend area:
   a. Typically, a directive from an Executive level with intent to reduce costs or improve process:
      i. Should match corporate objectives;
   b. Must have Executive sponsorship and endorsement;
2. Create sourcing team:
   a. Cross-functional participation (e.g. finance, accounting, engineering, maintenance, operation, HR, tax, R&D, IT, health & safety, marketing, sales...) with buy-in:
      i. Communicate to managers the impact to day job (gain buy-in);
   b. Develop team strategy and communication plan:
      i. Formalize a charter/mission statement with goals and objectives;
      ii. Timeline to achieve objectives;
      iii. Communication Plan to broadcast progress and updates – intent is to keep organization informed as well as maintain credibility of the project;
3. Assess current spend within the specified spend area:
   a. What is bought, where, what price? Overspend? Duplicated efforts?
4. Assessment of supply market:
   a. Who offers what?
   b. Distribute Request for Information (RFI) to gather supplier data (quality programs, financial stability, service capabilities, plant locations, client references, organizational structure...):
      i. Who is the current supplier? Who else is appropriate (interview before sending RFI; look local, regional, ...)?

---

97 https://www.instituteforsupplymanagement.org/files/Pubs/Proceedings/FBEngel.pdf

5. Identify suitable suppliers:
   a. Develop supplier portfolio from RFIs – identify organizations with potential to be developed locally, regionally, globally, company-wide…;
   b. Distribute the Request for Proposal (RFP) to those who appear to offer the greatest potential for the sourcing initiative (RFP includes pricing and commercial proposals);
6. Develop the 'To-Be' State (cost and performance analysis):
   a. Develop business case, perform a gap analysis, calculate financial information, determine performance metrics:
      i. Total Cost of Ownership (true cost = acquisition cost + operating cost + maintenance cost + training cost + warehouse cost – any salvageable value) – best value not lowest cost unit;
      ii. Total System Cost = Supplier costs + Supplier profit + interaction costs + buyer costs – consider the cost of doing business with the supplier base (interaction costs between organization and supplier; organization costs incurred maintaining relationships…);
      iii. Performance metrics – measure both the supplier and organization – on-time deliveries, warrantee issues, customer satisfaction, quality issues;
7. Develop and communicate the sourcing process based on three components:
   a. Vendor selection based on best value;
   b. Continuous improvement objectives must be established with supplier(s);
   c. Innovation from supplier(s) is the key to significant savings;
8. Negotiate and select suppliers based on value:
   a. Can be controversial with some managers as 'favored' supplier may not have made the list – communication is key and evidence from sourcing process is vital. If forced to add a supplier, better to do it here before the final 'short list' is announced;
   b. Principles to consider in this stage:
      i. Longer-term agreements – it takes time to develop trust, a good working relationship to realize savings from either improved processes or innovation (review 7b and c above);
      ii. Must develop higher levels of trust in the negotiations;
      iii. Agree performance metrics during negotiations;
      iv. Be committed;
   c. Products, service levels, pricing, geographies;
   d. Payment terms;
9. Go live with the new supply structure and manage via using supplier management or SIAM principles:
   a. Maintain the sourcing team for oversight of contract execution, effectiveness developments, other improvements;
   b. Track results; restart assessment – remember the value in the PDCA.

Glossary

Word or term	Definition
A3 problem solving	Ensures that a team solving the problem focuses on the essentials due to the limitation of the size of the paper (an A3 sheet). Information is generated throughout the improvement or problem-solving event and captured on the A3 as the event progresses, concisely and succinctly.
Adaptive leader	Learns through experimentation and manages the context, cultivates diversity of views to generate a multiplicity of options, leads with empathy, rewards accomplishment with autonomy and seeks winning solutions for all stakeholders.
Affinity mapping	An analytical tool to be used if lots of data are presented but not contextualized. Sort ideas or data into groups based on logical connections, relationships, dependencies, themes or some other criterion.
Autonomy	Giving employees the right to do the work they want, how they want and when they want. In an organization with employee autonomy, the focus is on what gets done (outcomes) as opposed to how it gets done. An autonomous team is one that is self-managing with little or no direction from a manager. When team members work well together, they can build on each other's strengths, and can compensate for other's weaknesses.
Behavior	Any observable activity of a living creature. Also referred to as operant behavior, because this type of behavior interacts with (operates on) the environment.
Burke-Litwin model	Utilizes twelve variables (it includes all seven from McKinsey's 7S) but posits that the external environment (e.g., markets, legislation, competition, economy) is the most powerful driver for organizational change. All factors interact and a change in one of them, can impact the others.
Business information plan	Defines the required business capabilities and services that are needed in the future.

Word or term	Definition
Business innovation circle (BIC)	An approach that leaves room for the use of different tools and techniques that best align with the company, product or service in question but defines measurable stage gates and timelines to ensure rapid and validated results; a way to embark on rapid product and service innovation, based on Lean and Agile thinking, requiring commitment, conditions and confirmation.
Business model canvas	A strategic management and lean start-up template for developing new (or documenting existing) business models. Canvas models allow organizations to understand needs and demands compared to competitive products that already exist. See also Operating model canvas.
Capability	The ability or the qualities that are necessary to do something -- see also digital capabilities and organizational capabilities
CAPEX	CAPEX, or Capital Expenditure, is a business expense incurred to create future benefit (i.e. acquisition of assets that will have a useful life beyond the tax year). See also OPEX.
Case response	From the Standard+Case model, this response presents an unknown or unfamiliar situation where there is no predefined process. Cases demand knowledge, skills and professionalism of the person dealing with them. They are best dealt with by Case Management, being knowledge-driven and empowering the operator to decide on suitable approaches, tools, procedures and process fragments. Agile thinking, swarming, and other adaptive dynamic approaches can be used. – See also Standard response
Collaboration	The action of working with someone to produce something.
Collaborative approach	An approach involving two or more people or organizations working together for a particular purpose.
Competence, -ies	The cluster of related abilities, commitments, knowledge, and skills that enable a person to act effectively in a job or situation.
Consumer	Provides the requirements for products and services, receives products and services, gives feedback, and participates in verify/review/improve activities.
Culture	The collection of written and unwritten rules, guidelines and practices that shape the behaviors of the people in the organization.
Customer	A type of consumer; often defined as the role that pays for or funds a product or service.
Customer centric (customer centricity)	Creating a positive customer experience at the point of sale and post-sale. A customer-centric approach can add value to a company by enabling it to differentiate itself from competitors who do not offer the same experience.
Customer experience (CX)	The entirety of the interactions, both qualitative and quantitative, a consumer has with an organization and its products or services. See also user experience (UX) and digital experience (DX)
Customer experience management (CEM)	The practice of designing and reacting to customer interactions to meet or exceed customer expectations and, thus, increase customer satisfaction, loyalty and advocacy.
Customer journey map	A tool for service design, Design Thinking, user experience design, and touchpoint management. It quite often leads to more detailed design like a service blueprint.

Word or term	Definition
Cynefin framework	Identifies five decision-making contexts or domains: obvious, complicated, complex, chaotic and disorder. The framework describes which methods, techniques or approaches would be most likely to work for each of these categories or domains.
Define	Part of the VeriSM model; the activities and supporting outcomes that relate to the design of a product or service.
Design Thinking	A human-centered approach to innovation that draws from the designer's toolkit to integrate the needs of people, the possibilities of technology, and the requirements for business success.
DevOps	The combination of cultural philosophies, practices, and tools from the development and operational areas that increases an organization's ability to deliver applications and services at high velocity.
Digital awareness	A curiosity and openness of mind toward technological innovation and its application to increase the value of a product or service.
Digital capabilities	Capabilities that enhance an organization's ability to produce and maintain digital products and services (digital culture??) • Consumer centricity and focus; • A focus on operational excellence; • An overall strategy defined in digital terms; • Leadership involved with and driving the organization from above; • Governance models and structures that support the new approach.
Digital center of excellence	Forum to review business opportunities and establish use cases incorporating emerging technologies and digital capabilities.
Digital channel	Any means an organization can use to interact with its consumers around its products and services.
Digital experience (DX)	Another name for user experience (UX).
Digital leader	Someone who has the core skills expected of any leader but emphasizes a collaborative style that includes the skills of delegation, is open to experimentation and understands a 'fail fast' risk approach.
Digital mindset	A 'digital first' mindset that leads to an increase of value to stakeholders across all services.
Digital native	An individual who has grown up using technology and includes technology in all aspects of their life -- socially and professionally.
Digital optimization	How organizations use innovative technologies to augment existing products and services.
Digital organization	An organization that uses technology as a competitive advantage to create or enable business models; an organization that reacts quickly to changes in the ecosystem based on consumer demand and changes in the business model.
Digital service	A service or product that is enabled by or only possible because of advances in technology.
Digital twin	A digital replica of what is in the physical environment that can be manipulated to find different ways of using or managing that physical object; used to experiment and learn for innovation purposes.

Word or term	Definition
Digital transformation	The changes associated with the application of digital technologies across all areas of an organization, from sales to marketing, products, services and new business models.
Digital use case	See Use case
Digitize / Digitalization	The transformation of physical products or services into digital products, services and experiences.
Disruptive innovation	Making products available and affordable. This type of innovation needs capital but creates jobs and growth – See also Efficiency innovation and Sustaining innovation
DMAIC	A problem-solving cycle approach often used in Lean IT. The acronym stands for: • Define: clarify the problem and break it down if needed, define requirements, set target and objective • Measure: validate the process, refine the problem, measure inputs, key steps and outcomes • Analyze: develop cause and effect relationships, identify the vital few root causes, validate hypotheses • Improve: develop ideas to remove root causes, test solutions, standardize solutions and measure results • Control: establish standard operating procedures to communicate the way of working and maintain performance and correct problems as needed
EDM model	A governance model from ISO/IEC 38500 that focuses on the evaluate, direct, and monitor activities.
Efficiency innovation	Helps organizations make more with less. This type of innovation can enable an organization to cope with increased growth without further capital or increases in cash-flow, but can destroy jobs – See also Disruptive innovation and Sustaining innovation
Enterprise governance	Defines the mission and vision for the organization as well as defining the purpose for existence and is typically owned by executive leadership (Board of Directors).
Fail fast strategy or approach	Found within the Agile growth mindset, where 'failure' is accepted and embraced (form of experimentation) as a natural part of learning and improvement.
Fintech	Used within the financial market to describe how new technology and innovation are combined to deliver financial services, disrupting traditional methods.
Flatter organization / flatter structure	Removes most hierarchical control and associated bureaucracy by empowering employees to make decisions and feel responsible for the organization's success. Characterized by better communication, greater democracy, and greater innovation.
Framework	A structure of principles and practices.
Five Why's	An effective way to get to the underlying cause(s) of a problem. It works by starting out with a description of what event took place and then asking, "why this occurred". The resulting answer is given, followed by another round of "why this occurred". Usually by the fifth iteration, the cause or causes will have been found.
Gap analysis	Compares the current state with a desired state, determines the gaps and then devises a plan to overcome those gaps.

Word or term	Definition
Governance	The underpinning system of evaluating, directing and monitoring, the activities of an organization. See EDM
Governance structures	Lines of communication and opportunities for internal role players to interact.
Hackathon	An organization wide competition which entices employees to think of new innovative ways of doing things.
Heuristics	An approach to problem solving, learning, or discovery that employs a practical method not guaranteed to be optimal or perfect, but sufficient for the immediate goals.
Holacracy	Another term for a flat organizational structure.
Hypothesis testing	Tests the assumptions (hypothesis) about the value of an outcome to consumers, such as A/B testing.
Innovation space	An isolated environment in which a plan or program can be executed without affecting the rest of the organization (e.g., sandbox or skunk-works).
Innovator's dilemma	The situation where the organization designs a product or service for one specific purpose or need and then later on, add valuable features and find the consumer is only interested in the original feature. See also disruptive innovation, sustaining innovation, efficiency innovation
Information radiator	Any public and visible means of communicating important information to the relevant stakeholders whether handwritten, drawn, printed or by means of electronic displays.
Ishikawa (fishbone) diagram	A method of documenting cause-and-effect situations; useful for problem-solving and improvements.
Issue	A product or service is not performing as agreed (incident), or the customer perceives the product or service to not be performing as agreed.
Iterative requirement gathering	The discovery and confirmation of a consumer need (the "what" and not the "how"). See also user stories.
Kaizen	The concept of making continuous improvement in small increments, involving everyone, managers and workers alike, every day, providing structure for processing improvement.
Kepner-Tregoe	A way of problem analysis that can be used to investigate deeper-rooted problems. Steps include: Define the problem; Describe the problem in terms of identity, location, time and size; Establish possible causes; Test the most probable cause; Verify the true cause.
Knowledge-centered service (KCS)	An approach for knowledge management typically managed by a small team and includes these elements: • Strategic framework • Communication plan • Measurement framework • Workflow or process definitions • Content standard • Adoption roadmap • Technology requirements.
Knowledge management	The process of capturing, developing, sharing and effectively using organizational knowledge.

Word or term	Definition
Lean management cascade	Defining a cascade for strategic intent ensuring that everyone in the organization works together to achieve the mission, values, and vision set by the organization.
Lean start-up	A tried and tested method which organizations can use to innovate and specifically to come up with disruptive innovation.
Management Mesh	How an organization combines its resources, environment, management practices, and emerging technologies to create and deliver products and services.
Management practices	Standards, frameworks, methodologies philosophies that can be applied to product and service creation. Examples include ITIL, ISO/IEC 20000, COBIT, SIAM, DevOps, Lean, Agile, and others.
McKinsey 7S framework	A technique to understand if the organization is positioned to achieve its objectives or to review underperformance of a single capability, team or project.
Mission	Articulates why the organization exists or the purpose of the organization.
Nadler-Tushman model (Congruence model)	Studies how the entire organization works together. The organization is viewed as a social system that is made up of four elements (people, work, structure, and culture) transforming inputs into outputs. The more congruence between these four elements, the better the performance.
Necessary but non-value adding (NNVA)	Actions that are wasteful but necessary, such as controls. See also Value adding (VA).
Network effect	When a product or service gains value as more people use it.
Non-value adding (NVA)	Actions that should be eliminated because they are wasteful, such as waiting. See also Value adding (VA).
Organizational capabilities	The capabilities that allow the business to remain viable. Capability areas are made up of people, knowledge, processes and could include HR, Finance, Sales, Marketing, IT, Manufacturing, Legal...etc.
Operating model canvas	A six-section canvas to describe and design the link between a defined strategy and operational activities. The six sections are: management system, organization, information, value delivery chains, suppliers, and locations. The operating model canvas links to the business model canvas. See also Business model canvas.
OPEX	Expenditures required for the day-to-day functioning of the business (e.g. wages, utilities, maintenance, and repairs). See also CAPEX.
Opportunity portfolio	A simple matrix that maps opportunities based on capability and market uncertainty.
Option space	The concept of treating strategic investments as financial options.
Organizational behavior management (OBM)	A sub-field of Applied Behavior Analysis. It is the proven and scientific approach for increasing and improving individual and team performance in an organizational context. Based on the scientific discoveries made by B.F. Skinner and others.
Organizational change management (OCM)	Practices that provide structure, preparation and motivation to give people the education they need to embrace and support change.
Organizational culture profile (OCP)	A profile based on seven different organizational cultural dimensions: innovative, aggressive, outcome-oriented, stable, people-oriented, team-oriented, and detail-oriented.

Word or term	Definition
Organizational portfolio	Provides the service provider with an enterprise view of their value proposition, their products and services.
Outcome	The end result of a consumer interacting with a product or service.
Output	A physical deliverable.
Pareto analysis	A technique for separating the most important issues from more trivial issues. This technique can be applied to decision-making, prioritizing activities, or problem solving.
PDCA (Deming's Quality Circle)	An improvement cycle based on the 'plan-do-check-act' set of activities.
PESTLE (or PESTEL)	Environmental analysis technique which explores: political, economic, social, technical, legal, environmental factors.
Platform business model map	Assists organizations in understand the dynamics of platform-based business models and can be used to analyze competitor's platforms or to conceptualize and design a platform model for the organization itself.
Porter's 5 Forces	Explores multiple aspects of the industry's competitive structure and economic environment which includes the bargaining power of buyers and suppliers, the threat of new entrants, competitive rivalry, and the threat of substitute products.
Produce	Part of the VeriSM Model; it describes the performing of build, test and implement activities, under the management of change control.
Product	Something that is created and offered to a consumer. See also Service.
Provide	Part of the VeriSM model; it describes that a product or service is available for consumption by the consumer and the service provider performs on-going maintenance and improvement activities.
Quality	How well a product or service meets the desired outcomes; quality is individually defined.
Request	Interaction with the consumer that is a question, or a requirement for new or additional functionality.
Requirement	Requirements describe problems ("what" needs to be solved or addressed) and can be divided into two groups: functional and non-functional.
Respond	Part of the VeriSM model; describes how the service provider reacts to service issues, inquiries and requests from the consumer.
Risk	Defined by ISO 31000 as the "effect of uncertainty on objectives".
Run-grow-transform (RGT)	Emphasizes investment decisions (invest to either run, grow or transform the business) are based on projected business value of the investment instead of regarding investment as costs.
Service	Fulfilment of a defined consumer need. See also Product.
Service blueprint	Design of a service containing, among others, master requirements, design solution, procurement plans, build instructions and performance requirements.
Service Integration and Management (SIAM)	A management methodology that defines a set of principles, practices and approaches used to manage, integrate, govern and coordinate the delivery of services from multiple service providers.

Word or term	Definition
Service management	The management approach adopted by an organization to deliver value to consumers though quality products and services.
Service management principles	High level requirements that apply across all products and services, providing guardrails for the management mesh.
SIPOC	A context diagram, identifying Suppliers, Inputs, Process, Outputs and Customers.
Six Sigma	A disciplined, data-driven approach for eliminating variability, defects and waste that undermine customer value.
Solution	A combination of products and / or services that fulfils a desired consumer outcome.
Source event	The root cause, or causes, of something that has happened. May be referred to as 'problems'.
Stakeholder map	Tool to understand interactions between stakeholders and the importance of these interactions.
Stakeholder value chain	Used to understand the dynamics and relationships between suppliers, the organization and its customers.
Standard response	This is a predefined response because it deals with a known situation. It uses a standardized process (procedures and scripts) to deal with the situation. It can be modelled. See also Case response.
Strategic sourcing	An organization-wide collaborative activity that leverages consolidated purchasing power across all capabilities to find the best possible value from services and service providers in the marketplace.
Sustainable development	Economic development which can be sustained in the long term; ecological use and development of natural resources in ways which are compatible with the maintenance of these resources, and with the conservation of the environment, for future generations.
Sustaining innovation	Management focus that makes good products better (i.e., better margins and improved market share). See also disruptive innovation and efficiency innovation.
SWOT analysis	Examines the organization, project or proposed line of business from internal (strengths and weaknesses) and external (opportunities and threats) perspectives.
Systems	Systems are generally described in two ways: • a set of things working together as parts of a mechanism or an interconnecting network; a complex whole or more operationally • a set of principles or procedures according to which something is done; an organized scheme or method.
Systems of differentiation	Applications that enable unique company processes or industry-specific capabilities.
Systems of engagement (SoE)	Decentralized IT components that incorporate technologies such as social media and the cloud to encourage and enable peer interaction.
Systems of innovation	New applications that are built on an ad hoc basis to address new business requirements or opportunities.
Systems of record (SoR)	An information storage and retrieval system that provides a centralized, authoritative source of data elements in an IT environment containing multiple points of data generation.

Word or term	Definition
Tacit knowledge	Knowledge which is known but not realized until questioned.
Technical debt	Reflects the extra development work that arises when code that is easy to implement in the short run is used instead of applying the best overall solution.
Technology business management (TBM)	Seeks to drive and instrument how the business and consumers are receiving value from technology services, and to understand and impact those value chains and their corresponding demand behavior.
T-shaped professional	A professional with a specialist area of expertise, plus general knowledge of other organizational capabilities.
Total quality management (TQM)	A management approach to long–term success through customer satisfaction based on improving processes, products, services, and organizational culture.
Use case	A modelling technique that describes, visually or through narration, a user's perspective of how they would interact with various systems to achieve a specific goal.
User	A type of consumer; often defined as having little to no control over the products or services they use.
User experience (UX)	The experience of interacting with a product or service focusing on usability and aesthetics (e.g., user interface, touch-and-feel of the interaction, graphics, content, features, ease of use…). Sometimes known as the digital experience (DX). See also Customer experience.
User journey	A visualization of the process that a user goes through to complete a task. It builds a step-by-step view, not of what users are expected to do, but what they are actually doing when they interact with the service or product.
User story	Captures a single consumer need in the structure: As a <who>, I want <what> so that <why>.
Value	How consumers perceive the products and services offered (e.g., "Your service offers great value.").
Value-adding (VA)	The conversion of raw materials (data is also a raw material) and changing it into something for which the customer will pay. See also Non-Value Adding (NVA).
Value proposition	An articulation of the value (by product and service) a service provider creates to meet the needs of its consumers.
Value proposition canvas (VPC)	A form of Business model canvas. Understanding the value proposition of products and services is essential when designing new or changed products or services. The intent of the canvas is to observe and understand customers and their requirements before starting to design products and services.
Value stream	The sequence of activities required to deliver a good or service to a consumer. It includes the dual flows of information and material. Most value streams are cross-functional; the transformation of a consumer request for a good or service flows through many functional capabilities within an organization.
Value stream mapping (VSM)	Visual representation of how value is created from consumer request to consumer request fulfilment.

Word or term	Definition
Value-to-cost metric	From the Option Space tool; the predicted value of the asset that will be built or acquired, divided by the present value of the expenditure necessary to build or buy that asset. See also Volatility metric.
VeriSM™	An approach to service management for the digital age with a focus on a value-driven, evolving, responsive and integrated service management approach.
VeriSM™ model	Visual representation showing how the organization delivers on its strategy and provides value to its customers through products and services.
Vision	An existential statement of what an organization aspires to be.
Volatility metric	From the Option Space tool; how much change can occur before an investment decision must be made (lower volatility, the less time one has to make a decision; higher volatility, more time to manage the option before a final decision). See also Value-to-cost metric.
VUCA	Used as a method to better understand the context in which the organization operates (volatile, uncertain, complex and ambiguous world) and which helps to frame responses to challenges.

Bibliography

. (2009). *Oxford English dictionary* (2nd ed.) [CD-ROM v4.0]. Cary, NC: Oxford University.

. (2011, May 24). *Adaptive leadership: Dealing with the unknowns*, (Online). http://www.firefighternation.com/articles/2011/05/adaptive-leadership-dealing-with-the-unknowns.html. [2018 January].

. (2016, March 23). *How cities score*, (Online). https://www.economist.com/special-report/2016/03/23/how-cities-score. [2018 January].

. (2003, October 30). *How to write your mission statement*, (Online). https://www.entrepreneur.com/article/65230. [2018 January].

. (2010). 8.4 Measuring organizational culture, (Online). From *Principles of Management* (University of Minnesota Libraries Publishing; Creative Commons license). https://open.lib.umn.edu/principlesmanagement/chapter/8-4-measuring-organizational-culture/. [2018 February].

. (No date). *What is self-management?*, (Online). http://www.self-management institute.org/about/what-is-self-management. [2018 April].

. (No date). *An inside look at a flat organization that serves millions*, (Online). http://firstround.com/review/An-Inside-Look-at-a-Flat-Organization-That-Serves-Millions/. [2018 April].

. (No date). *Burke-Litwin: Understanding drivers for change*, (Online). https://www.exeter.ac.uk/media/universityofexeter/humanresources/documents/learningdevelopment/understanding_drivers_for_change.pdf. [2018 March].

. (No date). *Five configurations*, (Online). https://www.provenmodels.com/22/five-configurations/henry-mintzberg. [2018 January].

. (No date). *Motivation-hygiene theory*, (Online). https://www.provenmodels.com/21/motivation-hygiene-theory/barbara-snyderman--bernard-mausner--frederick-herzberg. [2018 January].

. (No date). The entrepreneurial mindset: Strategies for continuously creating opportunity in an age of uncertainty, (Online). http://www.columbia.edu/~rdm20/emsumm.doc. [2018 March].

. (No date). *Theory X & Y*, (Online). https://www.provenmodels.com/20/theory-x-&-y/douglas-mcgregor. [2018 February].

. (No date). *Three generic strategies*, (Online). https://www.provenmodels.com/27/three-generic-strategies/michael-e.-porter. [2018 January].

Agutter, C. (2017). *Service integration and management (SIAM®) foundation body of knowledge*, (Online). https://www.scopism.com/free-downloads/. [2017 January].

Agutter, C., England, R., Van Hove, S. D. & Steinberg, R. (2017). *VeriSM™: a service management approach for the digital age*. Zaltbommel, Netherlands: Van Haren.

Amar, A. D., Hentrich, C., & Hlupic, V. (2009). *To be a better leader, give up authority*, (Online). https://hbr.org/2009/12/to-be-a-better-leader-give-up-authority. [2018 February].

AXELOS. (2010). *Management of Value (MoV®)*. London: TSO.

AXELOS. (2015). *Adopting service governance: Governing portfolio value for sound corporate citizenship*. London: TSO.

Bennet, N. & Lemoine, G. J. (2014). *What VUCA really means for you*, (Online). https://hbr.org/2014/01/what-vuca-really-means-for-you. [2018 March].

Besner, G. (2015, June 3). *The 10 company culture metrics you should be tracking right now*, (Online). https://www.entrepreneur.com/article/246899. [2018 March].

Birkinshaw, J. & Goddard, J. (2009). What is your management model?. *MIT Sloan Management Review*, **50**(2), 81-90.

Blain, T. (2006, November 21). *Ten requirements gathering techniques*, (Online). tynerblain.com/blog/2006/11/21/ten-requirements-gathering-techniques/. [2018 February].

Bonnet, D., Westerman, G., & McAfee, A. (2014). *Leading digital: Turning technology into business transformation*. Boston: Harvard Business Review.

Bossidy, L., & Charan, R. (2002). *Execution: The discipline of getting things done*. New York: Crown Business.

Bouman, J. F., Teunissen, W., Eusterbrock, T., van Steenbergen, M., & Flikweert, J. (2017, September 30). *Imperatives of a digital enterprise*, (Online). https://bouman.home.xs4all.nl/Artikelen/20170930_Sogeti_Imperatives_of_a_Digital_Enterprise.pdf. [2018 April].

Bradberry, T. & Greaves, J. (2009). *Emotional intelligence 2.0*. San Diego, CA: TalentSmart.

Brechner, E. (2017, June 1). *It's business time*, (Online). https://blogs.msdn.microsoft.com/eric_brechner/2017/06/01/its-business-time/. [2018 March].

Brooks, P. (2006). *Metrics for IT service management*. Zaltbommel, Netherlands: Van Haren.

Brooks, P. (2013). *An integrated requirements management process: Governing cost & risk in business analysis*. Amazon: CreateSpace Independent.

Burke, W. W., & Litwin, G. H. (1992). A causal model of organisation performance and change, *Journal of Management*, **18**(3), 523–545.

Campbell, A., Gutierrez, M., & Lancelott, M. (2017). *Operating model canvas*. Zaltbommel, Netherlands: Van Haren.

Caramela, S. (2017, July 5). *Techniques and tools to help you make business decisions*, (Online). https://www.businessnewsdaily.com/6162-decision-making.html.
[2018 March].

Chatman, J. A., & Jehn, K. A. (1991). Assessing the relationship between industry characteristics and organizational culture: How different can you be? *Academy of Management Journal*, **37**, 522-553.

Ciborra, C. U., Braa, K., Cordella, A., Dahlbom, B., Failla, A., Hanseth, O., Hepsø, V., Ljungberg, J., Monteiro, E., & Simon, K. A. (2000). *From control to drift – dynamics of corporate information infrastructures*. New York: Oxford.

Conlin, M., (1999, Nov 1). *Religion in the workplace*, (Online). https://www.bloomberg.com/news/articles/1999-10-31/religion-in-the-workplace. [2018, January].

Data Freaks. (2104, September 25). *Motivating employees has everything to do with giving them feelings of ownership*, (Online). https://www.forbes.com/sites/datafreaks/2014/09/25/motivating-employees-has-almost-nothing-to-do-with-their-attitude-and-almost-everything-to-do-with-feelings-of-ownership/#102957531140. [2018 May].

de Goede, T., Hesp, T., Meek, T., & Ten Tije, A. (2016). *Lean Six Sigma: Green & black belt* (2nd ed.). Amsterdam: Lssa B. V.

de Kock, R. (2017). *Digital Transformation Enablement: An assessment of IT Service Management as an enabler*. Unpublished master's thesis, University of Northampton, Northampton, United Kingdom.

Dekker, S., Spear, S., Cook, R., & Kim, G. (2017, November 15). *DevOps Enterprise Symposium: Lean, Safety and DevOps*, (Online). https://www.youtube.com/watch?v=gtxtb9z_4FY. [2018 March].

Dehra, N. (2011, May 19). *Techniques used in business requirements gathering*, (Online). https://www.brighthubpm.com/project-planning/60264-techniques-used-in-business-requirements-gathering/. [2018 February].

Deloitte. (2018, May 15). *The Deloitte millennial survey 2018*, (Online). https://www2.deloitte.com/global/en/pages/about-deloitte/articles/millennialsurvey.html. [2018 May].

Drucker, P. (1954). *The Practice of Management*. New York: HarperBusiness.

Drucker, P. (1996). *Landmarks of tomorrow: A report on the new*. Piscataway, NJ: Transaction.

Earl, M. J., & Scott, I. A. (1999, January 15). *What is a Chief Knowledge Officer?*, (Online). https://sloanreview.mit.edu/article/what-is-a-chief-knowledge-officer/. [2018 May].

England, R. (No date). *The Standard+Case approach to response management*, (Online). http://www.basicsm.com/standard-case. [2018 April].

England, R. (2017, September 18). *A project is a wave in a product structure*, (Online). http://www.itskeptic.org/content/project-wave-product-structure. [2018 March].

England, R. (2017, December 5). *Project management was the worst thing to ever happen to IT*, (Online). http://www.itskeptic.org/content/project-management-was-worst-thing-ever-happened-it. [2018 February].

Engle, R. J. (2004). *Strategic sourcing: A step-by-step practical model*, (Online). https://www.instituteforsupplymanagement.org/files/Pubs/Proceedings/FBEngel.pdf. [2018 March].

Expert Program Management. (2017 September). *Gap analysis*, (Online). https://expertprogrammanagement.com/2017/09/gap-analysis/. [2018 February].

Ferris, K. (2011). *Balanced diversity: A portfolio approach to organizational change.* London: TSO.

Fisher, S. (2016, September 8). *Using 'Run-Grow-Transform' to change your business*, (Online). https://www.laserfiche.com/simplicity/using-run-grow-transform-to-change-your-business/. [2018 April].

Florentine, S. (2016, May 11). *More than half of IT projects still failing*, (Online). https://www.cio.com/article/3068502/project-management/more-than-half-of-it-projects-still-failing.html. [2018 January].

Fried, E. (2003). *Strategy as a portfolio of real options*, (Online). https://maaw.info/ArticleSummaries/ArtSumLuehrman98.htm. [2018 March].

Friend, T. (2017, March 20). *Agile project success and failure (The story of the FBI Sentinel program)*, (Online). https://resources.sei.cmu.edu/asset_files/Presentation/2017_017_001_495733.pdf. [2018 January].

Galbraith, J. R. (2016, January 6). *The Star Model™*, (Online). http://www.jaygalbraith.com/images/pdfs/StarModel.pdf. [2018 March].

Garr, S. (2014, December 18). *The gift of clarity (and using goals to provide it)*, (Online). http://blog.bersin.com/the-gift-of-clarity-and-using-goals-to-provide-it/. [2018 April].

Gartner. (2012, February 14). *Gartner says adopting a pace-layered application strategy can accelerate innovation*, (Online). https://www.gartner.com/newsroom/id/1923014. [2018 February].

Ghosh, M. (2003). *Knowledge management in the digital age: Challenges and opportunities in India*, (Online). https://www.researchgate.net/publication/264496706_Knowledge_Management_in_the_digital_age_Challenges_and_opportunities_in_India. [2018 April].

Gordon, L., Gordon, C. (Producers) & Robinson, P. A. (Writer/Director). (1989). Field of dreams [Motion picture]. United States: Universal Studios.

Gore. (No date). *Our beliefs & principles*, (Online). https://www.gore.com/about/our-beliefs-and-principles. [2018 February].

Gore. (No date). *Working at Gore*, (Online). https://www.gore.com/about/working-at-gore. [2018 February].

Greenleaf, R. K. (1970). *The servant as leader.* Atlanta: Robert K. Greenleaf.

Grossman, L. (2010, November 10). *Nov. 10, 1999: Metric math mistake muffed Mars meteorology mission*, (Online). https://www.wired.com/2010/11/1110mars-climate-observer-report/. [2018 March].

Hamel, G. (2010, September 23). Innovation democracy: W.L. Gore's original management model, (Online). https://www.managementexchange.com/story/innovation-democracy-wl-gores-original-management-model. [2018 February].

Harrison, K. (2017, November 17). *What is a value chain analysis?*, (Online). https://www.businessnewsdaily.com/5678-value-chain-analysis.html. [2018 March].

Harschnitz, L. (2011, October 14). *Gathering effective requirements*, (Online). https://www.sas.com/content/dam/SAS/en_ca/User%20Group%20Presentations/Hamilton-User-Group/LesleyHarschnitz-EffectiveRequirements-October2011.pdf. [2018 January].

Hartley, A. (2012). *Requirements lifecycle management*, (Online). http://annehartleyconsulting.com/Requirements%20Lifecycle%20Methodology%20Guide%20-%20AHC%20-%20v%201.4.pdf. [2018 February].

Harvey Nash, & KPMG. (2017). *2017 CIO Survey*, (online). https://assets.kpmg.com/content/dam/kpmg/xx/pdf/2017/07/harvey-nash-kpmg-cio-survey-2017.pdf. [2018, March].

Haughey, D. (no date). *Requirements gathering 101*, (Online). https://www.projectsmart.co.uk/pdf/requirements-gathering.pdf. [2018 February].

Hebert, T. (2010). *To run, grow and transform, focus on the business value of your company's IT*, (Online). http://www.thoughtleading.com/Articles/th_RunGrow_BRUSA_10_05.pdf. [2018 April].

Hinchcliffe, D. (2015, August 29). *What is digital transformation*, [Online]. https://www.cxotalk.com/video/what-digital-transformation. [2017, June].

Hirsch, J. (2013, November 22). *10 steps to successful requirements gathering*, (Online). https://www.phase2technology.com/blog/successful-requirements-gathering. [2018 February].

Hunter, R. (2012, July 18). *A few things about running, growing, and transforming in the cloud*, (Online). https://blogs.gartner.com/richard-hunter/a-few-things-about-running-growing-and-transforming-in-the-cloud/. [2018 April].

Hunter, R., & Westerman, G. (2009). *The real business of IT: How CIOs create and communicate value.* Boston: Harvard Business Review.

ISACA. (2012). *COBIT® 5: A business framework for the governance and management of enterprise IT.* Rolling Meadows, IL: ISACA.

ISO. (2018). *ISO 31000:2108 – Risk management – Guidelines.* Geneva: ISO.

ISO/IEC. (2015). *ISO/IEC 38500:2015 – Information technology – Governance of IT for the organization.* Geneva: ISO.

K, A. (2017, July 10). *Uber operators must apply for operating licences – Transport minister*, (Online). https://mzansionline.co.za/uber-operators-must/. [2018 April].

Kastelle, T. (2012, 16 January). *Eight models of business models & why they're important*, (Online). http://timkastelle.org/blog/2012/01/eight-models-of-business-models-why-theyre-important/. [2018 January].

Kelly, T. (2010, April 8). *No more heroes: Distributed leadership*, (Online). https://www.managementexchange.com/blog/no-more-heroes. [2018 May].

Kim, G. (2015, February 25). *Mastering performance and collaboration through DevOps*, (Online). https://www.youtube.com/watch?v=cWpPmO6l064. [2018 March].

Kotter, J. P. (1996). *Leading change*. Boston: Harvard Business School.

Kotter, J. P. (2014). *Accelerate*. Boston: Harvard Business School.

Kruit, R. (2013, December 3). *The 7 keys to deliver better applications faster through effective IT/Business collaboration*, (Online). https://www.mendix.com/blog/7-keys-deliver-better-applications-faster-effective-itbusiness-collaboration/. [2018 February]

Kyriazoglou, J. (2012, December 22). *Strategy assessment methods: PEST*, (Online). http://businessmanagementcontrols.blogspot.com/2012/12/strategy-assessment-methods-pest.html. [2018 February].

Kyriazoglou, J. (2012, December 22). *Strategy assessment methods: SWOT*, (Online). http://businessmanagementcontrols.blogspot.com/2012/12/strategy-assessment-methods-swot.html. [2018 February].

Kyriazoglou, J. (2013, January 17). *Strategy assessment methods: Gap analysis*, (Online). http://businessmanagementcontrols.blogspot.com/2013/01/strategy-assessment-methods-gap-analysis.html. [2018 February].

LaMorte, W. W. (2016). *Diffusion of innovation theory*, (Online). http://sphweb.bumc.bu.edu/otlt/MPH-Modules/SB/BehavioralChangeTheories/BehavioralChangeTheories4.html. [2018 March].

Little, J. (2014). *Lean change management: Innovative practices for managing organizational change*. Happy Melly Express.

Luehrman, T. A. (1998). *Investment opportunities as real options: Getting started on the numbers*, (Online). https://hbr.org/1998/07/investment-opportunities-as-real-options-getting-started-on-the-numbers [2018 March].

Luehrman, T. A. (1998). *Strategy as a portfolio of real options* (Online). https://hbr.org/1998/09/strategy-as-a-portfolio-of-real-options [2018 March].

Mackey, J. (2010, March 9). *Creating the high trust organization*, (Online). http://www.wholefoodsmarket.com/blog/john-mackeys-blog/creating-high-trust-organization. [2018 February].

Mankins, M., & Garton, E. (2017, February 9). *How Spotify balances employee autonomy and accountability*, (Online). https://hbr.org/2017/02/how-spotify-balances-employee-autonomy-and-accountability. [2018 January].

Markgraf, B. (no date). *Tools for gap analysis*, (Online). http://smallbusiness.chron.com/tools-gap-analysis-46456.html. [2018 February].

Martin, K. & Osterling, M. (2013). *Value stream mapping: How to visualize work and align leadership for organizational transformation*. New York: McGraw-Hill.

Maylett, T. (2016, March 4). *6 ways to encourage autonomy with your employees*, (Online). https://www.entrepreneur.com/article/254030. [2018 April].

McCarthy, D. (2008, June 5). *The 10 greatest management theories, models, or methods*, (Online). http://www.greatleadershipbydan.com/2008/06/10-greatest-management-theories-models.html. [2018 January].

McChesney, C., Covey, S., & Huling, J. (2012). *The 4 disciplines of execution*. New York: Free Press.

McGrath, R. G. & MacMillan, I. (2000). *The entrepreneurial mindset: Strategies for continuously creating opportunity in an age of uncertainty*. Boston: Harvard Business Review.

Mifsud, J. (2013, May 20). *Requirements gathering: A step by step approach for a better user experience (Part 1)*, (Online). https://usabilitygeek.com/requirements-gathering-user-experience-pt1/. [2018 February].

Mifsud, J. (2013, May 27). *Requirements gathering: A step by step approach for a better user experience (Part 2)*, (Online). https://usabilitygeek.com/requirements-gathering-a-step-by-step-approach-for-a-better-user-experience-part-2/. [2018 February].

Mikolluk, K. (2013, July 25). *Gap analysis template: The 3 key elements of effective gap analysis*, (Online). https://blog.udemy.com/gap-analysis-template/. [2018 February].

Mind Tools Content Team. (No date). *Herzberg's motivators and hygiene factors*, (Online). https://www.mindtools.com/pages/article/herzberg-motivators-hygiene-factors.htm. [2018 March].

Mind Tools Content Team. (No date). *The congruence model: Aligning the drivers of high performance*, (Online). https://mindtools.com/pages/article/newSTR_95.htm. [2018 March].

Mind Tools Content Team. (No date). *The McKinsey 7-S framework: Ensuring that all parts of your organization work in harmony*, (Online). https://mindtools.com/pages/article/newSTR_91.htm. [2018 March].

Mochal, T. (2008, January 2). *10 techniques for gathering requirements*, (Online). https://www.techrepublic.com/blog/10-things/10-techniques-for-gathering-requirements/. [2018 February].

Moore, G. A. (1991). *Crossing the chasm (3rd ed.)*. New York: HarperCollins.

Moore, G. A. (2011). *Systems of engagement and the future of enterprise IT: A sea change in enterprise IT*, (Online). http://info.aiim.org/systems-of-engagement-and-the-future-of-enterprise-it. [2018 March].

Mulder, P. (2011). *Five product levels (Kotler)*, (Online). https://www.toolshero.com/marketing/five-product-levels-kotler/. [2018 March].

Nadler, D. A., & Tushman, M. L. (1980). A model for diagnosing organizational behavior. *Organizational Dynamics, **9**(2) 35-51.

Organizational culture. *BusinessDictionary.com*, (Online). http://www.businessdictionary.com/definition/organizational-culture.html. [2018 March].

Osterwalder, A. & Pigneur, Y. (No date) Business model canvas, (Online). https://strategyzer.com/canvas/business-model-canvas. [2018, March].

Osterwalder, A. & Pigneur, Y. (2010). *Business model generation*. New York: Wiley.

Osterwalder, A., Pigneur, Y., Bernarda, G., Smith, A., & Papadakos, T. (2014). *Value proposition design: How to create products and services customers want (Strategyzer)*. New York: Wiley.

Otchere, E. A. (No date). *Digitize services, capture value*, (Online). http://carrier. huawei.com/en/technical-topics/service/softwareservice/Helping%20Telcos%20 Digitalize%20Services%20%20Emma. [2018 January].

Palmer, T. H. (1840). *The Teachers Manual*, (Online). https://books.google.com/ books/about/The_Teacher_s_Manual.html?id=hSABAAAAYAAJ. [2018 March].

Radigan, D. (No date). *Product requirements documents, downsized*, (Online). https://www.atlassian.com/agile/product-management/requirements. [2018 April].

RealtimeBlog. (No date). *How to choose between Agile and Lean, Scrum and Kanban – which methodology is the best?*, (Online). https://realtimeboard.com/ blog/choose-between-agile-lean-scrum-kanban/#.WsY6cExFyUk/. [2018 March].

Ries, E. (2011). *The lean start-up – how today's entrepreneurs use continuous innovation to create radically successful businesses*. New York: Random.

Riordan, C. M. (2013, July 3). *We all need friends at work*, (Online). https://hbr. org/2013/07/we-all-need-friends-at-work. [2018, March].

Ross, L. (2017). *Hacking for agile change: With an agile mindset, behaviours & practices*. Amazon Digital Services.

Semler, R. (1989). *Managing without managers*, (Online). https://hbr.org/1989/09/ managing-without-managers. [2018 February].

Sieff, G., & Carstens, L. (2006). The relationship between personality type and leadership focus. *SA Journal of Human Resource Management*, **4**(1), 52-62.

Stewart, T., & Margolis, H. (1996, July 8). Company values that add value, (Online). http://archive.fortune.com/magazines/fortune/fortune_archive/1996/07/08/214342/ index.htm. [2018 February].

Taking Service Forward. (2014). *The adaptive service model: Architectural concepts, modelling language and principles*, (Online). https://docs.google.com/ document/d/1TcZqo71wDAzW2qQsAdEBE3WIFTEO34wSOygo6zGu2xA/edit#. [2018 February].

Thompson, S. C. (1999). Illusions of control: How we overestimate our personal influence. *Current Directions in Psychological Science*, **8**(6): 187–190.

Toffler, A. (1970). *Future shock*. New York: Bantam.

Tomaro, N. (2016, November 23). *9 proven business models to consider for your startup*, (Online). https://www.huffingtonpost.com/nina-tomaro/9-proven-business-models-_b_7949932.html. [2018 January].

Torres, R. & Rimmer, N. (2011, December 21). *The five traits of highly adaptive leadership teams*, (Online). https://www.bcg.com/en-au/publications/2011/ people-organization-five-traits-highly-adaptive-leadership-teams.aspx. [2108 April].

Trees, L. (2018, March 8). *Knowledge management experts on KM's role in digital transformation*, (Online). https://www.apqc.org/blog/knowledge-management-experts-km-s-role-digital-transformation. [2018 June].

Tuckman, B. W. (1965). Developmental sequence in small groups. *Psychological Bulletin*, **63**(6), 384–399.

University of Michigan-Administrative Services Transformation. (No date). *What is strategic sourcing*, (Online). http://ast.umich.edu/pdfs/What-is-strategic-sourcing-102811.pdf. [2018 March].

Vaes, K. (2013, June 13). *IT budget: Run, grow & transform*, (Online). https://kvaes.wordpress.com/2013/06/13/it-budget-run-grow-transform/. [2018 April].

Valve Corporation. (2012). *Valve: Handbook for new employees*, (Online). https://steamcdn-a.akamaihd.net/apps/valve/Valve_NewEmployeeHandbook.pdf. [2018 March].

Van Hove, S. D., & Thomas, M. (2016). *Pragmatic application of service management: The five anchor approach* (2nd ed.). Cambridgeshire, UK: IT Governance.

Van Vliet, V. (2011). *Five functions of management (Fayol)*, (Online). https://www.toolshero.com/management/five-functions-of-management/. [2018 March].

Wake, B. (2003, August). *INVEST in good stories and SMART tasks*, (Online). https://xp123.com/articles/invest-in-good-stories-and-smart-tasks/. [2018 April].

Waterman, Jr., R. H., Peters, T. J., & Philips, J. R. (1980). Structure is not organization. *Business Horizons*, **23**(3), 14-26.

Westerman, G. (2017, October 25). *Your company doesn't need a digital strategy*, (Online). https://sloanreview.mit.edu/article/your-company-doesnt-need-a-digital-strategy/. [2018 May].

Whale, S. (2017, August 2). *Adaptive leadership lessons from Trump and advertising*, (Online). https://www.campaignlive.co.uk/article/adaptive-leadership-lessons-trump-advertising/1441056. [2018 March].

Wilson, D. & Beaton, L. (2003). *Promoting institutional & organizational development: A source book of tools and techniques*, (Online). http://webarchive.nationalarchives.gov.uk/+/http:/www.dfid.gov.uk/pubs/files/prominstdevsourcebook.pdf. [2018 March].

Wysocki, R. K. (2008, May 14). *Effective requirements gathering and management need the skills of both the BA and the PM*, (Online). https://www.batimes.com/articles/effective-requirements-gathering-and-management-need-the-skills-of-both-the-ba-and-the-pm.html. [2018 April].

Zweidler, A., Wedge, C., & Metz, B. (2005). The "Real Options" approach to capital decisions: Planning for change, (Online). http://pkal.org/documents/RealOptions_CapitalDecisions.pdf. [2018 March].

Index